Teaching Reading & Thinking Skills

Teaching Reading & Thinking Skills

Myles I. Friedman

University of South Carolina

Michael D. Rowls

University of South Carolina

LONGMAN
New York and London

To Bob Rowls, Irene Rowls, and Betty Phifer

TEACHING READING AND THINKING SKILLS

Longman Inc., New York
Associated companies, branches, and representatives
throughout the world.

Development Editor: Nicole Benevento
Interior Design: Pencils Portfolio, Inc.
Cover Design: Edgar Blakeney
Manufacturing and Production Supervisor: Kris Becker
Composition: A & S Graphics, Inc.
Printing and Binding: Fairfield Graphics

Manufactured in the United States of America

Library of Congress Cataloging in Publication Data

Friedman, Myles I   1924–
    Teaching reading and thinking skills.

    Bibliography: p. 526
    Includes index.
    1. Reading. 2. Study, Method of. I. Rowls,
Michael D., 1947–   joint author. II. Title.
LB 1050.F69   428′ 4′07   79-15788
ISBN 0-582-29006-6

9 8 7 6 5 4 3 2 1

CONTENTS

PREFACE

The authors of this text—a reading specialist and a psychologist—have collaborated because we are interested in developing a psychologically sound and thorough approach to the teaching of reading. The book is comprehensive, as all basic reading texts must be. It covers the various reading and thinking skills reading teachers may be responsible for teaching. It is also designed to be an effective instructional aid and is replete with prescriptions for teaching reading. The book delves deeply into essentials of reading instruction, especially the diagnosis of readiness for reading, reading comprehension, and the planning of reading instruction. We did not want to oversimplify the teaching of reading. The student who learns from a textbook that oversimplifies reading instruction may understand the text but will not be able to teach reading effectively.

We begin the book with an introduction to the integrating theme that unifies the ideas presented throughout the book— prediction. We emphasize prediction as an important human trait and show how it applies to daily living, to reading, and to the teaching of reading. To show how the integrating theme of prediction applies to the teaching of reading, we show throughout the book how the prediction process is related to particular reading skills. For example, in chapter 7 when we discuss reading comprehension skills we include a section on the relationship between reading comprehension and the prediction process. In chapter 8 when we consider study skills we show the relationship between study skills and the prediction process.

In Part II we deal with the learning of words. We show how word identification skills are taught. In addition, we delve into vocabulary building and the thought processes involved in understanding words.

In Part III we probe deeply into reading comprehension, devoting four chapters to the subject (chapters 5, 6, 7, and 8). We discuss and evaluate various views on reading comprehension. Then, we enumerate reading comprehension skills and show how these various skills can be taught as concepts. Finally, we consider how study skills may be used to facilitate comprehension. The student is shown how to teach reading comprehension, skill by skill.

We stress the teaching of reading comprehension because although more Americans than ever before are exposed to reading instruction, an incredible number of students still graduate from high school illiterate. We believe that in order to correct this critical problem teachers must be better prepared to teach reading comprehension, to teach students to comprehend an author's message.

Reading comprehension skills are not only discussed in the text, but the reasoning processes that underlie these skills are analyzed. The student is shown how to teach the reasoning processes that lead to reading comprehension. Technical psychological terms have been avoided, and no attempt has been made to explain the neurological functions associated with reading comprehension. Emphasis is placed on the reasoning procedures followed in order to extract meaning from words. The reasoning procedures for such reading comprehension skills as "getting the main idea," "distinguishing fact and fantasy," "evaluating reading," "identifying supportive information and details," and many others are illustrated.

In Part IV we devote three chapters to diagnosis as the basis for prescribing reading instruction (chapters 9, 10, and 11). We devote an entire chapter to the diagnosis of the readability of reading materials. Then, we discuss the fundamentals of diagnosing reading skills so that the student will understand the scientific basis for diagnosis. After establishing this foundation, we deal with specific diagnostic instruments and techniques used to diagnose particular reading skills. Diagnosis deserves the intensive treatment we give it because diagnosis is the basis for prescribing reading instruction. Students must be able to diagnose readiness for learning before they consider instructional alternatives.

Part V focuses on the preparations required to deliberately and effectively teach reading. First, students are shown how to establish instructional goals. Then, the various goals of reading instruction are described and discussed. Next, students are shown how to plan reading instruction, and they are acquainted with the "mastery learning" approach to instruction. The planning of reading instruction is treated thoroughly because effective teaching is based on sound planning.

In Part VI we consider the teaching of reading in the content areas. We describe the desired learning outcomes in the major subjects. Then, we move to a discussion of the writing patterns in the content areas. Next, we deal with problems in reading content materials. Finally, we show how content is and can be organized in the various subjects.

All in all, we attempt to comprehensively cover the basic reading skills the reading instructor teaches. In addition, we deal intensively with the teaching of reading comprehension, diagnosis, and the planning of reading instruction. Our prescription for teaching reading is soundly based on research evidence and will lead to the improved teaching of reading.

We have gone to great lengths to provide teaching aids to help students understand the material in the book. The selection and design of the teaching aids is based on research findings and current instructional theory. Our application of the teaching aids in this text serves a dual purpose. It helps students learn the material in the text, and it provides illustrations of how they may use these teaching aids in their own instruction. Advance organizers are presented before each chapter, and summaries and review questions are presented at the end of each chapter. This prepares the student for the content of the chapters, displays the content from different perspectives, and provides the redundancy that is necessary to facilitate learning.

The teaching aids for each chapter incorporate the same devices we advise the students to use. In the text we suggest that the student establish purpose for reading when teaching reading. In the advance organizers for each chapter we present both the general purposes of the chapter and the more specific purposes by enumerating the desired learning outcomes for each chapter. In the text we advocate the preteaching of unfamiliar and difficult material before immersing the student in it. In the advance organizers we indicate the new information students will encounter in the chapter and particular words that may be unfamiliar to them. This enables the instructor and students to focus on the new content and discuss it before the students cope with it in the context of the chapter. We also advocate in the book that the hierarchical relationships among topics be shown to students to facilitate the learning of content. We display the hierarchical relationships among important topics in each chapter. In addition, we emphasize in the text the importance of basing new learning on students' experiential background. In the advance organizers we show the connection between the new material in a chapter and the previous knowledge that supports it. Finally, when we discuss reading and study skills we stress the importance of summarizing and reviewing material in order to learn and remember it. We present at the end of each chapter a summary of the chapter along with review questions for the student. So each teaching aid is designed to serve a particular purpose, although students may not need to utilize all the teaching aids.

In the appendix we provide a current list of instructional resources that are available commercially to aid the teaching of reading skills, and we offer the names and addresses of publishers of the instructional resources as well as publishers of tests we mention in the book. Also, a glossary is provided to clarify the meaning of many central terms used in the text.

The reading teacher is reponsible for teaching many skills. This book not only discusses these skills in a comprehensive way, but also shows the teacher how to plan for their instruction. After completion of the material in this text, the teacher should be able to:

- teach the word identification and study skills that enhance reading comprehension
- teach the reading comprehension skills and thinking procedures necessary to extract meaning from written words
- teach the application of reading comprehension skills and thinking procedures to the various content areas
- design instruction for both the teaching of reading skills and the comprehension of reading materials in the various content areas
- diagnose reading problems and prescribe instruction to alleviate those problems

We wish to thank Betty M. Phifer for offering her expertise as a public school reading teacher. The many hours she spent critiquing the book and making it relevant to the realities of classroom instruction contributed immensely to the instructional value of the text. We also wish to thank Dr. Paul C. Berg and

Walter L. Procko for their editorial assistance, and Gloria Nichol-
son and Loriene Hubbard for their secretarial services.

In addition, we wish to express our appreciation to Kenneth
Goodman and Frank Smith for the pioneering work they did in
relating reading to the prediction process. They provided a solid
foundation for the theme of the text. Finally, we are grateful to
Benjamin S. Bloom for his contributions to instructional planning
and mastery learning. We incorporated many of his principles in
recommending techniques for planning and teaching reading.

Introduction
Methods and Background

We have included in this textbook certain teaching aids known to facilitate learning. Each chapter begins with organizers that introduce and orient the reader to the subject matter. At the end is a summary of the major points in the chapter and review questions. These aids systematize the subject matter in each chapter.

Repetition facilities learning in many instances. Therefore, major ideas in each chapter have been repeated in the teaching aids. As you will learn, however, too much repetition produces boredom. Select those aids you think will benefit you in learning the material. If the content seems difficult, you may want to use them all.

ADVANCE ORGANIZERS

The purpose of the advance organizers (Ausubel, 1960) in each chapter is to help you learn the content of the chapter. We have selected advance organizers known to ready students for learning. They are (1) a statement of the purpose of each chapter, (2) a brief discussion of the information you already have concerning the topic of each chapter and the new information that will be presented, (3) a list of key terms that may be unfamiliar to you, and (4) the desired learning outcomes you are expected to achieve. A brief examination of each advance organizer will emphasize its purpose and importance.

Purpose

Knowing the purpose for reading and understanding material you are required to learn is very helpful. It gives the student a reason for becoming involved in certain instructional activities, and students must become involved if learning is to take place. We emphasize throughout the book that reading teachers must inform their students of the purpose of a particular reading assignment.

Background and New Information

Students' previous experiences greatly influence their ability to understand particular reading materials and their potential for learning new information. The knowledge students already have provides a foundation for new learning. Teachers can facilitate learning if they base new material on students' previous knowledge. We therefore attempt to acquaint you with those facets of your past experience that provide a foundation for learning the new material in each chapter. We also point out relevant information in previous chapters that supports the learning of the new material. The new information for each chapter is previewed by introducing the important topics that will be discussed and their organization.

Key Terms

The field of reading and reading instruction, like most disciplines, has its own special terms. Even words that may seem familiar may be defined in an unfamiliar way. By listing terms that may be troublesome, we alert the student to be on the "lookout" for them. A glossary at the back of the book also provides a handy reference for the meanings of puzzling words.

Desired Learning Outcomes

Desired learning outcomes are what we hope students will achieve as a result of instruction. Desired learning outcome statements are nothing more than elaborations of the general purpose of instruction. They state more specifically what the learner should know and be able to do at the end of an instructional unit. We present the desired learning outcomes at the beginning of each chapter so that you can see beforehand what you should know and be able to do after learning the material in each chapter.

HIERARCHICAL CHARTS

Charts showing the hierarchical relationships among important topics are inserted near the beginning of each chapter to facilitate learning. In chapter 4 we explain why displaying hierarchical relationships among topics facilitates learning, and cite supporting research. Here is an example of a hierarchical display.

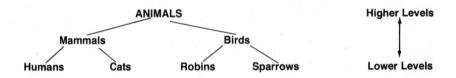

As you can see, each word in the hierarchy represents a category of things, and the lower level categories are subcategories of the higher level categories. Humans and cats are subcategories or types of mammals. Robins and sparrows are subcategories or types of birds, and birds and mammals are subcategories or types of animals. You are familiar with this kind of organization. You were already aware that mammals and birds are types of animals, that humans and cats are types of mammals, and that robins and sparrows are types of birds. What you may not have been aware of is that information or content is often organized in this way because it facilitates the storage and retrieval of the information. The information and books in the library are organized in hierarchical form to facilitate storage and retrieval. The Dewey Decimal system is nothing more than a numerical way to identify categories and subcategories of books. Also, the table of contents of a book forms a hierarchy of topics. Because the evidence indicates that the organization and presentation of information or content in this way aids storage, retrieval, and learning, we will use this format to show the relationship among important topics in each chapter of this text. In addition, we will discuss the importance of organizing information into hierarchies in several chapters of the book. This is merely an introduction to the concept.

REVIEW

Following each chapter is a summary and a set of review questions, study aids that have been shown effective in facilitating the learning and remembering of new material.

Summary

The purpose of the summary is to point out the most important topics dealt with in the chapter in a clear and concise way. It highlights and emphasizes central issues in terse, compact terms. It should help you to crystallize in your mind the major kernels of information presented in the chapter and to understand the overall framework within which the specific points and topics are presented.

Review Questions

The purpose of the review questions is also to highlight the most important points in the chapter, as well as to provide the reader with a tool for reviewing the information at a later time. After reading the chapter and summary, attempt to answer each review question. If you cannot give a comprehensive and precise answer to each question, review the corresponding information in the main body of the chapter.

PREDICTION

This book emphasizes the importance of prediction in living and in learning. Although students are not generally taught to predict in most subject areas, reading specialists have recognized the importance of predicting for some time. They have developed instructional activities to teach students to predict. For instance, an activity may require a student to read a paragraph of a story and predict what will happen next. In learning the importance of being able to predict coming events you will gain a new teaching perspective.

In the educational literature, much of the work related to prediction has been conducted under the heading of *expectancy*. E.C. Tolman (1951, 1959) was reponsible for achieving a theoretical legitimacy for the concept of expectancy. Tolman contended that if two stimuli are paired, expectancy is the situation in which the individual behaves in the presence of stimulus 1 as if stimulus 2 will be present.

McCorquodale and Meehl (1954) formalized expectancy theory. They contended that there are three components to an expectancy—S_1, the elicitor of the expectancy, R_1, a response following the expectation, and S_2, the fulfillment of the expectation. The expectancy process can be diagrammed as S_1–R_1–S_2. For instance, S_1 might represent the knob on a television set which elicits the expectancy that when the knob is turned (R_1), the television picture will appear (S_2). If watching television is the goal, then the expectancy process is activated.

Robert C. Bolles (1972: 402) has proposed this primary law of learning:

> What is learned is that certain events, cues (S), predict certain other biologically important events, consequences (S*). An animal may incidentally show new responses, but what it learns is an expectancy that represents and corresponds to the S–S* contingency.

Some animals, according to Bolles, are able to appreciate new environmental contingencies. In other words, their behavior is mainly a function of their expectations.

William K. Estes (1972) uses the word "anticipation" to explain behavior that does not fit neatly into the animal-laboratory-oriented reward/punishment model. Estes maintains that in the "case of a normal human learner a reward does not necessarily strengthen, nor a punishment weaken, the response which produces it. . . . In any choice situation the individual is assumed actively to scan the available alternatives and to be guided to a choice by feedback from anticipated rewards" (1972: 729).

There have also been a number of studies of behavior that have given credence to Tolman's statement about expectancy.

> One of the earliest and most striking observations of reward expectancy was that of Tinklepaugh. In his experiment, food was placed

under one of two containers while the monkey was looking but prevented from immediate access to the cans of food. Later the monkey was permitted to choose between the containers and showed skill in choosing correctly. The behavior which is pertinent here occurred when, after a banana had been hidden under one of the cups, the experimenter substituted for it a lettuce leaf (a less preferred food). The monkey rejected the lettuce leaf and engaged in definite searching behavior. Somewhat the same sort of behavior was found by Elliott when the food in the goal box of a rat maze experiment was changed from bran mash to sunflower seed. More systematic experiments have been carried out since with chimpanzees (Cowles and Nissen). There is little doubt that animals have some sort of precognition or expectancy of goal objects. (Hilgard, 1975)

Levine (1970) showed the importance of hypothesis testing in human problem solving. Using human adults, he validated the notion that problem solving is achieved through testing a group of predictions against feedback. When the subjects' predictions are tested and confirmed, they accept them as correct. When they are told that their predictions are wrong, they choose and test other hypotheses. They continue this lose-shift/win-stay strategy until they eventually solve the problem. Glassman and Levine (1972), in a later study, added support to this contention. This research and line of reasoning led to the development of what Levine (1974) calls H theory. The H stands for hypothesis theory. Hypothesis theory is reviewed by Brown (1974).

It is generally held that people do solve problems by sampling and testing hypotheses. Not only are individuals motivated to make predictions, but once they make a prediction, they are motivated to confirm it. It is through the confirmation of their predictions that individuals learn that their perceptions of reality are correct.

The tendency to confirm one's predictions was evidenced in a series of studies conducted at the Foxboro Company under the direction of Dr. Harry Helson (1949). The studies were concerned with the performance of machine operators. Helson found that operators set a performance standard which they expect to meet. When their performance falls below this standard, they expend greater effort to reduce the error. He labeled this the anticipation dimension of performance. It suggests that people tend to make predictions about their performance and work to confirm the predictions they make.

Further research findings on anticipation indicate that machine operators use advance information to predict future events as a basis for preparing for the coming events. Adams and Xhig-griesse (1960) showed that accurate anticipation increased with the predictability of the task, and through pretraining, which made the task more predictable to begin with. Thus, people try to predict to improve their performance, and the predictability of the task at hand aids them.

Prediction is an important human trait and is the integrating theme of this book. If you should wish to probe more deeply into the psychological implications of prediction, consult *Rational Behavior: An Explanation of Behavior That Is Especially Human* (Friedman, 1975). Let us now examine the relationship between prediction and reading.

PART I
PERSPECTIVE AND ORIENTATION

CHAPTER 1
A Promising Approach to
Reading Instruction

PURPOSE

1. To introduce you to important issues concerning reading and reading instruction.
2. To acquaint you with the concept of prediction.

BACKGROUND AND NEW INFORMATION

Being able to make accurate predictions contributes substantially to success of any kind.

Your own experiences remind you that people are interested in prediction. They bet on their predictions in certain games and sports. Mysteries are popular because people like to predict the outcome of the story before the author reveals the solution.

You make attempts to confirm your own predictions in order to solve everyday problems. You predict that a particular route will get you to school and confirm this prediction by your arrival at school. You may predict that the use of particular study procedure will result in a passing grade. Whatever it is you wish to accomplish, you select procedures that you predict will lead to your goals. The confirmation of your predictions results in the attainment of your goals.

Your own experiences as a reader prepare you to understand a great deal about the reading process. The courses you take in preparation for becoming a teacher also provide a foundation for teaching. These two experiences combine to aid you in learning to teach reading. They provide ample background for you to learn the more technical aspects of reading and reading instruction.

We begin this chapter by discussing the importance and purposes of reading. Next we consider the relationship between predictions and reading. Then we show how self-confidence and the pursuit of personal preferences tie into the reading-prediction process. Finally, we discuss the importance of optimizing predictability in reading and reading instruction.

KEY TERMS

optimum predictability
psycholinguistics
defensiveness
self-concept
readability
basal readers
the Directed Reading Activity method
the SQ4R study method
decoding

DESIRED LEARNING OUTCOMES

The student will be able to:

1. Describe the importance and purposes of reading.
2. Describe the relationship between reading and prediction.
3. Describe the relationship between reading, predicting, and self-confidence.
4. Describe the relationship between personal preference and reading.
5. Explain the importance of optimal predictability in reading and reading instruction.
6. Describe the three elements of instruction and their importance in optimizing predictability in the classroom.

The 1950s and 1960s saw a large-scale movement toward the improvement of reading instruction and, therefore, reading by the children in this nation's schools. The Right to Read proclamation of the U.S. Office of Education and the subsequent flood of federal monies into special programs in reading reflected the seriousness with which educators and citizens in general approached the reading problems in this country.

Briefly, three general perspectives governed and still govern the concern with reading as a skill to be taught in the public schools. First, reading was seen as an important facet of achievement in all school subjects. That is, a child with reading problems was immediately handicapped in math, science, and social studies—to name just a few achievement areas. Generally, failure in such content areas was associated in large part with deficits in reading ability. Second, reading was seen as a very important means by which people obtain information about their environment, helping them to interact successfully with their environment, especially the environment outside the realm of school. A recent study funded by the U.S. Office of Education and conducted through the University of Texas has indicated that from 13 to 30 percent of the adults in this country cannot adequately perform tasks like addressing an envelope, determining "best buys" from quantitative information on products, or reading a paragraph stating their rights under the Constitution. Third, reading was seen as an indispensable skill in terms of entertainment. Increased leisure time magnifies the importance of reading in this regard. Through reading, a person can experience ideas, adventures, feelings, and situations not available in the everyday real world. Like movies, television, staged events, and so forth, reading is an outlet, a form of diversion. The importance of reading to our daily lives has been well established. What we need to do now is continue to develop improved methods for teaching reading.

PREDICTION AND READING

A promising approach to psychology and to reading has been emerging and gaining popularity in recent years. From this perspective, reading and thinking are viewed as involving predic-

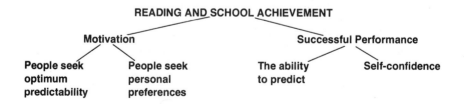

FIGURE 1-1 A hierarchy of topics in chapter 1

tion. We predict while thinking and while reading. The ability to predict is an essential factor in effective thinking and reading. Good thinkers and readers are good predictors. Relating thinking and reading to prediction yields an enormous potential for understanding thinking in general and reading in particular. It is the purpose of this book to tap this potential so that we may understand reading better and teach it more effectively.

Predicting the future is not the exclusive domain of clairvoyants and weathermen. It is something we all must do in order to live and read effectively. Some of us are better at predicting than others. The important point is that the ability to predict can be taught and improved throughout one's life. Increased attention is at present being paid to the relationships between reading and prediction, and there is mounting evidence that the ability to predict is an essential reading skill.

Goodman (1965; 1970) emphasizes the important connection between prediction and reading by insisting that reading is a "psycholinguistic guessing game." Goodman maintains that reading is not the precise, detailed, and sequential perception of letters and larger language units that other researchers have described it to be. Instead, Goodman says that reading is a process by which

> available language cues are selected from perceptual input on the basis of the reader's *expectations*. As this partial information is processed, tentative decisions are made to be confirmed, rejected, or refined as reading progresses. (Goodman 1970:260)

For Goodman, then, reading as a psycholinguistic process is the interaction between thought and language. The skilled reader makes use of minimal language cues in order to *hypothesize* about what he or she is reading, and ultimately to confirm these hypotheses. In short, according to Goodman (1973:295), "The proficient reader uses the least amount of information to make the best possible guesses."

The connection between the psycholinguistic approach to reading and prediction may be expressed in terms of the skilled reader who engages in the following activities:

1. Scanning the reading material.
2. Processing familiar cues (letters, words, phrases, sentences) that elicit ideas suggesting what the reading passage is about.

3. Attempting to predict the coming message in order to extract meaning.
4. Unable to make a prediction, looking for additional cues.
5. When a prediction is made, looking for confirmation as he or she continues to read.
6. As predictions are made and confirmed, assimilating meaning from the reading material, based upon what has been read as well as his or her own experiential background.

Although we are superimposing our own ideas of the importance to reading of the ability to predict on a model of reading that is not our own, researchers who attempt to describe the linguistic and psycholinguistic nature of reading consistently refer to a set of activities based on this important ability. Terms like "reader's expectations," "hypotheses," and "guesses" are common in the literature of psycholinguistics and reading. And common to all these activities is the ability to predict. Goodman (1973) more recently refers to the spiral of "prediction, sampling, selecting, guessing, and confirming" activities in which the skilled reader engages. We maintain that a more unifying and clarifying term to describe this process is that of *prediction*. "Guessing" implies uninformed or random prediction. Goodman consistently makes the point that the skilled reader is operating on the basis of "minimal" amounts of information; the less information required to make accurate predictions, the better the reader. The point is that readers do indeed act on information—their own and that contained in the reading material. Therefore, readers, especially skilled readers, make predictions and *not* guesses. Skilled readers constantly engage in the active process of making predictions.

In describing the process of reading, Goodman emphasizes the assimilation of meaning and deemphasizes processes that are strictly of a decoding nature. He describes the use of context in identifying words and obtaining meaning from them as the single most important skill in the class of word analysis skills. The use of context is simply the ability to use the grammar of the language and the meaning contained in the words and sentences in order to make predictions concerning what has been and is being read and what is yet to be read.

Those who have had experience with teaching reading to slow-learning youngsters are often struck by the fact that, even as poor readers read, they are unable to assimilate meaning. They are so engrossed in the decoding process that meaning and the assimilation of meaning become secondary, if not impossible. For them, the perceptual and decoding aspects of reading take so much time and energy that comprehension is precluded and impaired. Typically, these readers have a great deal of difficulty recalling freely what they have read and predicting what is to come. We are often fooled into thinking that they are reading and comprehending by their ability to recall isolated and specific bits of information from their reading.

If, for the moment, we accept Goodman's description as a reasonably accurate portrayal of the processes in which one engages during reading, what are the implications for reading instruction and how does the ability to predict relate to reading?

A number of researchers have offered support for the psycholinguistic model that tends to extend the model. The findings emphasize the importance of prediction in reading. Goodman (1965) himself presented subjects in grades one through three with words in isolation, asking them to pronounce the words. Then he placed those words the subjects missed in a meaningful context and examined their ability to identify the words successfully. He discovered that as age level increased, the children became increasingly more efficient in using cue systems outside the word itself to predict successfully the meaning of the unfamiliar words. After examining a group of fourth graders, Benz and Rosemier (1968) found that the ability to use context to predict the meaning of words was the single word analysis skill that best differentiated poor, average, and good comprehenders. Klein, Klein, and Bertino (1974) studied the developmental trend in the use of context for purposes of word identification. They, too, found that as children mature in reading ability, more variance in word identification ability is accounted for by the ability to use context clues in predicting word meanings.

Thus, it seems that there is a great deal of validity to the argument Goodman and others make concerning the nature of the reading process and what skilled reading entails. That is, the reader—both on a perceptual level and a cognitive level—formulates predictions about the material read. As he or she processes information during reading, these predictions are confirmed, rejected, or refined. On partial information and minimal available language cues, the reader predicts what will be found in the next string of letters and words, then proceeds to judge these predictions as he or she processes that information.

Research along other lines of inquiry also tends to support the notion that the ability to make accurate predictions and reading ability are highly related and go hand in hand. Greeno and Noreen (1974) had subjects read in order to develop expectations (predictions) concerning the material yet to be read, then supplied additional material that was either consistent or inconsistent with the material already covered. They concluded that inconsistent reading material (that is, material of low predictability) significantly increased the amount of time required to do the reading. Henderson and Long (1968) conducted an interesting study investigating the relationship between reading ability and the ability to predict story outcomes. They had readers at various levels of proficiency read the title of a story and rate thirty possible outcomes in terms of their likelihood. Then, all subjects read half of the story and rated a second set of outcomes in the same manner. Henderson and Long concluded that superior readers had much greater recognition of plausible outcomes, or ability to predict, than did poor or average readers.

The preponderance of evidence indicates that prediction is highly involved in reading and that good readers are good predictors. The growing trend to relate reading and prediction is clearly warranted. There is much to be gained by focusing on prediction in the teaching of reading.

READING AND SELF-CONFIDENCE

The ability to predict is necessary but insufficient for successful living in general and successful reading in particular. The ability to predict may be thought of as the cognitive or intellectual component of success. The affective component of success is, from our perspective, *self-confidence*. The ability to predict contributes to success because it is an index of the individual's belief that he or she can succeed, which is manifested in his or her persistence in trying to succeed. Although we may have the intellectual capacity to succeed, we cannot succeed if we do not try. Self-confident persons persist in their attempt to make and confirm their predictions; therefore, they will succeed more often and gain valuable practice in the ability to predict. To succeed in school and in reading, a student must have the cognitive capacity to learn, which is reflected by the ability to predict and the self-confidence to persist in trying to learn.

Anderson (1976) concludes that the time a student attends to a learning task contributes most heavily to the amount learned. A student who lacks self-confidence is not motivated to persist at a

learning task. He or she is likely to be distracted and to withdraw
from the challenge of learning. Further, he or she may disrupt the
teacher and other students.

In terms of disruptiveness, aggressiveness, and socially unac-
ceptable behavior, Feldhusen et al. (1967) found the incidence of
these kinds of behaviors to be much higher in poor readers than in
good readers. Similarly, Athey and Holmes (1969) found poor
readers to be more socially independent, lower in self-concept,
and to exhibit more school-related dislikes than average and good
readers. Frerichs (1971) determined that good readers were
higher in self-esteem than poor readers, and Rupley (1971) discovered that as reading achievement level goes down, frequency
of behavior problems goes up.

Bazemore and Gwaltney (1973) concluded that poor readers
tended to be less conscientious than good readers. Carter (1967),
using the *Vineland Social Maturity Scale,* found poor readers to
be less well adjusted socially than good readers. Henderson and
Long (1966) uncovered data indicating that good readers were
more socially oriented and saw themselves as both different and
complex, when compared with the self-evaluations of poor
readers. Woolf (1965) ascertained that poor readers were higher in
anxiety and lower in self-concept than good readers.

It is tempting to look at the apparent consistency of this research and say that poor reading causes people to have low opinions of themselves as well as a variety of undesirable and unac-
ceptable defensive behaviors. Such is not necessarily the case.
Strong inference, however, does tell us that the role of reading
ability and school achievement in general is an important factor in
the development of confidence in one's abilities and worth.

The pattern—and it has been recognized by many other writers
and researchers—is clear. Reading ability is vitally important to
success in nearly all facets of school achievement. Thus, impair-
ment in reading ability is, in large part, responsible for school
failure in general (Penty, 1956). In turn, school failure in general
and reading failure in particular are associated with low self-
regard and low self-confidence. The extent to which reading disability causes or is simply a result of low self-confidence is not
clear.

In any event, poor readers attempt to cope with the school environment in a variety of ways. Chief among these ways of coping
with a school environment that is highly unpredictable and associated with failure is withdrawal from or avoidance of that environment. This is evidenced by attendance figures for poor

readers; much more school time is missed by students who exhibit reading problems than by those who do not. If the environment contains too little predictability, the individual seeks to es-
cape the environment. Withdrawal and avoidance can also be
accomplished by means of disruptive behavior. These kinds of
behaviors are in a general class of defensive behaviors that provide the students a means of escaping situations that require
reading.

PERSONAL PREFERENCE AND READING

We said that people are motivated to predict. In addition, we
must consider that once they are able to predict, they are interested primarily in pursuing their preferences. So in order to
keep students motivated to learn, we must help them make and
confirm predictions that will help them obtain their preferences
from the environment, remembering that personal preferences
vary from one individual to another and for the same individual
over time. If we can achieve these goals, learning will remain
relevant to the student, and we will have increased the probability
that students will continue to engage in learning.

The concept of motivation is very complex. Postman and Weingartner (1969) see the question of the relevance of what is taught
as central to education and motivation. You will recall that two of
the general objectives in teaching pupils to read were to get information and to read for enjoyment. Reading to get information is
largely the objective of reading as it is at present taught in the
schools. Reading for enjoyment is less emphasized. In their book,
Teaching as a Subversive Activity, Postman and Weingartner
present a sample lesson that seems to be very progressive and
relevant as it involves students working in small groups and doing
projects. However, they emphasize that their sample assignment,
like most assignments pupils are required to do in school, is irrelevant. They insist that a game is being played with students:

> The game is called "Let's Pretend," and if its name were chiseled
> into the front of every school building in America, we would at least
> have an honest announcement of what takes place there. The game
> is based on a series of pretenses which include: Let's pretend that
> you are not what you are and that this sort of work makes a differ-
> ence to your lives; let's pretend that what bores you is important,
> and that the more you are bored, the more important it is; let's

pretend that there are certain things *everyone* must know, and that both the questions and answers about them have been fixed for all time; let's pretend that your intellectual competence can be judged on the basis of how well you can play Let's Pretend. (Postman and Weingartner, 1969:49)

Consequently, the relevance of the curriculum of the school—that is, what is taught and what is learned—is an important variable within the framework being offered here. This concern with relevance supports the argument of many reading teachers who openly say they do not care what children read (within bounds), as long as they *do* in fact read. The reading material can be *Popular Mechanics,* so long as it is something the student likes to read. With the information explosion and the acceleration of change in today's society, it is difficult to rationalize the teaching of a particular content, set of knowledges, or specific discipline to all students. John Dewey long ago emphasized this point. It is important to teach basic communication skills, of which reading is one. It is important to teaching thinking skills, for they will affect the quality and effectiveness of communication. What is being offered here is the idea reflected in the term *content area reading;* that is, the content itself (English, science, social studies, and so on) is less important than the communication and thinking skills that underlie the content. The content, then, is a vehicle for the teaching of these skills. Students should have a hand in the *what* of learning so that learning is relevant; so that when they read to get information, they see a relationship between their own needs and preferences and the information they obtain; so that they are able to answer some of the questions that will help them to integrate themselves into their environment and their society. Students find learning relevant when they can see how learning improves their ability to predict and to acquire their preferences—whatever they may be. The improvement of predictive ability improves students' ability to master their environment in general and to acquire their preferences in particular. Obtaining what one prefers brings personal pleasure. As learning achieves these ends, the student's self-confidence will grow.

OPTIMIZING PREDICTABILITY IN READING

During reading, an individual seeks optimal predictability in order to maintain harmony within a particular instructional or learning event. When optimal predictability does not exist, the student experiences either boredom or confusion. In the one instance, if the instructional material or the task is too simple, too repetitive, or too low in interest level, the student becomes bored with the task and withdraws from it.

This sort of behavior can be evidenced in the motor activity of driving. Driving requires a constant effort to predict. The driver must predict what other drivers are doing and what they intend to do, and what possible hazardous situations might develop at any given moment. He or she must continually process a host of information to make innumerable predictions. With the advent of the interstate highway system, a new and hazardous driving phenomenon was created—boredom in driving. With few stoplights, crossroads, bends, curves, and other physical features that help to keep concentration and attention on driving at optimal level, we tend to be hypnotized by the monotony and boredom of interstate driving so that when a hazardous situation does develop, we are not prepared for it and can easily make a serious driving error we might not make otherwise. In like manner, when individuals find themselves reading material that is too predictable (perhaps they have read it before), they become bored. Less concentration is required and their attention wanders. For whatever reason, the individuals are not challenged by the material or task at hand and tend to withdraw from it.

On the other hand, when too little predictability exists, individuals are thrust into a state of confusion. Using the example of the driver, imagine a novice driver in heavy traffic or a practiced driver on a curving and unfamiliar road. The mass of other cars, the abundance of information signs, and the complexity of three and four street intersections confuse the novice. In a more predictable situation, the novice driver would probably perform adequately. In a situation that possesses little predictability, the novice might withdraw by pulling off the street or become so confused that he or she makes a serious driving error. The practiced driver on an unfamiliar and highly unpredictable road faces the same dilemma. Most of us have had the experience of looking for a particular street or exit ramp that was poorly marked or completely unmarked. Oftentimes in order to "make" the turn or exit, we've had to change lanes hastily and engage in other hazardous driving behaviors simply because predictability was too low. In reading, when predictability is too low, perhaps because the material is too difficult or unfamiliar, confusion is also created for the individual. When this happens, the reader, like the novice driver, tends to withdraw from the situation that is creating the confusion. Over a long period of time, the individual constructs certain defenses and engages in certain behaviors that will remove him or her from the confusing situation or task, that is, reading.

Reading experts gives us two important observations regarding students who have reading problems. First, the reading problem does not "strike" a student as a disease might. It begins to develop, in most instances, early in the primary grades. Without remedial help, the gap between the achievement of the student with reading problems and the achievement of the student who has no reading problems continues to widen as they progress through school. Second, the earlier a reading problem is identified and dealt with, the better is the outlook for the reading problem to be successfully remedied.

This second observation is important in terms of the concept of *defensiveness*. If students experience too little predictability regarding the reading tasks in which they engage, they will avoid the situation and seek familiar kinds of stimulation. When a child is confronted daily with reading tasks that are too unpredictable, too difficult, and hold little chance for experiencing success, the negative effects on the child are enormous. This sort of vicious cycle over an extended period of time takes its toll on the child's self-confidence, natural curiosity, and eagerness to learn, and attitude toward all facets of the environment. A cycle of failure soon becomes evident in which the student predicts failure; a self-fulfilling prophecy of failure then governs his or her school environment and spills over into other elements of the environment. In order to satisfy their basic need to make predictions and confirm their predictions, these children predict failure for themselves, predictions that are all too often correct. It is not surprising that the later remedial efforts to teach reading are begun, the less chance for success exists.

OPTIMIZING PREDICTABILITY IN THE CLASSROOM

Attempting to define the environment in which we operate is an arduous task. Attempting to describe how we successfully interact with our environment becomes even more difficult. That part of the environment outside the realm of school is extremely important, for what happens in that realm greatly affects the interaction between children and their school. It is our contention that much can be done within the school environment to enhance the way in which students interact with all elements of their environment. The supportive nature of this enhancement process is particularly exciting, for by improving the interaction of the student with the school environment, the groundwork is laid for improving the interaction of the student with all elements of the environment. This contributes to successful living.

In this book, discussions of the environment will be largely limited to the central influences of the school environment. The school environment can be viewed as a combination of three elements: the teacher, the student and the student's peers, and the tasks and materials used in the teaching-learning process. Each of these aspects of the school environment can be optimized to improve the student's ability to predict.

The Teacher

Increasingly, educators are coming to realize that the teacher, more than the methods or materials, is the most important variable in an instructional situation. Bond and Dykstra (1967), in their report of the Cooperative First Grade Studies, concluded that little support exists for the use of one instructional procedure over another. Myers (1978) echoes this point in a review of studies of different teaching methods in reading. He concluded that different teaching methods seldom result in a lasting positive effect on reading achievement when compared to other methods. Rather, the teacher seems to be the determining factor regarding the quality and effect of reading instruction. This trend can also be evidenced in the research literature of the last several years.

Rosenthal and Jacobsen (1968) also draw attention to the potent effect the teacher has on learning. They maintain that teachers' expectancies regarding students have an extremely important impact on learning and achievement. By expecting students to do well, teachers can positively affect achievement. Although the research conducted by Rosenthal and Jacobsen has been hotly criticized and a number of studies have been conducted that do not support their contention, logic and experience dictate that a certain amount of truth is evidenced by their arguments. Individual students differ such that the teacher's expectancies will have minimal effect on some and maximal effect on others. The predictions a teacher makes affect self-confidence and self-esteem. Teacher predictions are an outward manifestation of the attitudes teachers have about students and the extent to which these attitudes reflect acceptance of students as people, as human beings, as individuals in their own right, and as worthwhile members of society, rather than as individuals the teacher has to "put up with."

Humanists like Carl Rogers emphasize this point to the extreme, but that emphasis is not necessarily unwarranted. It is important that teachers develop a certain empathy with their students. It is important that they be aware of the kinds of problems that confront their students. It is important that teachers be aware of the disparate backgrounds from which their students come. It is important for teachers to understand the needs of their students, not all of which are school related. It is important that teachers learn what motivates individuals, what individuals are interested in, what is important to individuals. It is important that teachers respect children. These human considerations a teacher can show for students are the determinants of self-confidence and a sense of worth—those factors that seem to be strongly related to reading ability and the ability to predict. The role the teacher plays as a socializer of students is an important and often overlooked role.

Another major task of the teacher in the school environment is to insure, from an instructional standpoint, an optimally predictable environment. This includes, as we have seen, the consideration of curricular relevance. Optimal predictability can also be enhanced by the careful choice of reading materials. A very important function a teacher must fulfill in this regard is that of continually defining and clarifying what students are to do. Too often, teachers make incomplete assignments like, "In one page, compare Macbeth and Hitler," or "For Monday read chapters seven and eight." In the first example, little information is given as to what aspects of the two men ought to be compared. One can bet that the student who comes in with a comparison of Macbeth and Hitler in terms of their physical features will be fortunate to get a good grade. In this example, the teacher probably meant "compare and contrast," rather than just "compare." The student who compares *and* contrasts the two men will probably receive the better grade. In the second example, no attempt is made to prepare students for the material, to help them formulate ideas about what they are reading to find out, or to pique their interest in any way. In each instance, an additional five minutes on the part of the teacher could make the assignment much more optimally predictable for students. For example, the teacher might add, "When you do your comparisons of Macbeth and Hitler, think about these three things . . ." or, "Before you write your paper, be sure to reread Macbeth's speech on page seventy-seven." The same procedure can be used in the second example: "As you read these chapters, think about these questions . . ." or "After you read chapter seven, see if you can think of why the author might have placed it *after* chapter six; is there a better spot in the book for this chapter?" In each of these examples, predictability is being optimized to further insure successful completion of the task.

Another method that has gained considerable impetus during the past several years as a way of optimizing predictability concerns the use of instructional objectives. Although research has been inconsistent regarding the extent to which instructional objectives facilitate learning, one strength associated with their use is that of clarifying exactly what the student is to learn and specifying the level of performance he or she is expected to achieve. The teacher, then, by using instructional objectives, can keep students constantly informed concerning the nature of the learning tasks they are attempting. The teacher can further communicate to the students how well they ought to do on a given task. Finally, instructional objectives tend to break a complex task down into more manageable units or steps, providing more and continual feedback to students regarding their performance of the task.

Student and Peers

As we have seen, the student's sense of well-being and self-confidence has a great effect on performance in a school situation. The attitude of self-confidence is significantly influenced by the social nature of the instructional environment; that is, the student's peers. If a student is embarrassed or belittled in front of peers, for whatever reason, the effect may be devastating on his or her self-confidence. Often, this happens inadvertently by requiring a student to read orally in class, or by pressuring a student for an answer he or she does not know.

When self-confidence is low, the ability to predict successfully is lowered. This affects school performance and achievement.

When the classroom or school becomes anxiety-producing and lacking in predictability, the student will withdraw from and avoid the situation.

Instructional Techniques and Materials

The most common complaint of teachers in general is that they either do not have at their disposal a wide range of materials on a variety of reading levels or that they are not proficient at matching students to materials in terms of readability level. Readability level (the ease with which materials can be read) is assessed in numerous ways. We will be concerned in later chapters with factors that affect readability. For now, consider readabilty as an index of predictability.

If you were handed a book about laser optics and their application to holography, you might have trouble reading it, if you were even motivated to read it in the first place. The task of reading the book would be an arduous and confusing one, for the book, in your case, would be extremely low in predictability. Reading materials that are too difficult for students are also confusing, thwarting, and something to avoid. The careful choice of materials in terms of readability, then, becomes an important instructional consideration. Furthermore, the use of one textbook for a group of twenty-five or thirty students with a variety of reading levels is rarely acceptable or defensible.

Different kinds of instructional materials have been developed to deal with the problem of optimal predictability. Basal readers in the elementary and middle grades have long been the vehicles used to maintain control of readability levels and to make sure that some sort of sequence in teaching reading is adhered to. The central concern of basals is vocabulary control. We know that vocabulary difficulty contributes heavily to general reading difficulty. Some have hypothesized that if new vocabulary is introduced systematically and at a comprehensible rate, students will learn it thoroughly before going on. This would appear effectively to deal with the maintenance of optimal predictability. However, it is commonly known that the stories in basals range across as many as four to six grade levels in terms of readability. Further, the introduction of new vocabulary is largely arbitrary. Finally, the usefulness of the basal reader is compromised if all students are reading at the same point in the readers.

There are a number of instructional techniques exemplary of the effort to promote optimal predictability in reading and study assignments. Stauffer's (1959) Directed Reading Activity is one example.

The Directed Reading Activity (DRA) is an attempt to impose a structure on a given lesson in order to optimize the student's ability to perform the requirements of that lesson, particularly the reading required by the lesson. Briefly, the DRA is made up of four steps. The first step, "readiness," can be dealt with in a variety of ways. Essentially, the task of the teacher in establishing readiness to do the reading is to (1) match the reading materials to the reading level of the student, (2) stimulate an interest in the new material by relating it to previous work, (3) build a background of concepts or key ideas, (4) introduce new vocabulary, and (5) set a purpose for reading the new material. The subsequent steps of the DRA are concerned with guiding reading and helping students set their own purposes for reading, extending the development of important concepts through discussion and related activities, and providing follow-up activities to extend and refine the skills being taught in the DRA. Similar methods are much the same as the DRA in that they are initially concerned with establishing a background for reading, establishing an interest in the reading, and directing reading toward the attainment of specified goals and knowledges. Study methods are dealt with in detail in chapter 8.

In essence, instructional formats, such as the DRA, are aimed at increasing the predictability of reading materials. This is accomplished by familiarizing the student with the material to be read *before* actual reading takes place, by getting the student to predict what is contained in the reading material and what ought to be paid attention to during reading, and allowing circumstances in which the student can confirm his or her predictions (for example, follow-up activities).

Along the lines of research in prose learning, several investigators have proposed and studied devices that, in effect, are simply designed to promote optimal predictability. Ausubel's (1960) concept of an advance organizer (as used in this text) is one such example. The advance organizer is a specially constructed reading passage about one-tenth the length of the reading materials on which it is based. It is conceived to provide a conceptual framework, giving students an organizational aid to help them in their reading.

Another related area is that of research in adjunct questions.

Frase (1968), Rothkopf (1965), and others saw the instructional utility in the use of questions. They interspersed questions directly in reading materials with the idea that the questions would guide reading and force students to engage continually in behaviors that would lead to the answering of the questions. Additional research has investigated how a host of adjunct aids and manipulations of reading materials such as underlining, emphasis of important words and phrases by other means, and a number of prereading activities, affect comprehension.

A common thread in this kind of research is evident. The various textual manipulations and prereading activities that have been investigated are, in large part, attempts to enhance predictability of reading materials. Like the Directed Reading Activity, much of this research relies on either establishing "mindsets" for reading or guiding the reader while he or she is actually reading. In both situations, the reader's attention is being directed in an effort to improve his or her ability to predict or to add predictability to the materials being read. In the chapters that follow, we will stress the relationship of prediction to reading and ways in which predictive abilities can be enhanced.

SUMMARY

1. The purposes of reading are to gain information and enjoyment.

2. Reading is important because the ability to read correlates highly with success both in and out of school.

3. People are motivated to predict. They are interested in making predictions and in confirming the predictions they make.

4. The ability to predict contributes to successful reading and successful living.

5. Self-confidence also contributes to successful reading and living. In addition to being able to predict, it is necessary to be self-confident so that one will persist in making predictions and in attempting to confirm the predictions made.

6. Once people are able to predict, they are interested in using their powers of prediction to acquire their personal preferences. Knowledgeable reading teachers encourage reading by determining what reading material their students enjoy and allowing them to make selections from among alternatives. This insures that the student will consider the reading materials relevant.

7. The reader seeks optimum predictability while reading. The reading material should not be so unfamiliar that the reader is confused, yet should be sufficiently novel and informative to be challenging.

8. The teacher should optimize predictability in the classroom. This amounts to structuring the relationships among the teacher, the students, and the instructional program so that the students are able to predict and confirm successful academic achievement. The learning tasks should not be too unfamiliar and difficult for the students to master. On the other hand, the tasks should be sufficiently advanced to generate growth in reading and learning.

REVIEW QUESTIONS

1. Why is reading important?
2. What are the purposes of reading?
3. Why is predictive ability valuable?
4. What is the relationship between reading and prediction?
5. Why is self-confidence important in reading and predicting?
6. What does optimizing predictability mean?
7. Why is it important to optimize predictability in reading and reading instruction?
8. What factors contribute to optimizing predictability in the classroom?
9. How is personal preference related to reading?

CHAPTER 2

Prediction and Reading Instruction

PURPOSE

1. To describe more specifically the reading process, the prediction process, and the relationship between them.
2. To apply the prediction process to the teaching of reading.
3. To show how predictability can be optimized in the classroom to promote learning.

BACKGROUND AND NEW INFORMATION

To understand the content of chapter 2, you need to know the importance and purposes of reading and predicting, the importance of optimizing predictability in reading and reading instruction, and the role that personal preferences play in reading and reading instruction. This information was presented in chapter 1.

Chapter 2 begins with a discussion of the elements of reading instruction: (1) students' reading vocabulary, (2) word identification skills, (3) reading comprehension, (4) students' experiential background, (5) purpose for reading, (6) readability of reading material, and (7) students' study skills. Then the reading process and the prediction process are described. Next, we show how the prediction process meshes with the reading process.

In the last part of the chapter we deal with implications for reading instruction. This includes a consideration of (1) how prediction skills can be taught and (2) how the prediction process applies to reading instruction (that is, to reading material, to the learner, and to the teacher). The chapter ends with a discussion of how optimal predictability can be insured in reading instruction.

abstraction
structural abstraction
contextual abstraction
phonic identification
reading vocabulary
syntax
program
reality criterion
root words
phonic generalizations

DESIRED LEARNING OUTCOMES

The student will be able to:

1. Explain the relationship between experiential background and reading.
2. Enumerate the word identification skills that are used to regain meaning when the meaning of the author's message is lost.
3. Explain the relationship between the readability of reading material and reading.
4. Explain the relationship between study skills and reading.
5. Explain the relationship between establishing purpose for reading and reading.
6. Describe the reading program and the prediction program.
7. Explain how the prediction program can function within the reading program and how programmatic skills can be taught.
8. Describe how the prediction program relates to reading.
9. Describe how optimal predictability can be insured in reading instruction.

ELEMENTS OF READING INSTRUCTION

Reading Vocabulary

Reading is the extraction of meaning from written words and symbols conveying an author's message. In order to read one must understand the word combinations presented by the author—the paragraphs, sentences, and phrases. Sometimes a short phrase conveys the author's meaning. Sometimes it takes larger units of prose. Often, the message an author wishes to convey extends across pages, chapters, and even books. However short or extensive, ultimately it is word combinations that convey the author's message.

To understand word combinations it is necessary to understand the words contained in them; in learning to read, a great deal of time is spent learning the meaning of words. When one has learned the meaning of words, they become a part of the reader's vocabulary. Then these words can be read and retrieved to help him or her understand the message whenever the author uses the words. For this reason an important part of reading instruction is the extension of the student's reading vocabulary. It is the teacher's goal to increase students' reading vocabulary to the point where they become independent readers and learners. That is, they know the meaning of, and can recognize during reading a sufficient number of words to be able to understand a variety of reading materials, with only the occasional assistance of the teacher or other resources. When students become independent readers, they also become independent learners because they can learn without the immediate assistance of others. Vocabulary building is discussed in chapter 4.

Word Identification Skills

In addition to using reading vocabulary and the dictionary to get the meaning of the message, proficient readers develop a number of word identification skills that enable them to unlock the meaning of words without the assistance of the dictionary. The meaning of unfamiliar words can be abstracted from the context in which the unfamiliar words are contained and from the way the words are structured. Consequently, considerable time is spent in reading instruction teaching students how to use word structure and context to abstract meaning from print.

Abstraction is the process of making identifications and predictions from limited clues or features. In *contextual abstraction* readers get the meaning of words from the clues they abstract from the surrounding words. For instance, if a sentence is not understood the reader can get clues to its meaning from the topic sentence at the beginning of the paragraph, the chapter heading, and the subheading in the chapter preceding the unfamiliar words. In *structural abstraction* readers abstract the meaning of words from the structural components of the words. For example, if the word "trimotor" is unfamiliar, we can abstract its meaning if we know the meaning of the root word "motor," the prefix "tri," and that prefixes modify root words.

Another element of reading and reading instruction is the alphabet. To identify words it is important to be able to identify the letters from which they are composed. Children first learn how to pronounce the letters of the alphabet, then to recognize them in print. Eventually they learn how to identify an unfamiliar written word by pronouncing the sounds of the letters in it. This skill is called *phonic identification.* Pronouncing a word will convey its meaning if the word is in the reader's oral vocabulary and he or she establishes an association between the oral symbol and the written symbol. *Phonic identification, then, can be defined as the association of written symbols with their associated oral symbols for the purpose of identifying written words.*

Individuals' potential for capitalizing on their ability to read and learn independently is enhanced immeasurably when they learn how to use authoritative sources to obtain information. In addition to learning how to use the dictionary, they should learn how to use the thesaurus and the encyclopedia, and how to gain access to the wealth of information contained in the library. Because a major purpose of reading is to obtain information, the reading teacher necessarily becomes involved in teaching students how to use authoritative sources to obtain information. These word identifications skills will be elaborated and explained in chapter 3.

Reading Comprehension

The author's message can be understood in many different ways and on many different levels. The reader may be able to recall what the author said and retell the events of a story in the order in which they occurred. This does not mean that the reader understands what the author is saying explicitly or what the implications of the author's message are. A considerable amount of the reading teacher's time is spent teaching reading comprehension because it is the ultimate aim of reading to understand the author's message. Part III of this text is devoted to the teaching of reading comprehension. The list of reading comprehension skills taught by reading teachers is sizeable. Such skills dealt with in the following chapters are: getting the main idea of a story; identifying the motives of characters in a story; detecting the mood the author is conveying; and many more.

Teaching vocabulary, word identification skills, and reading comprehension constitutes a major part of the reading teacher's responsibility. However, there are other factors that affect reading that the reading teacher must be concerned with. Four major factors are the reader's experiential background, the purpose for reading, the readability level of reading material, and the student's study skills.

The Reader's Background of Experience

The relationship between reading and experiential background cannot be overemphasized, for students' background of experiences is a potent factor in their subsequent success in school. Time and time again, we find that students who are retarded in reading have a paucity of experiences—the kinds of experiences that allow them to interact with their environment, to explore and discover new aspects of that environment, to make generalizations, and to discover a sense of order and a sense of predictability in their environment. These experiences are enormously important to students, for they help to determine their ability to predict successfully their relationship to the various aspects of their environment.

The background of experiences students bring with them to school affects the quantity and quality of the ideas they possess and can subsequently relate to words, phrases, and sentences. At the identification level, words can be viewed as stimuli that elicit ideas; obviously, if experiential background is limited, words will fail to elicit ideas. When this happens, the identification level of reading is hampered, as are all subsequent levels of reading. Finally, it is the ideas a person possesses that determine the quality and effect of any given communication. Reading is a form of communication that involves the interaction of the reader's ideas and experiences with those of the author. We can enhance the quantity and quality of these ideas and experiences in a school situation. In order to optimize the teaching of reading at any level, we should be cognizant of the fact that the nature of the student's experiential background will have a great effect on the development of reading skill. Jensen (1978) admonishes researchers to devote more consideration to what the reader reads and brings to the reading situation in the form of experiences, if they are to learn to improve the teaching of reading.

The Purpose for Reading

The purpose for reading is relevant to reading instruction in two ways. First, students must have a purpose for reading. If they do, to some extent, they will be interested in reading. If they do not, they will have little reason to read. We said that there are two general purposes for reading—information and enjoyment. When students learn to read for enjoyment and to gain information, their motivation to read is increased. Second, the teacher has a purpose in assigning particular reading selections to students, presumably to move them toward an instructional objective. Conveying to students the purpose of a reading assignment enables them to see what the teacher wants them to achieve. Consequently, they can plan and organize their efforts to achieve the objective.

Readability of the Reading Material

Another factor that affects reading is the readability level or difficulty level of the reading material assigned to students. Some reading selections are more difficult to read than others. The teacher must be sensitive to this factor and select reading materials that correspond to the students' reading level. If reading material is too difficult (too unpredictable) for them, they will become confused and will be unable to understand what they are reading. If reading material is too elementary (too predictable) for students, they will become bored. In chapter 9 we discuss readability and show you how to match the readability level of reading materials to the students' reading level.

Study Skills

Students' study skills affect their ability to comprehend what they read. An important skill is reading flexibility—the ability to adjust rate of reading to the difficulty of reading materials and the purpose for reading. Reading materials such as the newspaper can be read rapidly, while difficult textbooks must be pondered slowly. Also, students read more carefully if they are to be tested on the reading material than if their reading is solely for enjoyment. Study skills also involve the use of study methods to improve comprehension. Chapter 8 deals with the various study skills that can be used.

THE PROGRAMMATIC NATURE OF READING AND PREDICTION

Throughout our lives, we are constantly engaged in the process of developing routines. Sometimes these routines, or *programs*, are taught to us; other times, we develop them on our own. We have a particular program for tying our shoes. There are a number of individual movements that we engage in when we tie our shoes, and many are reasonably flexible. It matters little, for example, which finger we use in tucking one lace under another in order to draw both of them into a tight knot. It does matter that we draw the knot tightly *before* we attempt to loop the laces into a bow. This part of the "shoelace tying program" is relatively inflexible.

We might use another example—that of riding a bicycle—to extend the idea of our daily use of programs. Riding a bicycle is a complex motor skill composed of many subskills. All these subskills, taken together, comprise the total skill of bicycle riding. But for the moment, let's concern ourselves with only one of the subskills required for riding a bicycle—that of mounting the bicycle. It makes no difference if the rider mounts the bicycle from the left or the right, or the rear for that matter. Nor does it matter if the rider mounts the bicycle by parking it under a tree, climbing the tree, and subsequently lowering himself or herself onto the bicycle. This aspect of the "bicycle riding program" is fairly flexible. It is a certainty, however, that the rider must mount the bicycle *before* riding it. This part of the "bicycle riding program" is entirely inflexible. One simply cannot ride a bicycle before mounting it; there exists a sequence of steps in this instance that must be followed. Deviation from this prescribed sequence is impossible, and attempts at deviation will result in failure.

Similarly, both learning in general and reading in particular involve the understanding of sequences and the discovery of how

things, events, and ideas are ordered, patterned, and programmed. The discovery of patterns and sequences underlies our
ability to make accurate predictions. In reading, for example, we
make identifications of words and extract meaning from combinations of words. Extracting meaning from word combinations involves the discovery of programmatic sequences, as in the way
the events in a story unfold. Once we have perceived pattern and
sequence in the events of a story, we can then predict coming
events in the story. As we read further, we gain more and more
information from the story, and we modify our predictions as we
read, ultimately searching for confirmation of our predictions. We
engage in this process in many of our daily activities.

In a sense, language itself is sequenced and programmed.
There is a particular pattern or order in the way in which letters,
words, and word combinations are sequenced. Linguists call this
patterning *syntax*. The more knowledgeable we are about how
language is sequenced and structured, the better able we are to
make accurate identifications and predictions about language.
Since reading is a language skill, this holds true for reading.

Reading Skills as Programs

Skills are executed programmatically. That is, when we exhibit
a skill we follow a programmatic procedure. As we indicated, to
manifest skill at bicycle riding one follows the bicycle riding program. Similarly, skill in reading requires the execution of a program which we will describe shortly. However, to be skillful at
reading one must master a number of subskills. The mastery of
the subskills requires the execution of corresponding programs.
For instance, there are a number of word identification skills related to reading, each of which requires the mastery of a particular
word identification program. In addition, a number of reading
comprehension skills are related to reading. Each of these requires the mastery of a program. We will discuss these subskills at
length in later chapters, but the point to be made here is that the
skillful reader masters all these subskills and integrates them into
the total program of reading.

As you can see, we are describing reading as an integrated process. If we look at the subskills involved in reading separately, we
run the risk of aiding and abetting what Palmer (1974) calls the
"rip-off in reading." Palmer cites the "skills sleuth" who is con-

stantly concerned with discrete skills. However, he points out, "there is nothing wrong with breaking the teaching of reading into parts so long as the parts are put back together again" (Palmer, 1974:41). If we spend our time breaking reading into parts and assigning the parts to various levels (Palmer's "hierarchical hack"), we reduce the probability of producing critical readers who enjoy reading.

Palmer also makes reference to the "deliberate deceiver" who does not realize that "reading is more than a simple mechanical skill" (Palmer, 1974:44). This leads to the setting of unrealistic expectations for many students, and ultimately these students will be frustrated by reading. Should we finally manage to teach them to read with even a limited proficiency, we can rest assured that reading will not be among their desired or preferred activities.

So, what do we know about reading? We know that to divide reading up into these subskills without showing their relationship to the total reading program is to impose an artificial and even questionable structure on reading. More importantly, this procedure, if taken to the extreme and not used intelligently, can actually be detrimental to our efforts to teach students how to read to get information and how to read for enjoyment.

If we are to teach reading intelligently, there are several serious blunders we ought to avoid. First, although there are some invariant aspects of reading, individual differences in teachers and individual differences in students must be taken into account in order for them to learn to read. Second, we can divide reading into numerous and different subskills, teach mastery of those skills, and mistakenly make the assumption that the student has mastered the total skill of reading. However, the *integration* of all those subskills into one complex behavior is our goal in teaching reading. The student who learns and masters the individual skills has not necessarily mastered the total skill. In reading, we sometimes get so caught up in teaching all the skills that we forget to provide the opportunity to practice those skills in a real reading situation. The integration of the individual skills is our ultimate goal and, according to some researchers, is extremely difficult and perhaps impossible to teach. We may only be able to optimize the conditions under which the integration and practice of skills takes place; that is, we can motivate students, provide for their preferences, teach them the various skills, give them opportunities in which to practice those skills, and so on. In the final analysis, however, it is the student who is responsible for integrating the skills into the total behavior. We can get students to see a need for reading, we can get them to want to read, we can teach them the skills required to read, and we can supply them with books or stories they prefer, but, finally, the student must do the reading.

The programs we use in all levels of reading comprehension will be defined by the purpose or purposes for which we are reading to begin with. We might employ one program to deal with the learning of new words. We might read a selection in a content area with the intention of learning the meanings of new words so that they will become part of our reading vocabulary and ultimately a part of our speaking vocabulary. We might employ a different program that will allow us to recall facts. Memorizing names and dates, especially for tests, would be an example. We might employ still a different sort of program in order to read a selection and be able to retell what we have read in its totality. The purpose one has for reading in the first place has a great effect on what type of program is utilized. In short, what the teacher wants the student to know or be able to do, and what the student wants to know or be able to do as a result of reading, has direct bearing on the program used.

It might be helpful to look at reading in terms of a *reality criterion*. As we have said, reading is getting meaning from the printed page, either for purposes of informational needs or for purposes of entertainment. Anything that we teach, anything that we have students do in a classroom situation, anything that we associate with reading that does not ultimately fulfill this reality criterion, is *not* reading.

This simply means that when we discuss, teach, and test word identification skills, we are not really teaching reading—at least according to our reality criterion. We are, at this point, dealing with skills associated with reading. The student who can sound a word out or use structural clues in the word to predict its meaning is not necessarily reading. The unit of reading is not the word, but word combinations. Words contain meaning, but word combinations contain thoughts. We must always be cautious of the tendency to deviate from this reality criterion regarding reading. For example, teaching a student to sound out a word by a phonics approach is once removed from that reality criterion of getting meaning from print. Students who can sound out words and correctly pronounce them are not yet reading. Even if they can then tell the meaning of the words, they are still not reading. Now, if we teach students phonics generalizations, for example, we are twice removed from our reality criterion. We are now teaching a generalization that we predict will help students sound out words and ultimately result in students getting meaning from print, which they may not necessarily do.

While this is a very brief introduction to some of the skills and processes utilized in reading, it serves to point up the fact that reading is a very complex activity made up of a host of skills and subskills. Traditionally, reading is divided into many subskills to facilitate teaching. Skills like recognizing compound words, using context clues, knowing phonic rules, getting the main idea, making inferences, using an index, and so on appear frequently in the literature of reading instruction and in instructional materials themselves.

From a practical standpoint, a skills approach to the teaching of reading makes a great deal of sense. At the same time, however, we must be familiar with some of the problems associated with this approach to teaching reading. A great deal of discussion in this book will be devoted to clarifying the many skills and subskills of reading and fitting them into a logical and coherent framework. The following description of the reading program is an initial step in this direction.

THE READING AND PREDICTION PROGRAMS

The Reading Program

Now that we have described and discussed reading we can describe the reading process as a three-stage program.

Stage 1: Spontaneous Reading

Spontaneous reading is the continuous assimilation of the author's message as the reader perceives the words on the page. In this stage reading proceeds without interruption because the reader is able to extract meaning from the printed words and has little difficulty understanding what is being read.

Stage 2: Loss of Understanding

Loss of understanding occurs when the reader is unable to extract meaning from the words on the page. Either the printed

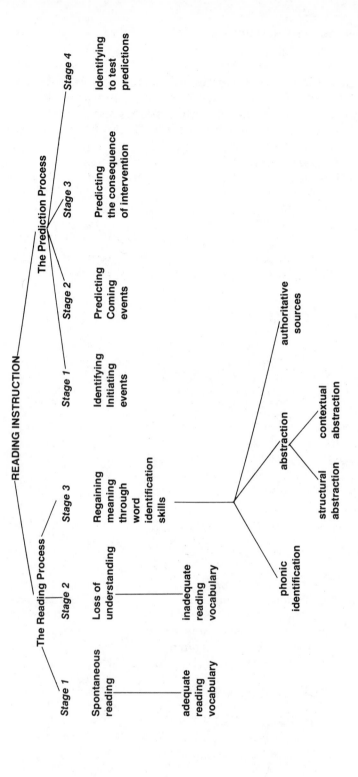

FIGURE 2-1   A hierarchy of topics in chapter 2

words are unfamiliar, or the way the author is using them is unfamiliar. In either event, the words do not bring ideas to the reader's mind revealing the author's message; the reader becomes confused, and reading is interrupted.

Stage 3: Regaining Meaning

To continue reading, once reading is interrupted, the reader must reestablish an understanding of the author's message. To accomplish this word identification skills are used. The reader may use phonic identification, structural abstraction, contextual abstraction, or a combination of these skills and programs. Or he or she may consult an authoritative source such as a dictionary.

Figure 2–2 shows the three stages of the reading process. Stage 1 represents spontaneous reading. In this phase words elicit ideas that convey meaning, and reading progresses without interruption. Stage 2 denotes that words no longer make sense, the meaning of the author's message has been lost, and reading is interrupted. Then the reader enters stage 3 in which phonic identification, structural and contextual abstraction, authoritative sources, or any combination of these is used to regain understanding. Once understanding is regained, the process moves back to stage 1 again, and reading continues spontaneously.

It is important to understand that readers are at one stage or another during their reading. They are either in the process of spontaneous reading in which they have little difficulty in understanding the author's message, or they are in the process of intervening to regain their understanding of the author's message. In either event, the reader's knowledge of the skills of reading and his or her experience in both predicting the meaning of the author's message and how to regain understanding when the author's message is no longer comprehended will determine proficiency in the skill we call reading. In an instructional situation we can enhance the reader's ability both to identify and predict the author's message. As teachers we must (1) create an optimally predictable instructional situation for the student; (2) encourage the development of skill in reading and prediction; and (3) recognize those student behaviors that tell us that the learning tasks and/or the instructional situation is too low in predictability.

The Prediction Program

The prediction program takes place in four stages.

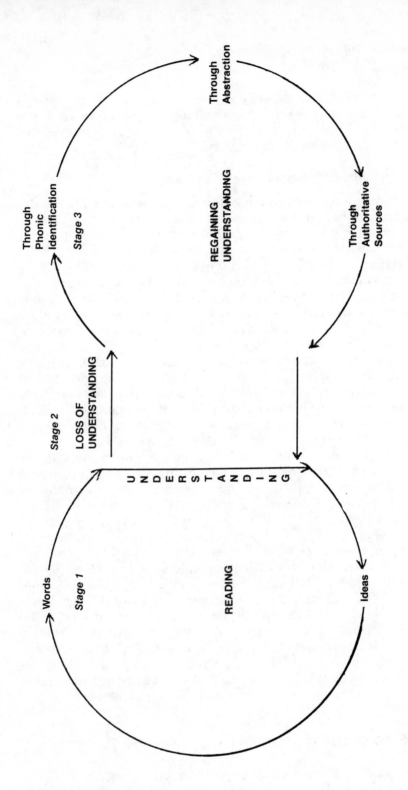

FIGURE 2-2 The reading program

Stage 1: Identifying Initiating Events

Initiating events are the things that stimulate our interest. We attempt to identify them in order to deal with them.

Stage 2: Predicting Coming Events

Once we have identified what is happening, we are prompted to predict what will happen. We look for current trends as a basis for making predictions.

Stage 3: Predicting the Consequences of Intervention

Forces are always intervening on the current trend. People take actions to change the course of events. We note the interventions that are intruding and modify our predictions accordingly.

Stage 4: Identifying to Test Predictions

After predictions are made we monitor ensuing events for feedback to determine whether our predictions are correct.

Figure 2–3 reveals pictorially how the prediction program proceeds.

THE RELATIONSHIP BETWEEN READING AND PREDICTING

Now that we have described the reading and predicting program we can show how they are related by discussing the four stages of the prediction process within the framework of the reading process.

Spontaneous Reading

Stage 1: Identifying Initiating Events

In reading, the initiating events are the words being read and the meaning they convey. The words continue to be initiating events as long as the reader remains interested in the reading material and is able to understand what is being read.

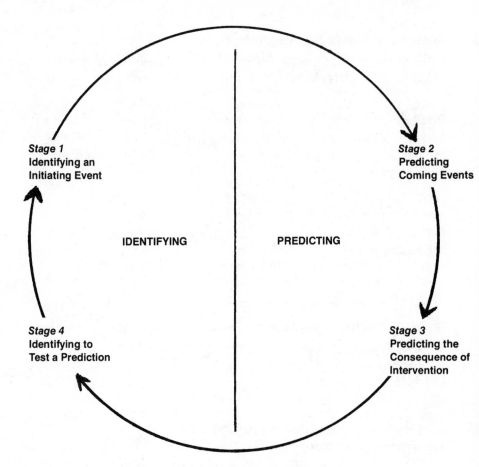

FIGURE 2–3 The prediction program

Stage 2: Predicting Coming Events

The individuals' interest in predicting will cause them to predict the author's coming message based on the meaning they get from the words they are reading. Such is the case when we read a sentence like, "The boys are going surfing." We expect them to load their surfing equipment in a car or truck, travel to the ocean (or other suitable body of water), unload their equipment, enter the water, and start surfing.

It is indeed amazing how one thought can elicit a program indicating an extended sequence of events to occur. The sentence, "I am going on vacation," conveys a thought that matches a program generating a sequence of expectations. We expect the person to pack, to leave home, to take some means of transportation, to arrive at a vacation spa, to seek fun, to return home, and to resume the usual routine. Although particulars may vary, we expect this general sequence of events to occur.

Predicting coming events is so natural that we often overlook it as an important mental function or tend to believe that it is a great intellectual feat achieved only by geniuses. The ease with which one can predict is illustrated in the above examples. To hone our powers of prediction we try to make predictions based upon less and less information. Mystery stories are conceived to strain and test our powers of prediction. As the author presents the mystery, one clue after another is revealed. We find out at the end of the story "who done it." The better predictors uncover the culprit earlier in the story from very few clues. Students who receive high grades often brag that they did little studying. This suggests that they were able to predict the correct answers on the teachers' examinations from a negligible amount of information, and with little effort.

Stage 3: Predicting the Consequences of Intervention

As the author's message unfolds, new information is given which intervenes on our thinking. As a result we attempt to predict the consequences of these interventions. As a story is told, trends keep shifting because the characters in the story are intervening and taking action to produce the outcomes they prefer. In reading a mystery story we may first predict that one of the characters is guilty because of his suspicious actions. Then another character begins to act suspiciously, and we change our mind and predict that she will turn out to be the culprit.

Stage 4: Identifying to Test Predictions

The testing of predictions involves the monitoring of feedback. In spontaneous reading, readers need only to go on further to find out whether their predictions of coming events in the story come true. If the difficulty level of the words in the story remains within their level of comprehension, they should have little difficulty in testing their predictions.

LOSS OF UNDERSTANDING

When the words on the page do not bring ideas to mind conveying the author's message, there is a loss of understanding; the reader becomes confused, and reading is interrupted. This is because the words themselves are unfamiliar. Or, the words may be familiar, but the reader does not have the experiential background to understand them in the way that the author is using them. In either case the words will not bring ideas to mind revealing the author's message.

Loss of understanding can occur because the reader does not understand a word or combination of words conveying a thought. This might be because a single word, phrase, or sentence is not understood. Sentences convey thoughts and ideas. There are a number of reasons a sentence may not be understood. The reader may not understand a key word in the sentence or may know the meaning of each word individually but does not understand them as the author has combined them. Perhaps the author is writing in an idiom or dialect, and the reader is not familiar with the idiom. It is foreign to his or her experiential background. The words. "hankering" (desiring) and "moseying" (walking) have meaning for those who are familiar with Western culture. The words "yonder" (over there) and "you all" have meaning for those familiar with Southern culture. An example of how the reader can understand individual words—but not word combinations—can be seen in the sentence "The boy has gone off." The word combination "gone off" in the Southern idiom means left or departed. It is possible to understand the meaning of each of the two words without understanding them in combination.

Another reason readers may lose their understanding of the author's message is that although they understand the individual thought conveyed by the author, they do not understand the relationship between thoughts. The author's thoughts may seem disconnected to the reader because, in fact, they are or because the reader misreads the words. On the other hand, the reader may not understand the context in which the author is writing or the author's purpose.

In most writing, a paragraph concerns a particular topic, and the sentences in the paragraph are related in that they pertain to the topic. In certain forms of poetry and prose, however, the author foresakes this logical composition to convey personal feeling and mood. Although the sentences in a paragraph may not be related logically with respect to content, they may be related in that they convey similar feelings to create a mood. If readers are not familiar with this kind of writing, they may not understand it. Reading is also interrupted when the reader predicts the coming message, the predictions are not confirmed, and no plausible explanation is given by the author. In short, the material is unpredictable to the reader.

As readers continue to identify the meaning of the words in a passage, they attempt to predict coming events because they are interested in predicting. As the story unfolds, they will be able to make predictions. For instance, the phrase "The boy . . ." does not facilitate a prediction. However, the sentence "The boy is going to the store" does facilitate a prediction. Readers can anticipate that coming events in the reading passage will place the boy in a store and perhaps reveal how he got to the store. Also, one might anticipate a possible commercial transaction while he is at the store. Readers continue to read to test their prediction. They compare ensuing events with their predictions to see if the boy gets to a store. If he does get to a store, events in the story are predictable. If the boy does not get to the store and the story does not explain why, then events are unpredictable, and reading will be interrupted.

Unpredictability causes reading to be interrupted. Such interruptions indicate that readers do not understand what they are reading. In this example, reading is interrupted because events did not turn out as predicted and the reader finds the passage incomprehensible. Thus one aspect of understanding a reading passage involves the confirmation of predictions that reflect cogency and continuity in the passage.

REGAINING MEANING

To describe how meaning is regained we return to the four stages of the prediction process.

Stage 1: Identifying an Initiating Event

Readers become aware that the meaning of the author's message is lost because the words are unfamiliar. Meaning cannot be extracted from the words.

Stage 2: Predicting Coming Events

Because readers are confused by the unfamiliar words, they predict that they will be unable to continue reading unless they find the meaning of the words.

Stage 3: Predicting the Consequences of Intervention

Readers now can exercise choice. If they prefer, they can stop reading. On the other hand, if they prefer to continue to read and have learned programs to identify the meaning of unfamiliar words, they are able to predict that the use of these skills will result in finding the meaning of the puzzling words, enabling them to continue reading. So, if readers possess phonic identification skill, structural and contextual abstraction skills, and know how to consult the appropriate authoritative sources, they can regain meaning. However, they must be sufficiently motivated to read the material they are reading to choose to employ these word identification skills.

Stage 4: Identifying to Test Predictions

When readers employ a word identification skill that they predict will enable them to regain meaning, they must monitor ensuing events to see whether the skill or program is working. To do this they employ the word identification skill and monitor feedback to determine whether or not the skill is unlocking the meaning of the unfamiliar words. If the particular skill is not working, readers can shift to another program and try it. Students are taught a number of word identification programs and their appropriate uses. As they become more proficient in using these skills, they will be able to regain meaning more efficiently. If one word identification skill does not work, a reader can and should be encouraged to try another.

The prediction process permeates all areas of teaching and learning. Students are required to identify and predict in math, social studies, science, and English. Whatever the content area, learning to identify and predict within that content area is essential for students. Furthermore, they must learn to test and confirm their predictions.

TEACHING PROGRAMMATIC SKILLS

When students acquire a programmatic skill, they have learned the program conceptually; that is, they understand the sequence they must follow and why the sequence is arranged the way it is. In addition, they have learned to execute the program. One mistake we often make is to teach only for a conceptual understanding of a program. We do not follow through to insure that the student can execute the program. It cannot be assumed that students who understand a program can execute the program efficiently. The smooth execution of programs requires practice. It is important that the teacher first insure that the students understand the program and how it is to be executed. Then the teacher must guide the student in practicing the execution of the program and then monitor and correct the student's execution of the program until he or she becomes efficient.

It is also an error to teach students to execute a program without giving them a conceptual understanding of how and why the program works. Without a conceptual understanding of a program, students are unable to correct their mistakes when they make them. In teaching a skill such as structural abstraction, it is important to teach the student both to execute the program and to understand how and why it can be used to identify the meaning of an unfamiliar word. In essence we are referring to the difference between training and education. In education we teach a conceptual understanding of a skill as well as the execution of it. In training, only the execution of a program is taught. Such is the case when we teach a dog to fetch a stick when we throw it. The dog learns to execute the program on its master's command, but it is not taught to understand why its actions work or why it is important to learn the skill in the first place.

TEACHING STUDENTS TO IDENTIFY PROGRAMS

As we indicated earlier, there are two skills involved in identifying programs—identifying sequences and identifying the consequences of intervention.

Identifying Sequences

This topic may be approached by explaining to students that many events in their lives occur in a fixed order. The sequence of events that occurs in their school day may be given as an example. We can also explain how assignments given to them often require them to proceed in a sequential order. To offer an example, we can explain that they are often required to read a chapter and then answer the questions at the end of the chapter. We might also explain that the parts of complex words are sequenced in the following order: prefixes, root words, and suffixes. Additionally, authors often present their arguments in sequences. They first introduce a problem. Then they discuss various possible solutions and the ramifications of pursuing each solution. Finally, on the basis of the evidence, they present in conclusion the solution they propose.

Students should also be shown how the events in stories are sequenced and how it is necessary to sequence events in order to tell a story. Most stories can be used to illustrate these points, providing they are at the appropriate readability level. In addition, there are many published instructional exercises that require students to detect sequences in stories. Finally, students should be taught that, although all programs represent fixed sequences of events, there often is flexibility within the fixed sequence.

Identifying the Consequences of Intervention

After students learn to identify sequences, they should be informed that some programs represent cause-effect relationships. They should be given examples contrasting sequences to cause-effect relationships. They might be told that a time sequence does not specify a cause-effect relationship. One o'clock does not cause two o'clock, nor does morning cause afternoon. On the other hand, turning on the ignition of a car is a cause of the car starting, and the sun rising is a cause of it becoming bright outdoors.

These cause-effect principles can now be applied to reading. The student can be told that there is a cause-effect relationship between employing word identification skills and unlocking the meaning of troublesome words. A person who knows how and when to use word identification skills possesses important tools for controlling the acquisition of information. In addition, authors often present cause-effect statements to buttress their conclusions. An author might argue that government spending is the cause of inflation and conclude that to reduce inflation we must reduce government spending. Finally, the student should be taught that cause-effect relationships abound in most stories. Each character in a story is intervening and affecting the outcome of the story. Every intervention can affect the trend and outcome of the story.

A contrast might then be made between reading and using

word identification skills. Students understand that they cannot cause a change in the author's message or the outcome of a story they are reading. On the other hand, they can control the information they acquire through the use of word identification skills and such factors as speed and thoroughness of reading.

USING PROGRAMS TO PREDICT

As we said, programs can be used to make predictions based on a current trend or based on the effects of intervention.

Predicting Coming Events

Students are taught that their knowledge of sequences can be used to predict coming events. Knowing that the teacher required them to answer questions after reading the chapters in the textbook, students can predict that this trend will continue. This skill is then related and applied to reading. Students might be shown how syntactic clues are gained from a knowledge of the way the language is programmed; syntactic sequencing provides a basis for making predictions while reading. Understanding that titles and headings come before and cue the meaning in subsequent paragraphs, students are then able to read the heading and predict the coming message. Knowing that a story has an introduction, a middle, and an outcome, students are able to predict that they can read the end of the story to find out about the outcome any time they choose. Finally, students can be shown how events are sequenced in stories and how this sequence is essential to storytelling.

Predicting the Consequences of Intervention

To introduce this skill and to introduce all topics, the teacher should begin by showing the relevancy of the topic or skill to students' lives. Students can be reminded that they learn to predict based on current trends. For instance, they learn to predict that the sequence of school events will be the same tomorrow as it has been in the recent past. However, they should be told that the principal can intervene to change the school schedule. Knowing that the principal has the authority to change the schedule, one can predict that it will be changed if he or she chooses to change it. In this instance we are predicting the consequence of intervention.

Students should be taught not only how to use word identification skills, but also how to predict how and when they will lead to finding the meaning of troublesome words. As a result they will gain control over the acquisition of information. The teacher can review with the students the various word identification skills they have learned and their appropriate application.

Students then are taught that the interaction of the characters in a story changes the trend of the story. Students must be alert to the actions of the characters and change their predictions of coming events in the story based upon the characters' actions. The teacher can then demonstrate how the actions of characters in various stories changed the trend of events.

In summary, in teaching programmatic skills the teacher should teach students:

1. that it is necessary to identify what is happening in the present in order to predict what will happen in the future;

2. that the identification of programmatic sequences is the basis for making predictions;

3. to identify sequences, which involve students in identifying trends;

4. to identify the consequences of intervention, which involve students in identifying cause-effect relationships;

5. to predict coming events based on an understanding of sequence, which involves students in making predictions based on the identification of trends; and

6. to predict the consequences of intervention, which involve students in making predictions based on the identification of cause-effect relationships.

APPLYING THE PREDICTION PROGRAM
TO READING INSTRUCTION

The four stages of the prediction program are applicable and relevant to the teaching of reading. Let us first look at the prediction program from the standpoint of the reader. Then, we can view the prediction process from the perspective of the learner in the classroom. Finally, we can show how the prediction program applies to reading instruction.

Reading and the Prediction Program

In chapter 1 we cited the work of Goodman and a number of other researchers who have investigated the skills and processes of reading. Learning to read and developing skill in reading are governed to a very great extent by the learner's ability to predict. Therefore, understanding the prediction process and how the learner engages in predicting is important to understanding the nature of reading and how to teach reading. Let us now describe the stages readers go through in using their ability to predict during reading.

Stage 1: Identifying an Initiating Event

In terms of the act of reading itself, an initiating event is nothing more than the material the student reads. An initiating event in reading, then, consists of the letters, words, and word combinations contained in the material. If, for example, students are assigned a short story to read, the short story becomes the initiating event, and the students' ability to make identifications of words and word combinations governs to a very great extent their ability to predict the author's message. If the short story is far above the students' effective reading level, they will be unable to gather enough information from the story to predict the message. Let's assume that we are reading a short story within our ability range about a young man named Bobby Marshman who is speeding down a mountain road.

Stage 2: Predicting Coming Events

As pointed out in chapter 1, we are constantly engaged in the process of predicting future events. Our knowledge of how events are programmed or sequenced permits us to make these predictions. As we identify events in the present, we search for patterns and sequences that will enable us to make predictions. For example, we might hear someone counting "1, 2, 3, 4." Our knowledge of and familiarity with the counting sequence allow us to predict that the next numbers in the sequence will be "5, 6, 7" and so on. In this example, we identified the initiating event (the numbers 1, 2, 3, 4), discovered a sequence, and predicted coming events (the numbers 5, 6, 7).

In the same way, we search for programmatic sequences in the information we gain from reading so that we can predict the author's message. Our ability to make identifications is crucial in this respect. In reading the short story about the young man driving down the mountain road, we automatically begin making predictions about the coming events in the story. Based on only the information we have so far, we might make a prediction that the young man in the story is going to be involved in an accident. As we continue to read, we learn that the brakes on the automobile fail and that our prediction appears to be an accurate one.

Stage 3: Predicting the Consequences of Intervention

We know that as the story unfolds and we gain additional information, we may modify our predictions of coming events. As we read the short story, we learn that the young man is a professional race driver. This new information causes us to change our prediction: he will come very close to having an accident, but his driving skill will help him avoid the accident. The author has intervened and supplied us additional information, and we have used that information in altering our prediction so that it is more likely to be confirmed.

Stage 4: Identifying to Test Predictions

At this point we have made predictions about coming events in the story and modified our predictions based on new information we gained from the story. Ultimately, we finish the short story and test the predictions we made. As it turns out, our original prediction was not quite accurate, but our modified prediction was, and we are finally able to confirm it. Had certain words *not* been in our reading vocabularies so that we could identify them (for example, "race," "driver," "brakes"), our ability to make accurate and plausible predictions of coming events would have been greatly hampered. On the other hand, if our ability to make identification had been at a very high level, our early predictions might not have required modification. While we were able to identify the words "Bobby Marshman," they contained little meaning for most of us. Racing enthusiasts would have identified Bobby Marshman as a professional driver and would have predicted early in the short story that there would be no accident, even though the automobile's brakes failed.

The Learner and the Prediction Program

In an instructional situation, learners constantly seek optimal predictability. They want to know what they are to do, how doing particular learning tasks will help them gain their preferences from the environment, and how best to go about the learning tasks they are assigned by the teacher. When learners are not aware or informed of these kinds of things, the classroom becomes low in predictability, and they can become either confused or bored. Learners' natural inclinations are to alleviate that confusion or boredom, and they will typically engage in a variety of behaviors to maintain optimal predictability. On the one hand, learners may predict failure for themselves and withdraw from the situation or even disrupt the classroom. These behaviors are indicators that optimal predictability does not exist in the classroom for some students. The following is a description of the prediction process and how the learner attempts to achieve predictability in the classroom learning situation.

Stage 1: Identifying an Initiating Event

As we pointed out in chapter 1, maintaining optimal predictability in an instructional situation is important for a number of reasons. When learners find a particular learning task low in predictability, they will avoid the task. If the task is too difficult, unclear as to what the learners are to do, lacks familiarity or interest for the learners, or lacks purpose and practical utility in the way the learners perceive it, learning and achievement will be hampered.

What we as teachers do to help students identify and clarify the learning tasks we assign (that is, initiating events) can greatly enhance learning and achievement. As students are actively involved in learning, learning becomes purposeful. As learning becomes purposeful, achievement is enhanced. As achievement is enhanced, students' self-confidence is bolstered, which in turn enhances learning and achievement.

Stage 2: Predicting Coming Events

When students are unable to identify an initiating event or learning task for any one of the reasons stated above, they are subsequently unable to predict coming events in the classroom. For example, if students are assigned to read a short story but no particular purpose is established for reading the short story (for example, "read the story for enjoyment," "read the story since you will be tested on it," "read the story to find out . . ."), then students are less able to predict how they should go about the reading task and what they will ultimately be expected to do. Less able readers will be particularly at a disadvantage in this respect.

Stage 3: Predicting the Consequences of Intervention

When the instructional situation is low in predictability, learners are motivated to intervene in order to change the situation. At this point learners may predict that the task expected of them is too difficult, lacks structure and purpose, and so on. One way in which learners might intervene is to withdraw from the task, having already predicted failure and frustration for themselves. Learners might also recognize the fact that they are not clear about what the teacher expects of them or how to do this task, in which case they can seek clarification by questioning the teacher or other classmates.

In an actual reading situation, readers can also predict the consequences of intervention. Learners may encounter unfamiliar words in their reading, resulting in a loss or interruption of meaning. In this case, the learner may employ any one of a number of word recognition skills, consult a dictionary in order to regain meaning, or consult the teacher. In any event, the learner has encountered difficulty in making identifications—and, therefore, in predicting coming events—and has taken action (intervened) in order to restore predictability in the instructional situation. It is important for the teacher to realize that the learner can intervene to add predictability to the instructional situation by engaging in either adaptive behaviors (asking questions to clarify the task, using the dictionary, and so forth) or maladaptive behaviors (disrupting the class, gazing out of the window, going to the bathroom, and so on).

Stage 4: Identifying to Test Predictions

Finally, the prediction process as it applies to learners specifies that they will seek to test and confirm the predictions they have made, both with regard to reading and the total instructional situation. For example, if readers encounter an unfamiliar word and consult the dictionary for its meaning, they have predicted that the dictionary will provide them enough information to regain meaning. If this is the case, they are able to test and confirm their prediction in this respect. The dictionary may present several meanings for the unfamiliar word, however, and learners may be unable to predict which meaning is most appropriate in the immediate context of what they are reading. Learners, in this instance, may have to intervene again by consulting the teacher, predicting that the teacher will provide the needed information about the unfamiliar word. On the other hand, learners may have predicted failure for themselves; in this instance, the final stage of the prediction process gives them the opportunity to confirm that prediction also.

The Teacher and the Prediction Program

The essence of teaching is the teacher's ability to maintain optimum predictability for students in the classroom instructional situation. There are many teacher behaviors that can contribute to or work against establishing optimum predictability. Below is a description of how the stages of the prediction process apply to what the teacher does in the classroom.

Stage 1: Identifying an Initiating Event

A most important facet of teaching is preparing students to engage in a particular learning task. The actions of the teacher in this respect are extremely important to student learning and achievement in the classroom since the teacher's actions are themselves initiating events (for example, "read chapter 9," "work problems 1 through 5 at the end of the chapter," "if you have trouble with the assignment, raise your hand and I'll help you"). At least four general categories of teacher behaviors (initiating events) have a great effect in enhancing learning and achievement. In other contexts, the behaviors have been referred to as "readiness activities" that are designed to make clear the purposes for reading and learning and to provide motivation for reading and learning.

Establishing familiarity and appropriateness of new content. The first decision teachers must make involves the appropriateness of a particular learning task; the task must be within the ability range of the students so that they can successfully engage in the task, and the task must not be beyond their experience. Secondly, it is important that the teacher demonstrate to students that they already know something about the new content or task and that it is not completely new or unfamiliar to them. This is important since as human beings we tend to withdraw from completely unfamiliar tasks and situations that are low in predictability.

Establishing interest in the task or new content. It goes without saying that if a student is interested in reading and learning, he or she is

177 630

much more likely to engage in those behaviors. Interest and motivation are such potent factors in learning that often we are able to engage in learning new skills or information far beyond the apparent limits of our ability simply because we are highly interested and motivated. It becomes important, then, for the teacher to capitalize on students' interests and motivations in order to insure optimum learning and achievement.

Establishing the importance and practical utility of the task or new content. Often, students do not perceive relevance or practical value in the tasks they do, the material they read, or the skills they learn in school. If the teacher takes care to communicate to students why a task or skill is important, how it is useful, and how it will fulfill students' needs, learning and achievement can be optimized.

Establishing and clarifying the task. We have pointed out several times that when a learning task is not clear in the mind of a student, the instructional situation lacks predictability and learning is hampered. It is, therefore, extremely important that the teacher communicate to the learner the goals and objectives of the learning task, requirements of the learning task, and expectations once the task is completed.

Stage 2: Predicting Coming Events

The teacher, like the learner, must predict coming events in the instructional situation. For example, after assigning a particular learning task, the teacher must anticipate which students will have difficulty in successfully completing the task so that extra help and guidance can be provided to those students. Many of the predictions the teacher makes are dealt with in identifying the initiating event. For example, the teacher may predict that certain vocabulary items will create reading problems for students and preteach those words before students begin their reading. Also, the teacher needs to predict the amount of time a learning task will take and the materials required.

Stage 3: Predicting the Consequences of Intervention

All of the teacher's actions and behaviors in the instructional situation can be viewed as interventions. Preteaching new vocabulary words is an intervention on the part of the teacher. Providing extra help to slower or less able readers is an intervention by the teacher. The teacher must also intervene at other times during the instructional situations as a result of new information. For example, a student may engage in disruptive behavior the teacher had not anticipated. The teacher then must eliminate the disruption and involve the student in the learning task.

Stage 4: Identifying to Test Predictions

Much of what the teacher does along the lines of testing is an attempt to confirm predictions that students will successfully master the learning task or new content. If the teacher's predictions are confirmed, then instruction continues to the next step, level, or unit. If the teacher's predictions are not confirmed, he or she may decide to intervene by spending more time on a particular task, eliminating the learning task or content from the instruction program, and so on.

INSURING OPTIMUM PREDICTABILITY IN READING INSTRUCTION

Based on the preceding discussion, we can make some specific recommendations for optimizing predictability for the student. To insure optimum predictability the reading teacher attempts to make reading interesting and challenging rather than boring, and manageable for the student rather than confusing.

Enhancing Student Readiness

We have indicated that the preinstructional behaviors or initiating events in which the teacher engages before students begin a particular reading or learning task have a great effect on subsequent student achievement. The degree to which the teacher insures that a task is appropriate for students, contains a certain amount of familiarity, is perceived by students as interesting and relevant, and is clear to them in its objectives, will govern student achievement. In other contexts, these preinstructional teacher behaviors have been called "establishing purposes for reading" and "establishing readiness for reading and learning."

A list of questions the teacher can ask of a particular learning or reading task, as well as the way in which the students are prepared or readied to engage in the task, follows. While it would be virtually impossible for the teacher to deal with every question from the list regarding every reading and learning task assigned to students, it is important for the teacher to consider these questions and attempt to deal in some way with each of the four major areas for enhancing student readiness.

A. Establishing familiarity and appropriateness of new content
    1. How does new material fit in with material already studied?
    2. Do students have knowledge of new material?
    3. Have students mastered the reading/thinking skills required to deal effectively with the new material?
    4. Do students possess the experiential background required to deal adequately with the new material?
    5. What aspects of the new material (vocabulary, concepts, specialized reading skills like map reading, and so forth) are sufficiently difficult and/or unfamiliar to necessitate preteaching and extra instruction?

B. Establishing interest in new content
    1. Are there aspects of the new content that students will find interesting?
    2. Is there anecdotal information the teacher can use to stimulate interest in the new content?
    3. Will the new content fulfill students' recreational reading needs in any way?
    4. What questions or other techniques can the teacher use to arouse interest and curiosity in reading the new material?

C. Establishing the importance and practical utility of new content
    1. Will the information contained in the new content fulfill students' informational reading needs? Will it help them gain their preferences?
    2. Is the new content useful to students beyond the classroom?
    3. Will the information contained in the new content be useful in helping students deal with day-to-day problems they encounter?

    4. How does the teacher rationalize to students the learning of new content?

    5. How does the teacher establish usefulness of the new content?

    6. What circumstances might necessitate knowledge of the new content?

D. Establishing and clarifying the task

    1. Have students been informed of the general and specific goals and objectives of the reading assignment?

    2. Do students know how to approach the assigned task? Are they aware of the different reading and study strategies required by the task?

    3. Do students know what is expected of them, what they are expected to know, and what they will be required to do once they have completed the assignment?

    4. Has the teacher involved the students in establishing reading purposes, objectives, and goals for the assignment?

Enhancing Students' Ability to Predict

To make reading predictable to students, they should be informed that spontaneous reading is interrupted when the reader does not understand the author's message. They should realize that loss of understanding while reading happens to everyone. As students attempt to improve their ability to read and to predict, they deal with increasingly difficult material. Meeting the challenge is necessary for learning and self-improvement. The students should then be informed that to continue to read and to learn, it is important to master word identification skills which enable them to regain meaning. Reading becomes predictable when students learn that loss of understanding is an inevitable part of the process and that when it occurs they can predict the regaining of meaning, if they master important word identification skills.

The students' ability to predict can be further enhanced if they become familiar with the prediction process. They should be taught that identification is prerequisite to prediction and that reading involves both identification and prediction. In order to read, one must identify the meaning of words. While reading, one attempts to predict the coming message. An example can be traced that shows students how, while reading a story, the reader makes predictions based on identifications, and how, as he or she continues to read, predictions are modified based on new information introduced by the author. Recall the example of the race car driver.

We have shown how the ability to predict is important to the process of reading and to maintaining optimum predictability in the instructional situation. We have also indicated that a very important aspect of teaching is the teacher's ability to predict which students require extra instructional guidance, which students will have difficulty with a particular reading or learning task, and in general to anticipate those problems that might interfere with learning before they arise. The teacher can engage students in the prediction process during reading by utilizing the following procedure:

1. Have students read the title of the story or textbook chapter they will be assigned.
2. Have students make predictions based only on the title of the story or chapter, knowledge of the author, or perhaps the first few introductory paragraphs:
   - What do you think this story/chapter is about?
   - What new vocabulary words do you think might be in the story/chapter?
   - What do you think you should look for in this story/chapter?
3. Have students read the initial portion of the story. (In the case of a textbook chapter, have them skim the entire chapter for three to five minutes.) Then, have students make additional predictions about the content of the story/chapter and have them modify, if necessary, the original predictions they made:
   - Have you changed or added to your ideas about this story/chapter? How?
   - Are there any more new words you think might be in this story/chapter? How?
   - What do you think are the most important things you should be on the lookout for?
4. If the reading assignment is lengthy, the teacher may repeat step 3 at appropriate intervals.

5. Enhance students' readiness to read the story/chapter using the appropriate techniques described in chapter 2.

Enhancing Students' Ability to Confirm Predictions

During reading, as well as during an instructional lesson, the student makes predictions and seeks to confirm those predictions. The procedures and techniques we have described thus far are designed to engage the student in the process of making predictions, help the student make increasingly more accurate predictions, and maintain optimum predictability in the instructional situation.

In the final analysis, students' ability to confirm their predictions will be reflected in their achievement of the objectives of a learning task and the degree to which they have mastered the new content being taught. Therefore, the tests and follow-up activities the teacher assigns to students become, themselves, methods by which students confirm their predictions. We will have a great deal to say about the measurement and assessment of student achievement in later chapters. For now, the following guidelines should govern those tests, follow-up activities, and assignments the teacher uses in evaluating student achievement.

1. All follow-up activities should logically relate to the material being read and studied.
2. All follow-up activities should relate to the original purposes that were established for reading.
3. In most instances, follow-up activities should not come as a surprise to students; students should be made aware of the general nature of the follow-up activities before they begin their reading, since this knowledge will guide the way in which students go about the reading task.
4. Like the learning and reading assignments themselves, follow-up activities should be within the experiential and ability ranges of the students.
5. All follow-up activities should be made very clear to students, and they should be prepared and readied (see techniques for enhancing students' readiness) to engage in the activities.

Finally, the student should be informed that the primary purpose of follow-up activities is feedback. It is on the basis of feedback that we correct our errors so that we eventually can confirm our predictions. Students must be taught that they should not be discouraged if their predictions are not confirmed on the first attempt, as we are seldom right the first time. The important thing is to correct our mistakes so that we can eventually confirm our predictions. Also, it is on the basis of testing and follow-up activities that teachers gain diagnostic feedback to help students correct their mistakes and confirm their predictions.

SUMMARY

1. The individuals' experiential background contributes to and limits their school success in general and their reading success in particular. If the words being read do not elicit ideas of past experiences, individuals will not understand what they are reading.

2. Word combinations convey the author's message. Therefore, it is important that we increase students' reading vocabulary to the point at which they become independent readers and learners.

3. Word identification skills are employed to regain understanding when the meaning of the author's message is lost. Word identification skills include (a) phonic identification, (b) structural and contextual abstraction, and (c) the use of authoritative sources.

4. Reading materials may be comprehended in different ways and on different levels. Therefore, students' reading comprehension skills affect substantially their ability to understand what they read.

5. Establishing a purpose for reading affects reading because it creates interest and gives direction to reading.

6. The readability of reading material affects reading because, in order for students to understand what they are reading, the material must correspond to their reading level.

7. Students' study skills affect their reading in that appropriate study methods aid comprehension.

8. Programs are sequences of activities. All processes, procedures, methods, and routines are programs.

9. The reading program contains three stages: Stage 1—spontaneous reading; stage 2—loss of understanding; and

stage 3—regaining meaning. Spontaneous reading continues until there is a loss of understanding. Then, word identification skills are employed to regain meaning. When meaning is regained spontaneous reading resumes.

10. The prediction program consists of four stages: Stage 1—identifying initiating events; stage 2—predicting coming events; stage 3—predicting the consequences of intervention; and stage 4—identifying to test prediction. The initiating events that attract our attention must be identified before coming events can be predicted. The prediction of coming events is based on the recognition of an emerging trend. Predictions of coming events must be altered as factors and forces intervene to change a trend. After predictions are made they are tested by monitoring environmental feedback (identifying to test predictions).

11. The prediction program can be applied within the reading program to improve our understanding of reading and reading instruction. The prediction program applies to spontaneous reading and the regaining of meaning when the meaning of the message is lost.

12. To teach students how to apply the prediction process to learning and to reading, we must teach them identification and prediction skills. With respect to identification skills, the student must learn to identify sequences and to identify the consequences of interventions. With respect to prediction skills, the student must learn to use programs to predict coming events and to predict the consequences of intervention.

13. To better understand reading and reading instruction it is helpful to apply the prediction program from the viewpoint of the reader, the learner in the classroom, and the teacher. The reader engages in the prediction process while reading as he or she attempts to identify and predict the message. The learner in the classroom employs the prediction process in an attempt to optimize predictability in the learning situation. It is the teacher's job to apply the prediction process to maintain optimum predictability for the student.

14. Predictability can be optimized in the classroom by (a) enhancing student readiness, (b) enhancing students' abilities to predict, and (c) enhancing students' abilities to confirm predictions.

REVIEW QUESTIONS

1. How does the learner's experiential background affect his or her success in school and in reading?

2. Why is the understanding of word combinations more important in reading than the understanding of individual words?

3. What word identification skills can be used to regain meaning when the meaning of the author's message is lost?

4. How do students' reading comprehension skills affect their reading?

5. How does establishing purpose for reading affect reading?

6. How does the readability level of reading materials affect reading?

7. How do students' study skills affect their reading?

8. What are programs?

9. What are the stages of the reading program? How are they related?

10. What are the stages of the prediction program? How are they related?

11. How does the prediction program pertain to the stages of the reading program?

12. How can we teach students the skills necessary for them to predict? Specifically, how can we teach them to (a) identify sequences; (b) identify the consequences of intervention; (c) use programs to predict coming events; and (d) use programs to predict the consequences of intervention?

PART II
LEARNING WORDS

CHAPTER 3
Word Identification and Prediction Skills

PURPOSE

1. To describe in greater detail the major word identification and prediction skills used in reading.
2. To discuss the rationale behind and limitations of the various word identification skills.
3. To provide an extended example of how a reader loses and attempts to regain meaning using word identification skills.
4. To describe practical techniques for teaching word identification skills.

BACKGROUND AND NEW INFORMATION

In chapter 2 we introduced and defined most of the word identification skills we will consider in this chapter: phonic identification, structural and contextual abstraction, and the use of authoritative sources. These skills will be dealt with more comprehensively in this chapter.

As we delve more deeply into word identification skills, we will consider the rationale behind and the value and limitations of sight identification, phonic identification, structural and contextual abstraction, and the use of authoritative sources. We will also show how syntax and semantics aid in the abstraction of meaning from words, and how the various word identification skills are used in combination. We will then describe aids and strategies for teaching each word identification skill.

KEY TERMS

configuration analysis
semantics
blend
whole word method

DESIRED LEARNING OUTCOMES

The student will be able to:

1. Explain the value and limitations of sight identification in reading.
2. Explain the value and limitations of using phonic identification to regain meaning.
3. Explain the value and limitations of both structural and contextual abstraction in reading and in regaining meaning when the message is lost.
4. Explain the value and limitations of using various authoritative sources to gain information.
5. Explain how word identification skills can be used in combination to extract the meaning of words and word combinations.
6. Describe aids and strategies for teaching the various word identification and prediction skills.

In chapter 2 we learned how reading involves the reader in extracting meaning from printed symbols (letters, words, and word combinations). We also described three stages of reading—spontaneous reading, loss of meaning, and regaining meaning—and showed how the reader must necessarily be involved in one stage of reading or another. During spontaneous reading, the reader is able to identify words and word combinations with sufficient proficiency and has no trouble in understanding the author's message. On the other hand, the reader often encounters words and word combinations that are unfamiliar, resulting in a loss of meaning. When this occurs, the reader's task is to regain meaning. The competent reader has a number of word identification skills that help in identifying both the pronunciation and meaning of unfamiliar words and word combinations in order to regain meaning.

As we discuss the various methods of word identification, three things should be kept in mind. First, each particular method of identifying a new word is only one method, and it is not useful in *all* situations requiring the student to unlock a new word. That is, a number of such skills exists, and the student must possess them all. If students are handicapped with regard to any one specific word identification method, it will reduce their ability to deal with words, both singly and in larger contexts. Second, the student must be taught the ability to determine when one particular method is more useful than another in identifying an unfamiliar word. Often we spend large amounts of time in teaching students each word identification method, but we fail to teach them how to select the method that is most relevant to the unfamiliar words they are dealing with at any given time. Third, each word identification method can be viewed as a sort of "minicomputer program" in that it involves a sequence of steps that must be carried out. The flexibility of the order in which they are carried out will vary with the skill and the immediate task. In viewing the word identification methods as programs, it can be said that each individual method is designed to identify either the pronunciation or the meaning of a word or both. The student is faced with the task of determining which method or program will yield the most accurate pronunciation and/or meaning of a new word. Finally, the extent to which a particular word identification program is useful depends upon the relative degree of familiarity or unfamiliarity of the word or word combination the reader must deal with. While reading, the reader's task is to extract meaning from the printed symbols, and each word or word combination contains clues that help the reader get meaning. If readers possess adequate skill in identifying words, then they can make use of the clues. If they do not possess adequate facility in word identification programs, the clues available to them are of little use, and they, therefore, have fewer clues to use in identifying words, getting meaning from words, or in regaining meaning from words once it is lost.

WORD IDENTIFICATION AND PREDICTION PROGRAMS

Sight Identification

Sight word knowledge or sight vocabulary does not involve analytic abilities on the part of the student, at least once the particular words become part of the sight vocabulary. Sight vocabulary words are those words the student knows instantly on sight. No analysis is necessary because they are known instantly.

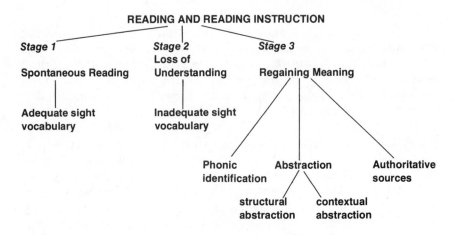

FIGURE 3-1   A hierarchy of topics in chapter 3

The rationale behind teaching sight words has been with us for many years. Several decades ago, researchers began to isolate those words—from a variety of sources—that appeared in print most often. Basic word lists of the 200 or 300 or 600 most frequent words were constructed and circulated among teachers. It was estimated that the 200 to 250 most frequent words accounted for around 60 percent of all the words contained in printed materials. When we test children who have reading problems, a consistent finding is that reading disabled students generally possess poor sight vocabularies.

The line of reasoning was soon advanced that perhaps we should teach all words by a sight vocabulary or "whole word" method. It was discovered that in general children learned the first 200 or 300 words quickly by this particular method, but learning rate and efficiency dropped off rather dramatically after that. We know that the general shape of a word, or configuration, is an important cue in learning words by the sight method; perhaps there exists a finite number of distinct word shapes, or some upper limit with regard to the number of words that can be committed to memory and recognized by sight. Teaching words as wholes is not an acceptable method for teaching reading if it precludes the teaching of other more analytic word identification programs.

Phonic Identification

A great deal of confusion surrounds phonetic analysis and the teaching of phonics skills. Phonics, very simply, is the recognition of visual symbols and their association with the auditory symbols for which they stand. When the student knows the meaning of an auditory symbol and the connection is made between the auditory symbol and its corresponding visual symbol, the meaning of the visual symbol is known.

One reason readers may not understand a passage is that they have misread the words. They may have misread only one word in a sentence and yet lost its meaning. In the sentence "The house is on fire," readers may read the word "house" as "horse." They might correct their mistake by rereading the sentence in order to find a phonic identification error. They may regain understanding by sounding out the words, pronouncing them out loud or subvocally. As we said, pronouncing words will restore understanding if a word is in the reader's oral vocabulary and he or she establishes an association between the oral symbol and the written symbol.

The rationale for teaching reading via a phonics approach has centered around the fact that children who enter first grade already have a large speaking vocabulary at their command, and that teaching phonics capitalizes on that fact. Experts (Harris, 1961) estimate that children entering first grade have somewhere between a 2,500- and 23,000-word speaking vocabulary. By teaching them phonics identification skills, we then teach them the visual symbols for those words they already know as well as a technique for unlocking unfamiliar words. Nearly every teacher of beginning reading will agree that phonics skills are important and should be taught. In fact, Bond and Dykstra (1967) found in their study that even when teachers were assigned to other teaching methods, they introduced phonics instruction because they felt their students would be handicapped without it.

There is one problem, however, connected with teaching phonics. There are approximately forty-three different sounds in the English language, all of which must be represented by twenty-six letters. In addition, letters in different positions in words, and letters preceded or followed by other specific letters, have different sounds associated with them. This sort of variance in the sounds that letters make creates many problems for a large number of children beginning to read. This problem is compounded for children from linguistically different backgrounds.

Dealing with this problem of variance in sound-symbol relations involves the question whether or not to teach phonic generalizations. Clymer (1963) analyzed the utility of a number of phonic generalizations as they applied to words found in primary grade reading materials. More recently, Emans (1967) assessed the utility of forty-five phonic generalizations using words from reading materials above the primary grade level. Emans found that eighteen of the generalizations were applicable in more than 80 percent of the instances.

While general phonic analysis skills involve making the required associations between the visual symbols and the auditory symbols for which they stand, another important related skill is *blending*. Once students have identified the visual/auditory relationship between letters and sounds, they must then synthesize the sounds into syllables and the syllables into words. In order to learn how to blend sounds into larger units, students must first be able to hear the separate sounds that comprise syllables and words. Often, a poor reader may demonstrate a thorough knowledge of letters and letter combinations and the sounds for which they stand, but remain unable to combine the separate sounds into syllables and words.

Decoding is a term that is often used to describe the process of phonetically identifying words. The term decoding implies nothing more, however, than pronouncing the word correctly. One can decode a word and still have little or no idea of what the word means, what the word stands for, or what the word is a label for. Suppose that a student has correctly decoded the word "cat." At this point, we have no idea if the student knows what a cat is; all we know for certain is that he or she can pronounce the word. If the student has had experience with cats, that is, has seen them in the neighborhood, seen them on television, or seen pictures of them, then "cat" will have meaning. The degree to which the student has had experience with cats will greatly affect the efficiency with which the word "cat" is learned. If the student's family has a pet cat that the student is particularly fond of, the word "cat" may have special meaning. Thus, experience underlies reading and learning in general; without it, more often than not, teaching is an arduous task and learning lacks purpose and direction.

Using Word Structure to Identify and Predict

The structure of words suggests clues that can be used in identification and prediction. Configuration analysis is used in teaching sight vocabulary. Certain words can be recognized from their shape and form. The student is taught to recognize these words from their structure. For example, at the primary level, the word "pup" might be outlined as follows by the teacher:

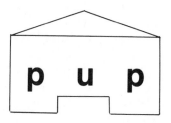

The student might be taught to associate the word "pup" with the shape of a doghouse. The mnemonic device helps the reader recognize the word when it is seen. However, it is most useful when a word has a stylish shape. This type of structural analysis only aids word recognition and has obvious limitations. It does not convey the meaning of the word.

Word structure also is used as a tool to aid in phonic identification. The structure of a word indicates how it is pronounced. The student is taught that structural components of words are pronounced in certain ways. By learning the pronunciation of the structural components of a word he or she can pronounce it more readily. The way in which words are syllabilized represents a structural feature in words that can aid in pronunciation and phonic identification. By identifying separate syllable or sound units in a word, the reader has available a method of analyzing or breaking the word down into its component parts.

Structural analysis also involves the identification of familiar letter patterns and patterns of letters that appear in words with high frequency. In either instance this usually involves identifying the "little word in the big word" for the purpose of correctly pronouncing the unfamiliar word. For example, the reader might recognize the little word "lap" in the larger word "collapse." The word "lap" is not a clue to the meaning of "collapse" but does aid the reader in identifying the pronounciation of the new word. Then, if the reader can attach meaning to the oral symbol for the new word, meaning can be extracted from the printed symbol for the new word. Reading materials that utilize the "linguistic" approach in teaching reading often present those letter patterns that occur most frequently in words, allowing the student to build knowledge of "word families" where words are related according to the letters from which they are composed (for example, "at" is a high frequency letter pattern that is utilized in thousands of words: cat, mat, fat, and so on). This approach is often used as an alternative to the phonic approach since it emphasizes visual rather than auditory analysis of words, and therefore it is generally considered more appropriate for students from linguistically different backgrounds. The identification of familiar letter patterns also includes the recognition of inflectional variations in words that involve person, gender, case, tense, number, and superlatives. Some of the more common inflectional endings include -er, -est, -s, -es, -ed, and -ing.

Structural Abstraction

We said that abstraction is the process of identifying and predicting events from limited clues and features. We gain an understanding of what is happening through abstraction by observing only some of the features associated with the event in question. In spontaneous reading, we use abstraction to identify the meaning of the author's message from minimal word clues. During spontaneous reading we encounter highly familiar words and word combinations and therefore do not need to identify each letter and each word in order to understand the author's message. This use of abstraction allows us to skim or scan words, selecting out the information we wish to acquire from our reading. In spontaneous reading abstraction is also used to predict the coming message. Such is the case in reading mystery stories. Reading that a man buys a gun and a face mask and inspects the blueprint of a bank might lead the reader to predict that the man will attempt to rob the bank as the story unfolds. The clues that prompt this prediction may be interspersed with a great deal of description and dialogue. The reader abstracts these pieces of information from the story as a basis for making a prediction. Finally, abstraction contributes to flexibility during spontaneous reading. Rapid reading skimming and scanning are dependent upon the ability to abstract meaning from minimal word clues. The fewer clues readers need, the faster they can read. However, they adjust their reading speed to get the meaning of the author's message. If they are not using sufficient clues to get the message they read more slowly to pick up additional clues.

Abstraction is also used to regain meaning when the meaning of the message is lost. An unfamiliar event may not be totally unfamiliar; it may have some familiar features. In abstracting to derive understanding one looks for familiar features that pertain to an unfamiliar event in order to derive some understanding of the event. This application of abstraction is slow and deliberate. In using abstraction to unlock the meaning of unfamiliar words readers inspect the passage for familiar features. If they gain sufficient information from fragmentary clues, they can infer the meaning of the unfamiliar word or words.

We constantly make identifications and predictions using our facility in structural abstraction. For example, we might encounter an unfamiliar animal and inspect the animal's structural features in order to identify it. If we find that the animal has structural features like fins and gills, through structural abstraction we can conclude that the animal is a fish. In a similar manner, unfamiliar words may have familiar structural components that enable the reader to identify their meaning by means of structural abstraction. If the word "semiannual" were unfamiliar but the reader knew that the root word "annual" means yearly, the prefix "semi-" means half, and that prefixes appear before and modify root words, he could identify the meaning of "semiannual" through structural abstraction. Similarly, if the word "supersonic" were unfamiliar, but the reader knew the meaning of the root word "sonic" and the prefix "super-," she could decipher the meaning of "supersonic" through structural abstraction.

Readers, then, can structurally abstract the meaning of unfamiliar words with their knowledge of word parts that contain meaning. When loss of understanding occurs, the reader can identify the meaning of a word based on knowledge of prefixes, roots, and suffixes. This becomes a powerful tool in word identification and in regaining meaning, since it permits the reader to make identifications regarding word meaning when the unfamiliar word is not in his or her oral vocabulary.

Using Context to Identify and Predict

While structural abstraction involves observing the internal clues of an unfamiliar object or event in order to identify it, contextual abstraction involves observing clues external to the unfamiliar object or event. The learner inspects the immediate surroundings of the unfamiliar event or object for familiar features in using contextual abstraction. For example, we might find a strange and unfamiliar animal that lives in the water. From the immediate surroundings or context (the water), we might identify the unfamiliar animal to be a fish. Using contextual abstraction, the reader has available a powerful tool for making identifications and predictions, as well as for regaining meaning during reading. If the reader is having difficulty understanding a particular sentence, he or she may get clues from the surrounding sentences or a heading that precedes the paragraph containing the puzzling sentence.

Syntax and Semantics: Aids for Abstracting Meaning

Using Syntactical Clues

Syntax refers to the way language is systematically ordered and programmed. In our discussion of structural abstraction we indicated that knowing that prefixes appear before and modify root words aids in abstracting the meaning of words from their structure.

Syntax is also an aid to contextual abstraction. English generally follows a subject-verb-object pattern; when we encounter unfamiliar words during reading, our knowledge of the way in which the language is programmed helps us to make identifications and predictions through our use of contextual abstraction. For example, suppose while reading we encounter an unfamiliar word represented by the blank space in the following sentence: The _____ bit the mailman. We know from our experience with and knowledge of the language that the unfamiliar word is a noun. We know that nouns usually appear in the first part of the sentence and, when used as subjects, precede the predicate. Since there is only one blank space, we can infer that the unknown word is not an adjective or adverb. Had the sentence contained two unfamiliar words as in "The _____ _____ bit the mailman," we might have inferred through contextual abstraction that one of the unfamiliar words was a noun while the other either modified the unfamiliar noun or the verb "bit."

Using Semantic Clues

The term semantics pertains to getting the meaning or sense of something. In our previous discussion of structural abstraction we showed how knowing the meaning of prefixes and root words within an unfamiliar complex word helps us abstract the meaning of the complex word.

Semantic clues also aid in abstracting meaning from context. We indicated how in syntactic context the position of an unfamiliar word in a sentence, relative to the rest of the words, yields us clues as to the function of the unfamiliar word. With respect to semantic context, knowledge of the meaning of surrounding words gives us clues to the meaning of an unfamiliar word. Consider again the sentence: "The _____ bit the mailman." By analyzing the semantic context, we infer that the unfamiliar word is probably an animal (due to the fact that it bites someone) and that the animal can be found in the same general vicinity as mailmen (due to the fact that it bit a mailman). With this information, we can narrow the choices down to words like "dog," "cat," "snake," and so on. Using other available clues, we can make a fairly precise identification. Now consider the same sentence with one minor change: "The _____ bit the swimmer." The semantic sense of the sentence now tells us that the unfamiliar words is some sort of aquatic animal like a shark, snake, or stingray.

The reader's facility in contextual abstraction is probably the single most important determiner of success in reading in the upper grades. Contextual abstraction, more than any other word identification skill, engages the reader in identifying and predicting the author's message and in ultimately extracting meaning from printed symbols. Wisher (1976) has shown that when a reader has prior knowledge of sentence syntax, this results in superior recall and decreased time spent in reading. Lopez (1977) demonstrated that children's pronunciation errors for Spanish words were cut in half when new words appeared in a semantic context rather than in isolation. Contextual abstraction does have its limitations and becomes less useful to the reader as he or she is required to gain precise meanings for words and word combinations. Contextual abstraction is of limited use, for example, when the reader encounters unfamiliar technical vocabulary in content area reading materials. These vocabulary terms underlie the concepts in the content areas, and therefore require the reader to gain exact and precise meanings.

Using Authoritative Sources in Identifying Words

The knowledge and lore of human culture is passed on from generation to generation. We can find meaning and regain an understanding of what we are reading by consulting an authoritative source. Libraries contain reference books of various kinds which contain definitions and descriptions of objects and events. In a good library one can find authoritative statements on most subjects. Dictionaries, encyclopedias, and text books contain socially agreed upon or standard definitions and descriptions. Perhaps one of the most crucial skills we need to teach students is how to use the library. Many students graduate from secondary schools with only a partial knowledge of how to tap the rich resources in the library.

An authoritative source such as the dictionary is useful for clarifying word meanings when a specific meaning is required, when an in-depth meaning is required, when subtle differences in word meanings must be checked, and when a precise pronunciation is required. Nevertheless, writers like Thomas and Robinson (1972) and Otto, McMenemy, and Smith (1973) warn us against overuse of the dictionary when dealing with words. This activity tends to become extremely boring for students if used too often or for too long a period of time. For many reasons, it is difficult to defend a practice such as requiring students to look up twenty words in the dictionary, write the definitions, syllabicate the words, and so on.

In addition to printed materials, there are human sources the student may consult to regain an understanding of reading material. These are the teachers of the culture. In secondary schools teachers specialize in various content areas. When they are certified for secondary school teaching they are in a sense publicly acknowledged as experts in a particular content area.

There are a number of circumstances in which it is wise to consult a teacher to regain an understanding of reading material. The teacher is usually the last source to consult when the student is unable to understand the author's message. But failing to regain understanding by rereading the passage, through phonetic identification, abstraction, and authoritative sources, the student must rely on the teacher to clear up misunderstanding.

USING WORD IDENTIFICATION AND PREDICTION SKILLS IN COMBINATION

Once meaning is lost, the reader must regain meaning if reading is to continue. Readers must employ a word identification program or programs that they predict will help them regain meaning. In this section, we present examples of how a competent reader employs word identification and prediction programs in order to understand the author's message.

Although these programs seem to be few in number, the complexity of programs in identifying words is very high since, in most instances, we utilize various combinations of programs. Furthermore, each separate program is made up of many steps or subskills. Finally, the ability to predict which particular program or combination of programs will unlock the meaning of a new word—that is, which program(s) to choose—is necessary. This latter ability must be mastered so that it becomes relatively automatic, if reading is to progress smoothly and accurately. Below is an extended example of how meaning can be interrupted when a single word is not understood and the various programs the reader may use to regain understanding of the author's message. Note that the programs for regaining understanding are intertwined. They are used in combination, and the use of one program often leads to and triggers the use of another program.

REGAINING MEANING OF INDIVIDUAL WORDS

Phonic Identification

Let's take the ability of phonic identification as an example. You will remember that in our discussion of phonic identification, the point was made that this particular ability is strictly a decoding process. That is, the student who effectively uses phonic abilities will ultimately be able only to pronounce the word. Facility in phonic identification implies nothing about extracting the meaning of the word. The assumption here is that if students can take an unfamiliar array of visual symbols and translate them into the auditory or sound equivalent of the word, they will have identified the word. If the sound equivalent of the word holds meaning for the students, then the visual equivalent will also. If the word is unknown to the students in its spoken form, however, it will surely be unfamiliar to them in the visual or printed form. Phonic identification, regardless of the degree of importance attached to it by teachers and other practitioners, is at the lowest end of the continuum in regard to the amount and quality of thinking ability it requires, as well as the extent to which it provides meaning clues to words. With this knowledge of the phonic identification program firmly in mind, let us examine an illustration.

Suppose for the present that a reader encounters the word "constabulary." At least for our fictitious reader, "constabulary" is a new word; our reader has never encountered the word in print before. He now engages his "phonic identification program" in order to get the pronunciation of the word. He predicts that once he pronounces the word, he will recognize the sound equivalent, and the sound equivalent will hold meaning for him. He now proceeds to process the familiar cues that are available—in this instance, the letters and combinations of letters. He probably begins with the initial consonant, making the sound of "c." Next, he recognizes the letters "on" as familiar letters that often appear together. You will notice that our reader is now, to some degree, using structural abstraction in decoding the word by looking for familiar letter patterns or "little words in big words." Our reader has thus far recognized the sound of "c" and the sound made by "on" and has combined them to make the sound of the first syllable of the word, "con."

Next our reader sees the blend "st" and immediately produces the sound for which "st" stands. Notice that our reader, who is a relatively good reader, did not try to combine "ns" for the sound these two consonants make. Our reader has internalized the phonics generalization that consonants are split when the word is pronounced, if they cannot be blended in speaking. Although "ns" appears in a number of words (for example, con science), our reader knows automatically that he will have much better luck at pronouncing the word if he deals with the blend "st" rather than the "ns" combination. This knowledge is a result of familiarity with the printed language and the proper use of all those "language generalizations" the reader has made through his experience with the language.

Now our reader sees "ab" and recognizes that "stab" is a word he already knows how to pronounce. He now has correctly decoded "constab." Next, our reader sees the "u" and does not know, perhaps, whether it will have a long "u" sound as in "mule" or a short "u" sound as in "but." In the first instance, he sees no "e" that might give him reason to invoke the old reliable "silent e rule." In the second instance, he does not see a double consonant following the "u." He does know that consonants usually go with the vowels that follow them, so he looks ahead to "lary" for help. Now "ary" is a common and fairly frequent combination of letters our reader has seen attached to words before (again, we are entering the realm of structural analysis). He can derive the sound "lary" makes.

Our reader is now ready to attempt to pronounce the word "constabulary." He will probably come pretty close to the correct pronunciation, even if he does pronounce the "u" like the "u" in "but."

If we were to show how a second reader might use the phonic identification program with the same word, we might come up with a few minor differences. For example, a student who has been taught by a strict analytic phonics approach might attempt to associate a sound with each individual letter and then blend all the individual sounds together (count them, there are twelve) for the correct pronunciation. If we were to show how a third reader uses the phonic identification program with the same word, we will again see some differences. Our third reader might regard the letters "con" as one unit for pronunciation, the letters "st" as a second, the letters "ab" as a third, the letters "ul" as a fourth, and the letters "ary" as a fifth. A fourth reader might use still a slightly different breakdown of letter units in identifying the word "constabulary."

What did our four fictitious readers have in common? What did they all do that exemplified the efficient use of one particular word identification program? First, they all decoded the word from left to right. That is to say, each reader began with the initial portion of the word, proceeded to the medial portion of the word, and finally dealt with the end portion of the word. In phonic identification, left to right analysis is fairly important since pronouncing the letters or syllables of a word out of order will seldom result in accurately identifying the word. Second, each of our readers broke the word down into its component parts. There was some variation among the readers in the way they went about this particular part of the "phonic identification program," but each reader broke the word down into letter and/or syllable units that he or she could deal with singly. Third, each reader, once the word was broken down into units, decoded the units, and went about the task of synthesizing or putting all the pieces back together again by pronouncing them all together—that is, blending them.

All four readers, then, engaged in an orderly and systematic program of identifying the word "constabulary" in order to correctly pronounce the word. Each reader predicted that by getting the correct pronunciation (or coming reasonably close) he or she would ultimately gain meaning from the word. Each reader engaged in relatively efficient phonics identification of "constabulary," and the entire program probably took from one to three seconds, for our readers, as we said, are reasonably good readers.

Now let us assume that even after the word "constabulary" is correctly identified, it does not match any of the words our reader has in his speaking vocabulary. That is, even though our reader can accurately, or fairly accurately, pronounce the word, he still doesn't know what it means. For the moment, "constabulary" is a blank space in the sentence he is reading.

Structural Abstraction

Although our reader has already used the "structural abstraction program" to some degree in his attempt to identify "constabulary," he has used it only to the extent that it might help him identify the word. That is, our reader has used his structural knowledge of words and the patterns of letters that make up words to pronounce the units of the word "constabulary" that he recognized from experience with other words—units like *con*, *stab*, and *lary*.

Now our reader looks at these units for the meaning they might contain individually in order to predict the meaning of the entire word. As an experienced and fairly efficient reader, our reader first goes to the root of the word—"stab." He knows what "stab" means but probably concludes that there is no relationship between a knife thrust and the meaning of "constabulary" (again, we are forced to spill over into another program, that of contextual abstraction; more will be said relative to this example and contextual abstraction). Our reader now searches his memory for other words that have the letter combination "stab" in them. He comes up with "stable." He again sees no relationship between a place where horses are kept and the word "constabulary" (the fact is, "constabulary" comes from "constable," which in turn comes from the Latin phrase "count of the stable"). He considers another meaning of "stable," that is, "unwavering." Again our reader doesn't see the connection, if in fact there is one at all. Now he searches his memory for additional words containing "stab." He comes up with "establish" and then "establishment." He suddenly has an insight that the word "stable" (unwavering) is probably related to "establishment."

Now our reader begins to make use of the information he has gained from using his "structural abstraction program." He pursues the structural abstraction of the new word. Now he looks to "con." He goes through essentially the same program steps he used with "stab." He goes to the prefix first because he has internalized the "rule" or "principle" that prefixes generally contain more meaning than suffixes, just as root words are likely to be of more help than prefixes. He searches his memory for other words that begin with "con." Our reader comes up with too many—constant, construct, concave, contain, contest, and so forth. He sees that in this instance at least the prefix is not of much help in predicting the meaning of the new word. Finally, our reader examines the suffix "lary." The suffix "lary" or "ary" could help him to an extent by providing him a clue to the function of the word in the sentence. Our reader finds little help here, however, as he considers the noun "seminary" and the adjective "contrary."

Thus, by using his structural abstraction program, our reader has accomplished a great deal toward predicting the meaning of the word "constabulary." Certainly the prefix and the suffix could have been a little more helpful; had the prefix been "com" instead of "con" our reader would have quickly seen that the word meant *with* something—perhaps *with unwavering something*. At any rate, our reader holds on to his prediction that "unwavering" or "constantness" is a clue to the actual meaning of "constabulary."

The example of several readers using the same word identification program we presented earlier in relation to the phonics identification program holds in the present instance of the structural abstraction program. A second or third reader might well execute the various steps of the program a little differently, or might even omit some of the steps (the analysis of "lary" and/or "ary" as meaningful clues is a step of the structural abstraction program that many proficient readers might omit). However, all our readers would have used the following steps. First, each reader would have analyzed portions or units of the word "constabulary" for meaning clues. Second, each reader would probably have made some tentative predictions regarding the meaning of individual units within the word. Third, each reader would probably have held on to his tentative prediction pending a chance to confirm or reject the prediction (by use of context or dictionary). Finally, each reader demonstrates proficiency in that upon finding that his phonic identification program does not unlock the meaning of "constabulary," he immediately goes to another word identification program in order to extract meaning from the new word. In short, each reader engages in an orderly and systematic analysis of the new word.

Our reader now possesses the correct (or nearly correct) pronunciation of the word "constabulary." He also has a couple of ideas about what the word means. The reader now resorts to his contextual abstraction program. The sentence containing the new word is "The local *constabulary* was intent upon depriving me of my freedom."

Contextual Abstraction

Our reader first examines the immediate context. He looks at two things. He looks to see where in the sentence the word is located (chances are our reader did this long before his close examination of the suffix "ary" for a determination of the function of the word). He is now examining the *syntactical context* of the new word. He knows from previous experience with the English language—both in spoken and in written form—that the subject of a sentence usually appears first, then the verb or predicate, and finally the object. He has internalized the linguistic principle that a basic order and sequence exist in the language, whether or not he can verbalize the exact nature of this order and sequence on a grammar test. Our reader knows now that "constabulary" is a noun; it is a thing, and possibly a place or event. Our reader knows for sure, however, that "constabulary" is not a verb or some sort of modifier.

Next, our reader scrutinizes the *semantic context* of "constabulary." He first looks at the immediate context, that is, the sentence in which the new word appears. Our reader predicts that "constabulary" is something that can cause a person to go to jail, or something like jail. However, a murder or some other crime can result in the same thing. But a "constabulary" can be *intent* upon forcing a person to go to jail, whereas a crime probably would not be *intent*. Our reader now predicts that a person or persons or something that possesses a will must constitute the "constabulary." Further, our reader sees that whoever constitutes the "constabulary" is a "local" entity. This leads our reader to believe that there are other "constabularies" and that they probably exist with a fair amount of frequency. Thus, on the basis of contextual abstraction, our reader now knows quite a bit about the meaning of "constabulary."

Our reader might go to the trouble of rereading the previous paragraph in order to provide himself additional contextual information that might help in predicting the meaning of "constabulary." He might also revert back to his structural abstraction program after gaining contextual information. He might suddenly remember a related word he had not considered—*constable*. He knows from his own experience and his previous reading that a constable is (at least in this country) some sort of public official who, among other things, can perform marriages. He might also recall that British policemen are called constables. Our reader was, perhaps, thrown off the track somewhat by pronunciation differences between "constable" and "constabulary." In any event, he has now attached additional meaning to "constabulary" via his structural abstraction program. Our reader now predicts that "constabulary" is another word for policemen or police department or some governmental agency concerned with the enforcement of laws.

Had our reader been less proficient in his use of the various word identification and abstraction programs, he might have been forced to employ still another program—the use of the dictionary. Had the programs he did employ been less helpful, which is often the case, our reader still might have had to resort to the use of the dictionary program. Had this been the case, our reader might have had to call upon his contextual abstraction program once again in order to determine which of several dictionary definitions (if there were more than one) was the most appropriate for the word "constabulary" as it was used.

Again, we make the point that our reader is still engaging in an orderly and systematic analysis of the new word. His ability to switch from one program to another and back again demonstrates that he is a proficient reader who has mastered not only a variety of word identification and abstraction programs, but who has mastered the ability to employ them efficiently and effectively. For the mature reader, our ultimate teaching goal regarding word analysis programs is to teach the student all the programs and how to use them, and to teach him to predict which programs are most appropriate and most likely to result in success in any given situation.[1] Again, we feel it necessary to emphasize that reading is a unitary process requiring the effective use of many programs and skills.

---

1. The efficient reader in our example most certainly would not have gone through all of the word identification programs, but would have gone immediately to contextual abstraction because it was the most appropriate and useful program in this particular situation.

REGAINING THE MEANING OF WORD COMBINATIONS

We have demonstrated how a loss of meaning during reading that involves only a single word can interrupt reading. We have also shown how an efficient reader engages in a variety of identification and abstraction programs in order to regain understanding. Now we will show how a loss of meaning involving larger units of prose like phrases, sentences, and paragraphs can interrupt reading. We will show also how a reader can regain understanding by using a repertoire of identification and abstraction programs when puzzling words are encountered.

Suppose our reasonably fluent reader from the previous "constabulary" example encounters the following passage in a short story:

> I had wandered through endless villages and settlements up and down the river. Now, ten years later, I can remember none of them in particular. I have in my mind's eye an amalgam of all the habitats of the river folk.
>
> The river people I met were, as a group, unlike any other people I had ever encountered. A "Devil may care" attitude pervaded them. They were generous to a fault and fiercely loyal. They basked in their freedom and could not comprehend a life that lacked that same complete and total liberty. Only the local constabulary was intent upon depriving me of my freedom. Being an outsider, I was probably the only person who would have allowed himself—under *any* circumstances—to be interfered with.
>
> Fortunately, my humble manner and ability to run very fast helped me to avoid most of the village pokies. However, when the strong arm of the law did descend, its enforcers usually threw the book at me.

Three ideas emerge as important in this passage, ideas the reader must assimilate:

1. The villages on the river were all alike.
2. The people on the river were different.
3. The only people who gave the author any trouble were local police, and they could give him a rough time.

Assimilating the First Major Idea

Phonic Identification Program

In order for our fictitious reader to assimilate the first idea, he will necessarily have to deal with the identification of two words that may be totally unfamiliar, "amalgam" and "habitats." If the words are familiar in a spoken sense, then phonic identification will help the reader to extract meaning. If the words are unfamiliar in both the printed and spoken format, phonic identification will be of little help. We have already shown how a loss of understanding involving a single word can interrupt reading. Although phonic identification is a useful program the reader may employ in his attempt to extract meaning from the rest of the passage, we will now concentrate on structural and contextual abstraction.

Structural Abstraction Program

If the reader is to assimilate the first major idea, he may attempt to extract meaning from "amalgam" through structural abstraction. Our reader might remember that industries sometimes use the word "amalgamated" in their company names and realize that such companies are organized into a conglomerate. As a result he might predict that "amalgam" means something like "composite picture."

Contextual Abstraction Program

As our reader engages in the process of extracting and assimilating the first major idea, he encounters the word "habitats." The subject of the entire first paragraph of the passage is the places where river people live. Our reader knows what villages and settlements are. If, through contextual abstraction, our reader sees that "habitats" is simply another way of saying "villages and settlements," he will be able to extract meaning. Should the above structural abstraction program not be employed with the word "amalgam," the reader can employ his contextual abstraction program to get meaning. If the reader can link the word "amalgam" to the idea that the author could "remember none of them [villages and settlements] in particular," then he will probably be able to attach a certain amount of meaning to the word "amalgam" so that he can continue his reading.

Additionally, our reader may have some difficulty with the idiom "mind's eye"; however, in this particular instance, the reader could simply ignore the idiom and consider only the word "mind" and still extract meaning. Finally, our reader may encounter some difficulties with the unusual syntactic pattern exhibited by the phrase "I can remember none of them in particular." A more familiar pattern, like "I can't remember any particular one," may well make the author's message more predictable.

In this instance, our fluent reader may have to regress and reread the sentence but will probably have little trouble in extracting meaning from it. Still, the fact remains that the reader can experience a temporary interruption in reading due to syntactical patterns of low predictability that make his contextual abstraction programs work less efficiently.

Assimilating the Second Major Idea

Phonic Identification Program

Now our reader must assimilate the second major idea, that the river people were different from others the author has met. The first sentence of paragraph two contains virtually all the information the reader requires in order to assimilate the second major idea. If there are any unfamiliar words in this sentence, the reader is likely to engage his phonic identification program.

Structural Abstraction Program

A key word in assimilating the second major idea is the signal word "unlike." Our fluent reader is probably familiar with this word, but may well encounter a problem if he ignores the prefix "un." This would distort the author's message a great deal and would prevent assimilation of meaning, at least correct meaning. Again, a more predictable way of stating this part of the idea might be "the river people were not like other people I have met."

Contextual Abstraction Program

The contextual abstraction program will certainly be important in assimilating meaning from the next two sentences since they contain words that may be unfamiliar to the reader ("pervaded" and "basked"). Like the other programs the reader might use, contextual abstraction can be used with any words or ideas that are unfamiliar to the reader. However, the next two sentences are relatively unimportant to assimilating the second major idea. These sentences simply tell how the river people were different. In terms of higher level comprehension ability, our reader may be asked on a test how river people are different from other people. In this instance, two idioms will have to be correctly abstracted by the reader: "Devil may care" and "generous to a fault."

Assimilating the Third Major Idea

Phonic Identification Program

We have already explained how phonic identification, as well as other programs, can be used to extract meaning from the word "constabulary." In assimilating the meaning of the third major idea, phonic identification can be used with those words that are unfamiliar to the reader. Again, if the words are unfamiliar in their spoken form, phonic identification will be of little use.

Structural Abstraction Program

Again, we have already explained how structural abstraction programs can be used to gain meaning from the word "constabulary." If the word "intent" is unfamiliar to our reader, he may well get meaning from it with his structural abstraction program by matching it to a more familiar word—intend—because of the similarity in their structure. The meanings of the two words are similar, and they differ only in their function in a given sentence.

Contextual Abstraction Program

In order for our reader to assimilate the third idea, he must have some understanding of the word "constabulary," the phrase "deprived me of my freedom," and the idiom "threw the book at me." He may achieve understanding of "constabulary" in all the ways we have already described. Now, with additional context, we can see that our reader can use contextual abstraction to accurately predict the meaning of "constabulary" and assimilate the third major idea. All our reader need do is extract meaning from "village pokies" and/or "strong arm of the law." Both phrases are excellent contextual clues to the meaning of "constabulary." Should the word "deprived" be unfamiliar, gaining meaning from the word "constabulary" will help in contextually abstracting it. Our reader may search his memory for information about "deprived" and recall that "deprived people" are generally poor and lack many advantages. With this information, our reader will be able to extract enough meaning from "deprived me of my freedom" to continue reading and assimilate part of the third major idea.

Finally, for our reader to assimilate the second part of the last idea, he must be able to extract meaning from the idiom "threw the book." Our reader, if he is unfamiliar with this idiom, probably realizes that no books were thrown in a literal sense. Even in this example, contextual abstraction will be of great help. We know that the author was usually able to avoid being jailed. By picking up on the signal word "however" our reader can predict that "having the book thrown at you" is the opposite of avoiding going to jail. In short, even if the reader is totally unfamiliar with this idiom, he can gain enough meaning through contextual abstraction to regain understanding and continue reading.

In this example, we have been primarily concerned with the reader identifying the author's message. What the reader is ultimately asked to do once he has identified the author's message is another matter. Although we specified what appeared to be the three major ideas from the passage, the teacher who teaches the short story containing this passage may well regard only the idea that the author spent much time among river people to be of interest. Teachers who wish to make the content and tasks they teach optimally predictable will communicate just what they expect the student to assimilate from the reading.

It is important to realize that students must learn to predict the reestablishment of meaning when meaning is lost, or they will become frustrated and thwarted in learning to read. To help make the regaining of meaning optimally predictable for students we must do more than teach them to use word identification and prediction skills independently. We must teach them when the use of each skill is appropriate and how to use the skills in combination as we have demonstrated (Frenzel, 1978). Then they will be able to predict when a particular skill or a combination of skills will unlock the meaning of words. They will become more successful in their attempt to extract and regain meaning, and more self-confident in their ability to read effectively.

AIDS AND STRATEGIES FOR TEACHING WORD IDENTIFICATION AND PREDICTION SKILLS

A Teaching Aid for Sight Identification

We know that certain words appear in print more often than others. The word "the" is probably the most common and frequent word we encounter in our reading. Students who can instantly identify those words that appear most frequently in print possess a good sight vocabulary and, therefore, a useful tool to aid them in word identification. Below is a combined list (Dolch, 1945; Kucera and Francis, 1967) of the 300 words that appear most frequently in printed materials. The first 220 words are in descending order of frequency according to the Kucera-Francis analysis (1967) while the last 80 words appeared on the original Dolch (1945) 220-word list but not in the Kucera-Francis analysis.

Teaching Strategies for Sight Identification

1. Particularly with less able readers, provide students with copies of the sight word list presented in this chapter. Explain to students the importance of these words (they account for well over half the words found in print) and the importance of learning to recognize these words instantly. Set reachable goals for students in learning these words by sight, emphasizing speed and accuracy in recognition.

2. Particularly with less able readers, work the words from the Basic Word List into spelling lessons. Work continuity into spelling lessons by (a) including in the same lesson words related in theme and meaning (states, American, government, public, united, and so forth); (b) including in the same lesson words related in terms of spelling pattern (small, tall, fall, call); (c) including in the same lesson words that are easily confused in terms of spelling and usage (were/where, to/too/two, fall/full).

3. Place sight words on index cards for individual and small group work (see chapter 11 for exposure technique). There are mechanical devices called tachistoscopes designed for teaching sight words. They control the amount of time a word is exposed to a learner for identification. More expensive tachistoscopes project words and phrases on a screen, while relatively inexpensive versions are hand operated. The teacher can construct homemade tachistoscopes with cardboard and paper.

4. Instruction in sight word identification can be carried out in a game format for the more reluctant readers. One successful technique can be used by (a) placing twenty-five to thirty sight words on cards and making two copies of each sight word card; (b) mixing cards up and placing them face down on a table or on the floor in rows and columns; and (c) having students one at a time turn one card over and attempt to match it with its buried counterpart sight word. This game parallels the television game show "Con-

Combined Dolch and Kucera-Francis Basic Word List

1. the	61. can	121. long	181. left	241. fast
2. of	62. only	122. get	182. number	242. five
3. and	63. other	123. here	183. course	243. fly
4. to	64. new	124. between	184. war	244. four
5. a	65. some	125. both	185. until	245. full
6. in	66. could	126. life	186. always	246. funny
7. that	67. time	127. being	187. away	247. gave
8. is	68. these	128. under	188. something	248. give
9. was	69. two	129. never	189. fact	249. goes
10. he	70. may	130. day	190. though	250. green
11. for	71. then	131. same	191. water	251. grow
12. it	72. do	132. another	192. less	252. help
13. with	73. first	133. know	193. public	253. hold
14. as	74. any	134. while	194. put	254. hot
15. his	75. my	135. last	195. thing	255. hurt
16. on	76. now	136. might	196. almost	256. jump
17. be	77. such	137. us	197. hand	257. keep
18. at	78. like	138. great	198. enough	258. kind
19. by	79. our	139. old	199. far	259. laugh
20. I	80. over	140. year	200. took	260. let
21. this	81. man	141. off	201. head	261. light
22. had	82. me	142. come	202. yet	262. live
23. not	83. even	143. since	203. government	263. myself
24. are	84. most	144. against	204. system	264. open
25. but	85. made	145. go	205. better	265. pick
26. from	86. after	146. came	206. set	266. play
27. or	87. also	147. right	207. told	267. please
28. have	88. did	148. used	208. nothing	268. pretty
29. an	89. many	149. take	209. night	269. pull
30. they	90. before	150. three	210. end	270. ran
31. which	91. must	151. states	211. why	271. read
32. one	92. through	152. himself	212. called	272. red
33. you	93. back	153. few	213. didn't	273. ride
34. were	94. years	154. house	214. eyes	274. round
35. her	95. where	155. use	215. find	275. run
36. all	96. much	156. during	216. going	276. saw
37. she	97. your	157. without	217. look	277. sit
38. there	98. way	158. again	218. asked	278. seven
39. would	99. well	159. place	219. later	279. shall
40. their	100. down	160. American	220. knew	280. show
41. we	101. should	161. around	221. am	281. sing
42. him	102. because	162. however	222. ask	282. six
43. been	103. each	163. home	223. ate	283. sleep
44. has	104. just	164. small	224. big	284. soon
45. when	105. those	165. found	225. black	285. start
46. who	106. people	166. Mrs.	226. blue	286. stop
47. will	107. Mr.	167. thought	227. bring	287. tall
48. more	108. how	168. went	228. brown	288. tell
49. no	109. too	169. say	229. buy	289. ten
50. if	110. little	170. part	230. call	290. thank
51. out	111. state	171. once	231. carry	291. today
52. so	112. good	172. general	232. clean	292. try
53. said	113. very	173. high	233. cold	293. walk
54. what	114. make	174. upon	234. cut	294. want
55. up	115. world	175. school	235. done	295. warm
56. its	116. still	176. every	236. draw	296. wash
57. about	117. own	177. don't	237. drink	297. white
58. into	118. see	178. does	238. eat	298. yes
59. than	119. men	179. got	239. eight	299. wish
60. them	120. work	180. united	240. fall	300. write

centration," and the object of the game is to make as many matches as possible. The student who acquires the most cards by the end of the game wins. The game is most suited for use with two to four players.

A Teaching Aid for Phonic Identification

We have explained how phonic identification is an important word identification skill and that there is a great deal of variance in the sounds that letters and letter combinations make. Often, we have students memorize phonic generalizations that will aid them in correctly pronouncing words. However, many phonic generalizations apply so seldom that it becomes a questionable practice to have students learn them. If the teacher deems it appropriate to teach phonic generalizations, the following eighteen generalizations that Emans (1967) found to apply most often should prove useful:

Generalization	Percent of Utility
1. The letters *io* usually represent a short *u* sound as in notion.	86
2. The letters *oo* usually have the long double *o* sound as in food or the short double *o* sound as in good. They are more likely to have the double *o* sound as in food.	100
3. When a vowel is in the middle of a one-syllable word, the vowel is short except that it may be modified in words in which the vowel is followed by an *r*.	80
4. When the vowel is the middle letter of a one-syllable word, the vowel is short.	80
5. When the first vowel in a word is *a* and the second is *i*, the *a* is usually long and the *i* is silent.	83
6. When the first vowel is *o* and the second is *a*, the *o* is usually long and the *a* is silent.	86
7. The vowel combination *ui* has a short *i* sound.	79
8. The two letters *ow* make the long *o* sound or the *ou* sound as in out	100
9. When *y* is used as a vowel, it most often has the sound of long *e*.	92
10. The letter *a* has the same sound (ô) when followed by *w* and *u*.	84
11. One vowel letter in an accented syllable has its short sound if it comes before the end of the syllable and its long sound if it comes at the end of the syllable.	78
12. One vowel letter in an accented syllable has its short sound if it comes before the end of the syllable and its long sound if it comes at the end of the syllable except when it is followed by an *r*.	92
13. When *y* or *ey* is seen in the last syllable that is not accented, the short sound of *i* is heard.	97
14. A-*tion* at the end of a four-syllable word indicates a secondary accent on the first syllable with a primary accent on the syllable preceding the -*tion*.	95
15. If the first vowel sound in a word is followed by two consonants, the first syllable usually ends with the first of the two consonants.	96

Generalization	Percent of Utility
16. Except in some words with a prefix, if the first vowel sound in a word is followed by a single consonant, that consonant begins the second syllable, and the vowel sound in the first syllable will be long; or if the consonant ends the first syllable, the vowel sound will be short.	84
17. A beginning syllable ending with a consonant and containing a short vowel sound is likely to be accented.	95
18. When a word has only one vowel letter, the vowel sound is likely to be short unless the vowel letter is followed by an *r*.	78

As you teach these generalizations, an example or application of each should be given by the teacher or the students so that the rules begin to have meaning for learners. As students learn and master these phonic generalizations, they will be able to produce their own additional examples and illustrations of the generalizations.

Teaching Strategies for Phonic Identification

1. If phonic generalizations are taught, insure that students learn a common example of each generalization along with the generalization itself. Encourage students to produce their own examples of the phonic generalizations they learn. Students can be encouraged to write words phonetically. Nonsense words written phonetically can be a challenging and enjoyable change for more able readers.

2. Often, retarded readers utilize their skill in phonic identification only in the initial portion of an unfamiliar word, then guess randomly at the pronunciation of the word. Encourage students to systematically use phonic identification skills on the entire word—syllable by syllable and letter by letter. A useful instructional practice for students in this respect is to have them cover the portion of the unfamiliar word they have identified, concentrating then on the next sound unit in the word. Once the student has correctly identified each sound element in the word, he or she should be encouraged to blend the separate elements together in pronouncing the word.

3. In presenting new vocabulary words, the teacher should place the words on the chalkboard and demonstrate correct phonic identification techniques in pronouncing the words. The teacher should insure that students not only hear the correct pro-

nunciation of words, but see the correct pronunciation of words by watching the teacher pronounce vocabulary words.

4. The teacher can also utilize oral reading of words and passages to demonstrate correct pronunciation. Oral reading of stories by the teacher as the students follow along is also an excellent instructional technique. Over-emphasis on oral reading by students is not desirable, since poor readers find oral reading a threatening situation and poor oral reading in a group situation provides other students a poor reading model. If a particular instructional activity necessitates oral reading with students who are not good oral readers, the teacher is wise to allow these students an opportunity to practice what they will read orally in front of the class beforehand. In any event, the teacher should not force students to read orally in front of other classmates.

5. Many drill activities for improving identification skills are available in the form of workbook exercises. Especially for older students who have significant reading problems, drill and workbook activities in phonic identification should be used sparingly and only for short periods of time (five to ten minutes).

6. There are many teacher-made and published games and activities for improving phonic identification skills. These are particularly useful with less able and reluctant readers who lack skill in phonic identification.

Teaching Aids for Using Structure to Identify and Predict

The ability to identify syllables in words can be a useful word identification skill as well as an aid to spelling. Some of the more useful rules for syllabication which are applicable a majority of the time are:

1. There are as many syllables in a word as there are vowels, except when two vowels are sounded as one and when the final *e* is silent.
2. Consonants usually go with the following vowels.
3. If the accent is on the first syllable, the following consonant is included in the first syllable.
4. Consonants are split if they cannot be blended in speaking.
5. Double consonants are split.
6. Prefixes and suffixes remain separate syllables.

7. If a consonant comes before *le* in a word of more than one syllable, this consonant goes with the *le* to form the last syllable.
8. When *ed* comes at the end of a word, it adds a syllable only when preceded by *d* or *t*.

Researchers have determined to a great extent which roots, prefixes, and suffixes appear most often in words. We can use this information in teaching the most frequently appearing word parts and letter patterns. Stauffer (1959) indicates that the suffixes which appear in the list below are most frequent and the prefixes listed below account for around 80 percent of all prefixed words.

Most Frequent Prefixes

ab . . . . . . .from	dis . . . . .apart	pre . . . . .before
ad . . . . . . .to	en . . . . . . .in	pro . . . . . .in front of
be . . . . . . .by	ex . . . . . . .out	re . . . . . . .back
come . . . .with	in . . . . . . .into, not	sub . . . . .under
de . . . . . . .from		un . . . . . . .not

Most Frequent Suffixes*

-able	-ary	-ic	-less
-age	-ate	-ical	-ment
-al	-ence	-ion, -tion, -ation	-ness
-an, -n, -ian	-ent	-ish	-or
-ance	-er	-ity, -ty	-ous
-ant	-ful	-ive	-y

*The five underlined suffixes are the most frequently used

MOST FREQUENT ROOTS

Root	Common Meaning	Example Word
capere	take, seize	precept
tenere	hold, have	detain
mitters	send	transmit
ferre	bear, carry	offer
stare	stand	insist
graphein	write	monograph
legein	say, study of	dialogue
specere	see	inspect
plicare	fold	complicated
tendere	stretch	extend
ducere	lead	produce
ponere	put, place	dispose
facere	make, do	sufficient
scribere	write	transcribe

Teaching Strategies for Using Structure to Identify and Predict

1. In teaching the common prefixes and roots listed in this chapter, encourage students to learn a common example word that clearly demonstrates the meaning of the prefix or root. For example, the prefix "sub" that means "under" is more clearly demonstrated in the word "submerge" than in the word "subtract," although the prefix has essentially the same meaning in both words. In teaching prefixes and roots, encourage students to produce examples of their own that demonstrate how prefixes and roots are used in and are clues to the meanings of words.

2. Once the meaning of a prefix or root is clearly established and students have had an opportunity to come up with their own examples, the teacher can place on the chalkboard relatively unfamiliar words using the same prefixes or roots. The teacher should then engage students in predicting the meaning of the word from the structural clues they have studied. Students' predictions can then be verified by both studying the word in context and consulting the dictionary.

3. Less able students should be encouraged to search for familiar letter patterns (the little word within the big word) contained in unfamiliar words. However, the teacher should make certain that the little words follow the same pronunciation. It can be confusing; for instance, finding the little word "in" in the word "pineapple" would not be appropriate. Again, you see the importance of structure as you first note that the word is compound, and each part should be examined separately and by utilizing a combination of identification skills. If one is not going to utilize the phonic generalization, a better approach than finding little words within big words is to teach word patterns like *ine, ank, ight,* and so forth. The creative teacher can initiate many games and activities in this regard with the more reluctant readers.

4. Even the most reluctant readers are intrigued by the etomology, history, and derivation of words. Searching out the history of words is a motivating instructional activity, if not used to the extreme. Discussions of word history utilizing new vocabulary terms contained in the reading assignments is a useful preinstructional strategy the teacher can use to generate interest in reading and learning. Additionally, showing how words change in meaning over the years is a word study technique that generates student interest.

Teaching Aids for Using Context to Identify and Predict

Contextual Clues

We have discussed two kinds of contextual clues: syntactic and semantic. The use of syntactic context is facilitated by the student's general familiarity with the structure of language; simply the position of an unfamiliar word in a sentence gives a clue to its function and usage. Word endings are also useful syntactical clues since they generally are clues to the function of words; for example, -y and -ly are usually clues to adjectives and adverbs, their function being to modify nouns and verbs respectively (as well as other adjectives and adverbs). Finally, function words that carry little meaning themselves (the, a, but, and, since, and so on) are important syntactic clues since they signal, bridge, and connect the language and thought units that do carry meaning. (In later chapters we will address the subject of "signal" words more extensively.)

The competent use of semantic contextual clues by the reader in gaining or regaining meaning during reading is a most useful word analysis and identification skill. There are a number of semantic contextual clues that aid the reader. Some of the more common ones are listed below.

(a) *Direct statement of meaning*. Often a writer will clarify and informally define words and word combinations that are of particular importance or that are apt to be misunderstood by the reader.

> *Holography*, or three-dimensional photography, has many industrial applications.

> The group finally reached a *consensus*. Everyone agreed to continue with the new project.

> *Kinetic* energy is energy of motion.

(b) *Statement of meaning by example*. An author uses examples to either define or clarify unfamiliar words, word combinations, and concepts. The author may also use examples to support a particular line of reasoning being advanced. In any event, the reader should pay particular attention to example clues as a means of gaining or regaining meaning.

> *U.S. imperialism* was perhaps best exemplified by Teddy Roosevelt's "gunboat diplomacy."

A common instance of *sublimation* occurs when dry ice goes from a solid to a gas, without passing through the liquid stage.

The letter *p* is a *voiceless consonant* while the letter *b* is a *voiced consonant*.

(c) *Statement of meaning by description.* An author often provides enough description so that the reader can infer meaning for unfamiliar words and word combinations. Description can be provided by comparing or contrasting an unfamiliar event with more familiar and known events.

The *Hindenberg* was a gigantic gray ship more than 400 feet long, with a pod on its underbelly designed to carry people. (straight description)

The *euphoria* was contagious. Soon Harry and Jim were acting like they didn't have a care in the world. (description by comparison)

Mary was always *adroit* in her dealings with others. Sandra, on the other hand, lacked Mary's social diplomacy. (description by contrast)

(d) *Statement of meaning by mood and tone clues.* Contextual clues of mood, tone, setting, and general feeling pervade literary selections but are seldomly used in more expository kinds of writing. Authors utilize mood and tone clues to establish the nature of characters and to establish the general air or mood in a particular situation.

She could not converse on a single subject for more than a minute before jumping to another wholly unrelated topic. That, and her *capricious* tendency to visually examine every object in the room while talking, became unnerving to me.

He bowed low and apologized for being late. His *self-deprecating* behavior seemed to contradict all of the things I had learned about him.

The cloze procedure as a tool for teaching use of context

The cloze procedure is a technique whereby words are systematically deleted from a reading passage, the student's task being to replace the deleted words. This technique is used a great deal in assessing student's facility in contextual analysis and can easily be adapted as an instructional method for teaching contextual analysis. There are many variations of the cloze technique in terms of the way it is used; a sample cloze passage using an every fifth word deletion pattern is presented below.

EXAMPLE 1

Although the United States _____ still in its infancy _____ the late 1700s and _____ 1800s, its leaders were _____ intent on expanding its _____ boundaries. Spain claimed ownership _____ much of the territory _____ the Gulf of Mexico. _____ the present state of _____ to the port city _____ New Orleans. Eventually, the _____ States simply added this _____ to its domain after _____ became evident that Spain _____ too weak to defend _____ claims. Soon after, Jefferson _____ the Louisiana Purchase with _____ French leader Napoleon.

In this particular cloze passage, every fifth word has been deleted. This is the most frequent deletion pattern generally used with cloze passages; deletion patterns usually have an every fifth word to every tenth word deletion, depending on the nature of the reading material and the students who are to work through the cloze passage. Other deletion patterns used with cloze passages include a staggered pattern where only key vocabulary terms are deleted. The previous example of a cloze passage using a staggered deletion pattern appears below.

EXAMPLE 2

Although the _____ _____ was still in its infancy during the late _____ and early _____, its leaders were nonetheless intent on expanding its territorial _____. _____ claimed ownership of much of the territory along the _____ _____ _____, from the present state of _____ to the port city of _____. Eventually, the _____ _____ simply added this territory to its domain after it became evident that _____ was too _____ to defend its claims. Soon after, _____ negotiated the _____ _____ with the French leader _____.

An additional way in which to use the cloze technique as an instructional tool is to construct a cloze passage deleting important signal words that express and clarify the relationships among the ideas in the passage. Below is an example of a cloze passage in which several signal words have been deleted.

EXAMPLE 3

_____ the United States was still in its infancy _____ the late 1700s and early 1800s, its leaders were _____ intent on expanding its territorial boundaries. Spain claimed ownership of much of the territory _____ the Gulf of Mexico, from the present state of Florida to the port city of New Orleans. Eventually, the United States simply added this territory _____ its domain _____ it became evident _____ Spain was too weak to defend its claims. _____. _____ _____, Jefferson negotiated the Louisiana Purchase with the French leader Napoleon.

In using the cloze technique as an instructional method, the teacher can construct a variety of different kinds of cloze passages. For students who have basic problems in using context clues and who need practice in contextual analysis, Example 1 of the cloze technique is particularly appropriate. Students who have mastered contextual analysis, but who can benefit from practice in the use of context clues, might benefit most from cloze exercises similar to Example 2. (Example 2 is also useful in situations where the mastery of content information is being stressed.) The cloze technique demonstrated by Example 3 is useful with students at nearly any reading level since attention to important signal words contained in reading materials is basic to both comprehension and study skills. In each instance, the teacher may wish to include with the exercise a list of words from which students can choose the most appropriate response. Some students may require the added help of such a word list while others do not, making the provision of such a word list an excellent way to individualize instruction.

In using the cloze procedure as an instructional tool to teach contextual analysis skills, the following guidelines should be kept in mind:

1. As students work through the cloze exercise or after they have completed the exercise, direct instruction should be provided by the teacher. This can be in the form of a class or small group discussion of the cloze exercise, including discussion of correct and incorrect responses and contextual clues in the cloze passage that help in making identifications of deleted words.
2. Cloze exercises should seldom be used to assign grades to

students. As achievement measures, cloze exercises are un-
reliable. Since students are generally interested in how well
they do on various learning tasks, the teacher can go ahead
and assign percentage scores to students based on their performance; however, it is not wise to assign grades based on
cloze performance.

3. When using a cloze exercise as an instructional method, it is
best to allow synonym substitutions where the synonyms
are close in meaning to the deleted word. By discussing why
or why not certain synonyms can be substituted for deleted
words, the teacher provides direct instruction in contextual
analysis. Additionally, students should be taught that it is all
right to skip unknown words and read ahead in order to
utilize the context.

Teaching Strategies for Using Context to Identify and Predict

1. Before students begin a particular reading task, have them
examine new vocabulary items in context. Have students predict
the meaning of new words and unfamiliar words from the way in
which they are used in context.

2. Point out to students the contextual clues that are available
to help them identify unfamiliar words. Elicit from students the
strategies they use in making identifications from context.

3. Particularly with less able readers, prepare exercises to teach
use of context that dramatically show how useful context can be
in identifying unknown words (for example, Mary's *weimaraner*
bit the mailman).

4. Observe students in a one-to-one oral reading situation in
terms of their use of contextual clues to identify unknown words.
Their oral reading will reveal a great deal about their facility in
contextual analysis.

5. With less able readers, select portions of the reading assignment and construct cloze exercises from them, or construct a
cloze exercise around a summary of the reading assignment. If
the cloze exercise is taken straight from the reading assignment,
allow students time to read the assignment, then have them work
through the cloze exercise without referring to the original passage. If the cloze exercise is based on a teacher-written summary
of the reading material, students can work through the exercise
while they do their reading or after they have completed their

reading. Regardless of how the cloze exercise is constructed, it should be accompanied by or followed by direct instruction.

A Teaching Aid for Using Authoritative Sources

The use of authoritative sources such as the dictionary is among the various word identification skills that students can use in regaining meaning. While the dictionary is an important source of information and a useful instructional tool, the teacher must take care not to overuse the dictionary or to use the dictionary as a basis for "busy work" assignments. There is little justification, for example, in having students look up a list of words in the dictionary and divide them into syllables. Such assignments tend to promote a negative attitude in students toward reading. There are three general kinds of dictionary skills that students should possess in order to make dictionary usage a viable word analysis skill to be used in regaining meaning. These include gaining correct pronunciation of words, interpreting and using derivational information, and selecting appropriate word meanings.

Gaining Correct Pronunciation

The purpose in gaining the correct pronunciation of an unfamiliar word is to determine if the word is familiar in a spoken sense; if so, the word will hold meaning for the student. Dictionaries utilize pronunciation keys, and often these pronunciation keys will vary from one dictionary to another. It is important for students to learn how to use pronunciation keys, and the following specific skills should receive instructional attention:

1. An understanding of how a dictionary uses phonetic respelling of words as a guide to gaining correct pronunciation.
2. An understanding of how word syllabication is indicated in a dictionary as a guide to gaining correct pronunciation.
3. An understanding of how primary and secondary accenting is indicated in a dictionary as a guide to correct pronunciation.

Interpreting and Using Derivational Information

Knowledge of structural features of words such as affixes and roots is an aspect of structural analysis. Since the dictionary contains a wealth of information about word derivations, it is important for the student to learn how to gain this information from the dictionary. The study of derivational information is also a helpful technique and aid in helping students to remember and retain new words they encounter. The following specific skills are important to the study of word derivations:

1. A knowledge of the location of derivational information within dictionary definitions and special sections of the dictionary devoted to word derivations.
2. An understanding of abbreviations used to communicate derivational information (for example, Gk = Greek; Me = Middle English; Lat = Latin).
3. An appreciation of the history of words and the changing nature of language itself through the study of word derivations.

Selecting Appropriate Word Meanings

Once students locate an unfamiliar word in the dictionary and must use the dictionary to get the meaning of the word, they often must select word meanings that are most appropriate to the context in which they found the word. Even with highly familiar words there is such variation in meaning that a "point" of law is simply not the same as a "point" in geometry. The following specific skills are important in choosing appropriate word meanings:

1. An understanding of abbreviations and terms that are clues to word meanings (for example, syn = synonym; anc = ancient; biol = biology; vb = verb; n = noun).
2. An understanding of how the order of word meanings is arranged in a dictionary (chronological, most common to least common).
3. An ability to select the meaning that best fits the unfamiliar word within the context it is used.

Teaching Strategies for Using Authoritative Sources

1. Utilize in instruction word history and derivation, using these as readiness activities and ways of presenting and introducing new words. Students generally find the study of word histories and derivations interesting and fun.

2. Avoid using authoritative sources like dictionaries for busy work. These kinds of activities tend to be drudgery for students and can easily turn students off to using dictionaries and other reference materials.

3. Many games and interesting activities can be utilized based on dictionary usage. Games centered around the use of guide words and facility in using alphabetical order are particularly appropriate for less able readers:

> *Spotting Guide Words*: Place on the chalkboard pairs of guide words (for example, June/justify; jerky/jigger; join/jostle). Then give students additional words requiring them to indicate between which pair of guide words the new words will be found. This game can be organized around teams where scores are kept or as a class activity.

Games that deal with word definitions can also be used to increase word knowledge:

> *Definition Game*: Provide each student with a dictionary, then have one student randomly choose a definition and read the definition to the class. If the word is used in the definition, the student should substitute the word "blank." The first person to correctly identify the word reads the next definition. This game, too, can be organized around teams or simply used as a class activity.

4. Have students keep a record of new words by placing them on index cards that include the word in context as well as a synonym for the new word. The teacher can provide various incentives to students for increasing their word files and for periodically reviewing words in their files.

5. Particularly with less able readers, the teacher should attempt to obtain copies of simplified dictionaries. Often standard and unabridged dictionaries will define unfamiliar words with synonyms that are equally unfamiliar to students. Simplified dictionaries are readily available from a variety of publishers.

A Teaching Aid for Direct Word Study

We have devoted a great deal of discussion to the various word analysis and identification skills students must possess in order to grow in reading ability. We have also made the point that competent readers use these word analysis skills or programs in combination when they encounter unfamiliar words. Often we find that while less able readers possess the word analysis skills to varying degrees, they fail to utilize them in a systematic way to unlock the pronunciation and meaning of unfamiliar words. For this reason, we include here a simple procedure for analyzing unfamiliar words that the teacher can use in teaching new words and students can use in dealing with unfamiliar words on their own.

1. *Try to pronounce the whole word.* Look for familiar syllables, familiar letter combinations, and "little words" in the unfamiliar word.
2. *Look at how the word is used.* If the word remains unknown, or you still need a better idea of what it means, look at how it is used in the sentence. Try to predict what it means from its context.
3. *Look for meaning clues in the word.* If you can't pronounce the word or after pronouncing it find you don't know it, try to predict what it means from its structure (prefix, root, suffix).

SUMMARY

1. Sight identification words are words the reader knows instantly on sight. The words need not be analyzed because they are instantly recognized. An adequate sight vocabulary permits the reader to read spontaneously.

2. Phonic identification is used to unlock the meaning of a visual symbol by pronouncing it and associating it with an auditory symbol for which the meaning is known. The value of teaching phonics is that the student can link visual symbols with the words already in his or her oral vocabulary. A problem in teaching phonics is the vast variation in the ways written symbols may be pronounced.

3. Word structure can be used to identify the meaning of words. The configuration of a word is used to teach sight vocabulary. Word structure also is used in phonic identification. In addition, the meaning of unfamiliar words can be identified through structural abstraction, if the meaning of structural components of the unfamiliar word is known (for example, prefixes, roots, and suffixes).

4. Contextual abstraction also is used to abstract the meaning of unfamiliar words. If the meaning of words surrounding an unfamiliar word is known, the meaning of the unfamiliar word can be inferred from context.

5. In addition to regaining meaning, structural and contextual abstractions are used in spontaneous reading when the meaning of the message is obtained from limited word cues. Thus the ability to abstract contributes substantially to spontaneous and flexible reading.

6. Syntax and semantics are important aids in abstracting meaning. Using syntactical clues one derives meaning from the

way in which the language is programmed. Using semantic clues one identifies the meaning of unfamiliar words by knowing the meaning of their structural components and/or the surrounding words.

7. Authoritative sources such as the dictionary and encyclopedia can be used to gain information and meaning. But it is important that the student be directed not to spend too much time using the dictionary lest he or she become bored.

8. It is important that students know when to use a particular word identification skill and how to use word identification skills in combination. Phonic identification and structural and contextual abstraction should be used in combination to extract meaning while reading.

Teaching Aids and Strategies

9. *Sight identification.* The student should know by sight the words most commonly used. The Dolch and Kucera-Francis word lists enumerate many common words. To teach commonly used words (a) stress the importance of learning them by sight, (b) use them in spelling lessons, and (c) involve students in games to teach the words.

10. *Phonic identification.* Emans's list of phonic generalizations is useful if the teacher wishes to teach phonic generalization. In teaching phonics have the student pronounce all the sound elements of a word and blend them. New vocabulary words should be placed on the chalkboard and pronounced by the teacher. Oral reading also helps students learn how words are pronounced. Workbook exercises also provide helpful drill activities in phonic identification. There are many games that provide practice in phonic identification.

11. *Using word structure to identify words.* Spache offers some rules for syllabication which are useful in spelling and word identification. Stauffer provides a list of common prefixes, root words, and suffixes which are useful in teaching how to derive the meaning of complex words from their structural components. In teaching common prefixes and roots the student should learn an example that clearly illustrates the meaning of the prefix or root. The teacher should engage students in predicting the meaning of unfamiliar words from their familiar structural components. Students can be motivated to study words and word parts by involving them in the etomology, history, and derivation of words.

12. *Using context to identify words.* Word endings and signal

words provide syntactic and semantic clues that aid contextual abstraction. Clues given by the author aid the reader in deriving the meaning of unfamiliar words through contextual abstraction. Paraphrasing, giving examples, providing descriptions, and conveying mood help convey meaning. The cloze procedure can be used to teach contextual abstraction skills. Having students examine new words in context is another good way to teach contextual abstractions. The teacher can provide and point out important contextual clues that convey the meaning of new words.

13. *Authoritative sources*. The use of authoritative sources such as the dictionary is an important word identification skill. There are three dictionary skills that should be taught: (a) gaining correct pronunciation of words, (b) interpreting and using derivational information, and (c) selecting appropriate word meanings. The teacher should teach word history and derivation to interest the student in finding the meaning of words, avoid using authoritative sources for busy work, involve students in games that require them to find the meaning of words, have students keep a record of the new words they are learning, and introduce students to a simplified dictionary at first.

REVIEW QUESTIONS

1. What are sight identification words and why is sight vocabulary important?

2. How does one use phonic identification to identify unfamiliar written words?

3. What are the values and limitations of phonic identification?

4. How can word structure be used to identify words?

5. How does one find the meaning of an unfamiliar word through contextual abstraction?

6. How does the ability to abstract contribute to flexible reading?

7. When should authoritative sources be used to gain information?

8. Why is it valuable to be able to use word identification skills in combination?

9. How can you teach sight identification?

10. How can phonic identification skills be taught?

11. How can you teach the use of word structure to identify words?

12. How can you teach the use of context to identify words?

13. How can you teach the use of authoritative sources to gain information?

CHAPTER 4
Vocabulary Building

1. To discuss and clarify the factors that affect vocabulary building and the understanding of words. Vocabulary building involves the teaching of words and their meaning. To have meaning, words must refer to objects and events.
2. To present the various references words may have and problems students have in understanding these word references.
3. To discuss the thinking involved in understanding words and their relationships.
4. To present teaching strategies for vocabulary building.

BACKGROUND AND NEW INFORMATION

Your past experiences with words and their meanings will go a long way toward preparing you to learn the material in this chapter. The discussion of abstractions in chapter 3 prepares you to understand how words represent abstraction categories, and the description of programmatic sequences and their relationship to identification and prediction in chapter 2 prepares you to understand how words may designate programs.

We introduce in this chapter the various references to reality; that is, objects and events that words may stand for. We consider (1) words as references to concrete events, (2) words as references to abstraction categories, (3) words as hierarchical references, and (4) words as programmatic references. In addition, we discuss the kind of thinking involved in understanding these usages of words and prescribe ways to teach students how to understand these word references.

KEY TERMS

  inductive reasoning
  deductive reasoning
  signal or function words

DESIRED LEARNING OUTCOMES FOR CHAPTER 4

The student will be able to:

1. Identify words that refer to concrete events and abstraction categories.
2. Distinguish between absolute and relative categories.
3. Describe the errors made in categorizing.
4. Diagram and describe how words may designate hierarchical relationships.
5. Explain the benefit of presenting new content to the learner in the form of content hierarchies.
6. Describe the various relationships that exist within the framework of a content hierarchy.
7. Explain how inductive and deductive reasoning help him or her draw conclusions about an author's message.
8. Describe how words may refer to programmatic sequences.
9. Describe how concepts or abstraction categories can be taught.

We said that reading is the extraction of meaning from words conveying the author's message. Therefore, it is essential in learning to read to become familiar with the meanings that words convey and ways of finding their meaning. We all know that we can find the meaning of words in the dictionary. We study the way words are programmed when we study grammar. For example, we learn that in the English language adjectives usually appear before the nouns they modify. We also learn types of words when we study the parts of speech. However, there are functions of words not often discussed in a grammar text or course that have substantial bearing on the assimilation of meaning while reading. Let us consider some of these word functions.

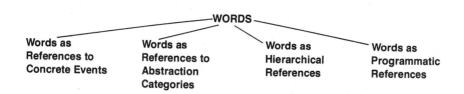

FIGURE 4–1   A hierarchy of topics in chapter 4

WORDS AS REFERENCES TO CONCRETE EVENTS

Some of the words we use refer to concrete, tangible events we experience. Proper nouns represent such words. Your name represents you. You are tangible. You can be experienced directly through the senses. You can be seen and felt. Each member of your family and your friends have names that represent them. They, too, are tangible. When you meet someone for the first time you introduce yourself by giving your name, and your new acquaintance introduces himself or herself by giving a name. Thereafter, you attach a name to the person, as the person does to you. When you meet again you greet and call each other by name.

Proper nouns may represent tangible objects other than people. The *Queen Mary* is a name representing a particular ship. Whirlaway is the name of a horse that won the Kentucky Derby. Louisville is the name of the city where the Kentucky Derby can be witnessed each spring. Personal pronouns also represent concrete events, simply because they may be substituted for proper nouns. Instead of referring to particular people by their names, we may refer to them as he or she.

WORDS AS REFERENCES TO ABSTRACTION CATEGORIES

Earlier we defined abstraction as the process of making identifications and predictions based upon limited features or clues. The process of abstraction is used to group concrete events into categories based on their common characteristics. A category is created when the common characteristics of concrete objects are enumerated and a word label is designated to refer to the category. For instance, the word "mother" is a word label for a category. The common characteristics of members of the category are (1) woman (2) with a child or children.

Categories are abstractions because they refer to only a limited number of features of a concrete event. For instance, the word "mother" as we have defined it refers to only two features. To be a member of the category you (1) must be a woman and (2) must have a child. Although any mother has these two features, a particular mother has many other features that make her distinct from other mothers. A mother may be tall or short, heavy or lean, and so on.

It is important to realize that most words in the dictionary are labels for abstraction categories. When we look up a word in the dictionary we are given a definition that specifies features or criteria for inclusion in a category. To be a member of the category, the person or item must meet the criteria for inclusion in the category.

Word combinations, too, designate abstraction categories. The statement "things that fly" identifies a category that includes such things as birds, bats, airplanes, and kites. The phrase "animals that live in the ocean" designates another category that includes fish, eels, whales, and so forth.

Since in reading it is words that convey meaning to the reader, it is necessary for the student to understand that all words except proper nouns and personal pronouns represent abstraction categories. Also, the student must learn that proper nouns and personal pronouns represent tangible things, whereas words designating abstraction categories do not. Only examples of the categories are tangible. In order to develop this skill it is necessary for a student to distinguish concrete events and the words that symbolize them from abstraction categories and the words that symbolize these categories.

Teaching Abstraction Categories or Concepts

Gibson and Levin (1975) point out the importance of abstraction to the initial stages of learning to read. Identification through abstraction is of primary importance in learning about and understanding how a printed language system works. This process of identification through abstraction is also of great importance to reading and learning in general because it allows systematic application of relationships without practice in each individual instance. For example, Velten's (1943) observation that by teaching the concept of voiced and voiceless consonant pairs with one clear-cut example, the concept of voice in consonants was transferred to other pairs—without practice.

Gibson and Levin go on to state that the process of identification through abstraction, or "high-level generalization," involves both aspects of associative learning (recognition of similarities) as well as discrimination learning (recognition of differences):

> one cannot perceive the likeness between two things unless he can at the same time perceive that they are different. Recognition of similarity is not the same thing as failure to discriminate. (Gibson and Levin, 1975:82)

Words and the abstraction categories they represent are often referred to as *concepts* in educational literature. In order to teach the meaning of such words it is necessary to teach the student: (1) the word label for a category; (2) the defining criteria for the category, that is, the criteria or required features for inclusion in the category; and (3) to distinguish examples from nonexamples of the category. Thus, if teachers wish to teach the meaning of the word "mother," they present the word "mother." They also define the word by giving the criteria for being a "mother"; that is, being a female with one or more children. In addition, they give the students practice distinguishing mothers from nonmothers until they become proficient at it. Only then can it be said that they completely understand the meaning of the word "mother." In order to teach the student to distinguish examples of a category from nonexamples it is often necessary to refine their understanding of the criteria defining a category.

Teaching students is aided by the students' tendency to organize information into categories. Preusser and Handel (1970) showed the tendency of people to organize information into categories. In related research, Johnson and Stratton (1966) compared five methods of teaching concepts: (1) subjects were given definitions of concepts; (2) concepts were used in relevant sentences; (3) subjects were given practice in classifying examples of concepts; (4) subjects were taught synonyms for the concept; and (5) subjects were given a mixed program employing all of the above techniques. The subjects given the mixed program performed significantly better than the other groups, indicating the importance of using a variety of approaches to teach the meaning of concepts.

Approaching the teaching of vocabulary from the standpoint that new vocabulary words are actually concepts has been demonstrated to be an effective method. McCann and Barron (1975) had average and below average tenth graders classify words by analyzing the new words and grouping them into different categories in order to reveal the vocabulary relationships. On follow-up vocabulary tests, the students who studied the new vocabulary words by conceptually analyzing them performed significantly better than students who studied the vocabulary words in a more traditional approach.

Students should learn that when they encounter words that are defined in many ways, they must rely on the context surrounding the word to derive the intended meaning of the author. Some words that represent abstraction categories have only one definition. For instance, mammals are defined as (1) animals that (2) nourish their young with milk secreted from mammary glands and (3) that have hair on the skin. Other words have a number of definitions. The word "run" is given more than 40 different definitions. Thus the word "run" can be used to represent more than 40 different categories of things.

Abstraction categories permit the individual to have ideas about the similarities and differences among events and objects. For example, if the abstraction "food" has been learned, the individual has knowledge of a group of alternative items that can be safely eaten. The person may then choose one item from among the alternatives when he or she is hungry.

Programs may also be categorized to form an abstraction. The programs would represent alternative methods of accomplishing something. The abstraction "recipes" represents alternative methods of preparing food. A given event can also be placed in a number of abstraction categories. For instance, a spider can be in the category "arachnids," the category "bug," the category "things that crawl," the category "scary things," and so on.

Teaching concepts requires the use of effective feedback/corrective procedures as well as an effective set of cues. The learner must be aware of all the relevant features of an event. Perhaps a child is shown a hamster and says "mouse." It is obvious that either his memory of "mouse" is faulty (it does not contain all the relevant features of mice, for example, the possession of a long tail), or he does not identify all the relevant features of hamsters (for example, he did not notice the absence of a long tail). Frequent opportunity for feedback from the teacher should help the student identify events correctly.

In teaching an abstraction, an example that belongs in the abstraction is memorized first. Then the student is taught that the object observed has features in common with other objects. The teacher must take care not to confuse an example that belongs in an abstraction with the abstraction itself. As we said, most words are labels for abstractions. When a child sees a particular robin and memorizes its features, it must eventually be made clear to her that it is a particular example of the abstraction "robin" and the more general abstraction "bird," and an example of the still more general abstraction "animal." Further, it must be made clear that examples of abstractions are observed, not the abstractions themselves.

It is generally the case that an event is similar to some events and different from others. For example, a diamond is like a stone in that they are both hard. They would thus belong in the category "hard things." Furthermore, a diamond is like an original oil painting by Rembrandt in that both are valuable. Therefore, both the diamond and the oil painting belong in the category "valuable things." Note, however, that this latter category would exclude "stone." Comparing and contrasting events according to their relevant features promotes the learning of concepts.

Once an abstraction category is formed, future events can be classified into one or more abstraction categories. This requires that the learner learn the necessary and sufficient criteria for inclusion in an abstraction. There may be several criteria which are sufficient criteria for inclusion, or there may be only one. For example, the abstraction "vegetable" requires several criteria: it must be edible, it must be a plant, and, more specifically, it must be a herbaceous plant. On the other hand, the abstraction "light" has only one defining criterion: it must illuminate.

There are two possible means of learning the necessary and sufficient criteria for inclusion into a particular abstraction. The learner can be given the necessary and sufficient criteria and be expected to memorize them, or the learner can infer the necessary and sufficient criteria from a set of events. The teacher, consequently, has two ways of teaching the criteria: (1) directly, using the memorization of the stated criteria and (2) indirectly, giving the student a set of examples of events.

It should be pointed out at this time that some abstractions are absolute abstractions and others are relative abstractions. An example of an absolute abstraction is "rational numbers." The necessary and sufficient criterion for inclusion is that a rational number can be transformed into a ratio of two integers. An event can always be classified into the abstraction rational number if it possesses this single criterion. What we mean to say here is that experts will agree on the criteria for inclusion in an absolute category.

A relative abstraction, on the other hand, is an abstraction whose criteria for inclusion are not universally agreed upon. The question of inclusion often depends on the degree to which a particular event differs from other events on the specific criteria for inclusion. The concept "small objects" is an example of a relative abstraction since whether an object is classified as a small object often depends on the individual's subjective viewpoint. Is a bird (for example, a swallow) an example or instance of a "small object"? That depends on whether your universe of objects contains microscopic organisms, airplanes, or insects.

We refer you to the work of Markle and Tiemann (1969), Tennyson and Wooley (1972), and Klausmeier and Feldman (1975) for additional information on how to refine discrimination in teaching concepts.

Problems in Learning Abstraction Categories and Concepts

Because most words represent concepts or abstraction categories, it is important for the teacher to know the kinds of errors that are made in the learning of concepts.

Erroneous Criteria

Criteria are specified for including an event in a category. If *erroneous criteria* are learned for a category, the individual will not be able to use the concept for accurate identification. For example, an individual would not be able to identify round shapes as circles if a criterion for the abstraction "circle" specified a four-sided figure.

Overgeneralization

Overgeneralization occurs when an identification is made on the basis of *insufficient criteria*. The result is that more things are included in the category than should be. For example, suppose we define only the following two criteria to describe the concept "square"; (1) four-sided figure and (2) the opposite sides are the same length. These criteria are insufficient, and overgeneralization would result. That is, too many objects such as rectangles and parallelograms would be identified as squares.

Children often overgeneralize because they do not have sufficient experience to discriminate properly. A child who believes that the concept "car" is defined by the criteria (1) four wheels, (2) engine and, (3) carries people down the street will tend to incorrectly identify certain trucks and buses as cars until he learns additional criteria to discriminate among them.

Overdiscrimination

Overdiscrimination occurs when an identification is made of an event and an abstraction on the basis of unnecessary criteria. The result is that more things are excluded from the category than should be. For example, suppose the following criteria are defined to describe the abstraction "spider": (1) eight legs; (2) oval-shaped body; (3) spins webs; (4) black. The criterion "black" is unnecessary and will result in incorrectly excluding certain spiders. For instance, if the individual saw a brown, oval-shaped, eight-legged, web-spinning creature, it might not be recognized and subsequently assigned to the category "spider."

Words as Hierarchical References

Words not only represent concepts, but they are often used to convey the hierarchical relationship among concepts. Organizing concepts into class inclusion hierarchies facilitates the understanding of the concepts and the relationship between them as well as the vocabulary used to describe the concept. Consider this example of a class inclusion representation hierarchy:

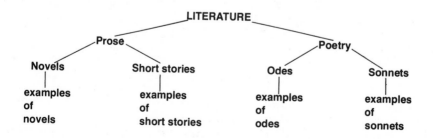

Each word in the class inclusion representation hierarchy is a label for a concept or abstraction category. However, the categories "prose" and "poetry" are subcategories of the more general category "literature." The categories "novel" and "short story" are subcategories of the more general category "prose." The categories "ode" and "sonnet" are subcategories of the more general category "poetry." This is a representational hierarchy because the lower levels are represented in the higher, more general levels of the hierarchy. An ode is a representation or subtype of poetry. Poetry is a representation or subtype of literature. Prose is also a representation or subtype of literature.

The arrangement of concepts into class inclusion hierarchies tends to facilitate the learning and understanding of the concepts. Bower et al. (1969) demonstrated that students recall two to three times more words if the words are presented to them in the form of a class inclusion hierarchy. Preusser and Handel (1970) showed that, given words and pictures of objects, students tend to organize them into class inclusion hierarchies.

Bower's findings indicate that information is more easily retrieved and remembered if it is presented in the form of a class inclusion hierarchy. Preusser and Handel's findings suggest that people tend to organize and store information in the form of class inclusion hierarchies. We can infer that information is stored in this form because it is more readily retrieved.

It is no wonder that public information is handled in this manner. The information in the library is stored in the form of class inclusion hierarchies for easy retrieval. Books and references are listed according to types and subtypes. Also, the table of contents of a book forms a class inclusion hierarchy as follows:

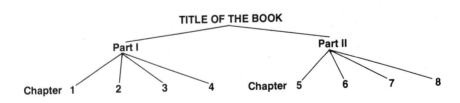

In addition, the chapters of a book are often subdivided by headings into subtopics of the chapter.

A table of contents is nothing more than a topic outline. All topic outlines form class inclusion hierarchies. When we teach study skills, we teach students to outline the material they are learning. Teaching them to form class inclusion hierarchies in this way facilitates their retrieval and understanding of the material.

Using Hierarchical Organization in Teaching

Hierarchical organization has implications for teaching, too. The teacher can facilitate the organization and understanding of information if he or she presents it in the form of class inclusion hierarchies. A teacher can teach students to understand what poetry is by defining it and distinguishing examples from nonexamples. However, it seems that students gain a more profound and comprehensive understanding of what poetry is if they learn that it is a type of literature, and if they learn how it is distinct from prose. Students learn even more about poetry when they learn that there exist various types of poetry, and when they learn how types of poetry are distinguished from one another. This expands the student's knowledge of the concept "poetry."

Understanding the relationship of categories within a class inclusion hierarchy provides a basis for answering "compare and contrast" questions about the content, which are often asked after reading material on a subject. After understanding the relationships within the above literature hierarchy, the student should be able to respond to directions such as, "compare and contrast odes and sonnets, or prose and poetry, or novels and short stories." This understanding prepares students to deal with similarities and differences in any subject area.

The illustration we gave shows how literature can be organized to form a class inclusion hierarchy. Subject matter in other content areas often can be, should be, and sometimes is organized and presented in this form. In math we might arrange concepts in a hierarchy such as the following:

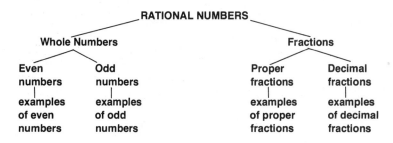

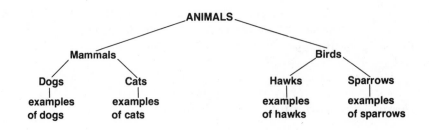

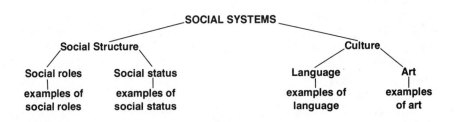

Class inclusion hierarchies are often called *content* hierarchies as well as concept hierarchies because they show the hierarchical relationships among units of content. We advocate that the content in the various content areas be organized and presented to students in this form. You will have noted that the first figure of each chapter is a class inclusion hierarchy of the material contained in the chapter. This is one way of using class inclusion hierarchies as teaching aids. It gives the student an overview of the material about to be learned and displays the relationship between one topic and another.

Teaching Hierarchical Relationships

Since many reading-thinking skills tests and activities require the student to understand class inclusion hierarchical relationships, it is important that the student be taught how to think within the framework of such a hierarchy. At the lowest level of a content hierarchy we have concrete objects and events that can be memorized and remembered because they are observable. As we proceed up the hierarchy we move to the abstraction levels where categories of events exist by virtue of definition. As we said, a category is a group of items with similar characteristics. In defining a category we stipulate the criteria for inclusion in the category. On this basis we can determine the items that fit a category. As we said, only the items that belong to a category are observable. The category itself is not observable. It exists by definition. The category "boy" may be defined as (1) young (2) human (3) male. These are the criteria for inclusion in the category. The category "boy" cannot be observed. Only examples of boys can be observed.

As we proceed up the content hierarchy to higher levels, we move from the specific to the general. The higher the level of the hierarchy, the more general the categorical references. At the lowest level we have specific examples. These examples are more generally referred to at the lowest level of abstraction. Because we are dealing with representational hierarchies, and lower levels are represented and included in the higher levels, the higher levels provide more general categorical references.

Consider the following content hierarchy:

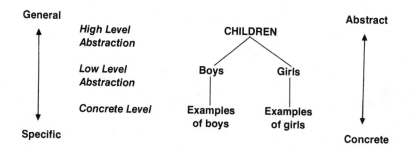

Examples of boys are represented in the abstraction "boys" and examples of girls are represented in the abstraction category "girls." Both the abstraction "girls" and the abstraction "boys" are included in the more general abstraction "children." As we proceed up our content hierarchy from the specific to the general, level by level, we are also moving from the concrete to the abstract. Content hierarchies may be derived by working *deductively* from the general to the specific, in which case we are deducing lower levels of the hierarcy from higher levels by subdividing the higher levels. Such would be the case if we subdivided the more general category "children" into the subcategories "boys" and "girls." Content hierarchies may also be derived working from the specific to the general. In this case we are *inducing* higher levels from lower levels. We are examining the things at a lower level to find common characteristics so that we can represent them in more general categories at higher levels of the hierarchy. As you can see, deductive thinking involves reasoning from the general to the specific, whereas inductive thinking involves reasoning from the specific to the general. We will clarify these processes of thinking as we proceed.

Once the relationships within a hierarchy are explained, the student can be introduced to the various reading-thinking skills that require an understanding of hierarchical relationships. Let us trace an example to illustrate the various hierarchical stages developed by our thinking.

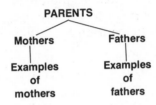

Underlying the ability to identify and predict and the organization of content hierarchies is the understanding of relationships. To identify relationships it is necessary to compare things for similarities and differences and to realize that the more similar things are to each other the more closely related they are and the less different they are. Conversely, the more different things are the less closely related they are and the less similar they are.

The ability to identify similarities and differences is the basis for answering compare and contrast questions and questions that ask the student to detect associations and contrasts and to discriminate or distinguish between one thing and another. Also, questions that ask students to group things together on the basis of their common characteristics or to form categories require the students to identify similarities and differences among items. In fact, the ability to identify similarities and differences is the basis for making any identification.

Here are some examples of words that are often used in reading material to signal similarities and differences:

Differences	Similarities
in contrast	likewise
conversely	similarly
however	in the same vein
but	comparatively
rather	alike
vice versa	in the same way
on the contrary	equally
on the other hand	correspondingly

Identifying the Relationships between Concrete Events

To prepare students to think within the framework of a content hierarchy, they must be able to inspect and compare concrete objects for similarities and differences. In the hierarchy we are dealing with, they must be able to see the relationship between men and women in order to identify mothers and fathers. This is because fathers are men with children and mothers are women with children. These are the defining criteria for inclusion in the two categories.

In order to identify the relationship between men and women, students compare them for similarities and differences. They learn that they both have such similar characteristics as arms, legs, a body, and a head. They also learn that they are different with respect to sexual attributes.

Identifying the Relationships between Concrete Events and Abstraction Categories

Once students learn how to relate concrete objects to one another in order to think within the framework of a content hierarchy, they must be able to see the relationships between concrete objects and categories. This requires them to compare the features of a concrete object with various abstraction categories for similarities and differences. They compare examples of "mothers" with the defining characteristics for inclusion in the categories "mothers" and "fathers" and note that the examples are more similar to the definition of "mother" than the definition of "father." They make the same comparisons with examples of "fathers" and learn that they are more similar to the definition of "father" and more different from the definition of "mother."

Identifying the Relationship between Abstraction Categories at the Same Level of a Content Hierarchy

To think in terms of content hierarchies students must also learn to relate one category to another. Using our example, students compare the categories "mother" and "father" for similarities and differences. They learn that mothers and fathers are different in that mothers are women with children and fathers are men with children. They learn that mothers and fathers are similar in that they are both adults with children.

Identifying the Relationship between Abstraction Categories at Different Levels of a Content Hierarchy

Students must also see the relationships between categories at different levels of a content hierarchy. In learning to compare a category at one level of a hierarchy with a category at another level they learn to make relative identifications with respect to generality and specificity. Returning to our example, students compare the category "mother" with the higher level abstraction category "parent." They learn that the defining characteristics of the two categories are similar because the criteria for inclusion in each is "adults with children." Students also learn that the defining characteristics for inclusion in the category "mother" are more specific in that they indicate a certain kind of adult, a woman. Conversely, they learn that because the defining characteristics for the category "parent" do not specify the additional criterion for inclusion, the category is more general. In essence, they can learn that higher level abstractions are more general references because they specify fewer criteria for inclusion in a category and lower level abstractions are more specific references because they stipulate a greater number of criteria for inclusion in a category. They also learn that more general categories include more items. Mothers and fathers both belong to the category "parent."

Teachers often teach students that words may denote more specific or more general references to events. When children refer to an object as a "thing," the teacher may teach them to make a more specific or precise word reference. Or if a teacher is teaching the parts of speech and a student refers to a noun as a word, the teacher may ask for a more precise identification. Conversely, teachers may wish students to make a more general reference.

They may wish to teach them that nouns, verbs, adjectives, and other types of words are all members of the category "words."

After understanding the relationships at different levels of a content hierarchy, students derive another skill used in thinking. They should be able to understand that all members of a subcategory are also members of a more general category of which the subcategory is a part, but not vice versa. For instance, they should understand that all nouns are words but not all words are nouns.

Identifying Absolute and Relative Degrees of Relationship

When people are asked whether or not two things are similar or different, they are being asked to make an absolute determination. On the other hand, when they are given more than two things to compare, they may be asked to determine relative degrees of similarity and difference. A person may be asked to indicate absolutely whether a particular individual is a mother or a father.

In teaching the meaning of words, it is the task of the teacher to teach students that certain words signal relative relationships, whereas other words indicate absolute relationships. The word "smaller" signals a relative relationship; the word "smallest" signals an absolute relationship.

Identifying New Categories

New categories are identified when the student examines items or categories and discovers similarities and differences among them. The student has identified a new category whether or not the category is public knowledge. New categories may be identified inductively and deductively.

Inducing new categories. Inductive reasoning proceeds from the specific to the general. When students categorize concrete items or form more general categories from more specific categories, they are identifying new categories inductively.

Students' ability to identify new categories of concrete items can be developed by showing them pictures of objects with common characteristics and asking them to determine what the pictures have in common. In this way students learn to form their own categories by determining the criteria for grouping similar objects together. They might be shown pictures of men with children and be asked what the people in the pictures have in common. They can be cued by the teacher until they understand. Then, they can be asked for the "word label" that represents the category. They are cued until they understand that father is the correct word label for the category.

To induce new categories from known categories students examine the known categories for similarities. If they find common characteristics, they can identify on their own a more general category at a higher level of a content hierarchy.

Students can be taught that they can induce a new category by determining what mothers and fathers have in common. They are cued until they understand that mothers and fathers are adults with children and can be grouped together because they share this common characteristic. Students then are asked to give the word label for the category. They are cued until they understand that the label for the category is "parents."

The students are then taught that the category "parent,' is a more general category than the categories "mother" and "father" because it contains a greater number of items; both mothers and fathers fit that category. Students then are shown the content hierarchy presented earlier and shown how they reasoned inductively from level to level to identify new categories.

There are many reading-thinking skills that require students to reason inductively. When we teach students to *generalize, summarize, synthesize,* or *determine the main idea* being proposed by an author, they must think inductively. They must examine specific pieces of information for similar characteristics. If they discover those similarities, they can summarize, synthesize, or generalize about the information. They get the author's main idea by generalizing about the specific statements the author makes. If the author's specific statements concern the child-rearing practices of parents, the students might generalize that the main idea is a discussion of types of child-rearing practices employed by parents.

Inductive reasoning is also taught when students are taught to identify the *mood* or *feelings* expressed by the author. Here again, the student is taught to reason from the specific to the general. A student may read a passage in which the author is reminiscing about childhood experiences. From the specific statements made by the author, the student may induce that the mood of the story is "nostalgic."

Deducing new categories. Students can learn to deduce new categories. They examine the characteristics of a general abstraction category for differences. If they find subgroups within the more general group, they have deduced new categories at a lower level of a content hierarchy. Students can also be taught to identify new categories by reasoning deductively as well as inductively. To reason deductively they look for differences in a category. They then can be asked to identify differences in examples that fit in the category "parent." With cueing, they should be able to determine that the category includes adult men and women with children and that men and women are different by virtue of the criterion sex.

Students are then asked to divide the category "parents" into two subcategories by identifying criteria for inclusion in each of the subcategories. They should be able to determine that men with children and women with children are the criteria for inclusion in each of the subcategories. The students are then asked to provide the word labels for each of the subcategories. They are guided until they associate the word "mother" with the criterion "women with children" and "father" with the criterion "men with children."

Although no further categories can be deduced, students should be encouraged to complete the deductive process. They are asked to look within the categories "mother" and "father" for differences. They are cued until they understand that although the examples in the category "mother" and examples in the category "father" are similar, they are also different. Each father is distinct, and each mother or father is a different mother or father. They are then shown the content hierarchy again and how they reasoned deductively, level by level, from the general to the specific.

When we teach students to *give illustrations or examples* we teach them to reason deductively. When we ask students to name the vowels in the alphabet, we are requiring them to give specific examples of the general category of "letters" called "vowels." When we teach students to identify subcategories of a more general category, we teach them to identify new categories deductively. When we ask students to inspect the letters of the alphabet for common characteristics and they discover that some are tall and some are short, they have identified subcategories on their own.

Students should be reminded that when they reasoned inductively from the specific to the general, they looked for similarities among events as a basis for grouping them together. When they reasoned deductively, they looked for differences within a category as a basis for dividing the more general category into sub-categories. They should also be informed that these are general rules for inductive and deductive reasoning.

Many reading-thinking skills activities and tests involve the student in drawing conclusions which require inductive and deductive reasoning. The conclusion is a product of such reasoning. In addition, many activities and tests involve the student in identifying inductive and deductive processes.

Still other tests and instructional activities involve the student in determining whether an author's reasoning is correct. Deductive reasoning is used by students when they are asked to identify whether a specific statement made by an author can be deduced from a general statement made. If the general statement made by an author is that communists are subversive, and he says that a certain person is a communist, then he can identify the person as subversive. However, if he infers that the person should be put in jail, his deductive reasoning can be challenged, because not all subversive persons are necessarily criminals. In addition to judging the validity of the author's inferences, the student may use deductive reasoning to determine whether valid inferences can be drawn from that which is not literally stated by the author.

Here are some words that signal inductive and deductive reasoning in reading material:

Inductive Reasoning	Deductive Reasoning
In summary and conclusion	For example
The main point is	For instance
To generalize	To illustrate
To synthesize	More specifically
In essence	To analyze the problem
To summarize	A kind of

A Procedure for Teaching Hierarchical Vocabulary Building

1. In presenting new vocabulary items to students, elicit from students themselves the defining criteria that are implicit in the new vocabulary words. For example, in teaching the vocabulary item "sedimentary rock," ask students what special characteristics make a rock a sedimentary rock, for example, it is comprised of minerals and is deposited by water, air, or ice.

2. Further, engage students in noting the similarities and differences between an example and non-example of the vocabulary item being taught. For instance, ask students how sedimentary rocks and igneous rocks are similar (perhaps in terms of color, texture, industrial uses, and so on) and different (igneous rocks are produced by intense heat). List on the chalkboard or have students list similarities and differences they identify:

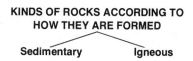

KINDS OF ROCKS ACCORDING TO
HOW THEY ARE FORMED

Sedimentary   Igneous

3. Encourage students to identify a category or word label in which the new vocabulary item would necessarily be a member. For example, help students understand that sedimentary and igneous rocks are each one kind of rock in terms of how rocks are formed and that "kinds of rocks according to how they are formed" can become a label for the new category:

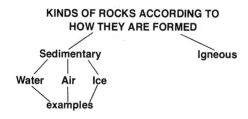

KINDS OF ROCKS ACCORDING TO
HOW THEY ARE FORMED

Sedimentary   Igneous

Water   Air   Ice

examples

4. Provide ample opportunity for students to make identifications based on their knowledge of the criteria for inclusion in a particular category. In this instance, provide students examples of rocks (or verbal descriptions or pictures) and ask them to assign each example to one of the categories previously identified. Those examples that are difficult to assign to one category or another can form the basis of extending the students' understanding of the criteria for inclusion in the categories "sedimentary" and "igne-

ous" rocks, thus teaching students to make finer and more subtle discriminations:

Sedimentary Rocks	Igneous Rocks
Deposited by water, air, ice	Produced by intense heat
Grainy texture	Smooth texture

Primarily dull gray or brown in
  color
	Usually shiny black, but
	  can be of many colors

Additional Strategies for Teaching Hierarchical Vocabulary Building

1. Point out to students those word identification and analysis skills that are useful in getting the meaning of new vocabulary words. Take students through the steps of structurally and contextually analyzing new vocabulary items (see chapter 3).

2. Engage students in deducing categories for words. Give students a general category and have them deduce words that are members of that category. For example, write on the chalkboard the category "things that fly," and have students think of as many examples as they can. Student examples might include birds, airplanes, insects, rockets, and so forth. Have students induce new categories by asking them if there is a way to group the examples they have deduced (for example, "animate" and "inanimate"). Continue to construct the content hierarchy that students produce on the chalkboard:

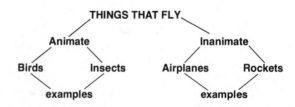

3. Engage students in inducing categories for words. Choose some general categories and as many examples of those categories as you can think of. One at a time, give students examples of the category you have chosen and ask them to think of the category. For example, cite "birds," "airplanes," "insects," "rockets," and so on until students induce the category "things that fly."

4. If you use a weekly spelling lesson, include in the lesson vocabulary words that are related in some fashion and use the technique described above with the spelling words.

5. Give students pairs of words and ask them to think of as many things the words have in common as they can. For example, present the words "pear" and "peach" and ask students what they have in common. Student responses might include: they are round, they are edible, they grow on trees, they are kinds of fruit, they have seeds, and so on. Discuss with students structural features (round, have seeds), contextual features (grow on trees), and functional features (edible) of the characteristics they think of. Discuss these characteristics as "criteria for inclusion" in the category "fruit." To increase the difficulty of this task, add words to the group of words you use (for example, "pear," "peach," and "banana").

WORDS AS PROGRAMMATIC REFERENCES

In chapter 2 we described programs and how they may be taught. We will deal further with programmatic sequences in chapter 16 when we discuss writing patterns in the content areas. Here we focus on the importance of words representing programs as they pertain to vocabulary building.

Since many thought patterns are sequential, the student must learn how the words of an author can convey sequences. For the student to have an effective vocabulary he or she must understand how words can describe (1) chronological sequences and (2) cause-effect sequences.

The student should be taught that chronological sequences are described when instructions or directions are given. The author or teacher giving the instructions is describing what is to be done and the sequence in which the activities are to be performed. In historical accounts the description of a chronological sequence plays a major role. Chronological sequences also are described in storytelling. Furthermore, many word labels identify chronological sequences. Words that identify procedures, methods, and skills stand for programmatic sequences. For example, phonic identification is a label for a programmatic sequence that is performed to identify words. The terms addition, subtraction, multiplication, and division are words identifying programmatic sequences, as are all names of math formulas. Scientific method is the name of a program for conducting scientific inquiries.

Words also describe cause-effect relationships as we have mentioned. To develop an effective reading vocabulary, the student must be sensitive to the activities an author describes and attempt to determine their impact on coming events. The student must be alert to the new information introduced by the author and attempt to predict how it may alter a current trend, whether the new information pertains to the characters in a story, or to a logical argument an author is presenting. While reading history students must not only detect chronological sequences, they must also look for cause-effect relationships being described by the author. In reading a science textbook, students may encounter procedures for conducting a laboratory experiment. They must understand that the author is describing certain causal agents that will produce an effect.

The following signal words indicate chronological and cause-effect sequences:

Chronological Sequences	Cause-Effect Sequences
first, second, third	therefore
next	thus
later	consequently
before	as a result
afterward	caused by
then	brought about
prior	the effect was

With respect to vocabulary building, it is a good idea for the teacher to first demonstrate how these signal words are used to describe chronological and cause-effect sequences. Then the students can use these signal words and others to describe chronological and cause-effect sequences.

TEACHING CONCEPTS

Since most words are labels for abstraction categories or concepts, in building vocabulary probably the most important skill the teacher must have is the skill to teach concepts. Although we have approached the topic from a variety of perspectives, our main focus has been on concept formation.

We dealt with the teaching of concepts when we considered words as references to abstraction categories or concepts. The skill involved is categorizing. When students understand a concept they can provide the word label and the defining criteria for it, and they can distinguish examples from nonexamples of the concept. In other words, they can correctly categorize members of the concept category.

When students can think correctly about a concept in each of the six ways we have stated, they know the concept thoroughly. If they can (1) remember the word label and defining criteria of the concept, (2) categorize examples of the concept, (3) deduce their own examples of the concept, (4) induce the concept given examples, (5) indicate how the concept is related in the sequence of time, and (6) indicate the cause-effect relationships that pertain to the concept, we can be assured that they have mastered the meaning of the concept.

It becomes clear that there is more to vocabulary building than memorizing the definitions of words. Memorizing is a necessary but insufficient skill for concept attainment. To build a vocabulary on a sound basis the additional five skills described above must be applied in the teaching of concepts and, therefore, vocabulary. In the following chapters, particularly chapters 6 and 7, we will greatly expand our discussion of concept development and the skills required for concept development. The six approaches to teaching vocabulary as concepts are summarized in the following chart.

CONCEPTUAL VOCABULARY BUILDING AND THE PREDICTION PROCESS

In chapter 3 we discussed word identification skills as those skills readers use in identifying unfamiliar words, their purpose being to aid readers in regaining meaning when their unfamiliarity with words brings about a loss of meaning. In this sense, word identification skills can be considered vocabulary skills since they aid readers in acquiring and adding to their reading vocabulary.

In this chapter, we have approached vocabulary building from another perspective; that is, the ways in which words are related in terms of their meaning and the reasoning skills we use and can teach as aids to vocabulary building. We have shown both how words are hierarchically related and how studying words in this fashion can result in increased learning and retention. The end result of learning more vocabulary words and extending meaning for vocabulary words is a decrease in the frequency with which

APPROACHES TO CONCEPTUAL VOCABULARY BUILDING

Skill	Identifying concrete events	Categorizing	Hierarchical Reasoning		Programmatic Reasoning	
			Deductive reasoning	Inductive reasoning	Chronological reasoning	Cause-effect reasoning
Provided for the student	The word label and defining criteria of a concept	The word label and defining criteria of the concept; examples and nonexamples of the concept	The word label and defining criteria of the concept	Examples of the concept	The word label and defining criteria of the concept	The word label and defining criteria of the concept
The student's task	Remember the word label and defining criteria of the concept	Distinguish examples and nonexamples	Produce examples of the concept	Produce the concept	Produce sequential attributes of the concept	Produce cause-effect attributes of the concept

the reader loses meaning. The more substantial the reader's reading vocabulary, the more predictable is the material he or she must read and comprehend.

Within the stages of the prediction process, we can look at the importance of reading vocabulary and how a sufficient reading vocabulary changes the way in which the reader goes about the task of reading.

Identifying Initiating Events

Words and word combinations remain the most important initiating event in reading. When words are relatively familiar to the reader, they elicit more ideas and contain more meaning for the reader. As readers build their reading vocabulary, they become increasingly independent in their learning and reading and require less guidance in an instructional situation.

Predicting Coming Events

As readers develop a substantial reading vocabulary, the nature of the predictions they make during their reading changes. Readers now can devote more of their predictive abilities to extracting meaning from the author's message and predicting coming events in terms of the ideas and concepts contained in the reading, rather than predicting which word analysis skill will help them regain meaning or deciding that the material is unpredictable. Readers' predictions of coming events can now be concentrated on extracting meaning, making judgments, reading critically, and generally comprehending what they read. Spontaneous reading is more likely, while loss of understanding occurs only infrequently. The reader becomes increasingly independent as his or her reading vocabulary develops.

Predicting the Consequences of Intervention

Similarly, readers who possess a substantial reading vocabulary make different kinds of interventions during their reading. The nature of the interventions readers make follows the nature of the original predictions they have made, so that increasingly their interventions have to do with extracting and extending the meaning of what they read. No longer must they spend substantial amounts of time making interventions like looking up words in a dictionary or seeking clarification from the teacher in order to regain meaning.

Identifying to Test Predictions

Finally, since the nature of the predictions and the interventions the readers have made changes, readers are free to seek confirmation of those predictions that deal largely with getting and extending meaning, rather than attempting to confirm predictions that deal with restoring and regaining meaning. Ultimately, readers' reading vocabulary has allowed them to devote more of their time and predictive abilities to the comprehension of the author's message—the paramount objective of reading in the first place.

SUMMARY

1. Most applications of proper nouns and personal pronouns refer to concrete events.

2. Most of the words in the dictionary are designations for abstraction categories. The definitions for words in the dictionary specify criteria for identifying members of the categories the word represents.

3. Some abstractions are absolute, others are relative.

4. The errors people make in categorizing are the result of (a) using erroneous criteria for inclusion in a category, (b) over-generalizing on the basis of insufficient criteria, and (c) overdiscriminating on the basis of unnecessary criteria.

5. Words are often used to convey the hierarchical relationships among abstraction categories. Such relationships form a concept, content, or class inclusion hierarchy which can be represented by a hierarchical tree.

6. The presentation of information as a content hierarchy facilitates the recall of the information.

7. Content hierarchies define general and specific relationships among the content contained in them. At the lowest, most specific level are concrete events. At the next higher level we have abstraction categories. At each succeeding higher level the categorical references become more general. The lower levels of a content hierarchy are contained or represented in the higher levels. For this reason content hierarchies are representational hierarchies.

8. Content hierarchies indicate relationships between (a) concrete events, (b) concrete events and abstraction categories, (c) abstraction categories at the same level of the hierarchy, and (d) abstraction categories at different levels of the hierarchy.

9. Absolute and relative degrees of relationships can be identified within the structure of a content hierarchy.

10. Hierarchical reasoning can lead to the formation of new categories. New categories may be inferred by reasoning inductively or deductively.

11. When we ask students to generalize, summarize, synthesize, or to determine the main idea, mood, or feeling an author is conveying, we require them to reason inductively.

12. When we ask students to give examples and illustrations or to analyze, we require them to reason deductively.

Teaching Aids and Strategies

13. To teach concepts or abstraction categories the teacher must teach the student (a) the word label for a category, (b) the criteria for inclusion in the category, and (c) to distinguish examples from nonexamples of the category.

14. To teach relationships in a content hierarchy the teacher should present the content hierarchy and show that the lowest level represents concrete events which are examples of the categories at the higher levels of the hierarchy. The teacher must show how the lower, more specific levels of the hierarchy are represented in the higher more general levels of the hierarchy.

15. To teach inductive reasoning the teacher must show the students how common characteristics may be found among items, or categories, and that these common characteristics are criteria for forming a more general category.

16. To teach deductive reasoning the teacher must show the students how a category may be subdivided into more specific categories. This is accomplished by identifying different groups that have common charactistics within the more general category.

REVIEW QUESTIONS

1. What kinds of words designate concrete events?

2. Why do most words in the dictionary represent abstraction categories?

3. Why are some abstractions absolute whereas others are relative?

4. What errors do people make in categorizing?

5. What is a content, concept, or class inclusion hierarchy?

6. What kinds of relationships are found in a content hierarchy?

7. How can inductive and deductive reasoning be used to infer new categories?

8. What questions require students to reason inductively?

9. What questions require students to reason deductively?

10. How can we teach concepts, hierarchical relationships, inductive reasoning, and deductive reasoning?

PART III
READING COMPREHENSION

CHAPTER 5
Views on Reading Comprehension
PURPOSE

1. To present popular views of reading comprehension and examples of reading comprehension skills.
2. To discuss the problems and limitations of viewing reading comprehension in these ways.
3. To consider some implications for teaching reading.
4. To provide a foundation for a description of reading comprehension skills as they apply to identification and prediction presented in chapter 6.

BACKGROUND AND NEW INFORMATION

Because you read and are confronted with problems of understanding what you read, you are sensitive to the issue of reading comprehension. Because you have read material that is easy to understand and material that is difficult to understand, you are aware that written material can make varying demands on your reading comprehension. The variety of test questions you have been asked about course material you have read sensitizes you to the different kinds of reading comprehension. Some questions you have been asked require you to remember what you have read. Other questions require you to make inferences and draw conclusions about the author's message. In this instance you must do more than remember what the author said.

Understanding the author's message is reading comprehension. Thus, everything mentioned in previous chapters that pertains to extracting meaning from written words concerns reading comprehension and prepares you to deal directly with reading comprehension in this and the next chapter. The last chapter provides a background for understanding our discussion of reading comprehension.

In this chapter we introduce some traditional views of reading comprehension and some different kinds of comprehension: (1) literal comprehension; (2) inferential comprehension; (3) evaluative comprehension; and (4) application. We discuss the reasoning skills related to the four kinds of comprehension and implications for teaching reading.

KEY TERMS

> literal comprehension
> inferential comprehension
> evaluative comprehension
> application

DESIRED LEARNING OUTCOMES

The student will be able to:

1. Explain the effects on comprehension of the (a) volume of information to be understood, (b) experiential background, (c) level of comprehension required, and (d) difficulty level of the reading material.
2. Describe traditional views of reading comprehension.
3. Describe literal comprehension and the thinking process involved in literal comprehension.
4. Explain inferential comprehension and the thinking process involved in inferential comprehension.
5. Explain application and evaluative comprehension and the thinking process involved.
6. Explain the implications that the various skills involved in comprehension have for the teaching of reading.

Probably the most essential responsibility of the reading teacher is to teach students to understand the author's message. If students are not comprehending what the author has written, they are not reading. When you are teaching reading your main goal will be to teach students how to comprehend what they are reading.

To understand the author's message students must be able to extract meaning from word combinations. Some writers in the field maintain that the unit in reading that we should be directing our attention toward is the sentence or the paragraph. Still others maintain that phrases and clauses contain messages, and that therefore units smaller than the paragraph and the sentence should be the focus of comprehension instruction.

The major point is this: reading is the acquisition of meaning from printed symbols, and meaning in this context is taken to be fairly complex combinations of information. That is to say, the word "tree" contains meaning; however, the sentence "The tree fell in the forest" contains a thought. In this sense, the acquisition of meaning during reading is the understanding of the relationships among the various words. We can ask a child who has read this sentence to tell us what a tree is. But he probably already knows what a tree is, and the sentence does not reveal what a tree is. A better probe for the total meaning of the sentence is "What happened to the tree?" or "What happened in the forest?" An even better question is "Why did the tree fall?" In this latter question, we are requiring the student to fuse the meaning contained in the original sentence as well as meaning contained in either previous sentences or sentences that follow.

Whatever we identify as the most important unit in reading (if we are indeed inclined to do so in the first place), that unit is not the word but rather a unit composed of combinations of words. Ultimately, then, improvement in reading comprehension follows three important thrusts. First, we must consider the *level* at which comprehension is taking place. This has to do with the notion of different comprehension skills that require different kinds and degrees of thinking ability. A great deal of discussion in this book will be devoted to this concept. Second, comprehension proceeds along a continuum regarding the length or *amount of information* the reader is required to deal with at any given time. That is to say, sheer volume of information will affect comprehension. Many students have little trouble with short reading selections; however, given a novel at the same level of difficulty, these students have enormous problems in reading and understanding the novel simply because of the amount of information it contains (Otto, McMenemy, and Smith, 1973). Amount of information greatly affects the accuracy of our comprehension measures, since standardized reading tests traditionally, and by necessity, are comprised of short reading selections not at all representative of the reading selections with which a student must deal in an instructional situation. Third, the factor of *difficulty level of material* affects comprehension. A number of subfactors operate to enhance and modify readability level of prose materials. We will discuss these factors in detail in a later chapter, but for now consider readability as primarily affected by sentence length and complexity and the number of new words being introduced (Klare, 1975). In addition to these three factors, experiential background is a readiness factor that will determine comprehension.

In this chapter we will be concerned primarily with describing reading comprehension in terms of the kinds of thinking skills required of the student. We will first discuss some traditional ways in which comprehension has been described and analyzed. We will ponder some of the practical shortcomings of looking at comprehension from these various perspectives. Then in the next chapter we will present several kinds of comprehension skills within the framework of the prediction process to organize, relate, and clarify them. We hope to impart to you, the reader, a way of looking at reading comprehension—a way to analyze reading comprehension for yourself in order to better understand this very important skill for the purpose of improving your ability to teach students to comprehend what they read.

TRADITIONAL VIEWS OF COMPREHENSION

A number of researchers have attempted to describe and type the processes of thinking, following the lead of Benjamin Bloom and his list of thinking skills. Writers and researchers in the field of reading have attempted to apply Bloom's list to reading com-

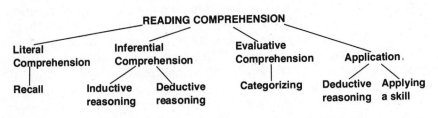

FIGURE 5–1 A hierarchy of topics in chapter 5

prehension; still others have constructed their own versions of reading comprehension.

Barrett (1968) has proposed a five-level structure including literal comprehension, reorganization, inferential comprehension, evaluation, and appreciation. Nila Banton Smith (1969) offers a four-level structure that is comprised of literal, interpretive, critical, and creative comprehension. She states that

> in literal comprehension the student tries to get the direct meaning of the author who wrote the text; in interpretation he tries to supply meanings to complete the author's text; in critical reading he evaluates, passes judgment on the author's text. In creative reading, however, the individual leaves the author's text and goes out on his own beyond the author's text to seek out or express new ideas, to gain additional insights, to find the answer to a question or the solution to a lifelike problem. (Smith, 1969:258)

Further, Smith offers some examples of each level of comprehension. Literal comprehension, Smith says, is exemplified by a question like "What did little brother want to eat?" whereas interpretive comprehension is called on in the question "Why was the cookie jar kept on the basement steps?" According to Smith, critical reading comprehension is required by the question "Did mother do the right thing in leaving the children alone?" Finally, creative comprehension is needed for answering the question "How would you have solved this problem?"

There has been a continuing effort to rank order comprehension into a hierarchy of prerequisite skills because if one skill is truly prerequisite to another, it must be learned before the other skill can be learned. Gagné (1965) states that "the subject of school instruction poses hierarchical organizations with respect to the required types of learning. Each can be analyzed to reveal prerequisite learnings that grow progressively simple . . .".

White's (1973) review of learning hierarchies provides evidence of the importance of teaching "prerequisite" skills first. White reports a study which demonstrated the importance of teaching lower level skills first. He also cites a study by Resnick, Segal, and Kresh in which two groups were taught two skills in a different order. One of the skills was logically prerequisite to the other. The group learning the lower level skill first learned the higher level skill in less time. Another study reported by White that supports this point of view was conducted by Merrill, Barton, and Wood. In this study a group of learners who mastered lower level skills in a hierarchy learned higher skills faster than a group who did not master the lower level skills first.

It should be noted that these studies do not prove that students who did not learn the lower level skills in the hierarchy could not learn the higher level skills. The studies demonstrate only that the learning of the lower level skills facilitated the learning of the higher level skills. The existing evidence also suggests that recall and learning are facilitated when the learner is shown the entire content hierarchy at one time, rather than the lower levels and then the higher levels, or vice versa.

At present there seems to be general agreement that literal comprehension or factual knowledge which is manifested by the recall of memorized information is the first level of comprehension. There appears to be little doubt that this is true, because we must be able to recall information before we can draw inferences about it or use it for any purpose.

The problem is in attempting to delineate among the higher levels of comprehension. We can say accurately that the literal level of comprehension is prerequisite to higher levels of comprehension. But we cannot rank higher levels of comprehension into a hierarchy of skills, one of which is prerequisite to another. For this reason, we will discuss different kinds of comprehension and the reasoning skills they require, without presuming to declare which is prerequisite to the other. These skills are found in many lists of comprehension skills.

TYPICAL COMPREHENSION SKILLS

Skills Required in Literal Comprehension

Literal comprehension is also referred to as the recall, concrete, factual, or explicit level of comprehension. If information is explicitly stated in the text and the questions we ask in a discussion or on a test simply require the student to reproduce that information, then we are operating at the literal level of comprehension. Again, two factors that will affect the quality of students' literal comprehension are the amount of information they recall and the level of sophistication of the materials from which they must gain a literal understanding.

Barrett (1968) refers to two essential skills of literal comprehension. First, students should be able to locate, recognize, and identify explicitly stated information with the information source in front of them. Second, students should be able to recall the information once they have read it. In the first instance, they are able to locate and identify the information they or the teacher deems appropriate. In the second instance, they must hold the information in memory pending a test, quiz, or other situation in which they must reproduce the information.

The skills required for literal comprehension more specifically involve the following:

1. Getting literally stated facts.
2. Deriving literal meaning from words, sentences, and paragraphs.
3. Choosing correct and applicable meanings for multimeaning words.
4. Following directions.
5. Being able to recall or retell information.

The process of synonym substitution will not affect the level of comprehension in most instances. For example, if the author stated that "Mary was angry," the student may recall that "Mary was mad." Although key words in this instance have been used interchangeably, the response remains at the literal level of reading comprehension. The following guidelines or rules of thumb should help in identifying comprehension questions and responses that are at the literal level.

1. Information is explicitly stated, in "black and white terms," by the author.
2. The student is required to locate the information or recall the information from memory.
3. The student is not required to "manipulate" the information in any way.
4. Paraphrasing the author's message or "telling it in your own words" is normally a literal level activity; however, paraphrasing does indicate a thorough literal understanding and can sometimes be included in the inferential level of comprehension.

Skills Required in Inferential Comprehension

Inferential comprehension requires the reader to go beyond the author's literal statements. The reader must draw inferences from the author's statements. The following are subskills that are often listed under inferential comprehension in descriptions of reading comprehension.

1. Interpreting the author's meaning.
2. Integrating new information with old.
3. Drawing inferences.
4. Deriving meaning from figurative language.
5. Weaving together ideas from content.
6. Recognizing the author's purpose, attitude, tone, or mood.
7. Identifying the author's style or technique of writing.
8. Sensing or following the organization of written material.
9. Predicting outcomes and solutions.
10. Making summaries.
11. Identifying character motives.
12. Seeing relationships among events, people, and ideas.
13. Distinguishing between real and unreal, fact and opinion, relevant and irrelevant.
14. Getting the main idea.
15. Analyzing the author's conclusions.

These fifteen skills are merely examples of reading comprehension skills found under the heading of inferential comprehension. They are not meant to represent an exhaustive list of those inferential skills that pervade various classification systems, reading tests, and published materials for teaching reading. If an exhaustive list of these skills were compiled, the number of skills would surely stretch into the hundreds. The important thing to note is that a potpourri of skills can be included under the heading of inferential comprehension. Some of these skills are quite different from others. They require different kinds of reasoning. Sometimes both identification and prediction skills are included under the heading. "Identifying character motives" is an identification skill which is sufficiently different from "predicting outcomes" to be distinguished from it. In addition, "getting the main idea" requires inductive reasoning, whereas "analyzing the author's conclusions" requires deductive reasoning. It is helpful to distinguish skills that require inductive thinking from skills that require deductive thinking as we did earlier and will do again in the next chapter.

Although the inferential level of reading comprehension involves a number of skills that range from seeing relationships to more complex reading-thinking skills that require inductive and deductive reasoning, the following guidelines should prove useful in identifying comprehension questions and responses that require inference.

1. Information is *not* explicitly or directly stated in the text; the student must "read between the lines" in order to correctly respond to an inferential question.
2. Often, students are supplied only partial information by the author and must supply missing information on their own.
3. Often, students are required to make connections and see relationships between seemingly unrelated facts, ideas, and events. Compare and contrast questions on essay examinations require students to deal with relationships.
4. Students are being asked to draw inferences inductively when they are required to generalize from specific statements made by the author, such as in summarizing, synthesizing, or determining the "main idea."

Skills Involved in Evaluative Comprehension

Evaluation may be defined as the description, comparison, and interpretation of an existing state and a criterion state. The criterion state is often a desired state. In evaluation one is usually comparing "what is" (the existing state) to "what ought to be" (the criterion state). Evaluation in reading involves the reader in comparing the author's position (the existing state) with a criterion. The criterion may be the reader's values or generally established values. For example, the reader might compare an author's position on the freedom of the press with the guarantees stated in the Bill of Rights. Or readers might compare a poem with criteria of good poetry given to them by their teacher.

Often evaluation involves us in making value judgments. The desired state is the valued condition we strive to achieve. When we compare an existing state to a desired state we are in a sense making a value judgment about the existing state. The closer the existing state conforms to the desired state, the more our values have been realized.

The skill involved in evaluation is categorizing. The criteria used in an evaluation are criteria for inclusion in a category. The evaluation compares some performance, object, or event to the criteria to see if it fits the category. For example, a teacher may establish that 80 percent correct answers on a test shall be the criterion for determining whether or not a student passes the exam. The students then are evaluated to determine whether or not they meet the criteria. Those that do, fit the category "pass."

Sometimes the evaluator is given the criteria for the evaluation. Then the evaluation only involves comparing a performance to the criteria defining the category. Such is the case when a student is given criteria for judging "good poetry" (the category in question) and is to decide whether specific poems fit the category. At other times the evaluator must determine the criteria for the evaluation as well as comparing performance against the criteria. Such is the case when a teacher establishes a score on a test as a criterion for "passing" and then evaluates students against the criterion.

Skills Involved in Making Applications

Application concerns the ability to apply what has been learned in two ways. First, application involves the correct utilization of information in different contexts. Readers should be able to demonstrate their ability to distinguish between a correct and an incorrect application of the author's statements. If the author is discussing dogs in a text, the reader should be able to understand that what the author concludes about dogs is applicable to dogs but not necessarily to all animals. When students read an author's conclusions about children, they should understand that the conclusions apply only to children and not necessarily to adults. Students demonstrate this skill when they are able to correctly apply a general conclusion to a specific situation or event and when they catch an author making an incorrect application.

Second, application involves the ability to demonstrate by our performance that we can correctly apply a skill we have learned. For example, students might be taught how to use the library. They would demonstrate that they knew how to use the library by applying correctly what they learned. To do this they would show their ability to find the information they needed in the library. Also, students who learn how words are structured in order to spell correctly can apply this skill to get the meaning of a word while reading.

Many writers have pointed out a number of problems that exist when one goes about the task of asking application level questions or requiring students to perform tasks at the application level. For example, students might read a book about how to build a house. They may comprehend the information contained in the book at all levels of comprehension. However, if we test their comprehension of that material at the application level by requiring them to actually go out and build a house, we are introducing a number of skills that are not necessarily related to reading. In this instance, the students must be able to use a tape measure, pound nails, and use a variety of tools adequately in order to perform the task of building a house. These skills are not indicative, however, of the ability to read at the application level of comprehension.

IMPLICATIONS FOR TEACHING READING

It is important that we as teachers examine the various comprehension skills in order to understand the thinking processes involved when students respond to our questions. For example, when we ask students to "draw an inference" about what an author has written, we are really asking them to read between the lines, to "fill in" the missing blank, to comprehend an implication of what the author has written, or to interpret the author's message. In this instance, there is not much difference among the skills "drawing inferences," "getting an implied meaning," "interpreting the author's meaning," or "inferring the author's message." In each of the above examples, some form of thinking is required. Inferential comprehension may require the student to merely see relationships, or inferential comprehension may require inductive or deductive reasoning.

Students are required to understand relationships when they are asked to "sense or follow the organization of written material" or to "see relationships among events, people, and ideas," or to "determine how story characters are alike or different." In addition, students are required to understand programmatic relationships when they are asked, for example, to determine the sequence of events that led to World War II.

Inductive and deductive inferences require students to use their knowledge of relationships to draw conclusions. In inductive reasoning the reader is expected to conclude by reasoning from the specific to the general. This way of reasoning is involved when students are asked to "get the main idea" from the reading or to "summarize the author's message." In either case they are required to integrate and generalize from specific statements the author has made. For example, an author might make a number of specific statements or present a number of specific examples of the wanton killing of animals. From these statements students can generalize that the author believes in the sanctity of life. It is in this way that they reason inductively to integrate specifics in order to summarize what the author is saying or to express the author's main idea.

To "draw conclusions" from general statements made by the author the student must often reason deductively, that is, from the general to the specific. For example, if the author made a general statement that he or she believed in the sanctity of human life, the student could reason deductively to conclude that the author would be against abortion (specific statement). Or if an author stated that he or she believed in democracy, the student could conclude deductively that the author would be against totalitarian forms of government.

We have already stated that both the amount of information a student must deal with, as well as the difficulty level of the reading material, will affect comprehension. Suppose, for the moment, that we want to teach a student to "get the main idea" from his reading. We could ask him to "get the main idea" from his reading. We could ask him to "get the main idea" from a paragraph, or perhaps from an entire chapter out of his textbook. In the first instance, the student will need to consider a relatively small amount of information in order to "get the main idea," whereas in the second instance, he will be required to manipulate a much larger amount of information. Although the process of "getting the main idea" is the same in each instance, simply the quantity of information the student must consider will affect his ability to perform this particular task.

Similarly, experiential background and the difficulty level of the reading material will affect the student's ability to "get the main idea." If difficulty level is high, the reading material probably contains new or unfamiliar words and longer, more complex sentences. These factors will also affect his ability to "get the main idea."

Finally, a number of comprehension skills which are concerned with things like "recognizing the author's style" are entirely dependent on the material being read. That is, a student may discern the differences between poetry and prose; this requires some discrimination. When students recognize the subtleties between Hemingway's style and Dreiser's style, they are exhibiting much more refined discrimination.

It is important to realize that comprehension is a product of thinking. Thinking enables readers to comprehend what they are reading. So when teachers teach comprehension, they are actually teaching the programmatic thinking skill that is used to comprehend the reading material. For instance, "determining the mood the author is creating" is a kind of comprehension a teacher may wish to teach. The thinking skill that must be taught to achieve this comprehension is the application of the inductive reasoning program. The student must be taught how to (1) look for specific feelings expressed in the statements of the author, (2) identify similarities among them, and (3) describe in words the common feelings prevading the author's statements. To demonstrate the skill the teacher might show a student a number of statements made by an author in which he or she describes exciting experiences. The teacher might then identify the general mood as "excitement" or "exhilaration" or use another appropriate word label.

Several studies point to the inadequacies of instruction beyond the literal comprehension level. Gallagher (1965) reported the results of a study designed to assess the level of comprehension dealt with most in the teaching of social studies. He found that literal understanding was the process observed most often. Davis and Tinsley (1967) conducted a study to determine the range of cognitive objectives manifested in secondary school social studies classrooms from questions asked by student teachers and their pupils. The results revealed that both teachers and pupils asked more questions involving remembering literal statements than all other questions combined. Similarly, a study by Pfeiffer and Davis (1965) revealed an overwhelming emphasis on the acquisition of facts in the analyses of ninth grade social studies examinations. Hunkins (1974) demonstrated that by changing the emphasis of questions on instructional materials to higher levels of comprehension, pupils' achievement in these areas can be increased.

In a study reported by Hogg (1973) it was found that 87 percent of the questions of the student teachers probed for factual knowledge.

The evidence indicates that although teachers tend to dwell mostly at the level of literal comprehension, involving students at higher levels of comprehension is beneficial to learning. Both teachers of reading and teachers in various content areas are interested in developing student capabilities at the higher levels of comprehension. It is important for them to learn how so that they can do more than question students for literal comprehension.

The development of lists of reading comprehension skills, combined with the move toward the use of behavioral objectives in education, has resulted in the "skills approach" in teaching reading. That is, exhaustive lists of reading comprehension skills have been constructed on which numerous standardized reading tests and classroom instructional materials have been based. These lists vary from test to test and among different kinds of instructional materials.

The different ideas regarding reading comprehension classification, the resultant skill listings, and the wording used to describe the skills have resulted in a multitude of problems for teachers. From a practical standpoint, an exhaustive list of reading comprehension skills is of little use simply because it is exhaustive. It would be extremely difficult, if not impossible, to plan instruction, conduct instruction, and evaluate instruction in all proposed reading comprehension skills for all students. Also, if teachers regard each skill as a separate skill and teach the skills independently, they may tend to overlook the importance of teaching students to use the skills in combination. A student may learn a multitude of subskills related to reading and still not be an accomplished reader.

Another problem is that we are immediately limited when we use words to describe reading comprehension skills. One person's idea of "drawing an inference" might be another's idea of what is involved in "getting an implied meaning." Problems in communicating definitions of skills and processes when investigating reading comprehension have probably contributed greatly to the notion that a myriad of discrete reading comprehension skills exists. The variation of meaning and overabundance of terms and jargon regarding reading comprehension has certainly been a major obstacle with which teachers have had to contend.

In addition to the problem of reconciling one list of comprehension skills with another, there are problems within lists. Although the purpose of a list of comprehension skills is to identify clearly different mental skills, some lists cause confusion. Some lists do not provide clear definitions for each category. Consequently, it is impossible to determine what to include in the category. Kinds of comprehension must be clearly defined; otherwise we cannot know what the composer of the list means by literal comprehension, inference, evaluation, application, creative reading, and so forth. The lack of clear definition sometimes leads to different kinds of comprehension being included in the same category. In a sense the composer of the list "mixes apples with oranges."

Finally, classification systems are limited with respect to describing comprehension skills. A classification system is a set of categories sometimes arranged in a hierarchical manner. Literal comprehension, inference, evaluation, and application are examples of categories of comprehension in a classification system. Classification systems allow us to identify a particular comprehension skill as a member of a category. Such is the case when we identify "getting the main idea" as an "inferential skill." However, classification systems do not indicate how a comprehension skill is taught or executed. Classifying "getting the main idea" as an inferential skill does not inform us of the procedures or programs involved in getting the main idea. In short, comprehension skills, like all other skills, are executed as a program. The teacher must know how a comprehension skill is executed in order to teach it. To teach this skill the teacher must know the program for getting the main idea and teach students how to execute it.

Although it may be important for us to be able to classify comprehension skills, it is more important for us to be able to identify those that are pertinent to reading and to be able to teach them. In order to be able to teach them we must know how they are executed programmatically. For this reason, we will present a list of comprehension skills in the next chapter which will help you understand the programs for executing important comprehension skills as well as a means of classifying the skills.

SUMMARY

1. Four major factors affect reading comprehension: (a) the level at which reading material is to be comprehended, (b) the amount of information that is to be understood, (c) the difficulty level of the material, and (d) the reader's experiential background.

2. A number of researchers have attempted to describe and categorize comprehension skills. Some have attempted to rank order comprehension skills into a hierarchy of prerequisites without too much success. The most we can say at this time is that literal comprehension is probably the lowest level comprehension skill. It remains to be determined if other comprehension skills form a hierarchy of prerequisites.

3. Literal comprehension involves remembering, recalling, or retelling what the author has stated explicitly.

4. Inferential comprehension requires the student to do more than remember explicit statements made by the author. The student must induce or deduce conclusions from what the author has said.

5. Evaluative comprehension involves comparing the author's statements against criteria to determine the extent to which the statements meet the criteria. Often the criteria specify a desired state.

6. The comprehension skill "making applications" has two references. First, application involves making a specific application of a general statement through deductive reasoning. Second,

application concerns the ability to demonstrate the correct application of a skill.

7. Comprehension is a product of thinking. Thinking is the general ability that enables the reader to understand the author's message. When teachers teach comprehension, they are actually teaching the thinking skill that is used to comprehend the reading material.

8. The evidence indicates that teachers mainly require and test for comprehension at the literal level and that requiring comprehension at higher levels is beneficial to learning.

9. The composers of classification systems of comprehension skills generate confusion about comprehension skills. Different composers may use different language to refer to the same skills. In addition, they do not supply clear definitions of the comprehension skills in their classification systems.

10. Although classifying a particular comprehension skill provides some information about the skill, the information is not sufficient for teaching the skill. To teach a comprehension skill the teacher must know how the skill is executed and communicate the procedure to the student.

REVIEW QUESTIONS

1. What four major factors affect reading comprehension?

2. To what extent can we presently rank order comprehension skills in a hierarchy of prerequisites?

3. What methods of thinking skills are involved in literal comprehension, inferential comprehension, evaluative comprehension, and in making applications?

4. What are some problems with present comprehension classification systems?

5. What must a teacher know about a comprehension skill in order to teach it?

CHAPTER 6
Reading Comprehension Skills

1. To present the many specific reading comprehension skills that are discussed and listed in the literature.
2. To describe six thinking procedures that underlie most reading comprehension skills.
3. To show the relationship between the six thinking procedures and the various reading comprehension skills.

BACKGROUND AND NEW INFORMATION

The prior discussion of identification and prediction skills prepares you to understand the four thinking procedures employed to make identifications and the two thinking procedures used to make predictions, which we discuss in this chapter. We are applying ways of thinking you have become familiar with (categorizing, inductive reasoning, and deductive reasoning) to reading comprehension.

You should be acquainted with terms such as drawing conclusions, reading critically, making applications, getting the main idea, classifying ideas, analyzing conclusions, evaluative reading, and making inferences. Most of these terms have been discussed in preceding chapters. In this chapter we deal with them in a new context.

At the beginning of chapter 6 we introduce a list of the reading comprehension skills commonly found in publications that discuss reading comprehension. Next we proceed to describe each of six thinking procedures: (1) identifying concrete events, (2) categorizing, (3) deductive reasoning, (4) inductive reasoning, (5) predicting coming events, and (6) predicting the consequences of intervention. As we discuss each procedure, we identify the related reading comprehension skills and show the relationship between the reading comprehension skills and the thinking procedure.

KEY TERMS

See lists on pages 163–64; 207.

DESIRED LEARNING OUTCOMES

The student will be able to:

1. Apply the procedure for identifying concrete events to comprehend reading material.
2. Identify the reading comprehension skills that require the reader to identify concrete events and describe the similarities and differences among the skills.
3. Apply the procedure for categorizing to comprehend reading material.
4. Identify the reading comprehension skills that require the reader to categorize and describe the similarities and differences among the skills.
5. Identify and apply the reading comprehension skills that require the reader to reason deductively and describe the similarities and differences among the skills.
6. Identify and apply the reading comprehension skills that require the reader to reason inductively and describe the similarities and differences among the skills.
7. Identify and apply the reading comprehension skills that require the reader to predict coming events and describe the similarities and differences among the skills.
8. Identify and apply the reading comprehension skills that require the reader to predict the consequences of intervention and describe the similarities and differences among the skills.

We reviewed the reading literature to find the reading comprehension skills most often dealt with. The following list summarizes our findings.

1. Comparing and contrasting reading selections and author's traits.
2. Recalling specific facts, details, names, places, events, dates, and so forth.
3. Following directions.
4. Recalling and retelling story events in order.
5. Paraphrasing what is read.
6. Classifying ideas.
7. Distinguishing fact and fantasy.
8. Distinguishing real and unreal.
9. Distinguishing fact and opinion.
10. Distinguishing relevant and irrelevant.
11. Integrating new information with old.
12. Evaluative reading.
13. Choosing correct and applicable meanings for multimeaning words.
14. Inferring details.
15. Making applications.
16. Identifying supportive information and details.
17. Analyzing conclusions.
18. Providing examples and illustrations.
19. Making generalizations.
20. Identifying character traits and motives.
21. Interpreting the author's style, bias, purpose, attitude, tone, or mood.
22. Getting the main idea.
23. Making summaries.
24. Interpreting figurative and idiomatic language.
25. Anticipating what will happen next in a story.
26. Making hypotheses.
27. Forecasting and predicting story outcomes.
28. Understanding the author's use of foreshadowing.
29. Making educated guesses.
30. Predicting cause-effect relationships.
31. Anticipating the effect of actions of characters in a story.
32. Predicting how a change introduced by the author affects events in a story.
33. Forecasting the effects of acts of nature in a story.
34. Making inferences.

35. Drawing conclusions.
36. Forming an opinion.

An analysis of these comprehension skills reveals that they require the reader to think about the author and the reading material or to go beyond the author and the message to draw a conclusion. Examples of comprehension skills that require the reader to think about the author are "interpreting the author's style, bias, purpose, attitude, tone or mood," and "comparing and contrasting reading selections and author's traits." Examples of comprehension skills that require the reader to think about the reading material are "recalling and retelling story events in order," "recalling specific facts, details, names, places, events, or dates," and "getting the main idea." Examples of comprehension skills that require the student to go beyond the author and reading material to conclude are "applying information gained from reading to a new situation" and "providing examples and illustrations." This suggests that when you teach reading comprehension you will instruct your students to consider something about the author, the reading material, or to relate something about the author or the reading material to their own experiences.

In the last chapter we pointed out that classifying a comprehension skill as one type or another may be helpful, but to teach a comprehension skill you must understand how it is executed. In this chapter we discuss thinking procedures that encompass most, if not all, of the comprehension skills presented in the preceding list. They are:

1. Identifying concrete events.
2. Categorizing.
3. Deductive reasoning.
4. Inductive reasoning.
5. Predicting coming events.
6. Predicting the consequences of intervention.

The first four are identification procedures. The last two are prediction procedures. It is our purpose now to describe the thinking procedures that pertain to each of the six skills and to relate the procedures to the preceding list of reading comprehension skills.

Underlying all comprehension skills is the ability to detect similarities and differences. The student must be able to inspect objects and events and enumerate the similarities and differences among them. This amounts to listing the features the objects and events have in common as well as listing the differences in their features. Compare and contrast questions require the student to enumerate similarities and differences. In reading we may ask students to compare and contrast authors' moods, styles, purposes, and tones. Or we may ask students to compare and contrast aspects of reading selections such as the traits and motives of characters and story plots and meanings.

The teacher begins to teach students to detect similarities and differences on a very simple level. To begin teaching similarities, the teacher shows students things that are similar with respect to only one easily distinguished feature. Once the students can identify simple distinct similarities the teacher introduces things that are similar with respect to two distinct features, then three, and so on.

To teach students to detect differences the same strategy is used. The students are first presented with things that are different in only one easily recognizable respect, then they are presented with things that are different in two distinct ways, and so on.

In order to illustrate the six thinking procedures we are about to discuss, we will use the stories "Goldilocks and the Three Bears" and "The Three Little Pigs." We have chosen these reading selections because we have advocated that in teaching skills the teacher should begin with simple content materials and progress to more difficult material after the student has shown mastery of a skill working with the simpler content materials.

THE THREE BEARS

Once upon a time there were three bears who lived in the forest. The three bears lived in a house in the forest. The first bear was called Father Bear. The second bear was called Mother Bear. And the third bear was called Little Wee Bear.

Father Bear had a very big voice. Mother Bear had a very big voice, too. But Little Wee Bear had a tiny wee voice. The three bears had three bowls. The Father Bear had a very large bowl. The Mother Bear had a big bowl, also. But Little Wee Bear had a little tiny bowl.

The three bears had three chairs. The Father Bear had a very large chair. The Mother Bear had a very large chair, too. But the Little Wee Bear had a little tiny chair.

The three bears had three beds. The Father Bear had a very large bed. The Mother Bear had a very large bed, also. But the Little Wee Bear had a tiny little bed.

One morning Father Bear could not eat his porridge. Mother Bear could not eat her porridge. And Little Wee Bear could not eat his porridge. The three bears could not eat their porridge. It was too hot.

So the three bears went for a walk. Father Bear went for a walk. Mother Bear went for a walk. And Little Wee Bear went for a walk. The three bears went for a walk in the forest.

Soon, a little girl came to the house in the forest. Her name was Goldilocks. Goldilocks went inside the house in the forest. Goldilocks saw the three bowls. Father Bear had porridge in his big bowl. Mother Bear had porridge in her big bowl, too. And Little Wee Bear had porridge in his tiny wee bowl.

Goldilocks said, "I will eat the porridge."

But Father Bear's porridge was too hot. And Mother Bear's porridge was too hot.

Goldilocks said, "I will eat the porridge in the tiny wee bowl." And she ate it all.

Goldilocks saw the three chairs. She said, "I will sit in the chairs."

But Father Bear's chair was too large. And Mother Bear's chair was too large. Goldilocks said, "I will sit in the tiny wee chair." And she did. Down it went. Bump!

Goldilocks saw the three beds. She said, "I will go to sleep."

But Father Bear's bed was too big. And Mother Bear's bed was too large. Goldilocks said, "I will go to sleep in the tiny wee bed." And she did. She went to sleep in Little Wee Bear's bed.

Then the three bears came home. Father Bear said, "I will eat my porridge now."

Mother Bear said, "I will eat my porridge now."

Little Wee Bear said, "I will eat my porridge now."

"Who ate some of my porridge?" said Father Bear in his very big voice.

"Who ate some of my porridge?" said Mother Bear in her very big voice, too.

Then Little Wee Bear said in his tiny wee voice, "Who ate all of my porridge? There is no porridge in my bowl."

"Who sat in my chair?" said Father Bear in his very big voice.

"Who sat in my chair?" said Mother Bear in her very big voice, too.

Then Little Wee Bear said in his tiny wee voice, "Who sat in my chair? My chair is broken!"

"Who was in my bed?" said Father Bear in his very big voice.

"Who was in my bed?" said Mother Bear in her very big voice, too.

"Who is in my bed?" said Little Wee Bear in his tiny wee voice. "A little girl is in my bed!"

Goldilocks sat up in the bed. She saw the three bears. She saw the big Father Bear. She saw the big Mother Bear. She saw Little Wee Bear, too. She jumped out of the bed and ran to the door.

Goldilocks ran out of the house. She ran, and ran, and ran. She ran all the way home. And she did not go again to the house in the forest.

THE THREE LITTLE PIGS

Once upon a time there was an old mother pig. She had three little pigs. The three little pigs ate and ate and ate. Then they played and danced.

The mother pig and the three little pigs lived in a house. The three little pigs ate and ate and grew and grew. They grew so big that they could not all live in the house.

One day the mother pig called the three little pigs together. She said, "You are too big and fat to live in my house. You must each get a house of your own."

"Where will we get a house?" asked the three little pigs.

"You must build your own house," said the mother pig. "You must build a strong house so the wolf cannot blow your house down and eat you."

Now the three little pigs hated to work. They did not want to build houses. So they played and sang all day long. The old mother pig became very angry.

She called the three little pigs together and said, "You must each build a house very soon. If you do not, the big bad wolf will catch you."

So the three little pigs left to build their houses.

The first little pig met a farmer with some straw. He said to the farmer, "Please, Mr. Farmer, let me have some straw so I can build a house."

The farmer gave him the straw, and the pig built his house with it. The little pig put a big door in the front of his straw house and a little door in the back. When he was done, he looked at his house and said, "I have a nice straw house and I am as safe as safe can be. When the big bad wolf comes, I'll laugh at him!"

The second little pig met a woodcutter with some sticks. He said to the woodcutter, "Please, Mr. Woodcutter, let me have some sticks so I can build a house."

The woodcutter gave him the sticks, and the pig built his house with them. The little pig put a big door in the front of the house and a little door in the back. When he was done, he looked at his house and said, "I have a nice stick house and I am as safe as safe can be. When the big bad wolf comes, I'll laugh at him!"

The third little pig met a builder with some bricks. He said to the builder, "Please, Mr. Builder, let me have some bricks so I can build a house."

The builder gave the third pig some bricks, and the pig built his house with them. The third little pig put a big door in the front of his brick house and a little door in the back. He also put big locks on the doors so the wolf could not get in. When he was done, he looked at his house and said, "I have a nice brick house and I am as safe as safe can be. When the big bad wolf comes, I'll laugh at him!"

All the little pigs had a house and felt as safe as safe can be.

One day the first little pig was in his house. He played and sang. Just then the big bad wolf came to the front door of the little pig's house. He knocked on the door and said, "Little Pig, Little Pig, let me come into your house."

But the little pig said, "No, no, by the hair of my chinny-chin-chin."

The wolf said, "Then I'll huff and I'll puff, and I'll blow your house down!"

The little pig was afraid but he did not let the wolf in.

So the wolf huffed and he puffed and he blew the house down. Down went the door in front. Down went the house made of straw.

The wolf looked for the little pig. But he could not find him. The little pig was not there. The little pig ran away. He ran out the little door in the back of the straw house.

All at once the wolf saw the little pig and ran after him. Away the little pig ran as fast as he could go. He ran to the house of sticks and went in the front door.

The wolf was very angry. He knocked on the door of the stick house and said, "Little Pigs, Little Pigs, let me in your house!"

But the little pigs said, "No, no, not by the hair on our chinny-chin-chins!"

"Then I'll huff and I'll puff and I'll blow your house down!" said the big bad wolf. He huffed and he puffed and he blew down the house of sticks.

The wolf looked for the two little pigs, but he could not find them. They were not there. The two little pigs ran away. They ran out the little door in the back of the house.

Away they ran to the house of bricks. They ran into the house of bricks as fast as they could go.

Before long the big bad wolf came to the front door. He knocked as hard as he could and said, "Little Pigs, Little Pigs, let me come into your house!"

But the three little pigs said, "No, no, by the hair of our chinny-chin-chins!"

"Then I'll huff and I'll puff and I'll blow your house down!" said the big bad wolf.

The three little pigs were afraid. They ran under the bed and hid. Then the big bad wolf huffed and he puffed, and he huffed and he puffed. But he could not blow down the house of bricks. Then the wolf tried to come in through the door. But the door had a big lock on it, and he could not get in. Soon the wolf gave up and went away.

The first little pig said, "Now we must each build a house of bricks."

So they all went to work, and in no time at all each little pig had a brick house of his own. Each little pig lived in his own brick house with big locks on the door. And the pigs were very happy because they were as safe as safe can be.

SIX IMPORTANT THINKING PROCEDURES

Identifying Concrete Events

Within the realm of reading comprehension, the term "concrete events" refers to words and word combinations. Concrete events consist of the facts, details, and ideas directly or explicitly stated in any reading selection. Thus, if the reader can identify the little girl in "The Three Bears," identify the kind of house the third pig had in "The Three Little Pigs," or identify each of the 50 states, he or she is identifying concrete events that were explicitly stated in a reading selection. In essence, the ability to identify concrete events corresponds to general literal level comprehension.

The problem for the student in identifying concrete events is to remember information in order to recognize, recall, or retell the information on a subsequent occasion. Based on research findings, we can recommend two aids for remembering information. First is the spaced review of the information, which simply means that new information is reviewed from time to time until it can be remembered and retained in memory. Spaced review aids remembering more than continuous review. There are a number of formal study skills procedures for spaced review of information. The SQ4R procedure is an example. In essence, it is a prescription for reviewing information in different ways such as surveying,

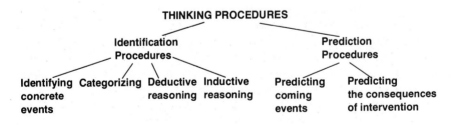

FIGURE 6–1   A hierarchy of topics in chapter 6

writing, and reciting the information to name three steps in the method. Reviewing information in a variety of ways reduces boredom and aids retention.

The second aid for remembering is the categorizing of new information, thereby making it meaningful. Suppose, for example, that the concept "personal pronoun" were new to you. You might review the definition of a personal pronoun again and again until you remembered it. However, if you already know what a "pronoun" is and are able to categorize the new concept "personal pronoun" as a type of "pronoun," the new concept would have some meaning for you. This would help you remember the meaning of the new concept (Ausubel, 1960). The summary offers an outline for teaching this comprehension skill.

Task: Remembering
Given: New information

A. Procedure for Performing the Task

1. Spaced review
2. Categorizing new information to make it meaningful

B. Comprehension Skills Involving Identifying Concrete Events

The following literal comprehension skills are among the most frequently mentioned skills that involve identifying concrete events:

1. Recalling a specific fact, detail, name, place, event, date, and so on.
2. Following directions.
3. Recalling and retelling story events in order.
4. Paraphrasing what is read.

Often, skills such as "following directions" are differentiated according to how many steps or parts are included in directions (for example, two-step directions; five-part directions). Teachers often complain that their students cannot follow directions. Students' difficulties in following directions are directly related to how many steps or parts the directions consist of and whether or not they must be followed in a particular order or sequence. Although a comprehension skill such as "following directions" is generally considered to be a literal level skill, the length (two-part; five-step; ten-step) and complexity (following the directions in a prescribed order) will affect the student's ability to perform this task. Similarly, "recalling and retelling story events in order" will be affected by the length and complexity of the story. Finally, a literal level skill such as "paraphrasing what is read" can easily be confused with "recalling and retelling story events in order." The factor that distinguishes these two skills is the student's response. If students paraphrase what they have read in such a way that they include in their paraphrasing inferences and conclusions they have made about what they read, a skill such as "paraphrasing what is read" can easily go beyond the literal or concrete level.

C. Sample Comprehension Tasks

There are hundreds of questions we could ask students after they have read "The Three Bears" that would require them to identify concrete events.

Recalling specific facts and details. In asking students to "recall specific facts and details," we should keep two general guidelines in mind: avoid asking students too many fact and detail questions, and avoid asking fact and detail questions that deal with trivial information. Using "The Three Bears" as a sample reading selection, the following are sample fact and detail questions:

- Where did the three bears live?
- What did the bears have for breakfast?
- Why couldn't they eat their breakfast?
- Who came to the bears' house while they were away?
- What did the visitor do?

Recalling and retelling story events in order. We pointed out previously that "recalling and retelling" what is read is a great deal like "paraphrasing" what is read. A skill such as "recalling story events in order" places a premium on the student's ability to recall the major events of a story in the same sequence in which they happened in the story. Some examples could include:

- What did the bears do after they decided the porridge was too hot to eat?
- What happened right after the bears left the house?
- What did Goldilocks do after she ate the porridge and broke the Wee Bear's chair?

Following directions. As we have said, "following directions" is a very generally stated skill and can take many forms. Within the context of reading comprehension, "following directions" would necessarily involve reading written directions and performing the activity called for in the directions. We might assume for the moment that the student has a worksheet or workbook containing various directions to be followed. Examples might include:

- Read the first two pages of the story, and write the names of the characters you find.
- Find out what the characters were having for breakfast, and look this word up in the dictionary to find what it means.

D. Factors Affecting the Identification of Concrete Events

For readers who have adequately mastered the word identification skills presented in chapter 3, two factors can significantly interfere with their ability to identify concrete events or comprehend at a concrete level what they read. First, the readers' ability to *recall or remember* what they read is important. Without the ability to recall the information they gain from reading, readers accomplish very little by reading in the first place. The amount of time readers must remember information they gain from their reading is, therefore, an important consideration.

Secondly, the amount and complexity of the information readers are expected to literally comprehend and subsequently remember is an important consideration. For example, in a social studies class the reader may be required to read a chapter about the different states that form the United States and perhaps do one of the following tasks:

1. Recall at least twenty-five out of the fifty states.
2. Recall all fifty states.
3. Recall all fifty states and indicate which were the original thirteen states.
4. Recall all fifty states in the order in which they were admitted to the Union.

As you can see, the task in each instance is at the literal level of comprehension requiring students to identify concrete events. However, the amount and complexity of the information that readers must recall will greatly affect how well they can do the task. This factor becomes increasingly important as we look closely at the range of comprehension skills; often we think of many comprehension skills as being beyond the literal level based on the language used to describe the skill. For example, a skill such as "perceiving sequential relationships" often involves only the literal understanding and recall of several facts or details in order. The task of recalling all fifty states in the order in which they were admitted to the Union could easily be identified as "perceiving sequential relationships," yet this skill is sometimes included among inferential comprehension skills. Regardless of the name of the comprehension skill, if the information is explicitly stated in the reading selection, then it involves only literal level comprehension.

Categorizing

Beyond literal level reading comprehension, the various comprehension skills require the reader to understand the author's message when it is implied and not directly stated. The reader's ability to categorize and classify events is basic to nearly all comprehension skills beyond the literal level.

The problem for the student in categorizing is to distinguish examples from nonexamples of a concept, given items, words, objects, events, or information to categorize. In order to categorize the things he or she is given, the student must have knowledge of the concept category to which the things belong. The student must know (1) the word label for the relevant concept categories and (2) the defining criteria or critical attributes of the categories. Students then match the items they are given with the criteria for inclusion in the categories. When an item matches the criteria for inclusion in a category, the student can conclude that it is an example of the category. When an item does not match the criteria for inclusion in a category, the student can conclude that it is not an example of the category. The reasoning procedure for solving the problem may be summarized as follows. The summary can be used as an outline for teaching students to categorize.

Task: Distinguish examples from nonexamples of a concept among items that are given.

Given: 1. Knowledge of the concept stated in the problem (that is, knowledge of the word label for a category and the criteria for inclusion in the category)

2. Items (ideas, statements, facts, information, and so forth)

A. Procedure for Performing the Task

1. Clarify the definition of the concept given in the statement of the task. That is, make certain of the criteria for inclusion in the category. Words can have multiple meanings.
2. List the defining criteria of the concept.
3. Match the items with the criteria to determine which meet the criteria and which do not. The items that match the criteria are examples of the concept. The items that do not match the criteria are nonexamples of the concept.

B. Comprehension Skills Involving Categorizing

There are a number of reading comprehension skills that are commonly included in various skill listings that require the student to categorize. These include:

1. Classifying ideas
2. Distinguishing fact and fantasy
3. Distinguishing real and unreal
4. Distinguishing fact and opinion
5. Distinguishing relevant and irrelevant information
6. Integrating new information with old
7. Evaluative reading
8. Choosing correct and applicable meanings for multiple meaning words

The reading comprehension skills "distinguishing fact and fantasy," "distinguishing real and unreal," "distinguishing fact and opinion," and "distinguishing relevant and irrelevant information" are categorizing skills that require the student to categorize reading material into one of two mutually exclusive categories. That is, the information gained from reading is either fact or fantasy, real or unreal, fact or opinion, or relevant or irrelevant. In each instance, the information must fit one category or the other; it cannot fit both.

"Distinguishing fact and opinion" is certainly an important comprehension skill since it underlies critical reading. In order to teach the reading comprehension skill "distinguishing fact and opinion," we must first teach the concepts of "fact" and "opinion." These two concepts become the categories readers will use to classify the ideas they gain from their reading. The terms "fact" and "opinion" are nothing more than word labels that represent these categories. When we teach the concepts of "fact" and "opinion," we are really teaching the criteria for inclusion in these two categories. At a very simple level, we might teach the following criteria for categorizing ideas as either "fact" or "opinion" and give students many examples to insure that they understand the concept:

FACT

Something that we *know* is true.

OPINION

Something we only *think* is true.

At this point, we have taught the students the word labels that denote the categories "fact" and "opinion" and the characteristics that make something a "fact" or an "opinion" (that is, the criteria for inclusion into the categories we have identified). Now we must see if the readers have mastered the comprehension skill of "distinguishing fact and opinion" by having them read a story or some other reading selection and classifying the ideas they gain from their reading as either "fact" or "opinion."

An important factor to keep in mind when teaching comprehension skills that require the student to categorize using existing categories is that the categories (like "fact" and "opinion") are provided for the student and the criteria for inclusion in the categories ("knowing something is true" versus "thinking something is true") are taught to the student. The students do not have to produce the categories or come up with the criteria for inclusion on their own. The students' only task is to correctly identify examples of a category. If an author makes a statement and says explicitly that the statement is his or her opinion, then only literal level understanding is required of students.

The categorizing skills "distinguishing fact and fantasy" and "distinguishing real and unreal" seem to be synonymous because they appear to represent the same mutually exclusive categories. The criterion for inclusion in both categories "fact" and "real" might be "something we know is true." The criterion for inclusion in the categories "fantasy" and "unreal" might be "something we know is not true." There may be, however, some slight semantic differences in the meaning of the words depending upon the definition one chooses to use.

"Distinguishing relevant and irrelevant information" is a

categorizing skill that requires the student to determine whether information pertains to or does not pertain to a particular issue. To exhibit this skill students must first know what the issue is. They then compare the information they glean from their reading to the issue. If it pertains to the issue it is categorized as "relevant." If it does not pertain to the issue it is categorized as "irrelevant." As you can see, the criteria for inclusion in the category "irrelevant" is "the information does not pertain to the issue in question." A teacher may, for example, ask students to determine which statements an author makes are relevant to the issue of communism. The important thing to remember about "distinguishing relevant and irrelvant information" is that students must be given the issue in question before they can determine what is relevant and what is irrelevant.

The skill "classifying ideas" is a very general reference. It might apply to any one of the more specific categorizing skills on the list we provided earlier. It simply refers to categorizing ideas of any kind.

"Integrating new information with old" suggests that students attempt to fit the new information they are reading into concept categories they already know so that the new information will have some meaning for them. We cited an example previously that is applicable here. We said that if students came across the term "personal pronoun" in their reading and it was unfamiliar to them, they could extract meaning if they knew the concept "pronoun" and identified "personal pronoun" as a type of pronoun.

"Evaluative reading" and evaluation of any kind is a categorization skill. By definition, evaluation involves the comparison of an event or an existing state to criteria defining a category. To evaluate whether or not reading material is factual, we use criteria for including reading material in the category "factual," that is, "events that actually happened." We compare the reading material to the criterion. If we determine that the reading material meets the criterion, we conclude that it is factual. Traditionally, comprehension skills that require the student to make evaluations are considered to be high level and difficult skills. But, as you can see, the ability to make evaluations might not be considered an exceptionally high level comprehension skill. Reading and thinking skills like making evaluations can be taught to children in the early elementary grades.

"Choosing correct and applicable meanings for multimeaning words" is a categorizing skill that requires the student to find the correct definition of a word based on the use of the word in context. Many words have more than one definition. Each definition represents a category the word label can represent. In order to demonstrate this comprehensive skill the student must compare the use of a word in a reading passage to the various definitions of the word to determine the meaning that is most appropriate. Usually contextual cues in the reading passage will be compared to the different definitions of the word. The definition of the word that best agrees with these cues will be selected.

C. Sample Comprehension Tasks

While not every comprehension skill can be taught using "The Three Bears," several are appropriate to this particular story. Below are sample comprehension questions based on "The Three Bears" that demonstrate various comprehension skills involving categorizing using existing categories. Remember that in each instance the categories (word labels) and the criteria for inclusion into the categories are taught to the students, their task being to correctly identify members of the categories being dealt with in the particular skill.

Distinguishing fact and fantasy. Assuming that the students have been taught the difference between a story that is factual in nature and a story that is fantasy, their task is to identify "The Three Bears" as fantasy using the criteria they have been taught. Sample comprehension question might include:

- The story contains talking animals. Does this tell us it is fact of fantasy?
- The bears lived in a house. Does this tell us the story is fact or fantasy?

Distinguishing relevant and irrelevant. As we pointed out, to distinguish relevant and irrelevant the student must be given the issue in question. In this instance, the teacher may want to establish that Goldilocks was not a particularly nice little girl. Those story events that support this contention (for example, Goldilocks went into someone's house without being invited) are relevant events while other events in the story (for example, Goldilocks had blond hair) are not. In this example, the teacher would tell the students that Goldilocks was not a very nice little girl then ask them whether specific statements of Goldilocks' behavior indicate whether she was nice or not.

- Does the fact that Goldilocks went into someone's house without being invited indicate whether or not she is nice?
- Goldilocks took porridge without asking. Does this tell us whether or not she is nice?
- Goldilocks broke one of the bears' chair. Does this tell us whether or not she was a nice girl?

Other relevant behaviors might be that Goldilocks slept in the bed without asking and ran away without apologizing to the three bears.

Evaluative reading. Remembering that evaluative reading involves the students in making comparisons between an existing and a desired or criterion state, there are a number of questions along these lines that might be based on "The Three Bears."

- Does the fact that Goldilocks fell asleep in the morning indicate that she is "strange"?
- When Goldilocks broke the chair was she being "nice"?

For all of the above tasks the teacher would clarify the definition of the concepts by enumerating their defining criteria. He or she would define fact and fantasy, relevant and irrelevant, strange, and nice.

D. Factors Affecting the Ability to Categorize

One factor that affects students' ability to categorize is accurate knowledge of the criteria for inclusion in a category. If they do not know the criteria attributes of a category, they cannot correctly classify members of the category. In chapter 4 we mentioned three mistakes students make in categorizing: (1) they use erroneous criteria; (2) they use unnecessary criteria which results in overdiscrimination; and (3) they use insufficient criteria which results in overgeneralization. We provided examples of these errors and will provide more in the next chapter.

Another factor that affects categorizing is the number of categories a student must deal with. It is easier to work with fewer categories. Also, if one is working with more than one category it is easier to categorize if the criteria for inclusion in the categories are distinctly different from one another.

Finally, the extent to which examples of a category may be clearly identified affects the student's ability to understand the concept. This is directly related to how distinctly examples of a concept can be experienced through the senses. The concept "dog" can be easily taught because examples of dogs can be seen, heard, felt, and so forth. The concept "patriotism" is not so easily learned because it is not so easy to identify examples and nonexamples of patriotism in the concrete. There are other concepts which are impossible to exemplify in the concrete. So far we are unable to provide concrete examples of the Freudian concepts "id," "ego," and "superego." Students learn the meaning of these concepts from their definitions. The concepts exist only by virtue of definition.

Deductive Reasoning

As we have shown, comprehension skills that require the student to reason from a general frame of reference to identify more specific details, information, facts, examples, or illustrations not explicitly stated in the reading material involve deductive thinking because the student reasons from the general to the specific. In reading the student is often required to reason from a general conclusion the author has stated to supportive details implied in the text or to go beyond the text to make specific applications of the author's conclusion. An important consideration in both teaching and evaluating deductive comprehension skills is the degree to which students must reason from the general to the specific to produce their own conclusion.

The problem for students in deductive reasoning is to produce their own examples of a concept. The concept is the general frame of reference given to students by the author in a reading passage. Students must know the meaning of the concept. That is, they must know the word label for the concept and the defining criteria of the concept. They then search for a specific object or event that meets the defining criteria. When they find one they have an example of the concept. They then describe the example to show how it meets the defining criteria. The following criteria summarize the deductive reasoning process and serve as an outline for teaching deductive reasoning.

Task: Produce example(s) of a concept
Given: Knowledge of the concept stated in the problem
        (knowledge of a word label for a category and the
        criteria for inclusion in the category)

A. Procedure for Performing the Task

1. Clarify the definitions of the concept given in the statement of the task. That is, make sure of the criteria defining the concept because words can have more than one
   definition.
2. List the defining criteria of the concept.
3. Search for items that match the criteria. This gives
   examples of the concept.
4. Describe the examples to show how they meet all the
   criteria.

B. Comprehension Skills Involving Deductive Reasoning

There are a number of reading comprehension skills that
require the student to engage in deductive reasoning. The
most frequently taught reading comprehension skills that
require deductive reasoning are included in the list below:

1. Identifying supportive information and details
2. Inferring details
3. Analyzing conclusions
4. Giving examples
5. Applying information gained from reading to new situations
6. Providing illustrations

One way of identifying reading comprehension skills that require deductive reasoning is to look for key signal words that signal deductive reasoning such as analyze, apply, exemplify, and
illustrate. Also, words that instruct the reader to identify specifics
or details suggest deductive reasoning. It also is important to remember that whatever signal words are used to instruct students
to reason deductively, the student will be required to produce one
or more examples of a given concept. Another important point to
remember is that the instructions eliciting deductive reasoning
may require students to produce an example that pertains to (1)
the reading material, (2) the author, or (3) their own experience.

Identifying supportive information and details. Identifying supportive
information and details is a deductive comprehension skill

that may be applied to a reading selection, to an author, or to one's own personal experience, depending upon what the details refer to. If we ask students to provide details and information that support the conclusion that the third little pig was wise, the student must provide examples from the reading material. After having read the story and being presented the concept "wise," students must identify statements in the story that illustrate that the third little pig was wise. To help the students the teacher would clarify the criteria defining the concept "wise," such as (1) planning ahead, (2) outsmarting an opponent, and (3) protecting oneself. After the students search the story for statements about the third little pig that illustrate his wisdom, they might come up with the following statements: the third little pig knew the wolf was vicious and would try to get him, or he built a house of bricks and put big locks on the door so that no one could get in. These are examples of characteristics that meet the criteria of being "wise." In "identifying supportive information and details" the student has reasoned deductively to provide specific examples of a general concept.

We can easily use the signal words illustrate, exemplify, apply, and analyze to instruct the student to reason deductively in the same way. We might instruct the students to find statements in the story that illustrate that the third little pig was wise. Or we might ask the students to analyze the actions of the third little pig to determine whether or not any of his actions indicate that he was wise. Or we might ask the students to determine whether or not the concept "wise" is applicable to the third pig. In each instance the student is being asked to find examples in the story that indicate that the third little pig was wise.

Applying information gained from reading to new situations. Applying information gained from reading to new situations is a deductive reasoning skill that specifically instructs students to provide examples from their own experience. After reading about and understanding the wisdom of the third little pig, the students might be asked to apply the concept "wise" to new situations. They could offer examples of wise behavior from any of their experiences. They could offer examples of their own wise behavior or examples of the wise actions of anyone they know or have read about. The students may also be asked whether or not an author is wise, in which case they would attempt to find characteristics of the author that exemplify wisdom. In addition, the students might be asked if they know anyone who is wise. In this case they would

attempt to find examples of behavior which meet the criteria for
being wise. These tasks require the student to reason deductively
in different contexts to produce examples of being wise.

Students can also be asked to reason deductively to identify
causal factors. They are given the word label "cause" and criteria
defining the word such as "forces that produce particular effects."
The students may then be asked to determine the cause of the
third pig's building a house of bricks and putting big locks on the
door. This, then, is the effect for which students must find a
cause. The students might cite the wolf's attack on the first and
second pigs as an example of a causal agent in the story. Remember, however, that if the story stated explicitly that "the
wolf's attack on the first and second pig caused the third pig to
build a brick house with big locks on the door," the conclusion
requires nothing more than literal comprehension. On the other
hand, if the teacher asks students whether or not the wolf's attacks on the first two pigs could be a cause of the third pig building a brick house with big locks on the door, the conclusion is
derived through categorizing. The students simply match the
statement about the wolf's attacks with the concept "cause" and
decide whether it meets the criteria of "forces that produce a particular effect." They are given both the concept and the statement
to be categorized. In deductive reasoning students are given only
the concept. They must produce their own example of the
concept.

C. Sample Comprehension Tasks

As we pointed out, there are a number of reading comprehension skills that require the student to engage in deductive reasoning. When we discussed categorizing we cited examples using the
concepts "fact and fantasy," "nice," and "strange." The student
was given the concept and particular statements in "The Three
Bears" and asked to determine whether the statements were
examples or nonexamples of the concepts. To contrast deductive
reasoning and categorizing we will use the same concepts. However, unlike categorizing, in deductive reasoning the student
must produce the statements in the story that exemplify the concept.

Identifying supportive information and details. The student might be
asked to find supportive details and information in the story
which indicate that (1) the story is either "fact or fantasy,"
(2) Goldilocks is a "nice" girl, or (3) Goldilocks is a "strange" girl.

Providing examples and illustrations. Here the instructions are slightly different, but the task is the same. The instructions might be, "Provide examples or illustrations in the story which indicate that (1) the story is either 'fact or fantasy,' (2) Goldilocks is a 'nice' girl, or (3) Goldilocks is a 'strange' girl."

Analyzing conclusions. In this case the instructions vary again, but the task is still one of deductive reasoning. The instructions might be, "Analyze the story to determine whether (1) it is 'fact or fiction,' (2) Goldilocks is a 'nice' girl, or (3) Goldilocks is a 'strange' girl."

Applying information gained from reading to a new situation. A we said, this deductive reasoning skill requires students to produce examples by applying a concept they encountered through reading to their own experience. After reading about Goldilocks and her strange behavior, the teacher might want to exercise the students' understanding of the concept "strange" by asking them to apply it to their own experience. The teacher might ask the student:

• Have you ever behaved strangely?
• Describe someone you think is strange.

To prepare students for deductive reasoning as well as for categorizing the teacher must make certain that he or she provides the defining criteria of the concepts in question.

D. Factors Affecting Deductive Reasoning

One factor that affects deductive reasoning is the students' understanding of the concepts in the reading selection. If they do not know the defining criteria of the concept they are required to reason from, they will not be able to produce an example of the concept. Another factor that affects deductive reasoning is the students' ability to determine the meaning of a concept from the structure and contextual clues in the reading selection when a word in the selection has more than one definition. The students' experiential background will also affect their ability to produce examples of a concept, simply because individuals with limited experiences will have fewer examples of any kind in their memory. Finally, the students' ability to critically compare the criteria of the concept with their experiences for similarities and differences and to detect similarities will affect their ability to reason deductively. If the students cannot accurately match the criteria of the concept with an experience, they will not be able to produce an example of the concept.

As you can see, many of the skills required for categorizing are required in deductive reasoning. Both reasoning processes require students to understand the concept in question, and both processes require students to be able to match objects and events with the defining criteria of a concept to determine whether they are examples or nonexamples of the concept. The difference between categorizing and deductive reasoning is that in categorizing, students are given objects, events, and concepts and asked to determine which objects and events are examples of the concept. In deductive reasoning students are given the concept, but they must produce their own examples of the concept.

Inductive Reasoning

As we have shown, those comprehension skills that require students to identify relevant details, facts, events, and so forth, then either identify or produce some sort of generalization that encompasses that information, involve inductive thinking since they move from the specific to the general. With regard to the broad spectrum of reading and thinking skills, inductive thinking is extremely important since we are constantly engaged in the process of making generalizations about language, about the world in which we live, and so on. In the same way, we utilize inductive thinking in dealing with and making sense from the ideas we gain from reading. An important consideration in both teaching and evaluating inductive comprehension skills regards the extent to which a particular skill requires students to move from the specific to the general in order to produce their own concepts.

The problem for students in inductive reasoning is to produce their own concepts with respect to the reading material, the author, or their own experience. They search for common characteristics among specific details, events, statements, or reading selections. Then they group together the subject matter they are inspecting, based on common characteristics. The identification of common characteristics gives them the critical attribute or defining criteria of their concept. Finally, they describe the defining criteria (common characteristics) of their concept. This gives them the word label for their concepts. The following outline summarizes the inductive reasoning process and serves as an outline for teaching inductive reasoning.

Task: To produce a concept
Given: Items (statements, ideas, and so forth)

A. Procedure for Performing the Task

1. Search for common characteristics among the ideas and statements in a reading selection.
2. Group items together based on their common characteristics. The common characteristics are the critical attributes or the defining criteria of the concept.
3. List the defining criteria of the concept.
4. Describe the defining criteria of the concept. This gives the word label for your concept.

B. Comprehension Skills Involving Inductive Reasoning

There are a number of reading comprehension skills that engage the student in inductive reasoning. The most frequently cited inductive reasoning skills are:

1. Making generalizations
2. Identifying character traits and motives
3. Interpreting the author's style, bias, attitude, tone, mood, and purpose
4. Getting the main idea
5. Making summaries
6. Interpreting figurative and idiomatic language

Some words often signal inductive reasoning. When students are asked to "generalize" or "summarize" they are required to reason inductively. Sometimes the words "integrate" and "synthesize" signal that inductive reasoning is required. When a signal word is used in questions and instructions that require students to reason inductively, the questions or instructions will require them to produce their own concept (the student is required to produce criteria defining a category and to give a word label for the category). Students may be asked to reason inductively with respect to (1) the reading material, such as in getting the main idea of a story; (2) the author, such as in determining the author's mood; and (3) personal experience, such as in generalizing about stories read.

Making generalizations. Making generalizations is a very general reference to inductive reasoning. It might pertain to any of the other inductive reasoning skills in the above list. One is making a generalization when he or she is "interpreting the author's purpose," "identifying character traits," "making summaries," "getting the main idea," and so on.

Identifying character traits and motives. Identifying character traits requires students to find similarities in the behavior of a character, to infer from these common characteristics criteria that type the character, and describe the criteria giving a word label for their concept. For instance, a student might read "The Three Little Pigs" and notice that the third pig knew the wolf had lied, built a house of bricks, put big locks on the door, and survived the attack of the wolf. From these observations the student may infer the criteria for his category: (1) the third pig outsmarted his enemy; (2) he planned ahead; and (3) protected himself effectively. The student would mull over these traits (criteria) and might decide they were criteria indicating wisdom. He would then state that the third pig is wise, offering his word label for the concept he produced.

Identifying the author's style, bias, attitude, tone, mood, and purpose. This is an inductive reasoning skill that requires students to produce a concept pertaining to the author. For instance, students might inspect the author's statements to detect the mood he is conveying. They might group mood statements together based on their common characteristics and infer that the criteria for their concept are "longing for the good old days." This might suggest to them that an appropriate word label for their concept is "nostalgic."

Identifying the author's purpose is another inductive reasoning skill that requires students to determine causality. Students must produce a concept that indicates why the author wrote the story. For example, they might be asked why the author of "The Three Little Pigs" wrote the story. To answer the question students would examine the effects the author created for common characteristics. They might realize that the first two pigs were almost eaten by the wolf because they were unwise. The students might decide that the author's purpose is to teach children not to be "unwise."

Making summaries. Making summaries is an inductive reasoning skill that involves the student in grouping the ideas in a reading passage into a number of groups. Each group has common characteristics that pertain to an essential point the author has made, and the different groups pertain to different essential points. To summarize the author's message the student describes succinctly each of the essential points the author is making. This gives the student word labels for each concept.

Getting the main idea. Getting the main idea is very much like summarizing. The only difference is that after the author's ideas are summarized into various groups of essential ideas, the student must determine which is the most important or main idea.

Interpreting figurative and idiomatic language. This inductive reasoning skill involves students in producing a concept that is synonymous or equivalent to a figurative or idiomatic statement they do not understand. For example, suppose that in reading the students come across the statement "fit as a fiddle" and do not know what it means. They begin to look among the adjacent statements that they can understand for common characteristics. If the statements refer to a character in a story they may read that the character is strong, has not been sick for a long time, feels good, and excels at athletics. This may suggest to the students the word label "healthy," which is synonymous with the idiomatic phrase "fit as a fiddle."

C. Sample Comprehension Tasks

The following are sample comprehension tasks that engage the student in various forms of inductive reasoning.

Identifying character traits and motives. In any kind of story-type reading selection, an author generally gives the reader a number of facts, details, and descriptive pieces of information about the characters in the selection. Most often, the reader's task is to pick up on these specific pieces of information and then generalize about the character by inferring criteria and a word label for a concept describing the character. Using the criteria of the bears from "The Three Bears," we might ask the student the following comprehension question:

- How would you describe the three bears?

The student might respond with the description "nice" based upon the fact that the bears did not do anything bad to Goldilocks or get her into trouble even though she went into their house uninvited, broke a chair, ate their food, and slept in one of their beds.

Identifying character motives involves the student in producing a concept that explains why or indicates a cause of a character's behavior. To engage students in this task we might ask a question like the following:

- Why do you think Goldilocks did the things she did?

The student might generalize from the facts that Goldilocks entered the three bears' home uninvited and inspected many things in the home. The student might then produce the concept "curiosity" to describe the cause of her behavior.

Identifying the author's purpose. This inductive reasoning skill also requires the student to produce a concept that indicates causality. However, in this case the student is to produce a concept that explains why the author wrote a story. Questions such as the following might be asked to engage students in identifying the author's purpose.

- Why do you think the author wrote "The Three Bears"?
- What was the author trying to do in writing this story?
- What was the author's purpose?

Upon examining the story the students may note that the character Goldilocks keeps intruding into the lives of the three bears; they then may produce the concept that the author's purpose is to teach children not to intrude on others.

Getting the main idea. Getting the main idea tends to be one of the more difficult comprehension skills to teach. It involves inductive thinking in the sense that the "main idea" statement is a generalization based upon the specifics in the reading selection. However, "main idea" also requires students to attach a priority to the generalizations they have made from their reading by requiring them to indicate "the most important idea." In the context of the story "The Three Bears," we might ask the students to state the main idea of the story by asking them the following questions:

- What is the main idea of "The Three Bears"?
- Can you think of another title for this story that would tell us more about the story?

As we pointed out, to get the main idea students summarize all the ideas in the story. Then they must judge which of these ideas is the most important one. If there is more than one basic idea in a story, different students may produce different main ideas. Such might be the case for the story of "The Three Bears." There are a number of major ideas that can be cited, including:

- People should mind their own business.
- People should stay out of others' business.
- People should always lock their doors when they leave the house.
- Little girls with blond hair are not to be trusted.
- Too much curiosity can get you in trouble.

Not all of these generalizations are necessarily accurate with respect to "The Three Bears." However, each is, in fact, a generalization that can be made based on the story. Which is the "main idea" or "most important idea" in the story? The generalization that "people should stay out of others' business" is probably the "main idea" of "The Three Bears." The point to remember is that in getting the main idea students make judgments in producing their concepts of the main idea. A student's concept of the main idea may not agree with the teacher's or other students' concepts. But if he or she summarized the various ideas in the story correctly and simply chose a particular idea as the most important idea, his or her disagreement with classmates and the teacher is judgmental; the student knows how to get the main idea. In teaching students to get the main idea, the teacher must focus on the student's reasoning. It is more important that the student reason properly than produce the same main idea as others.

D. Factors Affecting Inductive Reasoning

The first factor that affects inductive reasoning is the ability to detect similarities and differences and to group things with common characteristics together. Students will be unable to generate criteria for a concept if they cannot group similar things together. For instance, in "The Three Little Pigs," students must be able to detect that (1) building a brick house and (2) putting big locks on the door are similar in that they are ways of effectively protecting oneself. Finding this similarity gives them one character trait of the third pig and a criterion for the concept they are producing. The students must also be able to see that all of the third pig's protective actions were similar in the sense that they were taken before the wolf attacked. Finding this similarity enables them to infer another criterion for the concept they are producing—planning ahead. In order to infer that the third pig outsmarted his enemy (another criterion), the students must detect similarities in statements, such as he knew the wolf lied, and in events, such as he survived the wolf's attack.

Another major factor affecting inductive reasoning is the students' ability to produce a word label for their concept. It is not sufficient to be able to identify criteria; in addition, they must come up with a word label that describes the criteria. In the case of the third pig the students must understand that (1) protecting oneself, (2) outsmarting the enemy, and (3) planning ahead are criteria denoting a "wise" person. However, the students have options in producing a word label that summarizes their criteria. The words "intelligent" and "prudent" are also acceptable labels for the inferred criteria.

The students' vocabulary is also a factor in reasoning inductively. Clearly, if they must produce an appropriate word label for their concept, they must know the meaning of words that apply to the criteria they induce. If they are to reason inductively with respect to character traits, they must know the meaning of adjectives that are used to describe the traits of characters. In categorizing and deductive reasoning the students are given the concept, both the word label and the defining criteria. In inductive reasoning the students must produce the criteria and the word label. The larger the students' vocabulary the easier it will be for them to achieve this.

Predicting Coming Events

Up to this point, we have discussed a number of reading comprehension skills necessary to identifying the author's message. There are a number of additional reading comprehension skills that involve predicting the author's message. Typically, students engage in these comprehension skills after having read only a portion of a particular reading assignment and then making predictions regarding the information contained in the remainder of the reading selection.

An important consideration in teaching comprehension skills associated with predicting the author's message is how much information the student has available in order to make accurate predictions. The student may be able to make accurate predictions, for example, regarding the conclusion of a story after having read only the title or after having read the first half of the story. In the first instance, the student is demonstrating the ability to make accurate predictions based on fewer clues. This ability to make accurate predictions based on a minimum amount of information is an important aspect of growth in reading and thinking skills.

Another important point associated with the comprehension skills that involve prediction is that all of the identification skills we have already described can be viewed as prediction skills. If, for example, the student must "get the main idea" or "draw a general conclusion" after having read only a portion of a particular reading selection, then these comprehension skills involve the student in identifying *and* predicting. The following outline summarizes the procedures for predicting coming events and provides a guide for teaching the procedure.

Task: To predict from a current trend what will happen in the future
Given: A current trend of events

A. Procedure for Performing the Task

1. Note the current trend of events.
2. Project the trend into the future.
3. Predict what will happen in the future.

B. Comprehension Skills Involving Predicting Coming Events
The following are skills often referred to that engage students in predicting coming events:

1. Anticipating what will happen next in a story
2. Making hypotheses
3. Forecasting and predicting story outcomes
4. Understanding the author's use of foreshadowing
5. Making educated guesses

As you can see, words that signal that a prediction is required include anticipate, guess, predict, forecast, foreshadow, and hypothesize.

In predicting coming events from reading, the reader may base his or her prediction on (1) the reading materials, (2) the author's perspective, and/or (3) personal experience. A prediction about the content of a book can be based on the title of the book or the table of contents. Also, a prediction may be based on the author's purpose, bias, or the mood he or she is creating. In addition, readers may base a prediction on their own experience. If they have read murder mystery stories in the past and learn that the book they intend to read is a murder mystery, they can make predictions about the content and the sequence of events. They can predict that there will be a murder early in the story, an investigation following, and that the murder will be solved toward the end of the story.

Making hypotheses and making educated guesses. These are two general references to predicting coming events. They do not indicate specifically the kind of prediction that is to be made.

Anticipating what will happen next in a story. This involves the student in making short-range predictions of the coming events in a story. After reading about the wolf almost eating the first little pig the student might be asked:

- What do you anticipate will happen next in the story?
- What will the wolf do next?

Forecasting story outcomes. Much more complicated than "anticipating what will happen next in a story," here the student makes a long-range prediction of an end result. Typically, this is what one tries to do when reading a murder mystery. One attempts to predict who will turn out to be the murderer at the end of the story. In this case, readers continually try to zero in on the guilty person as they pick up clues the author provides. The good predictor will predict the culprit earlier in the story, therefore using fewer clues.

Returning to our example of "The Three Little Pigs," the student can be asked to predict the outcome of the story after reading that the first and second pigs had been almost eaten by the wolf. Based upon this trend and not knowing that the third pig was intervening to change the trend by building a house with big locks on the door, the normal prediction would be that the wolf will also blow down the house of the third pig; that is, if the current trend continues.

Understanding the author's use of foreshadowing. This involves the student in making predictions based on the author's purpose or the mood he or she is creating. If the author states a purpose for writing the text, prediction of coming events can be based on these statements. At the beginning of each chapter we state our purposes for writing the chapter. This foreshadows and helps the reader predict the content of the chapter. If students know that "The Three Little Pigs" is a didactic story before reading it, they can predict that the author will attempt to teach them something in the story. Consequently, they will be on the lookout for a moral and be more likely to detect that the story demonstrates that hard work leads to success. In general, the foreshadowing injected by the author makes the message more predictable for the reader and prevents confusion.

The mood that an author creates is often a basis for predicting the coming message. In writing novels the author often creates a mood at the beginning that enables the reader to predict whether the story will be a comedy or a tragedy.

C. Sample Comprehension Tasks

Although we have enumerated several comprehension skills associated with prediction, they are not significantly different from one another. Each involves the student in predicting the events and coming information in a reading selection based on having read only part of the selection. For example, we might have students read only the title of the story "The Three Bears," then ask them the following question:

Where do you think this story probably takes place?

After students have read further, we might have them stop at the point where the bears go for a walk and have them make additional predictions:

What do you think might happen next in the story?

Once students read to the point where Goldilocks goes to sleep, we might have them make further predictions about the events of the story:

Do you think the bears will find Goldilocks?
What do you think they will notice first when they return home?

D. Factors Affecting Students' Ability to Predict Coming Events

Underlying the ability to predict is the ability to identify trends. If students are unable to identify sequences of events, they have nothing on which to base a prediction.

Second, students must be able to project into the future the events that will follow, if the trend continues. This skill is to a great extent based upon the students' experiential background. Even if students detect a sequence of events in a story, they cannot predict coming events if the sequence suggests no prediction to them. In order to make a prediction after identifying a trend, they must have experienced previously where the trend leads. For instance, students may read that an airplane is losing altitude and heading toward an airport. To predict that the plane will land, students would need to have experienced the entire landing sequence. Only then will the sequence they identify indicate to them that the plane is probably landing.

Predicting the Consequences of Intervention

The final comprehension skill we will discuss is predicting the consequences of intervention. Predicting the consequences of intervention differs from simple prediction in the sense that readers are continually processing new information and altering their previous predictions based on the new information. In predicting the consequences of intervention, students' ability to perceive and understand cause-effect relationships and their ability to change their predictions when a new causal agent intrudes upon a current trend, are essential. Questions that probe this particular skill might include "How might things have turned out if _____?" or "Suppose _____, what do you think would have resulted?" Predicting the consequences of intervention is a very important skill in reading comprehension and in living. The good reader is sensitive to the new information the author injects and anticipates the effects it might have on coming events in the text. In one's personal life and in school, understanding cause-effect relationships is essential to success. In order to succeed in school, the student must be aware that reading, studying, and listening are causal agents that contribute to academic achievement.

The problem for students is to predict the effect that an intervening force will have on a current trend of events. First, students observe the impact of the intervening force on the present trend of events. Then they project into the future how the intervening force will change the trend. Finally, they predict the effect of the intervening force. For example, suppose students are reading about an airplane approaching an airport for a landing. This is the current trend. Suddenly, they read, another plane pulls into the runway in the path of the plane that is landing, and the control tower operator tells the pilot to abort his landing. This is the intervening force. The students consider the impact of the intervention and project into the future how the current trend will change. A reasonable prediction would be that the pilot will attempt to abort the landing.

The following is an outline of the procedure for predicting the consequences of an intervention. The outline may serve as a guide for teaching this skill.

Task: To predict the effect of an intervening force, a causal agent
Given: 1. A current trend of events
        2. An intervening force

A. Procedures for Performing the Task

1. Note the force intervening on a current trend of events.
2. Project into the future how the intervening force may change the current trend.
3. Predict the effect of the intervening force.

B. Comprehension Skills Involving Predicting the Consequences of Intervention

The following are reading comprehension skills engaging the student in predicting the consequences of interventions:

1. Predicting cause-effect relationships
2. Anticipating the effect of the actions of characters in a story
3. Predicting how a change introduced by the author affects events in a story
4. Forecasting the effect of acts of nature in a story

Predicting cause-effect relationships. This is the most general reference to this skill. It can pertain to predicting the consequences of any kind of intervention.

Anticipating the effect of the action of characters in a story. This skill focuses the attention of the reader on the actions of story characters as causal agents.

Forecasting the effects of acts of nature in a story. This involves the reader in predicting the consequences of acts of nature.

Predicting how a change introduced by the author affects events in the story. This skill focuses attention on the author's manipulations as a causal agent.

In predicting the consequences of intervention readers may base their predictions on the behavior of a character. The actions of one character in a story affect future events in a story. The fact that the third pig built a brick house with big locks on the door had a profound effect on events in the story. The reader must also be sensitive to natural causal agents in order to predict their effect on a story. In addition, predictions may be based on more subtle manipulations introduced by an author. The author may change the mood of a story to foreshadow a change in the plot. Happy endings are often foreshadowed by a shift to a happy tone. The author can also shift the scene in a story. This, too, can foreshadow a change in the plot. Any new information introduced may cause a change in the message. To predict the consequences of the author's interventions the reader must constantly be alert to the new information being introduced and anticipate its effect on coming events in the story.

C. Sample Comprehension Tasks

Comprehension tasks engaging students in predicting the consequences of intervention involve the student in detecting cause-effect relationships. The student must first detect a causal agent and then predict its effect. However, when initially acquainting students with this skill the teacher needs to focus the students' attention on the causal agent.

The teacher might pause at the point in "The Three Bears" where Goldilocks enters the three bears' house uninvited and ask:

- What effect do you think Goldilock's entrance into the three bears' house will have on coming events in the story?

Then, when the three bears return home, the teacher might pause again and ask:

• What will happen to Goldilocks now?

To focus attention of the students on the author's manipulation of story events as a causal agent, the students might be asked:

• Why do you think the author had the three bears go for a walk?
• What do you think will happen as a result?

D. Factors Affecting the Students' Ability to Predict the Consequences of Intervention

The students' experiential background will limit their ability to predict the consequences of intervention. If students are not familiar with the effect a particular cause produces they cannot predict the effect when the causal agent emerges. Students must know that a fire causes destruction and displaces people in order to predict the effect a fire can have on the lives of people. They must know that hostility begets hostility in order to predict that the hostile actions of one character in a story will usually cause the recipient to retaliate in kind.

All the factors that affect the prediction of coming events also affect predicting the consequences of intervention. Predicting of any kind necessitates the projection into the future of an outcome based on an emerging trend.

In this chapter we have described six thinking skills and provided an outline of procedures for teaching each skill, as well as associated comprehension skills. The following table summarizes the six thinking procedures.

A SUMMARY OF THINKING PROCEDURES

Skill	Identifying concrete events	Categorizing	Deductive reasoning	Inductive reasoning	Predicting coming events	Predicting the consequences of intervention
Task for the Student	To remember	Distinguish examples from non-examples	Produce your own examples	Produce your own concept	Predict a future event from a current trend	Predicting the effect of an intervening force
Provided for the Student	Material to remember	1. Concepts 2. Example and nonexample of the concepts	concepts	examples and nonexamples	A current trend of events	1. A current trend of events 2. An intervening force
Example of Comprehension Skill	Recalling a specific fact	Classifying ideas	Identifying supportive information and details	Making generalizations	Forecasting story outcomes	Predicting cause-effect relationships

SUMMARY

1. We have listed thirty-six skills involved in reading comprehension commonly found in lists and discussions of reading comprehension.

2. Most of the reading comprehension skills can be exhibited using six thinking procedures. The thinking procedures are (a) identifying concrete events, (b) categorizing, (c) deductive reasoning, (d) inductive reasoning, (e) predicting coming events, and (f) predicting the consequences of intervention.

3. Underlying all comprehension skills is the ability to detect similarities and differences.

4. *Identifying concrete events.* The identification of concrete events involves remembering, recalling, and retelling information that is explicitly stated by the author. The procedure for identifying concrete events is (a) the spaced review of the information to be remembered and (b) categorizing the information to be remembered in one's present framework of knowledge. Reading comprehension skills that are exhibited using the thinking procedure for identifying concrete events are: (a) recalling a specific fact, detail, name, place, event, date, and so forth; (b) following directions; (c) recalling and retelling story events in order; and (d) paraphrasing what is read.

5. *Categorizing* involves distinguishing examples and nonexamples of a concept. The examples and nonexamples are provided for the student. The procedure for categorizing is (a) clarify the definition of the concept, (b) list the defining criteria for the concept, (c) match the items under consideration with the criteria to determine which meet the criteria and which do not. Reading comprehension skills that employ the thinking procedure for categorizing are: (a) classifying ideas; (b) distinguishing fact

and fantasy; (c) distinguishing real and unreal; (d) distinguishing fact and opinion; (e) distinguishing relevant and irrelevant information; (f) integrating new information with old; (g) evaluative reading; and (h) choosing correct and applicable meanings for multiple meaning words.

6. *Deductive reasoning* involves students in producing their own examples of a concept they are given. The procedure for deductive reasoning is (a) clarify the definition of the concept; (b) list the defining criteria of the concept; (c) search for items that match the criteria; and (d) describe the examples to show how they meet the criteria. Reading comprehension skills that are exhibited employing the thinking procedure for deductive reasoning are: (a) identifying supportive information and details; (b) inferring details; (c) analyzing conclusions; (d) giving examples; (e) making predictions; (f) applying information gained from reading to new situations; and (g) providing illustrations.

7. *Inductive reasoning* involves the student in producing a concept, given examples of the concept. The procedure for inductive reasoning is (a) search for common characteristics among items (the ideas and statements in a reading selection); (b) group items together based on their common characteristics; (c) list the common characteristics or the defining criteria of the concept; and (d) describe the defining criteria of the concept. Reading comprehension skills that are exhibited employing the thinking procedure for inductive reasoning are: (a) making generalizations; (b) identifying character traits; (c) interpreting the author's style, bias, attitude, tone, or mood; (d) getting the main idea; (e) making summaries; (f) interpreting figurative and idiomatic language; (g) identifying the author's purpose; and (h) identifying character motives.

8. *Predicting coming events* involves the student in predicting what will happen, based on a current trend. The procedure for predicting coming events is (a) note the current trend of events; (b) project the trend into the future; and (c) predict what will happen in the future. Reading comprehension skills exhibited by employing the thinking procedure for predicting coming events are: (a) anticipating what will happen next in a story; (b) making hypotheses; (c) forecasting and predicting story outcomes; (d) understanding the author's use of foreshadowing; and (e) making educated guesses.

9. *Predicting the consequences of intervention* engages the student in predicting the effect of intervening forces on a current

trend. The procedures for predicting the consequences of intervention are (a) note the force intervening on a current trend; (b) project into the future how the intervening force may change the current trend, and (c) predict the effect of the intervening force. Reading comprehension skills employed in predicting the consequences of intervention are: (a) predicting cause-effect relationships; (b) anticipating the effects of the actions of characters in a story; (c) predicting how a change introduced by the author affects events in a story; and (d) forecasting the effects of acts of nature in a story.

10. *Giving clear instructions to students.* In teaching reading comprehension skills it is important to give clear directions that specify (a) what the student is to produce; (b) the thinking procedures used to produce the product; and (c) the content to which the thinking procedure is to be applied. A number of terms used in describing reading comprehension skills are vague and ambiguous and create confusion for teacher and student. Such terms are critical reading, making inferences, drawing conclusions, making judgments, and forming opinions. To give clear instructions to students these terms must be supplemented to specify the three ingredients mentioned above.

REVIEW QUESTIONS

1. What thinking procedures are employed in identifying concrete events and what reading comprehension skills are exhibited using the thinking procedures for identifying concrete events?

2. What thinking procedures are employed in categorizing and what reading comprehension skills are exhibited using the thinking procedures for categorizing?

3. What thinking procedures are employed in deductive reasoning and what reading comprehension skills are exhibited using the thinking procedure for deductive reasoning?

4. What thinking procedures are employed in inductive reasoning and what reading comprehension skills are exhibited using the thinking procedure for inductive reasoning?

5. What thinking procedures are employed in predicting coming events and what reading comprehension skills are exhibited using the thinking procedure for predicting coming events?

6. What thinking procedures are employed in predicting the consequences of intervention and what reading comprehension skills are exhibited using the thinking procedures for predicting the consequences of intervention?

7. In teaching reading comprehension skills, what should be specified in the instruction to students?

8. Why are terms such as critical reading, making inferences, drawing conclusions, making judgments, and forming opinions too vague and ambiguous as descriptions of reading comprehension skills and tasks?

CHAPTER 7
Teaching Reading Comprehension Skills as Concepts

PURPOSE

1. To show you how to teach reading comprehension skills as concepts, utilizing a variety of instructional techniques found to facilitate concept acquisition.

BACKGROUND AND NEW INFORMATION

The information in previous chapters on the teaching of concepts provides a foundation for teaching concepts of any kind. In this chapter we extend your ability to teach concepts and apply the teaching of concepts particularly to the reading comprehension skills we acquainted you with in the last chapter.

This chapter describes a procedure for teaching concepts in general, and reading comprehension skills as concepts in particular. The chapter begins with a method of teaching students the word label for concepts. Second, we show you how to teach the definition of concepts. Third, we demonstrate how the various thinking procedures discussed in the last chapter can be applied to the teaching of concepts. Fourth, we describe how the students' task can be simplified to teach concepts. Fifth, we indicate how the teacher provides feedback to the student in order to teach concepts. At the end of the chapter we apply the prediction process to reading comprehension.

KEY TERMS

literary definition
operational definition

DESIRED LEARNING OUTCOMES

The student will be able to:

1. Teach the word labels for concepts.
2. Teach the definitions of concepts, both the literary and operational definitions of concepts.
3. Apply thinking procedures to the teaching of concepts.
4. Simplify the learner's task in teaching concepts.
5. Provide effective feedback in teaching concepts.
6. Apply the prediction process to reading comprehension.

In chapter 4 we prescribed ways of teaching concepts and indicated that most words in the dictionary are labels for concepts. In addition, we mentioned terms used in reading, such as "word identification skills," that are concepts representing categories of things. Phonic identification and structural abstraction are examples of the concept "word identification skills."

In a similar manner, the various reading comprehension skills we have described are, themselves, concepts. This factor often contributes to the difficulty in teaching certain reading comprehension skills since students must learn and understand the concept of a particular comprehension skill before they will have success in performing the comprehension skill. Students must learn and understand the concept of "main idea" before they will have much success in identifying a "main idea."

In chapter 4 we showed how vocabulary terms may be taught as concepts, and we discussed six approaches to teaching concepts. To refresh your memory they are teaching students to (1) remember the word label and defining criteria of a concept; (2) categorize examples of the concept; (3) deductively produce examples of the concept; (4) inductively produce the concept, given examples; (5) identify sequential attributes of the concept; and (6) identify cause-effect attributes of the concept. It remains for us to show you how the teaching of reading comprehension can be approached in this manner. In addition, we prescribe procedures for providing feedback to students to help them learn concepts.

TEACHING STUDENTS THE WORD LABEL FOR THE CONCEPT

The first step in teaching the concept is to teach students the word label for the concept. The thinking procedure involved is literal or concrete level comprehension. The desired outcome is for the students to remember and understand the word label for the concept.

Spaced review of the word label will help the student remember it, where the word label is presented, reviewed, and reinforced periodically. Remembering is enhanced, and understanding can be achieved sooner if the new concept can be categorized within the framework of the student's present knowledge. The concept becomes meaningful when it fits a category with which the student is already familiar. If we are trying to teach students the concept "main idea" and they already know the meaning of the concepts "main" and "idea," the new concept will have meaning for them, and they will have less difficulty in remembering the new concept.

However, their understanding of "getting the author's main idea" will need to be sharpened because "main idea" is being applied in a particular way to reading material. One way of helping students understand the comprehension skill you are teaching

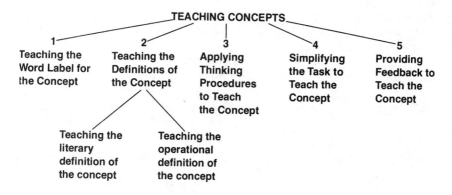

FIGURE 7–1 A hierarchy of topics in chapter 7

is to state it in various, simple terms. This optimizes students' chances of fitting the new concept into their own conceptual framework. Often the terminology the teacher uses is too abstract and sophisticated and prevents the student from understanding the concept; we must take care to insure that students understand the terminology of the skills we teach.

Clarifying the Word Label for the Concept

With particular reference to the higher-level reading comprehension skills, the terminology of the skills themselves is a major roadblock to teaching the skills. Terms like "main idea," "generalize," "conclusion," "paraphrase," "integrate," "distinguish," "apply," and so on, are not simple terms that are readily understood by students. Ofen we use the same terms in teaching these skills and in communicating to students what we want them to do. Further, we seldom stop to teach students what a "conclusion" or a "generalization" is, somehow expecting them to eventually learn these terms on their own. On the other hand, when we give time and provide instruction in the meaning of these abstract terms, we automatically engage in vocabulary instruction and begin to build a conceptual background for these terms.

For example, we may wish to teach the reading comprehension skills of "getting the author's main idea." Those students who do not understand the concept of "main idea" will have great difficulty in identifying "main ideas" and, therefore, in demonstrating this particular comprehension skill. However, there are other terms that we might use instead of "main idea" in communicating the comprehension skill we wish to teach. For example, we might call it "getting the most important idea." In many instances, "the most important idea" will also be "the main idea." In fact, the term "main" is often used to denote "most important." Students who do not possess knowledge of the concept of "main idea" may find "most important idea" easier to grasp and understand than "main idea." There are additional terms we might substitute for "main idea" like "high point," "moral of the story," and so on. Whatever terms we use to communicate the comprehension skills we wish to teach, we must insure that students understand the terms and possess the conceptual knowledge of those same skills.

Below is a list of the more abstract terms and phrases commonly used in reading comprehension skills statements and a parallel list of terms and phrases the teacher can substitute in questions and directions to students to help insure understanding of the concepts involved.

Abstract Terms and Phrases	Simplified Terms and Phrases
1. recall	remember; say from memory; tell
2. paraphrase	say in your own words; tell in your own words
3. correct/accurate	right; best
4. classify/categorize	group; place together; type; kind
5. distinguish/discriminate	separate; tell how they are different; tell what one has that the other doesn't
6. integrate/synthesize	tell how this fits in with that; tell how this relates to that
7. apply	tell how else is this useful; think of another way you can use this; why is it important to know this
8. information	facts; details; ideas; what you know; what the author tells you
9. infer/inference/conclude	what you think might be true; what you guess might be true; what you think is probably true
10. identify	point out; pick out; name; describe; define
11. supporting information/ supporting details	how you know this is to be true; what does the author say that tells you this is true; examples/reasons why this is true; illustrations
12. evaluate	compare this to that; tell if this is right/wrong, good/bad, ugly/pretty, fact/fiction
13. character traits/motives	things about the person in the story; what the man/boy/girl/woman looks like; what the person in the story thinks/feels/believes
14. style	way of writing; way of telling the story
15. bias	beliefs/believes; thinks; feels; attitude; loves/hates; views; viewpoint; reasons
16. purpose	reason for writing/reading; what the author was trying to do; why the author said this
17. tone/mood	feelings; sense(s); emotions; thoughts
18. summary/summarize	tell in a few words; briefly tell; tell in a sentence or two; shorten; make a brief statement that covers the subject

Abstract Terms and Phrases	Simplified Terms and Phrases
19. general/generalize/ generalization	state a rule/principle; give your overall impression
20. opinion	what you think; how you feel; what you believe; what the author thinks/feels and believes
21. main idea	most important idea; subject; high point of the story; what the author was really trying to tell us; emphasis; major point; focus; what the story is mainly about
22. predict/anticipate/ hypothesize	guess; educated guess; what will probably happen; what you think will happen next; what you will find later in the story
23. coming events/outcomes	how things will turn out; what will happen next; how the story will end

Besides learning how to ask comprehension questions that engage the student in the skills we wish to teach, it is important to learn how to "re-ask" questions or ask questions in different words. Often when we ask students a particular question, we get no response or an incorrect response simply because students did not understand the question—not necessarily because they were unable to answer the question. This is evidenced by long pauses after the teacher asks a question, completely inappropriate responses, and a general lack of student responses. It is important for the teacher to learn how to quickly rephrase poorly worded, awkwardly worded, and abstractly worded questions. Many of the simplified words and phrases in the above list can be used to this purpose.

DEFINING THE CONCEPT

Once the student remembers and understands the word label for the concept, it is necessary to clarify the definition of the concept. There are two ways of defining a concept: (1) providing a *literary definition* of the concept and (2) providing an *operational definition* of the concept. A literary definition, as we have said, provides the word label for the concept and the defining criteria of the concept. A literary definition is the type of definition that is found in the dictionary.

An operational definition specifies the operations or procedures one employs to produce a desired outcome. In chapter 6 we dealt with concepts such as "categorizing," "deductive reasoning," "inductive reasoning," "predicting coming events," and "predicting the consequences of intervention." To clarify the meaning of each of these thinking skills concepts we provided a set of procedures or operational definitions indicating how you proceed to categorize, reason deductively, reason inductively, and so on. Let us explain how literary and operational definitions may be provided for reading comprehension skills concepts.

Providing a Literary Definition of the Concept

In providing a literary definition of a concept for students, the task for the teacher is to compose a list of criteria that are accurate, necessary, and sufficient for distinguishing examples from nonexamples of the concept. If inaccurate, unnecessary, or insufficient criteria are given to the student, the student will not be able to distinguish examples from nonexamples as we will show later in the chapter when we discuss providing feedback for students.

The teacher may use the dictionary to help find appropriate criteria, but ultimately the teacher composes the list. This is because the dictionary provides definitions of single words, while most reading comprehension skills such as "getting the main idea" are communicated as statements. In composing a list of criteria defining the concept "getting the main idea," the teacher may find it useful to look up in the dictionary individual words contained in the comprehension skill statement. Considering the definitions of key words such as "main" and "idea" may assist the teacher in identifying defining criteria of the concept.

A good way for the teacher to identify criteria is to compare examples and nonexamples of the concept in reading selections. Then, the teacher inspects the examples of the concept for common characteristics. Each common characteristic is a criterion defining the concept and is placed on the list. For the concept "getting the main idea" the teacher identifies main ideas in reading selections and determines their common characteristics. Following this procedure the teacher might come up with a list of criteria like the following to define the concept "getting the main idea."

1. A general idea or theme of the story.
2. The most important general idea in the story.

3. Not a specific fact or detail.
4. Main idea statements can be used as the title of the story.
5. Main ideas encompass everything in the story rather than only parts of the selection.
6. Cues of the main idea often appear at the beginning of the message, for example, titles, headings, and topic sentences of paragraphs.

When the teacher believes he or she has enumerated criteria that will permit the student to distinguish examples from nonexamples of the concept, an adequate literary definition of the concept has been achieved. For some concepts it is difficult to derive adequate criteria, however. The literary meaning of some concepts is difficult to define. Further clarification of the meaning of concepts can be conveyed by means of operational definitions.

Providing an Operational Definition of the Concept

To develop an operational definition of a concept the teacher simply enumerates the steps in the procedure that are used to perform the task facing the student. As we indicated in chapter 6, summarizing and getting the main idea are inductive thinking skills. To summarize or to get the main idea of a story the student employs inductive thinking procedures. However, the operational definition or procedure for summarizing is slightly different than the procedure for getting the main idea.

Here is an operational definition or procedure for summarizing the author's message.

An Operational Definition of Summarizing

Step 1. Search for common ideas among the statements the author is making.
Step 2. Group statements together that convey common ideas.
Step 3. For each group of statements, briefly describe the common idea that is expressed.

As you can see, a summary consists of a brief description of each important idea the author is expressing. The operational definition or procedure for getting the main idea includes the same three steps as summarizing. One step must be added because in getting the main idea the student must decide which of the ideas the author conveys is the main or most important idea.

The operational definition for getting the main idea can be described as follows.

An Operational Definition for Getting the Main Idea

Step 1. Search for common ideas among the statements the author is making.
Step 2. Group statements together that convey common ideas.
Step 3. For each group of statements, briefly describe the common idea that is expressed.
Step 4. Decide which of these ideas is the most important idea the author is conveying.

The purpose of defining a concept is so that students will be able to distinguish examples from nonexamples of the concept. A literary definition of the concept provides criteria for distinguishing examples from nonexamples. An operational definition of the concept provides procedures for distinguishing examples from nonexamples. In giving students both a literary and an operational definition of a concept the teacher increases their understanding of the concept and maximizes their chances of distinguishing examples from nonexamples.

APPLYING THINKING PROCEDURES TO TEACH THE CONCEPT

The students' understanding of a concept can be sharpened if they are required to think about the concept in a variety of ways. To accomplish this the teacher engages the students in categorizing, deductive reasoning, inductive reasoning, chronological reasoning, and cause-effect reasoning.

Engaging the Student in Categorizing to Teach the Concept

Once the student understands the word label and definitions of a concept, the teacher involves the student in categorizing examples and nonexamples of the concept. However, if the student has difficulty understanding the defining criteria or critical attributes of a concept, it is not necessary to concentrate on the definition for an extended period of time. Students often understand the definition of a concept better after they are shown a number of examples and nonexamples of the concept and can see that the examples have the critical attributes of the concept and that the nonexamples do not.

In teaching students to distinguish examples and nonexamples of concept the teacher first provides examples of the concept and demonstrates to the student that the examples have the critical attributes of the concept. Then the teacher provides nonexamples of the concept and demonstrates that these do not have all of the critical attributes. If the teacher is teaching the concept "getting the main idea," he or she might show the student a title of a story that clearly expresses the main idea. Then the teacher shows the student that it meets the defining criteria. The title (1) expresses a general idea or theme of the story, (2) expresses the most important idea in the story, (3) encompasses everything in the story, and (4) is not a statement of a specific fact or detail. Next, the teacher might show the student a statement that describes a specific detail, perhaps a description of the clothes a character in the story is wearing. The teacher then explains to the student that the statement does not meet the criteria of a main idea statement.

After the students are shown examples and nonexamples of the concept as described above, they are ready to make their own discriminations with the teacher's guidance. The teacher in a discussion-questioning format might show the students a main idea statement and proceed as follows (see Singer, 1978).

Teacher: What is it about this statement that makes it the main idea of the story we just read?

Student: It covers everything the author said. The other statement only covers part of what the author said.

Teacher: That's correct. The main idea is more general. Is there anything else that tells us this is the main idea of the story?

Student: You could even use it for the title of the story.

Teacher: Yes, you could. Sometimes a story title is the main idea of the story, too. Is there anything else that helps us know this is the main idea?

Student: Well, there aren't any facts or details in the main idea statement.

Teacher: Yes, that's right. It's not a specific statement, but a more general statement, isn't it?

This gives the students practice in comparing statements to the defining criteria of the concept and encourages them to decide whether a particular statement meets the criteria of a main idea statement.

Engaging the Student in Deductive Reasoning to Teach the Concept

After the students are given examples and nonexamples of a concept by the teacher and are able to correctly distinguish examples from nonexamples, students are ready to be encouraged to reason deductively to produce their own examples of the concept. The teacher might ask a student to state the main idea of a story she has read. The student might think for a minute and refer to the book *Love Story*, indicating that the title of the book conveys the main idea of the story.

Following the student's reference to the title of the book, the teacher might wish the student to understand that titles are often examples of main ideas. The teacher might ask the student to give an example of a part of a book that often conveys the main idea of the book and guide the student until she indicates that the title often expresses the main idea.

Engaging the Student in Inductive Reasoning to Teach the Concept

When students are able to produce their own examples of a concept they should be encouraged to reason inductively to produce the concept on their own. Continuing with our example of the concept "main idea," the teacher should give students a passage to read and instruct them to state what the main idea of the passage is. To guide students toward this goal, the teacher reminds them that to determine the main idea they should follow the operational definition or procedure for getting the main idea. The teacher can review the operational definition.

We might also want to use the inductive approach to teach students the concept of "making a generalization" based on reading they have done. The first step for the teacher is to identify a "generalization" from the reading selection that he or she wishes students to make. Next, the teacher can present students with specific facts, details, and statements from the reading selection that support the "generalization" the teacher identified. In a discussion-question format, the teacher might use the following questioning strategy.

Teacher: What do all of these facts and statements have in common? How are they alike?
Student: They all come from the story we just read.
Teacher: That's right. Are they alike in other ways?
Student: Yes, they are all about the third little pig.
Teacher: They certainly are. And when we look at all these facts about the third pig, what do they all tell us about him?
Student: That he was pretty smart.
Teacher: Very good. Yes, he was smart, wasn't he? Is there another word we could use to describe the third pig? Do all of these things about him tell us anything else?
Student: He is also very wise.
Teacher: He certainly was. Very good.

In the above example, the teacher has involved the students in inducing the "generalization" (that is, the category and word label) that the third pig was wise by having them search for commonalities among the facts and events the teacher presented about the third pig from the story.

Engaging Students in Chronological Reasoning to Teach the Concept

By engaging students in chronological reasoning they gain a dynamic understanding of the concept and learn to see some of the functional attributes of the concept in the sequence of time. With respect to teaching the concept main idea the student should be informed that the main idea of a selection is often cued at the beginning of the message. Titles often cue the main ideas of books. Chapter headings cue the main ideas of chapters, and topic sentences most often appear at the beginning of a paragraph and cue the main idea of the paragraph. In teaching the concept "summarizing," the teacher would indicate that summaries appear at the end of the message for the purpose of reviewing the important ideas in the preceding passage.

Engaging Students in Cause-Effect Reasoning to Teach the Concept

Cause-effect reasoning is central to the understanding of concepts underlying many reading comprehension skills. To "identify character motives" students must understand that they are to find causes of the character's actions. The character's actions are the effect and the students' task is to identify the causal forces impelling the character to act in a certain way, as well as the effects of the character's actions.

To "interpret the author's purpose" the student also must engage in cause-effect reasoning. The student must figure out the cause of the author's writing the book. Sometimes the main idea indicates the effect the author was trying to create, and identifying the effect often cues the cause. For instance, if the main idea is a moral lesson the author expresses, then one infers that the author's purpose or the cause of the author's writing the book was to impart the moral.

SIMPLIFYING THE TASK TO TEACH THE CONCEPT

We have made the point in preceding chapters that the length and complexity of a particular reading selection can interfere with comprehension. For example, it would be a much simpler task to "get the main idea" of an article from a newspaper than from a novel like *David Copperfield* because the newspaper article is much shorter and less difficult to read. By the same token, it is a simpler task to "get the main idea" from a paragraph written at the third grade level as opposed to one written at the eighth grade level.

These factors become increasingly important as the reading comprehension skills we teach require increased thinking on the part of the student. For example, while the student may well be able to read *David Copperfield* and subsequently understand it at the literal or concrete level, the length and complexity of the book may make it impossible for the student to perform more difficult comprehension skills—particularly when the student does not have conceptual knowledge of the comprehension skills. Therefore, when we teach comprehension skills (like "getting the main idea") that the student is unfamiliar with, we should teach them using simpler reading materials (and in some instances using nonverbal materials like pictures). Once we have taught the concept of a particular reading comprehension skill, then we can teach the student to perform and apply the skill at increasingly higher levels of sophistication.

For example, we may wish to teach the comprehension skill of "getting the main idea." First, we should teach the concept of main idea using simple materials and examples. We might begin with a complex and lengthy sentence, having the student identify the main idea of the sentence:

> *The little boy* who lives down the street climbed a tree, then fell and *broke his leg.*

As you can see from the portion of the sentence that is in italics, the "main idea" or "most important idea," is that the little boy broke his leg. Once we have taught the concept of "main idea" at a simpler level such as this, we can extend the student's understanding of the concept of "main idea" by providing additional instruction using more difficult and sophisticated reading material. Next, we might graduate to teaching "main idea" using paragraphs and have the student identify the topic sentence, which is nearly always the "main idea" of the paragraph:

> There he stood dressed in the costume it had taken him days to make. *Tom was determined to win the prize for the best costume at the school's Halloween party.* He had on the tail he had found in Mr. Johnson's attic. And he even pasted fur on his hands to make himself more convincing.

Ultimately, we will teach students to apply their knowledge of "main idea" to one-and two-page stories, lengthier stories, and eventually to novels ("main idea" is normally referred to as "theme" when applied to pieces of literature and longer reading selections). Ideally, the concepts that underlie each of the reading comprehension skills should be taught using very simple materials and examples, then extended and refined using increasingly more difficult materials and examples. In this way, we greatly increase the likelihood that students will master the particular comprehension skills we teach by initially teaching them at a level they can successfully deal with. This is the essence of individualizing instruction in reading comprehension.

PROVIDING FEEDBACK

While we have spoken a great deal about the nature of comprehension skills and ways to teach them, a very important consideration in comprehension instruction is the nature of the student's response, for example, to a comprehension question we might ask. When we engage students in questioning as in the examples we presented earlier, we are constantly eliciting responses from them. The responses that students make to our questions are, in essence, predictions, and students constantly seek confirmation of their predictions. Therefore, the feedback we give students ("Yes, Johnny, that is correct;" "No, Mary, that's not quite right") helps students to confirm their predictions by telling them when they are correct or incorrect, and if they are incorrect by cueing the correct response.

The feedback we give students in this manner can also be viewed as *reinforcement* for their responses. As we have said, the confirmation of predictions is rewarding to the individual on its own. However, when the teacher provides students feedback, the feedback itself becomes a method of reinforcement. This is particularly important when we consider the nature of the comprehension and thinking skills we wish to teach and the range of student responses we can anticipate to the complex questions we will necessarily ask in teaching these skills. On the one hand, we run the risk of "turning students off" by giving them negative feedback to their responses in an instructional situation. For example, if we ask a student for a fact or detail that supports the generalization that the third little pig in the story "The Three Little Pigs" was wise, he might respond that "the third pig was a good house builder." While this may in fact be true, it is not a correct response to the question. One can be a good house builder without being wise. By saying to the student, "No, you're wrong" or "That's not something that makes him wise," we are not helping him master the particular comprehension skill we wish to teach and may ultimately cause the student to withdraw from the learning situation. On the other hand, if we say to the student, "Very good . . . are there any other things in the story that tell us that the third pig was wise?" we are, in essence, telling the student his response was correct when it was really incorrect. In this instance, we may not run the risk of "turning the student off," but we do run the risk of failing to teach him the comprehension skills by not providing him accurate feedback.

The Nature of Student Responses to Comprehension Questions

As we have pointed out, comprehension skills are similar in nature to teaching concepts because a skill like "getting the main idea" involves the understanding of the concept of "main idea." In concept learning, there are three kinds of categorizing errors students generally make: (1) categorizing on the basis of erroneous criteria, (2) incorrectly categorizing by overgeneralizing, and (3) incorrectly categorizing by overdiscriminating. By paying attention to the kinds of errors and inaccurate responses students make, we can alter our questioning and teaching strategies to help insure that students understand their errors and ultimately correct them in mastering the comprehension and thinking skills we wish to teach.[1]

Erroneous Criteria

In making categorizations regarding the concepts and comprehension skills we teach, students often utilize erroneous criteria for inclusion into a particular category. In the example above, the student thought "good house builder" was a criterion for inclusion into the category "wise." This is an example of using erroneous criteria in making a categorization. We can alter our questioning strategy in this example so that we do not cause the student to withdraw from the learning situation, and so that he will discover his own error and correct it. We can provide the student feedback regarding his response and follow up with additional questioning strategies:

- Yes, the third pig was an excellent house builder, wasn't he? But is that something that makes him wise? What are some of the things that the third pig did that tell us he was wise?

1. Smith (1978) has found that, generally, there is a direct correlation between the clause length and sentence length of the student's response and the cognitive quality of the response.

Notice in the questioning strategy above that we have not bla-
tantly communicated to the student that he was wrong. In fact, we
began by telling him that his response was accurate with respect
to story details, then we communicated to him that his response
did not correctly answer the question. Next, we re-asked the question in different words and simplified it somewhat by asking for
"things the third pig did that tell us he was wise" instead of "facts
and details from the story that tell us the third pig was wise."

Overgeneralization

Often, students make errors in learning particular concepts and
comprehension skills by using insufficient criteria. For example,
let us assume that the students we are teaching have already read
"The Three Little Pigs" and have learned that one reason (criterion for inclusion into a category) that the third pig was wise was because he planned ahead, and that this is often a criterion for being
considered "wise." Next, let's assume that the students read "The
Three Bears." After reading "The Three Bears" we might ask the
students to make a generalization about the bears. One student
may respond that the bears were "wise." When we ask the student
for reasons why the three bears were wise, she might observe that
the bears went for a walk in the forest in order to let their porridge
cool, and that this is an example of "planning ahead," which is
one criterion for inclusion into the category "wise." While in this
example the bears certainly were planning ahead, this is not evidence of their being wise. In this example, we can alter our
questioning strategies in the following manner.

- Yes, that is a good example of planning ahead. But is this the
  same kind of planning that the third pig used? What is different about how the pig planned ahead and how the bears
  planned ahead? Were the bears wise in the same way the
  third pig was wise? Is there another way you can describe the
  bears?

In the questioning strategy above, we have again avoided telling the student outright that she was incorrect and began by
indicating that her response was correct to some degree. Next, we
asked the student questions designed to sharpen her understanding of the term "planning ahead" and that will help her to understand that when we plan ahead, it does not always mean we are

"wise." Finally, we re-asked the question in different words and simplified it by asking for a "description" of the bears instead of a "generalization" about the bears.

Overdiscrimination

Finally, students make errors in categorizing when unnecessary criteria for inclusion into a category are used. For example, the student may have previously learned several criteria for inclusion into the category "wise," including the criterion of "not acting too quickly." Thus, someone who is wise, among other things, ponders and thinks through a particular problem before taking action. When we ask students for examples showing whether or not the third pig was "wise," they may respond that the third pig was not wise because he acted very quickly in building a house of bricks. Obviously, if the third pig had not acted quickly, the wolf would have gotten him. We can alter our question strategies in the following way:

- Yes, acting too quickly can *sometimes* be unwise. What might have happened to the third pig if he had not acted quickly in building his brick house? Yes, he might have been eaten. So you see, we may act quickly and still be wise. How quickly we act is not a reason for being wise. What did the third pig do that tells us he was wise?

Note again, that we have started by indicating to the students that their response, to some degree, was correct. Next, we have designed and asked questions to sharpen the students' understanding of the criteria for inclusion into the category "wise," showing that "not acting too quickly" is an unnecessary criterion. Finally, we re-asked the question in different words by substituting "what did the third pig do that tells us he was wise" for "examples showing whether or not the third pig was wise" to get the student on the right track.

Using Specific Questioning Strategies for Reinforcement and Feedback

In the preceding discussion of types of student errors, we have demonstrated a very useful questioning strategy for teaching concepts and comprehension skills. This questioning strategy can be summarized as follows:

1. Indicate the general accuracy of the student's response when possible. Above all, avoid telling the students they are wrong. Preface additional questions with phrases like: "Yes, but . . .," "that's very close . . .," "you're on the right track . . ."
2. Intervene with additional questions that will politely communicate to students that their response was inaccurate, and that will guide them in identifying and then correcting their error.
3. Re-ask the original question using different words and terms, simplifying and clarifying the original question when necessary.

When we look at the feedback we give students regarding the responses they make to our questions as reinforcement, it becomes apparent that our feedback is a powerful tool in teaching concepts and comprehension skills and in shaping student behavior. For this reason, it is important that the teacher adopt ways of responding to students that clearly communicate to the student the quality of the response the student has made. This applies not only to the oral responses students make in class, but to performance in a variety of situations and learning tasks.

Often we, as teachers, use a variety of terms that communicate to students the quality of their performance in a learning situation or with respect to a particular task. We use terms like "good," "very good," "excellent," "all right," and so on as judgments about the students' performance. If we take care to use these terms systematically, then the feedback we provide to students becomes much more instructive, and students have a much clearer idea of how they are performing in terms of particular skills and learning tasks.

For example, if we ask a student to give us one example of how the third pig was wise, he may respond "because he built a house of bricks." We might respond to the student with a term like "good," then ask how this shows that the third pig was wise. The student may then respond "because the wolf could not blow a brick house down." We might respond "very good" to this particular answer. Finally, we might ask the student how building a brick house shows that the third pig was wise, whereupon the student responds "because it shows that the third pig planned ahead." To this answer, we might respond "excellent." The point here is that, qualitatively, these various student answers are different from one another; some of these answers are better than others, although all the answers are correct. By using our verbal reinforcements systematically ("good," "very good," "excellent"), we can communicate to students the relative quality of their answers and differentially reinforce students according to the quality of their responses. This becomes a highly useful instructional technique for individualizing instruction.

READING COMPREHENSION AND THE PREDICTION PROCESS

We have reviewed the prediction process from many different perspectives. Now we will inspect its relevance to reading comprehension. In essence both indentification and prediction require that students extract meaning from or comprehend the selection they are reading.

1. Identifying Initiating Events

Again, the words on the page are the initiating events. They initiate thought on the part of the reader. However, the reader can comprehend the words in many different ways depending on the instructions given by the teacher. If the teacher asks the students to remember or recall what they are reading, then they are being required to comprehend the material on the concrete or literal level.

On the other hand, the teacher may require students to comprehend the selections beyond the literal or concrete level. The teacher might ask students to evaluate the reading selection to determine whether it is fact of fiction, in which case the readers become involved in categorizing. Or the teacher might ask the students to determine the main idea of the writing. In this case, the students engage in inductive reasoning. The teacher may also tell the students that the main idea of a story is that energy must be conserved and ask the students to apply this concept to their own experience. In this event students must reason deductively.

2. Predicting Coming Events

There are two applications to reading comprehension that are relevant to this aspect of the prediction process. First, any responses the students give to the teacher's questions, whether on a test or otherwise, should be regarded as predictions, in the sense that the students are predicting that their answers will be viewed as correct by the teacher. So when students identify initiating events under the instructions of the teacher, such as recalling information in the reading materials, evaluating, drawing a conclusion inductively, or drawing a conclusion deductively, they are predicting that their responses are correct. However, they must wait for feedback from the teacher to find out whether they understand.

Second, the teacher may give the students introductory sections of a story and ask them to predict what will happen next in the story. In this case, too, the students expect to test their predictions against feedback from the teacher or to be allowed to read the remainder of the story to see for themselves whether or not their predictions are correct.

3. Predicting the Consequences of Intervention

This part of the predictive process applies to reading comprehension because authors continually introduce new information that changes events and outcomes. In reading a text students must be aware that the author controls the text, be sensitive to the new information introduced, and change their predictions regarding the coming message accordingly. Predicting cause-effect relationships is a sophisticated and important comprehension skill.

4. Identifying to Test Predictions

As we said, the students' comprehension of reading material is manifested by the responses and answers they give about the reading selection. These responses should be regarded as their predictions concerning the meaning of the message. The teacher must make certain that he or she confirms the students' predictions when students accurately comprehend what the author is saying. The teacher must also indicate to students their misunderstandings. However, when the students misunderstand the author's message, the teacher must correct their misunderstandings. The teacher provides practice and feedback until the students comprehend what the teacher intends for them to comprehend.

SUMMARY

1. To teach reading comprehension skills as concepts the teacher must (a) teach the word label for the reading comprehension skill, (b) teach the definitions of the reading comprehension skill, (c) apply thinking procedures to teach the reading comprehension skill, (d) simplify the student's task in teaching the reading comprehension skill, and (e) provide effective feedback to the student.

2. To teach the word label for a reading comprehension skill the teacher (a) provides for spaced review and rehearsal of the word label, (b) clarifies the word label for the concept by offering simple synonyms for the more difficult terms in the word label, and (c) helps the student categorize the new word label within the framework of the student's present knowledge, making the word label meaningful to the student.

3. To define a reading comprehension skill, the teacher first provides a literary definition of the comprehension skill and then an operational definition of the skill. In order to provide a literary definition the teacher specifies criteria that enable the student to distinguish examples from nonexamples of the comprehension skill/concept. To offer an operational definition of the reading comprehension skill, the teacher stipulates the procedures for exhibiting the comprehension skill (that is, the tasks students must perform to exhibit the skill).

4. To teach a reading comprehension skill as a concept, the teacher must engage the students in applying thinking procedures. Students should be engaged in (a) *categorizing* examples and nonexamples of the reading comprehension skill given examples and nonexamples by the teacher; (b) producing their own examples of the reading comprehension skill through *deductive*

reasoning; (c) producing the concept through *inductive reasoning*, given examples of the concept; (d) *chronological reasoning* to identify functional attributes of the concept in the sequence of time; and (e) using *cause-effect reasoning* to further identify the functional attributes of the concept.

5. To simplify the student's task in teaching a reading comprehension skill, the teacher presents students with reading selections at a lower reading level. When the students adequately perform the reading comprehension skill with low-difficulty reading material, the teacher introduces more difficult reading material. In addition, the teacher initially presents students with short reading selections. When students exhibit the reading comprehension skill with shorter reading passages, the teacher increases the length of the reading selections.

6. To provide effective feedback in the teaching of reading comprehension skills, the teacher must diagnose accurately the types of errors the students make. The teacher must recognize when students (a) use erroneous criteria for a concept, (b) overgeneralize because they use insufficient criteria, and (c) overdiscriminate because they use unnecessary criteria. Appropriate questioning, reinforcement, and feedback strategies should be used to probe the student's understanding of a concept and to correct their misunderstandings. The teacher should (a) indicate the degree of accuracy of students' responses, (b) intervene with additional questions to steer students to the correct response when their responses are inaccurate, (c) re-ask questions using different words and terms to clarify the intent of the questions, and (d) encourage students to pursue the correct response.

7. Reading comprehension applies to the prediction process in that both indentification and prediction require students to extract meaning from or to comprehend the selection they are reading.

REVIEW QUESTIONS

1. What procedures should the teacher employ to teach reading comprehension skills as concepts?

2. How should the teacher teach the word label for a reading comprehension skill?

3. How may the various thinking procedures be applied in the teaching of reading comprehension skills?

4. How should the teacher simplify the students' task in teaching reading comprehension skills?

5. How should the teacher provide feedback to students in teaching reading comprehension skills?

6. How does the prediction process apply to reading comprehension?

CHAPTER 8
Facilitating Comprehension: Study Skills

PURPOSE

1. To discuss the various study skills used in reading and learning.
2. To suggest ways to use and teach these skills.
3. To show how study skills fit into the larger context of identification and prediction skills.

BACKGROUND AND NEW INFORMATION

Many of the study skills we discuss in this chapter will be somewhat familiar to you. This familiarity prepares you to delve more deeply and comprehensively into the broad range of study skills presented in the chapter. In addition, information about establishing purposes for reading and the effective organization discussed in previous chapters provides a foundation for learning the material in this chapter.

We begin this chapter by probing more extensively into how the teacher establishes purpose for reading. Second, we discuss skills involved in obtaining and organizing information. Obtaining information requires the use of reference sources, while organizing information concerns the development of notetaking and outlining skills. Third, we deal with reading flexibility more comprehensively, and fourth, with formal study methods. Our fifth concern is with the special problems of reading nonverbal material. Sixth, we consider other study techniques, specifically testtaking skills and study habits. The chapter closes with an application of study skills to the prediction process.

KEY TERMS

skimming
paperback scanning technique
study reading
flexible reading

DESIRED LEARNING OUTCOMES

The student will be able to:

1. Describe methods for establishing purpose for reading.
2. Describe skills involved in locating information.
3. Describe skills involved in organizing information, including a description of notetaking skills and outlining skills.
4. Describe the skills involved in flexible reading.
5. Describe the stages of the SQR4 study method (as an example of a formal study method).
6. Describe skills involved in test taking and in reading nonverbal material.
7. Describe effective study habits.
8. Describe how the prediction process can be applied to studying.

ESTABLISHING PURPOSE FOR READING

When reading proceeds without purpose, comprehension is greatly retarded. A student who reads without first understanding his purpose for reading or establishing for himself a purpose for reading will not know what particular reading programs and strategies to employ. A student who is not clear, for example, about why she is reading a chemistry textbook may well employ a reading program similar to one she might use in reading a newspaper. If this happens, her reading of the chemistry textbook will not be effective if her ultimate purpose is to pass an examination based on the text. It is important, therefore, to help students establish purpose for reading so that efficient reading can take place when the student reads independently.

Preteaching or preinstructional activities are an excellent way to establish purposes for reading. Any questioning or discussion that precedes reading will tend to guide and direct students' reading once they begin the task. Other methods such as previewing

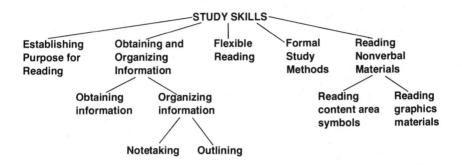

FIGURE 8-1   A hierarchy of topics in chapter 8

or surveying the reading material teach students to establish their own purposes for reading.

In preinstructional activities and in establishing purposes for reading, we should seek to clarify in students' minds the different kinds of reading materials and what purposes they normally serve. For example, consider the information we usually find in biographies, magazines, textbooks, brochures, encyclopedias, atlases, essays, pamphlets, novels, posters, legends, poetry, dictionaries, fables and myths, graphs, and so forth. Simply by being able to identify the reading material, the student will make a great deal of progress in establishing the purpose(s) for reading.

There are many questions that teachers can ask of students before they begin their reading that will help to establish purposes for reading and engage students in the prediction process. On the basis of a story or chapter title, the teacher might ask:

1. Can you predict from the title what this story is about?
2. Can you think of some words that might be in this story?
3. Can you think of another title that might be just as good?
4. Does the title tell you what might happen in the story?
5. What does the title remind you of? Another story you've read?

Whether students are reading fictional narrative material or content-based expository material, knowledge and discussion of the author can be used to establish purpose and direction for reading. Regarding the author, the teacher could ask the following questions of students:

1. Are you familiar with the author of this story? Have you ever read anything he has written before?
2. Do you think this author knows a lot about the subject?
3. What are some other things this author might have written about?
4. Did you like the other things you've read by this author?

Establishing the relatedness of new material to material that has already been read and to the experiences of the student is an important method of clarifying purposes for reading. In this instance, a teacher might ask:

1. What do you already know about this story (this subject)?
2. Have you ever been in a situation like the one described in the title?
3. How does this fit in with what we studied last week?
4. As you read the story, pretend you are the main character; would you have done things differently?

These sample questions are generalized to fit a variety of circumstances and can easily be adapted to the material being read and the level of the student you are teaching. See chapters 2 and 9 for additional discussion of setting purposes for reading.

OBTAINING AND ORGANIZING INFORMATION

Since all learning involves the processing of information, a most important study skill for students to learn is how to obtain the information they need and then how to organize information to facilitate comprehension.

Obtaining Information

In general, locating information requires the student to understand how information is organized. In fact, organizational systems like the Dewey Decimal System are nothing more than content hierarchies applied to virtually all human knowledge. Other organizational systems are utilized to retrieve information, such as alphabetical and numerical order. Students must understand and be able to use these organizational systems as they apply to everything from dictionaries to whole libraries.

Students must have knowledge of and the ability to use alphabetical, numerical, chronological, and other systems utilized in storing information. These organizational systems are usually applied to books, especially textbooks in content areas, and can be most easily taught using the student's textbook as the instructional vehicle.

First, students should have a working knowledge of book parts and publication information. Students should be able to effectively use the table of contents, the index, the appendix, the glossary, and publication information. They should understand what kind of information is included in each of these study aids, how to use each of these study aids, and they should be able to make accurate predictions regarding which of these study aids would most probably contain specifically needed information. Good teachers often spend several days at the start of the semester in getting their students acquainted with their textbook and in giving them practice in using study aids like the indices and glossary. The number and kinds of activities that can be used with students in this regard are virtually limitless.

Second, a complete understanding of how a textbook is organized requires that a student be able to use various study aids that authors build into textbooks. That is, students should be able to effectively use previews, summaries, headings, subheadings, and so on as study aids. The use of internal study aids such as these gives the student a powerful tool for conceptualizing the organizational format the author is using, which will in turn guide the student's reading by adding purpose and direction.

Finally, locating information requires the student to understand and use a variety of reference sources. We have already spoken about the organizational systems used in a library setting. Each reference source has a particular organizational format the student must understand in order to effectively use that reference source. Again, the student must understand what kinds of information different reference sources yield. A host of reference sources could be mentioned here; however, an examination of various study skills check lists reveals that the most often mentioned reference sources include the dictionary, encyclopedia, card catalogue, and *Reader's Guide to Periodical Literature*. Obviously, depending on the subject matter area, additional sources could be included. The reference sources mentioned above are those reference sources that should be dealt with first in a comprehensive study skills program. To generate interest in the use of reference sources, the *Guinness Book of World Records* has been used by many teachers to teach the basics of reference sources. Additionally, certain teachers need to teach the use of reference sources in highly specialized areas. For example, the autoshop teacher should be concerned with teaching students to use parts manuals and catalogues.

Specific instructional activities that can be used to teach the student locational skills and enhance the student's ability to locate information might include:

1. Locating specific information with a textbook index and/or glossary.
2. Locating chapters and major textual units that deal with particular topics or themes.
3. Locating specific information using the textbook table of contents.
4. Locating specific publication information and information about the author of a textbook.
5. Locating study aids such as introductions, summaries, discussion questions, and so forth in textbooks.
6. Identifying examples of the kinds of information contained in frequently used reference materials such as dictionaries, encyclopedias, card catalogues, and so on.
7. Predicting where specific kinds of information might be located and what types of reference sources are most likely to yield specific kinds of information.
8. Locating information contained in textbooks and reference sources given a limited amount of time.

In summary, the ability to locate information is extremely important to effective study. The ability to locate information requires the student to understand how information is organized, not only in textbooks, but in whole libraries; that is, both programmatic and hierarchical thought are required. It also requires the student to understand and be able to use reference sources of various kinds. Finally, the ability to locate information quickly is important. Again, there are numerous group and individual activities that can be designed around this very important ability.

Organizing Information

Within the context of skills associated with locating information, we indicated that it is important for the student to perceive and understand the ways in which information is organized. Many types of organizational systems are used in storing information from simple alphabetical and numerical organizations to organizational systems that resemble content hierarchies. However, when students are required to organize information, they must produce the organizational system themselves. That is, the students must create or re-create content hierarchies.

You will recall that in our examples of content hierarchies, categories of the hierarchy were arranged according to levels of abstraction. First, the label for the content hierarchy was presented, followed by categories that comprised the hierarchy and ending with examples of events in the various categories. One you may recall had to do with the content hierarchy "animals" and was portrayed in the following way:

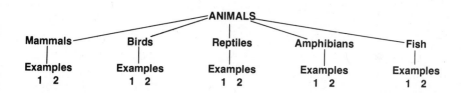

By arranging the content to be taught in this way, we can show the relationships among the categories in terms of levels of abstraction (birds comprise a subset of the entire content called animals), and we can show the similarities and differences among categories at the same level of abstraction by teaching the criteria for inclusion in a particular category (mammals are warm-blooded and they have hair). As we continue to analyze the content hierarchy, we discover that categories of the hierarchy can be related in other ways, such as sequentially or in terms of cause-effect. In general, we have imposed an organizational arrangement upon the content so that we might discover what reading-thinking skills are required in order to master the content and how best to teach the content.

In terms of higher-order study skills, students are required to impose organization in a similar way upon the content they study.

Up to this point, we have emphasized this procedure as a means for analyzing content in order to teach it. In the upper grade levels, it becomes important that we teach students not only to recognize the ways in which content is organized, but to impose their own organization on the content they study. These skills become increasingly important in the upper grade levels and are required when the student takes notes, studies a particular topic from a variety of sources, writes research papers and themes, and so on.

Notetaking as an organizational skill

Notetaking begins with good listening abilities. Although a student must take notes from oral presentations as well as from reading materials, most techniques for improving notetaking ability are applicable to taking notes in either fashion.

In taking notes students must continually evaluate information. That is, they must judge whether or not it is relevant, the degree of relevance, where it fits in with other information they have collected (classification and categorization), its general relation to other information they have gained, and so forth. Many of the higher-order thinking skills are involved, to some extent, in organizing information. Students' ability to recognize and understand relationships among events, people, ideas, and so on, is extremely important to their ability to organize information. As the level of the task increases, so too does the importance of these skills. In writing a research paper, these organizational skills are absolutely prerequisite.

Good notetaking, then, depends heavily upon the students' ability to summarize information, to sort out relevant from irrelevant information, and to translate information into their own language—all skills involving organizing information. Listening activities in the classroom followed by comprehension checks are an excellent means for developing these skills. Additionally, the following suggestions to students are helpful techniques for improving notetaking ability.

1. Sit in a position of physical alertness; do not slouch or get too comfortable as this will tend to lessen concentration. In general, be mentally alert and physically alert.
2. Be alert to the emphasis lecturers place on the ideas and concepts they talk about. If lecturers give clues about the content such as "This is important" or "You'll see this

later," make a note of these clues in class notes. Try not to allow the speaker's mannerisms and method of delivery to interfere with what you get from the lecture.

3. Jot down questions you have about the content in your notes. Try to resolve these questions in the lecture or in your study of the material later on.

4. Use abbreviations and your own "code" for taking notes to give you more time to listen actively.

5. Do not draw pictures or engage in other kinds of manual behaviors during notetaking that might interfere with concentration.

6. Circle or emphasize in some other way the assignments the lecturer might mix in with the lecture.

7. If you feel you have missed something during the lecture, leave a blank space and fill it in later.

8. Always record the examples the lecturer provides in class; these will help to clarify the content later.

9. Copy everything lecturers write on the board; assume that they are not writing information on the board simply because they like to write.

10. Don't depend heavily on getting the notes from someone else in class.

11. Review your notes soon after the lecture and then again at intervals that make sense, every two days or once a week; spaced practice like this will improve your retention a great deal.

Most of these techniques can be applied to taking notes from a textbook. In taking notes from a text, it is wise to develop a personal symbol system so that at one glance you can tell if what you have outlined or made a note of is very important or of only passing importance. In underlining, it is best to underline key words and phrases, not whole sentences and paragraphs.

Outlining as an organizational skill

Another study skill that requires skill in organizing information is outlining. Outlining requires the student, in essence, to perceive, produce, and sequence a content hierarchy. In constructing an outline, the student must identify major topical divisions that exist in the information being dealt with. Further, the student must be able to identify and categorize correctly additional divisions related to the major topics he or she has identified. The student, then, must be able to classify and categorize information and ideas according to their relatedness and understand the relationships that exist among the ideas and hierarchies contained in the information. The student is also required to evaluate information in this fashion in order to determine its applicability to the purposes for which the outlining is being done. The student must also judge the information outlined in terms of the degree to which it is relevant and useful to the purpose(s); this is reflected in the hierarchical organization of the information. Finally, the student must be capable of both deductive and inductive thinking in order to specify major (more general) topic divisions and minor (more specific) topical divisions.

Often students are required to outline information for purposes of study or for purposes of writing research papers. Too often, teachers are more caught up in insuring that students master the niceties of outlining skills, such as using Roman numerals for major topic divisions, capital letters for subtopic divisions, and Arabic numerals and lower case letters for still finer and more specific topical divisions. We often lose sight of the real value of teaching outlining skills—that is, as a tool for organizing information in a logical fashion and for teaching the many thinking skills we have described.

It is important for the student to realize that information tends to be organized hierarchically because it facilitates understanding. As we indicated in chapter 4, information is more readily recalled and understood when it is organized into content hierarchies which show the relationships between topics and subtopics of a body of content. This is why much of the material the student needs to locate is organized in this fashion and why the student, when taking notes, should organize the information being recorded in this manner.

It is also important for the student to understand that procedures for retrieving information most often are specified and executed programmatically. This is because the programmatic sequencing of activities involved in retrieval facilitates retrieval. Retrieval programs often are alphabetical sequences which are used to locate information in such references as the dictionary, the telephone directory, and the encyclopedia. For the purposes of locating historical information, the retrieval program often is chronological. At other times the retrieval program is arranged numerically. The chapters of books are arranged numerically, and to retrieve the information in a book, the reader is expected to read the chapters in numerical order.

Students should learn that to locate information they must follow a programmatic sequence. After retrieving the information they need they should study it as a content hierarchy so that they may see the relationship between the pieces of information and the total body of content. This will help them understand the information.

Further, students should be taught that when they record information, they should sequence it for purposes of retrieval and organize it in a content hierarchy for purposes of review and comprehension. This is precisely what they do when they outline information. The outline shows the hierarchical relationship between topics and subtopics. Specific pieces of information are retrieved by following the numerical sequence in the outline. The information under Roman numeral I is studied before the information under Roman numeral II.

When reading material such as the chapters of a book and notes are sequenced, there is the implication that reading and studying the material in the prescribed order will facilitate comprehension. The strategy for studying content is to obtain an overview of the content by inspecting the subject matter in a content hierarchy, then proceed to concentrate on specific pieces of information as they are sequenced.

FLEXIBLE READING

The Concept of Flexible Reading

Once students become proficient in the use of reference materials, know where to look for information to fulfill a specific need, and can use book parts and such as study aids, their ability to read flexibly plays a major role in the development of effective study strategies. The term "reading flexibly" is variously defined, but generally has to do with the adjustment of reading rate to purpose for reading and difficulty level of reading materials. Berg (1966:45) defines reading flexibility this way:

> In general, the term refers to the activity a reader is engaged in when he sets up various patterns of thinking relative to his reading needs and then selects the skills that best accomplish this purpose. The term also implies that the reader can carry out the reading activity selected with an optimum of comprehension for the time expended.

Many people are enamored with the concept of speed reading. Privately operated enterprises have attempted to capitalize on this fact by offering speed reading courses that are supposed to increase reading rates astronomically—from 2000 to 20,000 words per minute. Spache and others have determined that it is physically impossible to read more than about 800 words per minute; after that point, reading becomes a matter of selective perception in which the reader skips over words and phrases. This procedure is often referred to as skimming or scanning. In essence, the reader who internalizes the words of Francis Bacon—"Some books are to be tasted, others to be swallowed, and some few to be chewed and digested"—understands the concept of reading flexibility.

To be good readers, we must learn to read at different rates or speeds. The rate of our reading will be determined by our purpose for reading, our background of related information and experiences, and the material that is being read. We would not read the morning newspaper, for example, at the same rate we might read a chemistry text. This is true for a number of reasons. First, we know we will not be tested on the newspaper, whereas we will be tested on the material from the chemistry text. Thus, the purposes for reading the materials differ. Second, the material in the chemistry text is probably a great deal less familiar than the material contained in the newspaper. Thus, our background and fund of information are probably less for the material in the chemistry text than for the material in the newspaper. Third, the chemistry text will be, in terms of readability, at a much higher level of reading difficulty. Most newspapers are at or around the sixth grade reading level, while a college chemistry text would test out at around a twelfth grade reading level or higher.

Different Reading Rates Required for Flexible Reading

Generally speaking, three major reading speeds are required for flexible reading. Below is a description of each reading rate and examples of circumstances that might necessitate the use of one rate of reading over another.

Skimming

Skimming is a method of finding what one wants to know in a hurry. Readers should decide to skim the reading material if their purpose for reading it is:

- to find a single key word or name or number in a list
- to find several key words or a phrase in a sentence or paragraph
- to survey a book, magazine, or article

Rapid reading

Rapid reading is the rate of reading most often used in order to get the general idea of what the material is about or what the author is trying to say. It can also be used when the reader simply wants to understand how the reading material is organized before giving it a closer reading. Readers should use rapid reading if their purpose is to:

- get the general idea, organizational arrangement, or mood of a selection
- read for enjoyment
- select portions of the material to be read more closely at a later time

A number of researchers have observed that a reader's reading rate is essentially set by about the fifth grade or so. Normal reading rates average between 200 and 300 words per minute, and regardless of background and education, most people accomplish most of their reading at their average speed. Reading flexibly is among the last reading skills to develop. While many high schools have speed reading laboratories stocked with expensive equipment, few attempt to teach students how to read flexibly. Further, it is highly unlikely that any methods for teaching speed reading actually produce flexible readers, since the readers themselves must analyze their purpose for reading, their background in the topic they are reading about, and the difficulty level of the materials they are reading. If a reader is a flexible reader, rate training will provide him increased potential for variation of rate to purpose. If the reader is not a flexible reader, rate training will simply make him a faster inflexible reader, in which case he will tend to read all materials at the same rate.

One technique for teaching speed reading is called the Paperback Scanning Technique and requires no expensive equipment beyond books. Like most rate training methods, the Paperback Scanning Technique utilizes external pressure and easy material. That is, the material is covered at a rate the reader has no control over, and the material itself is usually two grade levels below the reader's effective reading level. Specifically, the steps in this technique are:

1. Have students select a paperback that is interesting to them, but most importantly, a book that is below their effective reading level. Some students may require assistance in choosing an easy text that requires no word recognition or comprehension skills beyond their attainment.
2. Inform students that they will read several pages of the book with a definite time limit on each page. Tell them also that they will be given a literal comprehension check after each page.
3. Give the students ten seconds to read the initial page. When time is called, students should turn the book face down. Ask three to five literal level comprehension questions about each page.
4. Give the students nine seconds to read the second page, eight to read the third page, and so on down to one second for the tenth page. Each page should be followed by a quick comprehension check.
5. Then, give the students the full ten seconds to read the eleventh page, and follow with the normal comprehension check.

To the students' surprise, they will have gained information from the pages of the book when they had only one, two, or three seconds to read it. They will be surprised when they find that the ten-second time limit for page eleven now seems much longer than the ten seconds they had to read page one. Students will also be surprised by the fact that in some instances their comprehension will increase even when they have less time to read. If students' reading rate goes up but their comprehension remains at about the same level, this still reflects improvement.

There are also many opportunities to give students practice in reading and locating information quickly. Preteaching activities before students begin their reading can easily deal with this important skill. For example, if the students are to read a chapter in social studies about labor unions, the teacher might introduce an important person's name from the chapter then ask students to see how quickly they can find out when he lived. Once several students have found the information, the teacher can call for the answer then discuss how they found the information so quickly

("I looked for a four-digit number"; "I looked for his name, then a date"). The practice of discussing reading strategies is useful in that it clues less capable readers into techniques for reading that they, too, can use.

Study reading

Study reading is careful and deliberate reading in order to understand and remember both details and major ideas presented in a text. It requires a good effort, clear purpose, and close concentration on the part of the reader. Study reading is most appropriate under the following circumstances:

to follow directions
to solve a problem
to remember details
to understand the material at the higher levels of
    comprehension
to gain a thorough understanding

Even with these various rates of reading, readers' rates will change depending on their familiarity with the material they are reading and its readability. No matter what kind of material readers are reading, they must start by knowing their purpose for reading in the first place. Once readers decide on their purpose for reading, then they can choose the reading rate that will best help them achieve their purpose.

FORMAL STUDY METHODS

A number of writers and researchers have proposed various highly structured study methods. Among these is the SQ4R Study Method. The steps in the SQ4R Study Method follow.

Survey

The general purpose of the survey step is for the student to quickly scan the material before reading in order to determine the structure, organization, or plan the author uses. In essence, the survey step is intended to give the student an overall picture of what is about to be read. The following specific activities comprise the survey step:

- thinking about the title and predicting what will be included in the reading
- reading the Introduction and Summary to get the main ideas contained in the reading
- reading the main headings to gather additional information about the main ideas, where they appear in the text, and what the relationships are among them

Question

Once a student has surveyed the reading material, she should predict what questions she thinks will or should be answered in the material. In essence, the student establishes her own purposes for reading by posing questions before she begins her reading. Having in mind these questions automatically steers the student toward finding answers, provides the student a criterion against which she can judge information as relevant or irrelevant in answering the questions and adds structure and direction to her reading. Specific activities in the question step include:

- reading questions at the beginning and/or end of the material and looking for answers while reading
- formulating questions by changing headings and subheadings to questions

Read

After a student has surveyed and questioned the material, he must read the material. If the initial steps have been performed faithfully, a selective reading of the material in order to (1) answer the questions already posed and (2) skip or skim over material that appears to be irrelevant is an excellent reading strategy.

Recite

Once students have surveyed, questioned, and read the material, they should close the book and recite as much of the material as they can that answers the original questions posed. This accomplishes two purposes: first, students are immediately aware of how much material they can recall without the aid of their books; second, the immediate review is very helpful in crystallizing the material in the students' mind for use later on.

"Rite"

The "rite" step of the SQ4R Study Method is an extended review of the material and provides additional opportunity to organize the material into a useful format. Generally, the best strategy here is to put down on paper, as briefly as possible, using key words and phrases, the information the student recited in Step 4.

Review

Since the recite and "rite" steps of the SQ4R Study Method are, in essence, immediate review strategies, the student still must engage in delayed review. The purpose of the review step is to go over the material that was read at a later time so that the positive effects of spaced practice can occur. The following activities are useful in the review step:

- rereading questions from the question step
- reciting the answers from memory using the written answers from the "rite" step as the criterion and as a cueing device
- additional review of the material at a later time

The SQ4R Study Method, as well as all other study methods, is an attempt to get the student to impose a systematic, organized, and sequential structure on studying. Obviously, the SQ4R Study Method is not useful or appropriate in all situations; the reading task and the tasks required of students once they have read the material will determine the extent to which the SQ4R Study Method is appropriate. In many instances, a shortened version of the SQ4R Method might be most appropriate—again, depending upon what the student must do with the information acquired from the reading. In this kind of circumstance, surveying, reading, and reviewing the material may suffice for the demands placed upon the student. In any event, surveying or previewing the reading material before reading is most important and yields a great deal in terms of improved comprehension and retention of reading material.

READING NONPRINT MATERIAL

Specialized Content Area Symbols

Content areas such as science, mathematics, and social studies regularly require students to read and interpret specialized materials. In mathematics, for example, students must read a variety of symbols other than the printed language, including numbers and symbolic information that have a highly precise meaning (+, =, −, %, #). These symbols are often mixed into expository materials like story problems, requiring students to have a firm knowledge of the meaning of the symbol and the function it denotes.

Graphic Symbols

We, as teachers, often make the mistake of assuming that students already know how to read graphic materials that appear in science, mathematics, and social studies such as charts, maps, diagrams, tables, formuli, atlases, and globes. Just as most of us would have great difficulty in reading a geologist's topographical map or a pilot's navigational map, students will encounter difficulties with graphic materials. To compound the problem, formal instruction in map reading skills occurs infrequently. Many of us learn on our own, for instance, that colors in maps can indicate altitudes and depths, or that the size and configuration of a circle denoting a city tells us the approximate population and whether the city is a capital. However, not all students learn these specialized reading skills on their own; many students require systematic instruction in these skills. As teachers, we should endeavor to teach the specialized reading-study skills required to deal effectively with the content students are to learn.

Maps

There are many different kinds of maps used for many purposes. For the most part, maps used in the various content areas are of five varieties according to Dale (1946): (1) Physical maps show geographical outlines and communicate physical features such as temperature and rainfall; they may vary greatly in terms of the amount and quality of the information they communicate, ranging from simple line drawings of countries to complex three-dimensional (topographical) maps: (2) Commercial or economic maps communicate product, import/export, and general industrial information regarding specific geographical regions: (3) Political maps show state, county, and ideological boundaries in specific geographical regions: (4) Special maps indicate such things as territorial changes, occupation, military campaigns, cultural information, and so on: (5) Combination maps utilize two or more of the presentations mentioned above.

Since there is great variation among different kinds of maps in terms of the information they contain and the way in which they present information, no specific procedure for teaching map reading skills is necessarily the best. Students should concentrate on the following generalized skills:

1. Getting the main idea of the map.
2. Gaining familiarity with symbols, colors, and so forth used in the map.
3. Locating specific information contained in the map.

Students, in getting the main idea of a map, should pay particular attention to the map title and look carefully at the map in order to get a broad overall understanding of what the map is all about. Secondly, students should search the map for the variety of symbols that are used in order to determine if they are familiar with them; in any event, students should then search the map for study aids such as keys, legends, and so on. Finally, students should be able to locate specific and relevant information using the map, such as city names, names of other geographical features, or any specific information contained in the map relative to the general purpose or main idea of the map.

Graphs and charts

Like maps, there exists a wide variety of graphs and charts. Basically, the same general procedures outlined in terms of map reading apply also to the reading of graphs and charts. Students should first search for the main idea or purpose of the graph or chart, gain familiarity with the specialized symbols used in the graph or chart, then be able to locate specific information contained in the graph or chart. While a great many varieties of graphs and charts are used, there is a general sequence to them in terms of their difficulty and complexity. This sequence can guide us in teaching the specialized reading skills required to deal with graphs and charts. Weintraub (1967) suggests that picture charts and pictographs—where symbols have a specific stated value—are easiest for students to learn to read. Next, circle and pie graphs are fairly easy for students to master. Weintraub points out that even students in the early elementary grades are capable of reading and understanding pictographs and circle and pie graphs. Next in terms of difficulty come vertical and horizontal bar graphs. Finally, two-dimensional graphs and line graphs tend to be the most difficult to read and understand. Generally, the more categories of information introduced in a graph or chart and the more specific the information, the more difficult it is to read.

OTHER STUDY TECHNIQUES

There are many more effective study techniques that deal with effective study habits, test-taking skills, and general kinds of organizational skills in preparation for studying. Those skills listed below are skills we should endeavor to teach and impress upon our students.

Test-taking Skills

General

1. Plan your time.
2. Make sure you understand the test directions.
3. Be equipped with the test-taking tools you need, for example, erasers, pens, pencils, rulers, compass, protractor.
4. Get enough rest the night before.
5. Study for the test with classmates as well as alone.
6. Preferably, space study over time, rather than cramming at the last minute.
7. Find out from the teacher beforehand the material that is to be covered on the test.
8. Go over old exams for clues about an instructor's exams.

Essay Exams

1. Study each essay question. Try to determine the different ways it might be interpreted and answered. Reread the question several times before answering.
2. If there appear to be different ways of interpreting the question or you are uncertain how to interpret it, ask the teacher for clarification. Pay particular attention to directional terms such as "describe," "trace," "compare and contrast," "justify," and so on.
3. Interpret the question before answering it. Even if you think you know how to interpret a question, explain your interpretation of the questions as an introduction before you begin your answer. This will prevent you from receiving no credit for an answer in case the teacher had something else in mind when he or she wrote the question.
4. Write your answer. Qualify your answers instead of guessing at specifics. Be general in your answer if you don't know specific supporting information.
5. Summarize your answer. While you are writing your answer your thoughts will become clearer. By summarizing you have a chance to crystallize and clarify your answer.

Objective Tests

1. Find out whether there is a penalty for answering questions incorrectly. If not, answer all the questions. If there is a penalty, do not guess at answers you do not know.
2. First go through the test answering the questions that you can answer rapidly.
3. As you go through the test, mark the questions that are very troublesome with an X.
4. The second time through the test, answer the questions that are not very troublesome.
5. Last, as time allows, try to answer the questions marked very troublesome.
6. If the correct answer on a multiple choice test is not apparent, you can often arrive at the correct answer by successive approximation. First, eliminate the answers that are obviously wrong. This often leaves two answers remaining. Choose the better answer of the two.

Effective Study Habits

Below is listed a number of effective study habits proven to be useful aids in reading and studying that can be turned into pointers we can give students to insure that they study as effectively as possible.

1. Before starting your study period, preview or survey all the material you plan to study during that period.
2. Acquire and have readily available the materials that will be needed to carry out an assignment before beginning so that your efforts will not be interrupted.
3. Try to study in the same place all the time; this practice makes studying the most appropriate behavior for the particular study place, and it becomes much easier to study and get to work quickly without wasting time. Select a location that is comfortable (but conducive to alertness rather than to relaxation), well lighted, and free of noise and activity.
4. Study your weakest subjects first, then go on to subjects you feel you do best in. Assign priorities to your study tasks and carry them out accordingly so that you do not become pressured at the last minute by having failed to survey the importance, magnitude, or time elements involved.
5. Allow an appropriate period of relaxation or physical exercise (a change from mental activity) before beginning a study period at home if you have been in a classroom all day.

Central to all the study skills discussed is the premise that students need to learn how to read and study effectively on their own. When students leave school, they will have information needs as well as needs regarding pleasure reading. You will recall our discussion of the reality criterion—reading for information and reading for pleasure—in making decisions about reading instruction and what we teach. The skills and abilities described in this chapter are those skills and abilities that students must possess, to relative degrees, in order to satisfy their reading needs. Students will not always have teachers standing over their shoulders telling them where to go to find information, for instance. For this reason, we must endeavor to impart these independent reading, thinking, and study skills to students so that ultimately they do not need us to guide them.

STUDY AND THE PREDICTION PROCESS

In chapter 2 we mentioned the importance of students becoming independent readers and learners. When students learn to study skillfully they have taken a giant step in this direction because, if they can study effectively by themselves, then they can learn by themselves. The following application of the prediction process makes this eminently clear. Within the framework we can see the decisions students must make to study effectively and how effective study facilitates learning.

Identifying the Initiating Event

The initiating event in reading and studying is to establish purpose. A student must decide whether he is reading and studying for his own enjoyment or whether he is attempting to gain information for some other purpose. If he is gaining information to achieve a grade, he must read and study to pass tests.

Predicting Coming Events

Once purpose has been established, a student predicts coming events. If she is reading solely for her own pleasure, she needs only to choose reading material which she predicts will give her pleasure. In addition, she would probably predict that a rapid rate of reading, with occasional skimming, will enable her to sufficiently understand the material. If she is reading a story she will also attempt to predict coming events in the story as she reads.

On the other hand, if the student is reading and studying to pass a test she may predict that a slower, more studious rate is the proper rate with which to begin. She might also predict that there will be times while reading that she will need to stop and take notes in order to record important information for later review. In addition, she might predict that there will be times when she will need to obtain additional information from reference books to fully understand the material she is studying. The student might also attempt to predict the important issues that will be dealt with in the reading material and which issues may be covered in the teacher's test. She may base her predictions from reading the introductory sections and surveying the text or from remarks the teacher may have made previously.

Predicting the Consequences of Intervention

If the student is reading for enjoyment he may need to intervene occasionally to look up an unfamiliar word in the dictionary.
Otherwise, his reading need not be interrupted. If the student is
studying for an exam he may intervene often to insure comprehension of the reading material. His interpretation of the relevancy and importance of each passage will govern his interventions. When he reads an important point he may slow his reading
rate, stop to underline a phrase, or take notes. When he believes
that a particular passage is not relevant he may skip it entirely.
Also, he may stop reading to consult reference materials when he
believes he needs additional information on a particular point.

Identifying to Test Predictions

The reader who is reading for enjoyment will monitor feedback
as she reads to determine whether the book is enjoyable as she
predicted. If not, she may stop reading or choose another book. If
she continues to read she will attempt to determine whether her
predictions of coming events are confirmed.

The studious reader will monitor feedback to determine
whether her predictions of the important topics to be covered in
the reading material were covered and whether the teacher asked
the exam questions she predicted would be asked. In addition, the
studious student monitors feedback to assess the consequences of
her interventions. Did her study regimen result in achieving high
grades on the test covering the material? Was she able to contribute more to the class discussion and answer the teacher's
questions correctly? Did she skim material which she should have
read more closely? Did she underline and take notes on the important topics?

The good student will regard the answers to these questions as
feedback and will modify his study regimen to improve his school
work. Learning to test predictions on his own and to correct his
mistakes on the basis of feedback contributes substantially to the
student's becoming an independent reader and learner. As he develops this ability, he will become less dependent on his teachers,
and he will be able to assume more initiative. In addition, he
should be able to confirm more predictions. This will make him
more successful and self-confident.

SUMMARY

1. *Establishing purpose for reading.* Prereading activities such as discussing (a) the type of reading material, (b) the probable content of the book based on the story or chapter title, (c) the relationship between the student's past experience and the new reading material, and (d) providing clear instructions for the reading help establish purpose for reading.

2. *Obtaining information.* To be effective in obtaining information from books the student should know how to use the table of contents, the appendices, the index, the glossary of books, as well as the study aids in textbooks. In addition, the student should know how to use a variety of reference sources such as the dictionary, encyclopedia, and library. Individual and group activities can be designed to teach these skills.

3. *Notetaking.* Good notetaking involves the ability (a) to listen and read well, (b) to evaluate information for relevance, (c) to classify information into categories, (d) to summarize information, and (e) to record information systematically, that is, programmatically and hierarchically.

4. *Outlining.* Outlining requires the student to (a) establish the purpose of the outline, (b) evaluate information for relevance, and (c) perceive and produce a content hierarchy in outline form. The content hierarchy indicates the relationship among topics and subtopics. The outline designations indicate the sequence in which the topics will be reviewed.

5. *Flexible reading.* Flexible reading refers to the adjustment of reading rate to the purpose for reading and the difficulty of the reading material. Skimming, rapid reading, and study reading are the three reading rates a flexible reader uses. Skimming is used to locate a particular piece of information or to survey the reading

material. Rapid reading is employed in reading for enjoyment, extracting a general idea, and locating information to be read more closely. Study reading is adopted to understand thoroughly and remember both details and major ideas in a text.

6. *Formal study methods.* The SQ4R method is an example of a formal study method. The steps in the method are: survey (the reading material); question (predict the questions the reading material will answer); read (the material); recite (the material that answers the questions posed); "rite" (the material that was recited); and review (the written material at a later time).

7. *Reading nonverbal material.* When special symbols are used in a content area (such as $+$, $-$, $=$, and $\times$ in math) the student should be taught the meaning of the symbols before reading a selection that contains them. The reading of graphics materials such as charts, maps, tables, and diagrams should be taught to students before they engage in reading selections that contain these graphic representations.

8. *Test taking.* Test-taking skills can be taught to the student. The student can learn general test-taking skills and particular skills for taking essay and objective tests.

9. *Effective study habits.* Effective study habits can be taught to students which will aid them in reading and in learning.

10. *Prediction process.* In applying the prediction process to study we can see the decisions the student must make to study effectively and how effective study produces independent readers and learners.

REVIEW QUESTIONS

1. What kind of activities can be used to establish purpose for reading?

2. What procedures must a student know to obtain information?

3. What skills are involved in effective notetaking and outlining?

4. What skills does a flexible reader possess?

5. What are the steps of the SQ4R study method?

6. What special programs emerge in reading nonverbal material?

7. What test-taking skills and effective study habits may be taught to the student?

8. How can the prediction process be applied to studying?

PART IV
DIAGNOSIS

CHAPTER 9
Diagnosing the Readability of Instructional Materials

PURPOSE

1. To highlight the importance of establishing the readability of instructional materials.
2. To discuss factors that affect readability.
3. To show how to estimate the readability of instructional materials.
4. To show how to make new content more readable.
5. To describe the relationship between readability and the prediction process.

BACKGROUND AND NEW INFORMATION

The many factors discussed in previous chapters that make reading more difficult and reading material less comprehensible or more boring affect the readability of reading materials. Knowledge of these factors establishes a foundation for the more penetrating discussion of readability in this chapter. The information you have gained from previous chapters pertaining to optimizing predictability in learning also provides background for understanding this chapter because, in essence, readability concerns optimizing the predictability of reading material for the student. In addition, aspects of the method proposed in this chapter to make new content more readable will be familiar to you. The method involves preteaching unfamiliar terms, providing struc-

ture for learning new content and establishing purpose and
interest.

vocabulary load
syntactic density
prepositional phrase
passive voice
inverted sentences
cloze procedure

DESIRED LEARNING OUTCOMES

The student will be able to:

1. Describe the factors that affect the readability of instructional materials.
2. Describe procedures for diagnosing the readability level of
reading material.
3. Describe how a teacher can make new content more readable.
4. Describe how the prediction process pertains to readability.

We have discussed the concept of optimum predictability in the
instructional environment in chapter 1. We said that when any
particular task is too high in predictability, the individual engaging in the task tends to become bored. Simply, the task represents
little or no challenge to the individual. On the other hand, when a
task is too low in predictability the individual tends to become
confused and ultimately to avoid a highly unpredictable, unstable
situation. You will recall our example of the novice driver in heavy
traffic presented in chapter 1. There are many aspects of the total
instructional environment to which we can apply this concept. A
very important consideration in terms of optimum predictability
in reading is the reading material to which students are exposed.

Traditionally, we have measured the degree to which reading
materials are optimally predictable with *readability formuli*. The
application of readability formuli to a textbook, for example, yields
a grade level reading difficulty score. The rationale is that if we
can assess readability of textual materials as well as reading levels
of students, then we can match students to materials and avoid
the pitfalls of placing students in materials that are too difficult

(low predictability) or too easy (high predictability). Probably the most common complaint of teachers today is that they have so few materials that are suitable for less able readers. Publishers have attempted to assess readability levels of instructional materials as a result. Cramer and Dorsey (1969), however, examined the readability of science books for grades one through six. None of the eighteen books they assessed with the Dale-Chall Readability Formula was on grade level. In fact, the reading level of these books ranged from three to seven grade levels higher than the publishers' estimates. This is a common occurrence in basal readers, trade books, and particularly in content area textbooks.

FACTORS THAT AFFECT READABILITY AND PREDICTABILITY

Readability is measured in a number of different ways, dependent upon which readability formula one uses (Klare, 1975). Readability formuli measure average word length, letter counts, syllable counts, ratio of "familiar" to "unfamiliar" words, average clause length, average sentence length, and so on. Nearly every readability formula, however, uses (1) an estimate of vocabulary load and (2) an estimate of the syntactical density which is usually attributable to sentence length and structure. Klare makes the point that no readability formula is necessarily superior to other formuli; one must choose a formula that fulfills a particular need. Using different readability formuli to assess the same reading materials often results in variations of up to three or four grades in terms of reading difficulty level. Further, few readability formuli have been shown to be valid in assessing difficulty level of content reading materials.

Many factors affect predictability or readability of printed materials; no single readability formula measures more than two or

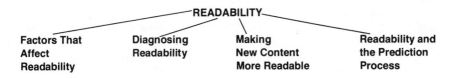

FIGURE 9–1   A hierarchy of topics in chapter 9

three of the factors associated with increased reading difficulty level of prose. An increased amount of research is being devoted to the linguistic and psycholinguistic analysis of printed language. However, many of the measures being used in this research are experimental, require much time and training to use and are not useful with all types of reading material. Additionally, many factors associated with readability defy measurement.

Some interesting research has been conducted with those factors that affect readability that are generally not measured by readability formuli. This research can guide us in making decisions about and selections of appropriate reading materials for students. For example, Weaver and Bickley (1967) found that by blocking out function words (that is, words like "but," "and," "or," and so forth) in passages taken from standardized reading tests, students' comprehension scores were significantly lowered. As we have said, these "function" or "signal" words are very important in communicating relationships among ideas in printed materials. Weaver and Bickley conclude, also, that function words apparently have a great effect on the extraction of conceptual meaning from text—that is, comprehension. Similarly, Stoodt (1972) determined that knowledge of conjunctions that signal relationships is highly related to reading comprehension.

Two studies point up the fact that one class of words—verbs—can significantly affect readability of and comprehension from printed materials. Blount and Johnson (1973) discovered that material written in the active as opposed to the passive voice was recalled significantly better. Emans (1973) found that verb simplification in printed materials resulted in increased comprehension. These two studies support the contention that narrative materials are generally easier to read than materials written in the third person or in passive voice. The use of active verb voice and simplified verb forms as in a narrrative selection reduces the word count, reduces average sentence length, and tends to clarify the relationships among the major elements in a sentence (subject, predicate, and object).

Other studies have indicated that a range of factors significantly affect readability and comprehension. Weaver, Holmes, and Reynolds (1970) found that deletion of punctuation significantly depresses cloze scores. Apparently, punctuation is among those "language cues" which has a potent effect on one's ability in predicting and extracting meaning from printed materials. Koenke and Otto (1969) determined that including pictures along with written material can greatly enhance comprehension. Edwards (1975) found that eighth graders did significantly poorer on comprehension tests when the passages contained idiomatic language such as "wild goose chase." It appears, then, that clarity of writing style, inclusion of graphic aids to reading, and use of unfamiliar and unique phrases all affect readability and comprehension. It is interesting to note that readability formuli measure none of these factors.

Regarding factors that affect syntactical difficulty, a number of research studies have demonstrated that type and sophistication of structural patterns of sentences affect readability and comprehension. Tulving and Gold (1963) gave subjects a task in which they were to find a particular word in context. They found that length and congruity of context had a great deal to do with how effectively subjects were able to perform the task. It might be inferred that reading skills like skimming and scanning, in which the quality of comprehension is not emphasized, are also affected by the clarity and style of the author's writing.

Ruddell (1965) compared students' performance on a task measuring contextual ability (cloze) with passages written in either high or low frequency oral language patterns. He found that cloze scores were significantly higher when students were dealing with the high frequency oral language patterns. Jongsma (1974), on the other hand, found no improvement in comprehension resulting from the use of high frequency sentence patterns in written materials.

The disagreement between these latter two studies, as well as other studies investigating language patterns as a source of comprehension difficulty, may well be explained by research along slightly different lines. Smith (1973), for example, took writing samples from students in grades four through twelve. He then determined their "productive syntactic levels" (that is, the sentence patterns students themselves use in their writing) and had students read passages written at, below, and above their own levels. He discovered that students read with the best comprehension those passages that were closest to their own syntactic levels. However, he also found that the simplification of the syntax or language patterns in the passages resulted in increased comprehension difficulty for older students whose syntactic levels were well above the levels of the passages they had read. Smith's findings are in agreement with our contention that reading materials that are either too high or too low in predictability will interfere with comprehension.

Other studies, like that of Kahn (1965), show that still other factors affect readability and comprehension. Kahn had good and poor readers make up and tell stories. He then analyzed the stories and found that good readers more often used future time perspectives in their stories. These findings may simply support other studies that have indicated that complex verb forms contribute to increased reading difficulty. On the other hand, it might be that students have more comprehension difficulties with materials that are removed from their own frame of reference in terms of time.

Finally, a number of research studies have conclusively demonstrated that interest level of reading material has a definite effect on comprehension, and is perhaps an important consideration when assessing materials in terms of readablity. These studies have provided convincing evidence that interest level of reading materials is a potent factor in comprehension performance. Estes and Vaughan (1973) found that materials high in interest level were comprehended significantly better than low-interest materials, even though the materials were equivalent in difficulty. Asher and Markell (1974) uncovered a strong interaction between interest level of reading materials and performance on a cloze test, with boys performing significantly less well after reading low interest material.

To summarize, the following factors negatively affect optimum predictability and readability, and therefore, comprehension:

1. Poor writing in terms of style, organization, and clarity.
2. Difficulty and abstractness of ideas and concepts and the vocabulary used to explain ideas and concepts.
3. Unfamiliarity of vocabulary.
4. Absence of good illustrative materials such as pictures, graphs, charts, and so forth.
5. Absence of appropriately placed and worded definitions.
6. Absence of good concrete examples.
7. Too many prepositional phrases.
8. Too many pronouns.
9. Too many complex verb forms.
10. Too frequent use of passive voice in verbs and use of negatives.
11. Too many complex, compound, and inverted sentences.
12. Poor punctuation, too much or too little punctuation.
13. Too frequent use of idiomatic language.
14. Sparse use of contextual aids.

15. Low interest level of material.
16. Material that is below the reader's effective reading level.

It is patently impossible for a teacher to consider all or even most of these factors when choosing instructional materials for students. However, we offer some suggestions for diagnosing both students and content instructional materials to insure a good match between the two so that we might optimize predictability for students in the instructional situation.

Perhaps the easiest way to detect poor writing in instructional materials is for the teacher to read them. Often, however, he or she may not be bothered by those aspects of poor writing that will interfere with students' comprehension. A number of factors listed above fall under the category of poor writing.

Pronouns

The following passage and comprehension question are taken from a well-known standardized group reading test. Although some of the words have been changed, it remains substantially equivalent to the original passage that appears in the test booklet:

Jerry was going to the ballpark to play an important game. It was for the first place in the league. He was the pitcher. Gordon was to be the starting catcher. They had planned out the signals for every type of pitch Jerry would make. Gordon had the mask and glove with him as he strolled to the field. He met Hank, the third baseman, and saw that he had forgotten his glove. Hank had his brother, Robert, run home to get it.

1. Who had forgotten his glove?
   a. Jerry
   b. Hank
   c. Gordon
   d. Robert

Notice that in the short space of about ninety words, four characters are introduced and fully ten pronouns are used—that is, over 10 percent of the passage consists of pronouns! In this instance, we are requiring the student to perform a very close reading of poorly written materials in order to answer a literal comprehension question. Any reader can become lost in a sea of pronouns like this; the less able reader is at even more of a disadvantage. By the way, Hank forgot his glove.

Complex and Passive Verb Forms

Complex and passive verb forms increase reading difficulty and lower predictability of written materials for a number of reasons. First, the sheer volume of words is increased when more complex predicates and passive forms are used. For example, consider the sentences:

1. It was decided by the group that Tom should receive the award.
2. The group decided Tom should receive the award.

Sentence 1 is written in the passive voice, while sentence 2 is written in the active voice. Notice that the word counts for the sentences are twelve and eight respectively. Now note that the passive form (1) requires the addition of an extra pronoun ("it"), an extra prepositional phrase ("by the group"), and an extra function word ("that") to connect the thought groups expressed in the sentence. Note also that the basic subject-verb-object pattern is altered, making sentence 1 less predictable. You will recall that both too many pronouns and too many prepositional phrases tend to increase difficulty. Thus, complex and passive verb forms raise readability levels and necessitate other changes in the writing that also increase readability levels and lower predictability.

Prepositional Phrases

The basic function of prepositional phrases is to modify or describe other elements in the sentence. For example, in the sentence, "The boy from Idaho won the prize," "from Idaho" is a prepositional phrase. It describes and tells about the boy in the sentence who won the prize. The inclusion of too many prepositional phrases signifies a great deal of description, perhaps too much description for the reader to deal with effectively. Consider the sentence with the addition of more prepositional phrases: "The boy with blond hair, about five feet tall, dressed in blue jeans, and from Idaho won the prize."

Negatives

A great deal of research has indicated that the overuse of negatives in writing increases difficulty level of reading material. The use of negatives increases reading difficulty for the same reason passive verb forms do. First, the number of words required to express a thought necessarily increases, for example:

1. "Please do not leave," she said.
2. "Please stay," she said.

Secondly, the use of negatives in writing resembles the use of a mixture of negatives and positives in an algebraic formula—one simply must keep all of them in mind. For example: "It was not hard to understand why they didn't ask him not to go." Put more simply without as many negatives, this sentence might read: "It was easy to understand why they didn't ask him to stay." Thus, the overuse of negatives can place an extra burden on the reader by making the material less readable and, therefore, lower in predictability.

Complex, Compound, and Inverted Sentences

We have described to some extent how syntactical difficulty of written materials increases reading difficulty. Complex and compound sentences serve to raise syntactical, therefore, readability levels since more thoughts and ideas are presented in one sentence. We have all encountered lengthy sentences in which we have lost the author's message simply because the sentence was too long. William Faulkner, in his short story "The Bear," holds, perhaps, the record for lengthy sentences with one that runs two and one-half pages—approximately 2000 words. Inverted sentence structures also increase reading difficulty, since an inverted structure is less familiar. For example, consider the two sentences:

1. Mighty oaks from acorns grow.
2. Mighty oaks grow from acorns.

In this example, we have again altered the basic subject-verb-object pattern (sentence 2) of the English language to one of subject-object-verb (sentence 1). By doing this, we have made the sentence less readable and less predictable. A great deal of poetry regularly uses inverted sentence patterns. Perhaps this is one reason why so many students dislike and have difficulty in reading poetry.

Idiomatic Language

The frequent use of idioms of the language, as we have seen, serves to increase reading difficulty. Often, authors introduce many idioms in the dialogue of their characters. Older reading materials will contain idiomatic language not commonly in use today, also serving to increase reading difficulty. Preteaching those idioms that might cause students reading problems is an excellent way to deal with them. Pointing out the idioms before reading and having students predict what they mean and how they came to be is an excellent method of generating interest in the reading material and the study of language in general. Edwards (1975) lists several common idioms, many of which are found in textbooks, that consistently cause comprehension problems:

Common Idioms in Texts	Other Common Idioms
pick up the scent	fly in the ointment
no time to lose	jump at an offer
hide the panic	hit if off with someone
in no time	live from hand to mouth
pick up a trail	lick into shape
catch them off guard	leave someone cold
held his breath	take issue with
breeze through	wild goose chase
mental storehouse	crow about something
key players	be at loose ends
took stock of . . .	lose face
he cleaned up on the deal	over their head
the right kind of head	be in the running
not to my taste	steal the show
blood ran cold	take someone in
drummed out of the army	red-letter day
candle was fully spent	off the top of her head
	draw the line
	feather in his cap

Author's Organization

Organization of written materials is also an extremely important consideration, particularly in choosing textbooks. Aristotle tells us that everything should have a beginning, a middle, and an end. And so it is with textbooks. Texts that have a great deal of running prose with no breaks in the form of new headings and such, create special problems for students. Chapter divisions, headings, and subheadings serve as places for readers to stop and reconnoiter—to regain their bearings. These chapter dividers serve also to break the chapter up into more manageable pieces—a principle on which programmed material is based. Chapter markers or dividers also serve as useful tools for students to use in previewing a chapter; by looking through the chapter before reading, the student can get the general picture or organizational structure which will be valuable when he or she begins reading. Short lead-in passages preceding each chapter, as well as chapter summaries, can also be valuable organizational tools. Finally, all the rules of good writing apply to authors of textbooks— particularly textbooks for students who have reading problems.

Often, instructional materials, although well written, lack features that would make them much easier to read and to understand. A well-placed picture, chart, diagram, or concrete example can literally be worth a thousand words. Well-placed and worded definitions are also a valuable aid to ease of reading. Key words and phrases that are underlined, italicized, or emphasized in some other way are important to optimum predictability. Some teachers have been known to sit for hours underlining key words and phrases in new textbooks to make them more readable—a laudable practice. Good teachers endlessly look for ways to supplement textbooks by providing as many concrete examples as are necessary to insure full understanding.

When textual materials contain too many unfamiliar words, difficult concepts, or a great deal of idiomatic language, the teacher is wise to preteach or in some way deal with these factors before students begin reading. It is a good idea to put the unfamiliar words or phrases on the board or in a handout with more familiar synonym equivalents. When students encounter trouble, all they need do is glance up at the board or read the handout. By the time they finish reading, they will have encountered the unfamiliar word or phrase a number of times. This repetition will help a great

deal in making new words or phrases a part of the student's reading vocabulary.

Sentence length and difficult language structures negatively
influence readability and predictability of reading materials. Too
many colons, semicolons, dashes, and such are a good indication
that difficult language structures are contained in the reading
material. It is difficult to say just what sentence length is optimal,
but materials that exceed an average sentence length of twelve to
fifteen words are usually high in difficulty level. Additionally, regardless of the average sentence length, materials that have a
high frequency of sentences exceeding eighteen to twenty words
will usually be high in difficulty level. These estimates, of course,
are dependent upon grade level of materials and students, clarity
of writing, and frequency of difficult vocabulary words.

DIAGNOSING THE READABILITY AND PREDICTABILITY OF READING MATERIALS

A simple method for assessing the compatability of students
and textbooks is suggested by Bormuth (1962). By choosing a
representative sample of 200 to 300 words of continuous prose
from the textbook, then deleting every fifth word, the teacher can
construct an informal test that will assess the appropriateness of
the textbook for students. After scoring only exact word replace-
ments as correct (giving credit for dropped endings, mispellings,
and incorrect verb tenses), a "cloze" score can be obtained for
each student. Bormuth reports the following cloze scores and
equivalent traditional comprehension scores:

Percent of cloze items judged correct	Percent of traditional comprehension items correct
50	95
40	80
30	65

Students who score in excess of 50 percent on the cloze test
may find that the textbook is too simple; that is, too predictable.
Students who score in the 40 to 50 percent range will probably
find the textbook to be of optimum predictability. If students'
scores drop much below 40 percent, the textbook may well be too
low in predictability and therefore too difficult for them. If all or
nearly all students score either very well or very poorly on the

informal cloze test, the teacher would be advised to try a different prose sample from the textbook as the original sample of prose may not have been representative of the entire book. We should caution you that little research is available that compares cloze score equivalencies with content reading materials. If you choose to try this method you may want to try the procedure several times and decide upon your own criteria for scoring it.

Another method of estimating readability of written materials is described by Singer (1975). Citing the cumbersome and difficult-to-use readability formuli available, Singer hypothesized that university students with no previous training could estimate readability using an informal technique that would yield valid difficulty levels for reading materials. Singer gave each subject in the study a set of graded paragraphs (grades one through seven), then had them estimate readability of unfamiliar materials by matching them to the examples in the set of graded paragraphs. He found that virtually all estimates done in this fashion were within one grade level of the readability level computed with well-known formuli. Singer concludes that this technique is valid, yields accurate information about readability and is much easier and quicker to use.

The following procedure can be useful in quickly estimating the readability level of reading materials:

1. Obtain a set of graded paragraphs or reading selections that range across grades one through eight (sources for graded paragraphs might include Silvaroli's *Classroom Reading Inventory*, or Woods and Moe's *Analytical Reading Inventory*.

2. Compare the reading selection to be estimated to the graded paragraphs in terms of (a) vocabulary load and (b) sentence length and difficulty.

3. By matching the reading selection to be estimated with a comparable graded passage of well-defined reading level, estimate the approximate grade level of the reading selection you wish to assess.

4. If the reading selection you wish to assess is a lengthy story or a book, randomly choose from two to ten paragraphs (depending upon the length of the selection) from the selection and estimate the readability of each in the manner described. Then, average the readability estimates you have made to produce one grade level index of the readability of the selection.

Singer's technique for assessing difficulty level of reading materials is an excellent way of diagnosing the optimum predictability of classroom instructional materials. We recommend this technique over Bormuth's cloze technique and traditional readability formuli since it is much easier to use and yields an accurate estimate of readability. This technique, combined with the knowledge of other factors that affect readability, provides the classroom teacher a powerful tool for matching students to reading materials and identifying potential trouble spots in reading materials where students may encounter reading problems and loss of understanding.

In using the Singer technique for estimating readability, it is assumed that the reading ability of students is already known, so that once the readability of instructional materials is estimated, the materials can be matched to the students' reading levels. However, the teacher must often match students to reading materials without a precise idea of the students' reading levels. In this instance, the following technique may prove helpful in insuring a good match between the reading levels of students and the reading levels of books.

1. Ask students to select a paragraph from the beginning, the middle, and the end of the book they have selected to read. Have students read these paragraphs to themselves or, in an individualized situation, to the teacher.
2. Have students count the total number of words they had trouble with in the paragraphs, that is, those words they could not identify or understand.
3. Have students count the total number of sentences that, because of their length or structure, they had difficulty in understanding.
4. Finally, let the students themselves decide if the book is too difficult to read and understand. If students have difficulty with three or more words per paragraph or in understanding the author's message, then the book is probably too difficult for them to read and understand.

MAKING NEW CONTENT MORE READABLE

Often, teachers in content areas find themselves in a predicament in which the textbooks and other supplementary reading materials they have available are too difficult for their students.

As we have seen, content area textbooks are often too difficult even for the grade levels for which they are intended. Additionally, local school policy sometimes dictates that teachers must use a particular textbook in, for example, the science course they teach. While some writers in the field of reading suggest that teachers rewrite materials in order to lower reading levels, this practice is not entirely realistic. Here are some suggestions for making unfamiliar content more readable.

In any given lesson or unit of instruction, the teacher can preteach concepts, content hierarchies, and new vocabulary. That is, by presenting an overview of the unit or providing concrete examples of content hierarchies before students read the related material, the teacher can (1) provide a structure students can follow during their reading, (2) establish purposes for reading the materials, and (3) establish interest in learning new content.

Providing Structure for Learning New Content

As we have said, by providing a structure or framework for students to follow we can make the new material to be learned more predictable. Also, by insuring that students know what they must learn, what they must be able to do after their reading, and what the teacher expects of them in general, we can enhance the predictability of the reading material. We must give students a set of directions or a program that adds structure to the content they are to study. Secondly, by insuring that students have a purpose or purposes for reading, we are simply communicating to them where they must go and what they must do during and after reading.

For example, suppose a teacher has just finished a unit in social studies about culture and the next teaching unit deals with urbanism. In preteaching the unit on culture, the teacher may have spent several class periods establishing the meaning of culture for the students. One way the teacher might have done this was to start with the culture of the students themselves, showing them how the holidays they celebrate, the food they eat, the clothes they wear, the way they think, and the attitudes they have are affected by their culture. Then, to introduce the unit on urbanism the teacher might begin with a discussion of how living in a city also affects these things, that is, that urbanism has a cultural impact on the way we live. This, then, establishes a structure students can follow and accents the interrelationships between culture and patterns of living.

Providing Reading Purposes for Learning New Content

The teacher can also establish purposes for reading the unit on urbanism at the same time. Questions such as "What causes cities to develop?" "How does living in a city affect what people do everyday?" or "What are some of the problems in living in a city?" will help to establish purpose for reading. By asking these kinds of questions, the teacher communicates to the students what he or she wants them to learn from their reading. This, in turn, guides students in their reading by making the reading itself and the tasks that will follow more predictable for the students.

Preteaching vocabulary will also serve to establish structure and purpose in a lesson or unit. For example, the term "urbanism" might well be new to the students. Making sure that students know this key term before they read the related material will insure increased understanding of the material. Other terms that might warrant preteaching could include migration, megalopolis, metropolis, metropolitan, cosmopolitan, demographics, urban flight, and so on.

Promoting Interest in Learning New Content

Preteaching any given lesson or unit can also be used as a vehicle for establishing an interest in the content to be learned. Often, the content we teach is seemingly unfamiliar to students, and as human beings, we all have a tendency to be uninterested in learning content that is totally unfamiliar. By establishing a background of information that is sufficient for students to understand new material before they begin their reading, we can motivate students to learn new content. To do this, it is necessary to constantly relate new content to content that has already been mastered, to demonstrate to students that they already know at least a little about new content they are to study, and to pique their interests by relating new content to their preferences.

READABILITY AND THE PREDICTION PROCESS

Stage 1: Identifying Initiating Events

We have said throughout the book that the author's words are the initiating events in reading. If the author's words do not convey meaning to the reader, the reader cannot begin to read. Implicitly, the readability level is too difficult, too unpredictable, too confusing. Given a readability level that is not too difficult the reader can begin to read. But he or she will not continue reading if the reading material is overly predictable and boring. To challenge the reader the reading material must impart new information. Readers will tend to be even more engrossed in reading if the material is of personal interest to them. Interest in reading material can be induced by providing readers with reading content they prefer to read. In order to initiate reading

1. The reading material cannot be too difficult.
2. The material must convey new information to be challenging.
3. The reader must be personally interested in reading the material.

Stage 2: Predicting the Coming Message

To predict the coming message readers must be able to identify trends in the author's message. If the author's organization is good, he or she will offer cues of the coming message with introductions, short lead-in passages, and topic headings. All these features make it easier for the reader to predict the coming message. Where the reading material contains too many idioms, prepositional phrases, long and complex sentences, pronouns, negatives, and passive verb forms, for example, it will make it difficult for readers to detect and maintain continuity as they read. Consequently, they will be unable to predict the coming message, and the reading material will be confusing to them.

Stage 3: Predicting the Consequences of Intervention

Readability affects the predictions readers make with respect to the consequences of their own actions. When the readability level of the material is too difficult, readers tend to become frustrated and feel that they will be unable to grasp the author's message no matter what they may do. If the teacher assigns such reading material, readers tend to believe that they are expected to be able to read it. If they cannot, they will tend to doubt their competency and lose self-confidence. In short, readers are victimized when they are assigned reading material that is too difficult for them to read.

On the other hand, if the·readability level of the reading material is optimally predictable, readers will be encouraged to intervene to regain meaning when meaning is lost. They will regard the new words and information they encounter while reading as challenging and seek understanding. They will be prompted to predict that a discussion with the teacher will be helpful in clarifying the author's message. They will be encouraged to use their repertoire of word identification skills to find the meaning of puzzling words.

Stage 4: Identifying to Test Predictions

Readers will monitor the ensuing message for feedback to see if their predictions are accurate. The author helps the reader with feedback cues by underlining important phrases, presenting graphic aids, and providing summaries. Of course, the problems mentioned with respect to predicting the coming message apply here also. To monitor feedback readers must be able to detect continuity and trend. Excessive idioms, prepositional phrases, long and complex sentences, negatives, and passive verb forms, for example, make it difficult for readers to detect continuity. Consequently, they will have trouble testing predictions.

SUMMARY

1. The challenge to the reading teacher with respect to readability is to make instructional reading material optimally predictable to the student, not too boring and not too confusing.

2. Factors that affect the readability level of reading material are (a) abstractness of ideas presented; (b) unfamiliarity of vocabulary; (c) absence of illustrations; (d) absence of good, well-placed definitions of terms; (e) too many prepositional phrases, pronouns, complex verb forms, complex, compound and inverted sentences, passive verbs, and negatives; (f) poor punctuation; (g) sparse use of contextual aids; (h) low interest level of material; (i) material that is substantially below the readers' effective reading levels; (j) author's organization and style; and (k) too frequent use of idiomatic language.

3. A method for assessing the compatibility of students and reading material with respect to readability is Bormuth's application of the "cloze" procedure.

4. Another method of estimating readability is described by Singer. In this procedure the reading material in question is matched with paragraphs for which readability level already has been established.

5. The teacher can make new content more readable by providing structure for learning the new content, purposes for learning new content, and interest for learning new content.

6. With respect to readability and the prediction process, if reading material is either too unpredictable (confusing) or too predictable (boring) readers will not be able to identify the author's message. Consequently, they will be unable to predict the coming message or the consequences of intervention.

REVIEW QUESTIONS

1. What is the connection between optimum predictability and the readability of instructional materials?

2. What factors affect the readability level of reading material?

3. What procedures can be used to assess the readability of reading materials?

4. What can the teacher do to make new content more predictable?

5. How does readability relate to the four stages of the prediction process?

CHAPTER 10
Understanding the Diagnosis of Reading Skills

PURPOSE

1. To acquaint you with the principles of educational diagnosis.
2. To acquaint you with diagnostic procedures and tests.
3. To show you how to judge and select diagnostic tests used in the diagnosis of reading skills.

BACKGROUND AND NEW INFORMATION

The knowledge you have acquired in previous chapters pertaining to reading skills prepares you to understand how these skills are diagnosed. In chapter 3 you learned about word identification skills, in chapter 4 about vocabulary skills, and in chapters 5, 6, 7, and 8 about reading comprehension and study skills. These are the reading skills you need to learn to diagnose.

The chapter begins with a discussion of the purposes of educational diagnosis. Second, we consider kinds of diagnostic observations. Third, we discuss making accurate diagnostic observations and show you how to judge the accuracy of an observation. Fourth, we deal with the accuracy of measurement and the criteria for judging the accuracy of a measurement instrument. Fifth, we discuss measurement instruments. Sixth, we deal with the crucial problem of selecting a measurement instrument. Finally, we apply the prediction process to diagnostic testing.

KEY TERMS

validity
reliability
objectivity
criterion-referenced tests
norm-referenced tests
direct observations
indirect observations
power tests
speeded tests
reliability coefficient
summative tests
formative tests

DESIRED LEARNING OUTCOMES

The student will be able to:

1. State the purposes of educational diagnosis.
2. Describe kinds of diagnostic observations.
3. State the criteria for judging the accuracy of an observation and explain how validity, reliability, and objectivity contribute to the accuracy of an observation.
4. Explain how the accuracy of a diagnostic test may be judged on the basis of validity, reliability, and objectivity.
5. Describe several diagnostic tests and the similarities and differences among them.
6. Describe a procedure for selecting an accurate diagnostic test.
7. Apply the prediction process to diagnostic testing.

PURPOSES OF EDUCATIONAL DIAGNOSIS

The term "educational diagnosis" implies that we study a student who is suspected of having some sort of learning problem so that we can determine the cause of the problem, the nature of the problem, or both. The end result of educational diagnosis, then, must be a program for alleviating those conditions that are suspected of causing the learning problem and a program of remedial action that we predict will alleviate the learning problem itself. To help you adopt a diagnostic perspective, let us begin with a form of diagnosis with which we are all familiar—medical diagnosis.

If we look at educational diagnosis from a medical point of view, we can gain valuable insight into the process of diagnosis. For example, it is not always necessary or even helpful that we determine the cause or causes of a student's learning problem. In the case of a medical doctor who has diagnosed his patient as having cancer, the doctor probably has little or no idea as to the cause of the cancer. However, this does not preclude treatment. Many cancers, especially if they are diagnosed early, can be successfully treated—even though the cause of those cancers remains unknown. Similarly, the cause of a physical injury often adds little or nothing to the doctor's diagnosis and subsequent treatment. A patient who has a broken arm, for instance, will be diagnosed as having a broken arm whether the patient fell from a tree, was hit by an automobile, or suffered the broken arm from some other cause. In this example, diagnosis and treatment are augmented little by knowledge of causative factors. However, if the patient breaks an arm by falling from a tree on several different occasions, the doctor can assume that the cause of the problem is important and include in the treatment directions to the patient to stay out of trees. Thus, spending a great deal of time and effort in investigating causes of learning problems may or may not be helpful. In any event, we should approach the study of causative factors intelligently and evaluate our efforts in this respect according to the extent that they help us plan successful remediation.

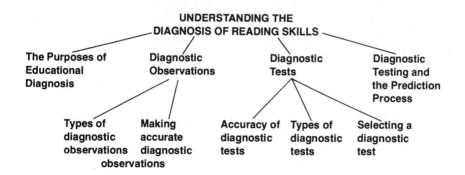

FIGURE 10-1 A hierarchy of topics in chapter 10

When we study the processes of reading and thinking from a diagnostic point of view, our aim should be to remedy the problem(s) we identify as well as those conditions that aggravate the problem, insofar as is possible. In order to diagnostically study the processes of reading and thinking, we must have a firm understanding of these processes, just as the medical doctor must have a firm understanding of human anatomy. For this reason, we have preceded our discussion of diagnosing reading and thinking skills with a lengthy discussion of what these skills are, how they operate, and how they can be identified. With a firm understanding of the processes of reading and thinking, diagnosis and remediation of deficiencies along these lines become a much simpler task. Lexier (1978) cautions that an overly simplified view of the processes of reading and thinking seldom results in effective diagnosis or teaching.

The teacher's primary job is to progressively increase learning and adaptive behavior through instruction. If we picture progressive desired learning outcomes as rungs in a ladder, it is the teacher's job to move the student up the ladder from one rung to the next. Only if the student fails to progress need the teacher become concerned with remediation. If the desired progress is not made on the first attempt, the teacher prescribes a new instructional plan for the student, and the student tries again. If the student fails to progress after the teacher has exhausted his or her repertoire of instructional strategies, the teacher refers the student to the "special programs" staff. Teachers need not know how to diagnose all learning disabilities. However, teachers need to know when the student is not progressing so they can refer the student to specialists for additional diagnosis. Generally speaking, when a teacher has attempted a number of times to individualize instruction for a student and the student is unable to progress from one rung of the learning ladder to the next, the teacher should refer the student for more penetrating diagnosis and possible special help.

For students who are progressing up the ladder of desired learning outcomes adequately, the teacher's primary diagnostic concern is with diagnosing a student's readiness for learning. If each rung of the ladder represented the attainment of the readiness requirements needed to proceed to the next higher rung of the ladder, then we would need only to start children in early childhood at the bottom of the various learning ladders, and we would know what they are ready to learn at all stages of their development by their position on the ladder.

Of course, education is not so neatly organized. Nor are the learning stages and steps so well defined and related to each other. More realistically, the teacher must prepare to diagnose student readiness within the framework of his or her instructional responsibilities.

DIAGNOSTIC OBSERVATIONS

Kinds of Diagnostic Observations

In diagnosing learning readiness, we must make observations of students. These observations can be done in many ways, since a myriad of variables affect learning. We have discussed a number of variables that affect achievement and learning such as self-concept, classroom social interaction, attitude toward school and toward learning, and so on. Observing these kinds of factors, in essence, is observing factors that we think are interfering with learning and achievement. Our observations in this respect may lead directly to action that can help to alleviate conditions associated with the problem. For example, we might observe that Johnny has a poor self-concept and a negative attitude toward reading. We might decide that these two factors are interfering with Johnny's progress and growth in reading. In order to treat Johnny's poor self-concept, we might give him added responsibility in the classroom, make an extra effort to praise him for the work he does in the classroom and generally try to instill in him that he is a worthwhile human being. In order to treat Johnny's negative attitude toward reading, we might make additional observations in order to collect information about his reading interests. Then, we can attempt to provide him reading materials that have high motivational value in an effort to demonstrate that reading can be fun and interesting.

However, if we fail to make observations regarding Johnny's attainment of certain reading and thinking skills, our efforts described thus far may fail. We may observe, for example, that Johnny has an intense interest in horses. We obtain, on the basis of this information, a book about horses for Johnny to read. However, Johnny's lack of skill in reading might make it impossible for him to deal with the book we identified. Therefore, we make observations of the learning problems and the processes involved so that we can treat those problems instructionally.

This is why we go through the painstaking procedure of analyzing the processes of reading and thinking and breaking them down into the component skills that, together, comprise these processes. In this way, we can pinpoint those reading and thinking skills that Johnny has not mastered, needs review in, or has mastered already. By doing this we can insure that Johnny gets instruction in those skills he has not mastered, and we insure that we do not waste time in teaching skills he has already mastered. Thus, in making diagnostic observations we are faced with the task of deciding what kinds of observations will yield us the most useful information regarding subsequent action.

Some of the observations we make are direct and some are indirect. We make direct observations of overt behavior. We can observe directly a student operating a teaching machine or dissecting a frog to diagnose his or her performance. On the other hand, reading, thinking, and learning are covert processes that are not directly observable. In order to diagnose reading, thinking, and learning we must make indirect observations, oftentimes with a paper and pencil test. We infer from students' answers to the questions we ask the extent to which they have achieved with respect to learning, thinking, and reading.

Making Accurate Diagnostic Observations

Accurate diagnosis must be based upon accurate observations. If an observation of a student's reading or thinking performance is inaccurate, the diagnosis of the student's readiness for learning will be inaccurate, and the instructional prescriptions based on the diagnosis will also be inaccurate. So, accurate observations provide the foundation for making accurate diagnoses and for prescribing instruction accurately.

Three factors contribute to the accuracy of an observation: validity, objectivity, and reliability. By demonstrating that an observation is valid, objective, and reliable, we demonstrate that it is accurate.

The Validity of an Observation

An observation is valid if we observe what we intend to observe. If a teacher intends to observe reading comprehension and in fact does, the observation is valid. A classic example of an invalid observation has to do with a poll taken of voters in 1936 in an effort to determine whether Alfred Landon or Franklin Roosevelt would win the presidential election. A telephone poll of voters was taken, and from the information collected, the pollsters predicted that Landon would win. However, only those who had telephones were sampled, and they were primarily Republicans because only the wealthier voters could afford telephones at that time, and they tended to be Republicans. This factor invalidated the observation resulting in the inaccurate prediction that Landon would win.

The Objectivity of an Observation

A second factor that contributes to the accuracy of an observation is objectivity. An observation is said to be objective when different people agree about the observation. For instance, if three teachers listening to a student read agree about a mistake the student made, there is objective evidence that the student made the mistake.

The Reliability of an Observation

A third factor that affects the accuracy of an observation is reliability. An observation is said to be reliable when the subject behaves in the same way from one observation to the next. Although different people may agree about a single observation, making the observation objective, the subject or thing they are observing may act differently from one moment to another. A student may take a test on a day when he is ill and score low. Given the test subsequently when he is feeling well and alert, he may score higher. People do vary in their behavior from time to time. When we attempt to observe a characteristic repeatedly, our conclusions about the characteristics are more reliable if our conclusions are the same from one observation to the next.

It is important to realize that the first thing to establish is the validity of an observation, because if an observation is invalid, it does not matter how objective or reliable it may be. The wrong characteristic is being observed. Once validity is established, then objectivity and reliability can be pursued. Teachers should not be dismayed because they must make subjective rather than objective observations. All professionals including doctors, diagnose based on their subjective observations. When the matter is serious and they are not certain of a diagnosis, they call in consultants in search of objective agreement.

DIAGNOSTIC MEASUREMENTS

Taking Accurate Measurements

One way of making an observation is through measurement. When we make an observation through measurement we observe quantities of a particular characteristic. We observe the characteristic weight in pounds, the characteristic height in inches and feet, and the characteristic intelligence in terms of IQ scores. The higher a person's IQ score, the more intelligent we say he or she is. The same three criteria are used for judging the accuracy of a measurement instrument that are used to judge the accuracy of any method of observation—validity, objectivity, and reliability.

Validity

The validity of the measurement instrument we use to assess reading and thinking skills is crucial to making decisions about the instruction we give our students. In chapter 3 we discussed the fact that in reading we rely heavily on our sight vocabulary to identify those words that appear in reading materials with great frequency. Sight vocabulary words, we said, were those words that we identify instantly; we do not need to engage in phonic or structural analysis of these words, nor do we need to study the context in which they appear. We know them instantly and do not need to analyze them in any of these ways.

Furthermore, we know that the competent reader must possess an adequate sight vocabulary and that there are methods of observing a person's sight vocabulary. One particular diagnostic word recognition test that is in current use contains a subtest entitled "Sight Words." The following example, although not taken directly from the test, illustrates the way in which this test measures "sight words."

| *knife* | kife | nife | kin |

In this particular subtest, the student is directed to circle the word in the group of three words that sounds like the first word.

In the above example, we have a subtest that supposedly measures "sight words" but in fact measures skills we associate with phonic identification. Based upon what we know about sight words and sight vocabulary, this particular subtest is entirely invalid. By no stretch of the imagination does it measure the skill it purports to measure. Students who perform poorly on this subtest are not necessarily deficient in their sight word vocabulary; more likely, they are deficient in phonic identification skills.

Now imagine a teacher who receives the results of a student's poor performance on the "sight words" subtest just illustrated. The teacher knows what sight vocabulary is and knows a number of instructional methods for teaching and increasing skill in sight vocabulary. However, the teacher may not be familiar with this particular test and has only the results to guide instruction. In this example the teacher may give the student hours and hours of instruction in sight vocabulary by using flash cards, a tachistoscope, and other sound methods of teaching sight vocabulary when, in fact, the student's sight vocabulary might be very good. Thus, inappropriate instruction was provided to the student based on an invalid observation.

There is another test in current use that contains a subtest called "basic reading vocabulary." Imagine the same teacher, who again is not familiar with this particular test, learning that several of his students performed very poorly on this subtest. The teacher has a very good idea about what kinds of words might be considered a part of the students' "basic reading vocabulary" and makes the assumption that the students who performed poorly on this test need to review those vocabulary words that appear in printed materials frequently. What the teacher does not know, however, is that uncommon words like "patrician," "meander," "missive," and "deft" actually appear on the "basic reading vocabulary" subtest. Again, an invalid observation leads to inappropriate instructional decisions.

Objectivity

Measurement contributes to the accuracy of an observation because it enhances objectivity. That is, it is more probable that people will agree on an observation, if the observation is made through measurement. For example, it is more likely that people will agree on the length of a table if they actually measure it than if they guess at its length. Similarly, it is more likely that people will agree on the intelligence of a student if they measure the student's IQ than if they do not use a measure of intelligence.

Objective tests are so called because they are accompanied by a scoring key. Different scorers using the key to score a student's test response will probably score the test the same. Hence, the test is objective.

Reliability

Tests constructed to measure a particular characteristic usually consist of a number of different test items. If people respond similarly to the items of a test that is constructed to measure a characteristic, we say that the test reliably measures that characteristic.

Types of Diagnostic Tests

We have said that in order to plan instruction in reading and thinking skills we must observe the extent to which students have mastered these skills. For the most part, reading and thinking skills must be observed indirectly with instruments we call "paper and pencil" tests. Literally thousands of paper and pencil tests exist, designed to diagnose and evaluate skills associated with reading and thinking. In fact, there are so many of these instruments available that choosing among them becomes a rather arduous task.

Most of the instruments available to measure reading and thinking skills can be classified as either *norm-referenced* or *criterion-referenced* tests. Norm-referenced tests are initially administered to a standardization sample (that is, a "norming sample") so that we can ultimately compare the performance of our own students to the performance of the students in the original standardization sample on the same test. Thus, norm-referenced tests yield us observations of the extent to which our students have achieved particular skills and abilities in comparison to the extent to which other students have achieved those same skills and abilities. This presents us with a logical dilemma. We are, in effect, using the norming information obtained from students in the standardization sample to judge our own students' achievement; however, our own students are probably not receiving the same instruction as those in the standardization sample and may well be much different from those students in some very important ways (experiential background, socioeconomic background, and so forth). Further, the observations we gain from the norm-referenced tests do not yield us much information about the instruction we should be giving our students. If, for example, we have ten students who score very low on a particular reading skill on the norm-referenced test, we still would have little information about the extent to which they have mastered that skill. All we know for sure is that in comparison with the students in the standardization sample, our students did less well. Thus, the criterion of performance is set by the performance of students in the standardization sample and not by knowledge of the level of performance a student must demonstrate in order to show mastery of a particular skill.

Criterion-referenced tests, on the other hand, are those for which some criterion of acceptable performance has been predetermined. We might make the decision, for example, that if Johnny can instantly recognize 75 percent of the sight words from the Dolch list of 220 most frequently used words, Johnny has demonstrated adequate mastery of basic sight vocabulary. If Johnny recognizes only 70 percent of the words on the Dolch list, he has not achieved the criterion we set, and he needs additional instruction in this particular reading skill. Most teacher-made tests are in reality criterion-referenced tests because they are keyed into the actual instruction the teacher is giving students, and some acceptable performance level is usually specified. There are some problems, however, with criterion-referenced tests. For example, in the situation stated above, is 75 percent performance on the sight vocabulary skill test really indicative of mastery of sight vocabulary? Is 70 percent really indicative of nonmastery of sight vocabulary? The real question here is how do we arrive at these criterion levels and how do we insure that they are meaningful?

As we said, there are many instruments available that we can use to observe reading and thinking skills. Most often, a distinction is made between *survey* tests and *diagnostic* tests. Standarized survey tests of reading and thinking skills are norm-referenced tests. That is, a student's performance on a standardized survey test is judged in comparison to how the norming sample performed on the test. Those tests referred to as "standardized achievement tests" are also norm-referenced. In general, achievement tests measure a broad range of skills often including reading, math, language skills, and so on. Usually they include two subtests of reading, one that deals with vocabulary knowledge and the other that deals with comprehension. Survey tests of reading skills, on the other hand, deal specifically with reading and reading-related skills. Ultimately, survey tests and achievement tests yield gross measures of a general nature. They are useful in charting achievement for an entire school district. Because they are generalized in terms of the skills they measure, however, they are of limited diagnostic value since they fail to pinpoint precise areas of strength and weakness in regard to reading skills.

Diagnostic tests of reading skills are highly useful in making diagnostic observations of these skills since they do attempt to measure subskills of these processes. Survey and achievement tests tend to measure broad skills that are comprised of a constellation of subskills, whereas diagnostic tests get at the subskills themselves. For this reason, diagnostic tests are seldom standardized to the extent that survey and achievement tests are. The underlying philosophy is that comparing a student's performance to that of students in the standardization sample does not yield us diagnostically useful observations. Instead, we want to observe the extent to which our students have mastered specific reading and thinking subskills we have identified as important to subsequent growth in the general processes of reading. This information is highly useful in guiding the instructional decisions we must make regarding reading and thinking. For example, a survey test might tell us that Johnny is reading at the fourth-grade level. This observation is not particularly useful in telling us what kind of reading instruction to provide or what specific skills Johnny has or has not mastered. A diagnostic test, on the other hand, may tell us that Johnny is reading at the fourth-grade level and that he is weak in contextual analysis skills, strong in phonic identification skills, needs practice in sight vocabulary skills, and needs additional instruction in comprehension skills beyond the literal level. These are diagnostically useful observations that will help us to make decisions about the instruction we should give Johnny, as well as the instruction we should not give him, and the extent to which we should emphasize the teaching of the specific subskills of reading and thinking.

Another important distinction between tests is the distinction between *summative* and *formative* tests. These two kinds of tests are usually used to assess the effects of instruction. A summative test is used to determine whether instruction has moved students to the achievement of a desired learning outcome as intended. Such a test summarizes student performance for the purpose of certifying mastery of the desired learning outcome. Summative tests often are used to assign a grade to students. Thus, most final examinations are summative tests.

Formative tests are used to determine whether the student has mastered a particular instructional activity. The instructional activity is one of a number that is prescribed to move students toward a desired learning outcome. A formative test determines whether the skills and knowledge required to achieve the desired learning outcome are forming. In essence, a formative test is a diagnostic-progress test the teacher uses to assess the progress the student is making and to diagnose the nature of a student's problems, if the student is not progressing adequately. Corrective activities are prescribed for students who are not progressing adequately to get them back on the track that leads to the achievement of the desired learning outcome.

A final general characteristic of observation instruments has to do with the amount of time they allow students to perform those tasks included on the tests. Some tests have no time limits or very lenient time limits that allow the student ample time to complete the entire test. Normally, these tests are designed to sample the range of a student's capacity regarding specific skills and abilities and are referred to as *power tests*. *Speeded tests*, on the other hand, place great emphasis on the number of tasks completed in a specified time period. Standardized survey and achievement tests normally have specific time limits during which the student can work at the test, but these may or may not be considered speeded tests. Diagnostic tests generally have lenient time allotments; however, how fast a student does a particular task can be considered very useful diagnostic information in many instances. Reading rate, for example, can be highly useful diagnostic information when we look at a student's total reading ability.

Selecting a Measurement Instrument

Above all, the test you choose must be valid. Tests are not valid in general. Rather, a test is valid for measuring a particular characteristic in a particular group of people. An IQ test is valid for measuring the characteristics of intelligence. However, different IQ tests have been constructed for different age groups. Before selecting a test you must determine the characteristic you wish to measure and the group to whom you intend to give the test. The test you choose is valid if it measures the characteristic you intend to measure in the group you intend to test.

To determine whether a test is objective you simply find out whether it is scored with a scoring key. If it is, it is an objective test.

In order to determine whether a test is reliable, check the reliability coefficient that should have been computed for the test. If the test has a reliability coefficient below .70 (closer to zero), then the test is not very reliable. This is a general rule of thumb.

Every published test should be accompanied by a test manual that gives information on the validity, objectivity, and reliability of the test. You can read the test manual without attempting to penetrate the statistical jargon and get some idea whether validity, objectivity, and reliability have been established for the test, as well as knowledge or information about the group of people for whom the test is valid. Presumably, in the development of the test, research was conducted to check the merits of the test and it was refined until it proved to be valid and reliable.

Reviews of many tests appear in *Buros' Mental Measurement Yearbooks*. Reading tests are also reviewed in a special edition of the book. The reviewers are test specialists, and you can read their reviews to determine whether the test you are considering is valid, reliable, and objective. The reviewers usually offer expert opinion on the merits of a test.

We have described different kinds of observations and tests and given you criteria and rules of thumb for making judgments when selecting tests. You must judge whether or not a particular test is valid for your purpose and for the students you wish to test. All teachers choose and construct tests, but many teachers are not formally trained in test construction. We have given you enough information to make judgments about tests. If in selecting a test you are uncertain of its merits or its appropriateness for your purpose, you can consult a test specialist in your school system or at a college nearby. Keep in mind that making accurate observations and diagnoses is the basis for making accurate instructional decisions.

DIAGNOSTIC TESTING AND THE PREDICTION PROCESS

The relationship between diagnosis and reading instruction can be clarified by viewing it within the framework of the prediction process.

Stage 1: Identifying Initiating Events

Since instructional decisions should be based on student diagnosis, diagnosis is the initiating event in teaching. Teachers must diagnose the present reading skills of their students before they can consider appropriate reading instruction. Among these skills are the various word identification skills we discussed in chapter 3—sight identification, phonic identification, structural identification, and contextual identification skills. In addition, reading teachers might wish to diagnose some of the reading comprehension skills we discussed in chapter 6. This decision depends upon the demands of the reading content teachers wish to introduce and the types of comprehension they wish to teach. Teachers may also wish to diagnose the students' interests so that reading material may be chosen to correspond with them. Published tests teachers can use to make such diagnoses will be considered in the next chapter.

Stage 2: Predicting Coming Events

To begin instructional planning the teacher makes predictions of coming events based on the obtained diagnostic information. The main prediction that needs to be made is that work on particular reading skills by particular students will improve their reading. Diagnosis may reveal that one student is weak in phonic identification, while another is weak in contextual identification. Still another student may need work on sight identification. Variation in student reading comprehension may also emerge from the diagnosis.

Stage 3: Predicting the Consequences of Intervention

The intervention that must be considered by the teacher is instructional intervention. In predicting coming events the teacher is involved with predicting what will improve student reading. In predicting the consequences of intervention the teacher is concerned with how to improve student reading. Essentially, the teacher predicts that particular instructional interventions will improve particular reading skills of particular students. To make such predictions the teacher must be familiar with the various instructional activities that can be used to teach the various reading skills.

Stage 4: Identifying to Test Predictions

The teacher tests instructional predictions for the purpose of confirming them. Now that the teacher has predicted that developing certain reading skills will improve student reading and that particular instructional interventions will perfect these skills, the teacher implements the instructional intervention and monitors feedback to test and confirm these predictions.

As a teacher proceeds with her teaching plan she monitors two factors. She makes sure that the instructional strategy is being implemented as intended because, if the strategy is not, she cannot expect to develop the particular reading skills for which the strategy was selected. Given the accurate implementation of the instructional interventions, the teacher monitors student progress to see if the strategy is working. She looks for signs of student progress, specifically an improvement in the particular reading skill.

If the student is proceeding toward mastery of the reading skill the teacher's prediction will be confirmed. If the student is not moving toward mastery, the teacher intervenes and employs corrective measures to get the student back on the track so that the prediction will eventually be confirmed.

Monitoring student progress is a form of diagnosis. In this case the teacher is diagnosing the effect on the student of the chosen instructional intervention. If the diagnosis reveals that the intervention is not working, the teacher must be flexible enough to choose another instructional strategy. A particular instructional strategy may not be effective for all students. Teachers must be sensitive enough to individual differences to vary instructional prescriptions based on student aptitude and interest until they find a strategy that suits the student's needs.

As you can see, in reading there are two kinds of diagnoses. Initially, the teacher uses diagnostic tests to determine the instruction to prescribe. Then, after the instructional intervention is selected and implemented, the teacher diagnoses student progress to determine whether the prescribed instructional intervention is working as predicted.

SUMMARY

1. The purpose of diagnosis is to assess the learning readiness of students in order to prescribe instruction for them.

2. When the teacher has attempted repeatedly to individualize instruction for a student and the student does not progress toward the teacher's learning objective, the teacher should refer the student for more penetrating diagnosis and possible special attention.

3. Some of the observations we make are direct and some are indirect. We make direct observations of overt behavior such as a student dissecting a frog or operating a teaching machine. We make indirect observations of covert characteristics such as reading, thinking, and learning because they are not directly observable.

4. To make accurate diagnoses the observations we make for diagnostic purposes must be valid, reliable, and objective.

5. In order to make accurate diagnoses based on information obtained from a testing instrument, the testing instrument must be valid, reliable, and objective.

6. Most of the instruments available for measuring reading and thinking skills can be classified as either norm-referenced or criterion-referenced tests. A norm-referenced test reveals the performance of the test taker relative to others who have taken the test. Criterion-referenced tests are tests for which a criterion of acceptable performance has been predetermined. We give a criterion-referenced test to determine whether or not an individual's performance meets the criterion of acceptability.

7. Survey and diagnostic tests can be used to measure reading and thinking skills. Survey tests are usually norm-referenced achievement tests that yield general information on a broad range

of skills. They are of limited diagnostic value because they do not pinpoint specific problems the student may be having. On the other hand, diagnostic tests are designed to identify specific problems and to reveal the nature of the problem so that remediation may be prescribed.

8. Summative and formative tests are used to assess the effects of instruction. Summative tests determine the extent to which students achieve a desired learning outcome. Formative tests determine the extent to which students master a particular instructional activity that leads to the achievement of a desired learning outcome. Formative tests are diagnostic-progress tests.

9. Power tests are designed to determine whether students can perform tasks without stringent time constraints. Speeded tests place emphasis on the number of tasks students can complete in a specified period of time.

10. In selecting a test the teacher should determine whether a test is valid, reliable, and objective. Above all, the test must be valid for the teacher's purpose and for the group of students he or she wishes to test. The validity, objectivity, and reliability of a test can be determined by reading the test manual or by consulting *Buros' Mental Measurement Yearbook*.

11. The relationship between diagnosis and reading instruction is clarified by viewing it within the framework of the prediction process.

REVIEW QUESTIONS

1. What is the purpose of educational diagnosis?
2. When should a teacher refer a student for special diagnosis?
3. When do we make direct and indirect observations?
4. How do we judge the accuracy of an observation?
5. How do we determine whether a testing instrument is valid, reliable, and objective?
6. What are the differences between norm-referenced and criterion-referenced tests? Survey and diagnostic tests? Summative and formative tests? Power tests and speeded tests?
7. What procedures should a teacher follow in selecting a test?
8. What is the relationship between diagnostic testing and the prediction process?

CHAPTER 11
The Diagnostic Testing of Reading Skills

PURPOSE

1. To consider the various reading skills that require diagnosis.
2. To discuss tests used to diagnose these skills.
3. To point out the limitations of some of the tests.

BACKGROUND AND NEW INFORMATION

In earlier chapters we familiarized you with the reading skills to be discussed in this chapter. In chapter 3 we considered word identification skills, in chapter 4 vocabulary, and in chapters 5, 6, 7, and 8 reading comprehension and study skills. In chapter 10 you learned about the general nature of educational diagnosis. In this chapter you learn about tests that will enable you to diagnose these skills.

The chapter opens with a discussion of tests used to diagnose word identifications skills. The diagnosis of the following skills are considered in this section: sight word identification, phonic identification, structural identification, contextual identification, and vocabulary knowledge. The second major section of the chapter deals with diagnosing reading comprehension. Third, diagnosing study skills is considered. Fourth, the diagnosis of reading potential is discussed. Fifth, we discuss informal diagnostic techniques in the content areas. Finally, diagnosing social relations, self-confidence, and interests is reviewed.

KEY TERMS

errors of confabulation
inflected word forms
derived word forms

DESIRED LEARNING OUTCOMES

The student will be able to:

1. Identify the various ways of diagnosing word identification skills, including sight word identification, phonic identification, structural identification, contextual identification, and vocabulary knowledge. In addition, the student will be able to recognize the appropriate uses of tests and methods for diagnosing these skills.
2. Identify tests for diagnosing reading comprehension and the appropriate uses of these tests.
3. Identify tests that diagnose study skills and the appropriate uses of these tests.
4. Identify tests that diagnose reading potential and the appropriate uses of these tests.
5. Identify tests that diagnose social relations, self-confidence, and interests, and the appropriate uses of these tests.

DIAGNOSING WORD IDENTIFICATION SKILLS

Sight Word Identification

From chapter 3 you will recall our discussion of sight word identification, its relationship to reading achievement, and limitations of sight word identification as a method of teaching children beginning reading. Few survey or diagnostic tests attempt to measure this particular skill, probably due to the fact that informal measuring devices are easily constructed by the classroom teacher. Most basic sight vocabulary lists are constructed on the basis of the frequency with which the words appear in print. Kucera and Francis (1967) have analyzed a corpus of well over one million words sampled from a broad range of printed materials (see chapter 3).

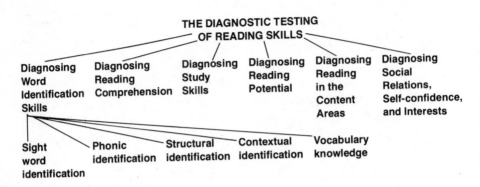

FIGURE 11–1   A hierarchy of topics in chapter 11

Examples of tests that include submeasures of sight word knowledge include:

1. *Dolch Basic Sight Word Test.* Arranges the Dolch basic sight list of 220 words for purposes of testing sight vocabulary (Garrard Press).
2. *Durrell Analysis of Reading Difficulty.* Test contains a cardboard tachistoscope for timed word presentation and stimulus words (Harcourt Brace Jovanovich).
3. *Instant Word Recognition Test.* A group test that measures a student's knowledge of 600 common words (Dreier Educational Systems).

The following procedure can be used in constructing a diagnostic measure of sight word identification ability.

1. Randomly select twenty-five words from the word list. Ideally, these words should represent a broad range of letter patterns, number of syllables, and so on.
2. Print the twenty-five words in lower case onto 3 × 5 inch cards so that the words can be seen easily from a distance of eighteen inches.
3. Construct a list of the twenty-five words on one sheet of paper that can be used as a score sheet. Leave two blanks following each word in order to write in student responses.
4. Give the student some practice with the task beforehand. Then, cover the word on the card with a blank card and hold

the card in front of the student. Moving only the blank cover card, expose the sight word to the student for an instant (approximately 1/10 to 2/10 of a second).

5. On the score sheet in the first blank indicate either that the student correctly identified the word orally or the student's response. This is the instant identification score.

6. If the student did not respond or responded incorrectly, show the word again for as long as he or she needs to see it in order to make a response (3 to 10 seconds). Record the student's response in the second blank; this is the student's untimed identification score.

7. After administering all twenty-five words, total the correct responses, giving full credit for instant identification and half credit for untimed identification.

Most authorities agree that 95 percent accuracy on a sight word identification test like this is an acceptable performance level, and the student who demonstrates 95 percent or better performance possesses an adequate sight vocabulary. We must stress that establishing a criterion level of performance of 95 percent may not be advisable in all situations. It is up to the teacher to establish an acceptable criterion level based on the characteristics of the task and the students being tested.

By returning to the response sheet where the student's incorrect responses were recorded, the teacher can examine these responses for patterns of error. In examining the error patterns, the teacher may wish to consider the following questions regarding the student's skill in sight word vocabulary:

- Were student errors more frequent in the initial, medial, or final position of the word?
- Did particular letters or letter combinations seem to account for more errors than we might expect?
- Did the words that were missed possess any additional factors in common? Number of syllables? Irregular letter patterns?

This particular method of diagnosing sight word identification skill can be used in other ways to assess knowledge of more content-specific vocabulary words. For example, the science teacher may wish to test students' sight identification of those science content words that appear most frequently in science materials. In this instance, the science teacher can follow the procedures outlined above using those words he or she defines as important in reading science materials. Again, the science teacher should exercise caution in establishing a criterion of acceptable student performance.

Phonic Identification

The extent to which a student has mastered the sound-symbol correspondences of the English language is an important consideration in making diagnostic observations regarding reading. In chapter 3 we discussed some of the factors that contribute to the debate that surrounds phonics instruction. Regardless of the degree to which phonics is emphasized instructionally, the student's phonic identification abilities should be observed diagnostically. Many of the suggestions we make in this chapter regarding the diagnosis of phonic identification skills will be most applicable to students in the lower grades and older students with very serious reading problems.

In observing the student's phonic identification skills, we should seek to answer some of the following questions:

- Does the student possess the concept that letters represent sounds?
- What is the extent and quality of the student's knowledge of sound-symbol correspondences?
- Where in the word does the student use or fail to use phonic analysis skills—initial, medial, final?
- Does the student exhibit a pattern of phonic identification errors? For example, does he or she have difficulty with particular letters and letter combinations: consonants, vowels, dipthongs, digraphs, two- and three-letter blends, highly irregular letter patterns, and so forth?

A number of diagnostic tests are available for observing the student's mastery of phonic identification skills. Listed below are several examples of such tests with brief descriptions and references.

1. *Botel Reading Inventory*. This diagnostic battery contains several subtests for observing a variety of reading related skills. The phonics subtest measures the student's

knowledge of consonant sounds, consonant blends, consonant digraphs, rhyming words, long and short vowels, and other vowel sounds (Follett).

2. *Cooper-McGuire Diagnostic Word-Analysis Test*. A group criterion referenced test containing three subtests, one of which deals with phonic analysis skills (Croft).

3. *Doren Diagnostic Reading Test of Word Recognition Skills*. A group test containing twelve subtests; phonic identification skills measured by this test include beginning sounds, speech consonants, ending sounds, blending, rhyming, and vowels (American Guidance Service).

4. *Durrell Analysis of Reading Difficulty*. An individualized diagnostic reading test that contains a number of reading subtests, including subtests that deal with hearing sounds in words (Harcourt Brace Jovanovich).

5. *Gillingham-Childs Phonics Proficiency Scales*. Contains individual subtests of letter-sound knowledge, consonant clusters, vowels, and spelling of nonsense words (Educators Publishing Service).

6. *McCullough Word Analysis Test*. A diagnostic battery of subtests including tests of initial blends and digraphs, vowel sound discrimination, sound-symbol knowledge, sounding whole words, and interpreting phonic symbols (Personnel Press).

7. *Phonics Criterion Test*. A diagnostic test of knowledge of many sound-symbol relationships using nonsense words (Dreier Educational Systems).

8. *Silent Reading Diagnostic Tests*. A group test that provides measures of several word analysis abilities, including phonics skills (Lyons and Carnahan).

9. *Sipay Word Analysis Test*. Contains sixteen subtests of visual and phonic analysis abilities and blending (Educators Publishing Service).

10. *Test of Phonics Skills*. A battery of nineteen individually administered subtests, most of which are concerned with knowledge of sound-symbol correspondences. Provision is made for measuring auditory discrimination ability in ten dialects (Harper & Row).

The tests listed above are only examples of the tests that are available for observing phonic identification skills; this is not intended to be an exhaustive listing. Additionally, there are many informal tests of phonic identification available. The teacher can gain much diagnostically useful information about the student's mastery of phonic identification skills from observing the student reading classroom materials and performing related exercises and tasks.

Structural Identification

In chapter 3 we emphasized structural identification as a skill important to identifying words. We said that structural identification involved the identification of familiar letter patterns and combinations that denote inflected forms (for example, -s, -es, -er, -est, -ed, -ing, and so on) and derived forms (those words that contain affixes, common roots, and contractions). There are a number of tests available that diagnose structural identification skills. Many achievement tests and survey tests of reading contain subtests with names like "Language Usage" or "Language Skills"; these subtests are generally measures of skills associated with structural identification. It is important for the teacher to differentiate among those tests that measure the finer and more subtle aspects of structural identification skills (for example, identifying the correct plural form of "baby" as either "babys" or "babies") and those that assess more basic kinds of structural identification skills (for example, recognizing the root word "depend" in the word "independence"). We also made the point that structural identification skills will range from strictly decoding skills to structural abstraction skills that involve extracting meaning from words and word parts. In making diagnostic observations of the student's mastery of structural identification skills, we should endeavor to answer the following questions:

- What is the extent and quality of the student's knowledge of compound words?
- What is the extent and quality of the student's knowledge of inflected and derived word forms?
- Is the student able to isolate discrete sound units (syllables) in words? Does he use this ability in analyzing new words?
- Is the student aware of familiar and frequent letter patterns that occur in a variety of words? Is she able to see the "little words in big words"?

- Is the student able to utilize meaning clues contained in prefixes, suffixes, and roots?

Below are listed several examples of tests that are useful in diagnosing skills associated with structural identification.

1. *Cooper-McGuire Diagnostic Word-Analysis Test.* A group criterion-referenced test containing several subtests that deal with structural analysis (Croft Educational Services).
2. *Doren Diagnostic Reading Test of Word Recognition Skills.* Contains several subtests dealing with structural analysis including words within words (American Guidance Service).
3. *Fountain Valley Reading Skills Test.* Samples a wide range of word recognition abilities with seventy-seven one-page criterion tests, including tests of structural analysis skills (Zweig Associates).
4. *Gates-McKillop Reading Diagnostic Test.* Contains a battery of diagnostic subtests including tests of spelling and syllabication (Teachers College Press).
5. *Lincoln Diagnostic Spelling Test.* Tests areas of difficulty in spelling associated with pronunciation and use of spelling rules (Bobbs-Merrill Publishing Company).
6. *McCullough Word Analysis Test.* Contains subtests of syllabication and knowledge of root words having affixes (Personnel Press).
7. *Stanford Diagnostic Reading Test.* Contains several subtests including one of syllabication ability (Harcourt Brace Jovanovich).

An additional diagnostic test of structural abstraction skills is the *Word Guessing Test: Part I* (Friedman, 1976). This test presents students with compound pseudo-words, requiring the student to identify the meaning of the pseudo-words. Two answered items are presented below.

1. *Curehide* means
   a. museum keeper
   b. secret
   c. leather
   d. curtain
   e. hidden
   f. ribbon

2. *Extrascarce* means
   a. afraid
   b. important
   c. weird
   d. distorted
   e. necessary
   f. rare

The *Word Guessing Test: Part I* diagnoses the student's ability to identify familiar features of unfamiliar compound pseudo-words, integrate the familiar features in terms of meaning, and identify the meaning of the compound pseudo-word.

The teacher can construct a number of informal diagnostic tests to assess students' skills in structural identification. The science teacher, for example, might wish to diagnose students' knowledge of those prefixes, suffixes, and roots that are common in science content materials.

Contextual Abstraction

In chapter 3 we discussed skills associated with identifying words through context. Many tests that contain subtests of skills called "word recognition" or "vocabulary" test the student's knowledge of words in context. That is, the stimulus word itself is presented in a meaningful context rather than in isolation. However, these tests generally tell us very little about the student's mastery of contextual skills.

Generally, oral reading tests are used as diagnostic measures of the student's ability to utilize contextual information in identifying unfamiliar words. In this instance, the student reads a passage orally while the examiner notes the student's oral reading errors on an identical passage. Using a predetermined marking system, the examiner notes oral reading errors such as regressions, repetitions, substitutions, mispronunciations, errors of confabulation, and so on. In terms of contextual identification, substitutions and confabulations are of most interest. Substitutions are evidenced when the student substitutes for a word in the text another word that is contextually correct. Replacing "home" for "house" is an example of a substitution error. Errors of confabulation are more serious and involve replacing words in text with words that are not contextually correct, for example, "three" for "there." Thus, oral reading tests measure a number of skills, among which is contextual abstraction.

An excellent example of a diagnostic instrument along these lines is the *Reading Miscue Inventory* (Goodman and Burke, 1972). However the RMI is an individualized and rather complex instrument that requires considerable expertise on the part of the examiner and, therefore, is of limited value to the classroom teacher. The classroom teacher can, on the other hand, construct less complex measures for diagnosing contextual identification skills. Using a cloze test as described by Bormuth (1962) and discussed in the chapter on readability, the teacher can gain much valuable diagnostic information. Harris and Sipay (1975:173) recommend the following scoring procedure for analyzing student errors in oral reading:

1. Count as one miscue each: (a) any response that deviates from the printed text and disrupts the intended meaning; (b) any word pronounced for the student after a five-second hesitation.
2. Count as one-half miscue each: any response that deviates from the printed text but does not disrupt the intended meaning.
3. Count as a total of one miscue, regardless of the number of times the behavior occurs: (a) repeated substitutions such as "a" for "the"; (b) repetitions.
4. Do not count as miscues: (a) miscues that conform to cultural or regional dialects; (b) self-corrections made within five seconds; (c) hesitations; (d) ignoring or misinterpreting punctuation marks.
5. Count repeated errors on the same word as only one miscue, regardless of the type of error made.

Harris and Sipay go on to say that two or three miscues per 100 words indicates that the reading material can be read independently by the student. When miscues reach the level of five to ten percent, the material is probably too difficult for independent reading but still appropriate with proper instructional guidance. Miscue rates above ten percent indicate the material is too difficult. After scoring miscues, the teacher should endeavor to examine the nature of the miscues in order to determine patterns of error. The following questions point up the nature of the diagnostic observations we should attempt to make regarding skill in contextual abstraction:

- When the student makes an oral reading error, to what extent is meaning preserved?
- What difficulty level (readability) of materials can the student effectively use context clues with?

- Does the student know the concept of context, but simply fails to use it during reading?

In using oral reading passages to assess contextual abstraction abilities, it is imporant that the teacher use passages of well-defined difficulty level. Oral reading tests that include passages over a range of reading levels include:

1. *Analytical Reading Inventory.* An individually administered test comprised of three sets of graded passages across readability levels 1.5 to 8.5 (Charles Merrill Publishing Company).
2. *Classroom Reading Inventory.* An individually administered test containing three sets of graded passages across eight grade levels (William Brown Publishing Company).
3. *Gilmore Oral Reading Tests.* An individual test of oral reading with passages across grade levels 1–8 (Harcourt Brace Jovanovich).
4. *Gray Oral Reading Test.* An individually administered test of oral reading passages across grades 1–12 (Bobbs-Merrill Publishing Company).

The *Word Guessing Test: Part II* (Friedman, 1976) also measures contextual abstraction skills. It is an adaptation of the cloze procedure. It should be noted, however, that validity, reliability, and objectivity have been established for the *Word Guessing Test: Part II* whereas validity, reliability, and objectivity have not been established for most adaptations of the cloze technique.

Here is the introduction of the *Word Guessing Test: Part II.*

In this test you read a story in which some of the words are missing. You are to guess the words that belong in the blank spaces. Every blank space is numbered, and there is a blank space in the column on the right side of the page with the same number. You are to write *one* word that you think belongs in the blank space in the story in the column where you see the same number.

Here is an example:

A crow is __1__ noisy bird. You can	1. _____
__2__ his caw when __3__ take a walk in the	2. _____
woods. He caws just __4__ fun, but he also	3. _____
hopes a lady __5__ will hear him.	4. _____
	5. _____

Vocabulary Knowledge

Many tests measure vocabulary knowledge, but there are a number of limitations to these tests when we look at the information they yield from a diagnostic viewpoint. First, vocabulary tests sample a limited number of vocabulary words in comparison to the number of words that comprise the English language. Second, tests seldom present a rationale for sampling one particular set of, for example, fifty words as opposed to some other set of fifty words. Third, as in the example given of the Basic Reading Vocabulary test in the first part of this chapter, some vocabulary tests tend to measure knowledge of words that appear very infrequently in print. Fourth, once we know, for example, that a student can identify forty out of fifty words on a vocabulary test, this provides little indication as to what should be done for the student instructionally.

Finally, vocabulary knowledge is measured in many different ways. One test may present a stimulus word and ask the student to pick from a set of four additional words the word that means the same or nearly the same as the stimulus word. Other tests present stimulus words in context and require the student to perform the same task. Still other tests present a sentence with a word deleted and ask the student to choose from a set of words the word that correctly completes the sentence. Thus, depending upon how vocabulary knowledge is measured by a particular test, we may obtain measures of a wide range of skills associated with word identification and vocabulary knowledge, including comprehension.

From a diagnostic standpoint, vocabulary tests that require students to deal with the relationships among words through categorization activities are of diagnostic utility. Two examples of such tests are presented below.

1. *Durrell Reading-Listening Series*. This test is available at several different levels and therefore uses pictures instead of words at lower levels. The student is presented a series of vocabulary words followed by three categories: his or her task is to assign each vocabulary word to the proper category. Separate test sections measure this ability when words are read to the student and when the student must read the words. This ability is also measured using sentences instead of single vocabulary items (Harcourt Brace Jovanovich).

2. *Differential Aptitude Test of Verbal Reasoning*. This is a

higher-level test that presents students with a pair of vocabulary items, then a third item for which the student must
choose a fourth word that demonstrates the same relationship demonstrated in the first pair. An example of the format
used might be: "dinner" is to "night" as "breakfast" is to
_____ (Psychological Corporation).

Tests such as these require the student to make categorical
identifications by means of abstraction categories. In the first
example, the student is provided the category and asked to place a
vocabulary item in the correct category. In the second example,
the student must abstract on the basis of the relationship between
and among words. He or she must identify a category that encompasses both "dinner" and "breakfast," then understand the relationship between "dinner" and "night," and, finally, abstract a
new category through contextual abstraction and identify a fourth
vocabulary item that fits the new category.

DIAGNOSING READING COMPREHENSION

There is a wealth of tests available that can be used to diagnose
reading comprehension. Basically, the teacher's task in diagnosing reading comprehension is twofold: (1) to determine the extent
to which the student has mastered the various comprehension
skills; and (2) to determine the reading comprehension level of
the student so that the teacher can place the student in materials
of appropriate difficulty.

Since the skills of reading comprehension are variously defined
and emphasized instructionally, reading comprehension tests reflect and measure a wide diversity of skills. Ultimately, the choice
of a particular reading comprehension test depends upon the content being taught and the objectives in teaching the content.
From a diagnostic standpoint, the choice of an appropriate reading
comprehension test (or tests) depends upon which comprehension skills are either prerequisite to successfully learning the new
content or which comprehension skills are to be taught with the
new content. Choosing an appropriate diagnostic test, then, is a
matter of matching the comprehension skills that are measured
by the test to those that are required in learning the new content.

Traditionally, we have used reading comprehension tests to establish students' reading grade levels. Johnson and Kress (1965)
define three reading comprehension levels: independent, instruc-

tional, and frustration. According to Johnson and Kress, the independent reading level is the grade level of reading materials the student can read with approximately 90 percent comprehension and no instructional guidance. The instructional level of reading comprehension is the grade level of reading materials the student can read with approximately 75 percent comprehension; this implies that the student can deal successfully with materials at his or her instructional level with appropriate instructional guidance. Finally, the frustration reading level is the grade level of reading materials that the student simply cannot effectively deal with either in an independent reading situation or with the teacher's help.

Most reading comprehension tests yield a reading grade level. The factor that separates tests in this respect is the accuracy with which they assess the reading grade level of the student. Individually administered diagnostic reading comprehension tests generally are more accurate in this respect than are group administered comprehension tests. However, to give an individualized test to all students, or even several students, is time consuming and expensive.

There are many informal tests available to assess reading comprehension level, and they appear to be at least as accurate as standardized group reading comprehension tests, and often are more accurate. If the purpose of giving students a test is to establish their reading comprehension levels, then an informal comprehension test may be just as appropriate as published diagnostic and survey reading tests. In fact, the content area teacher may do well to construct his or her own diagnostic reading comprehension test based on the material the student will be reading in that content area. In this way, the content area teacher may develop an instrument that will yield much better predictions as to how well students will be able to deal with the content being taught and the materials being used. In this instance, we refer you to a guide in constructing informal measures by Johnson and Kress entitled *Informal Reading Inventories* (International Reading Association).

In any event, there is a wide range of reading comprehension tests available that are useful in establishing comprehension levels. More diagnostically oriented tests yield estimates of independent, instructional, and frustration levels of reading. More group oriented (or survey) comprehension tests yield only one grade level score, which is commonly thought to be primarily an estimate of the students' frustration reading level. Below is a list of several examples of reading comprehension tests and tests that contain subtests of comprehension.

Individualized Reading Comprehension Tests

1. *Analytical Reading Inventory*. Contains three sets of graded passages from 1.5 to 8.5 readability grade levels (Charles Merrill Publishing Company).
2. *Classroom Reading Inventory*. Contains three sets of graded reading passages across eight grade levels (William C. Brown).
3. *Durrell Analysis of Reading Difficulty*. Contains reading passages at grade levels one through six, testing reading comprehension by means of free recall and traditional comprehension questions (Harcourt Brace Jovanovich).
4. *Spache Diagnostic Reading Scales*. Contains twenty-two reading passages across grades one through eight (California Test Bureau).
5. *Woodcock Reading Mastery Tests*. Contains a battery of individually administered tests including sentence comprehension (American Guidance Service).

Group Reading Comprehension Tests

1. *California Reading Tests*. Contains several levels, including grades six to twelve, with a vocabulary subtest and a comprehension subtest at each level (California Test Bureau).
2. *Davis Reading Test*. Contains two levels, grades eight to eleven and grades eleven to thirteen; yields scores of level of comprehension and rate of comprehension (Psychological Corporation).
3. *Diagnostic Reading Tests*. Contains levels including grades four to eight and seven to college. Some subtests are group oriented while others are individually administered, yielding scores for silent comprehension, general reading rate, and rate of reading in science and social studies (Committee on Diagnostic Reading Tests).
4. *Durrell Reading-Listening Series*. Contains intermediate and advanced levels covering grades three through nine, and yields vocabulary and science comprehension scores for both reading and listening (Harcourt Brace Jovanovich).
5. *Gates-MacGinitie Reading Tests*. Contains upper levels covering grades four through twelve; yields measures of

vocabulary, comprehension, and speed and accuracy (Teachers Publishing, MacMillan).

6. *Iowa Silent Reading Test*. Contains three levels covering grades six to college; the first two levels include subtests of vocabulary and reading comprehension (Harcourt Brace Jovanovich).

7. *Iowa Tests of Educational Development*. Designed for use in grades nine through twelve; yields a reading score based on vocabulary and comprehension of science, social studies, and literature materials (Science Research Associates).

8. *McGraw-Hill Basic Skills System*. Designed for use in grades eleven to fourteen; yields measures of vocabulary in subject matter areas and comprehension (California Test Bureau).

9. *Monroe Standardized Silent Reading Tests*. Contains levels that include grades six to high school; yields scores for rate of comprehension (Bobbs-Merrill).

10. *Nelson-Denny Reading Test*. Designed for use in grades nine to twelve; yields measures of vocabulary and comprehension (Houghton Mifflin).

11. *Nelson Reading Test*. Designed for use up to grade nine, yielding scores for paragraph comprehension (Houghton Mifflin).

12. *New Developmental Reading Tests*. A battery of tests including tests designed for use in grades four through six that assess reading for information, reading for relationships, interpretive reading, and creative reading (Lyons Carnahan Publishing Company).

13. *Reading/Everyday Activities in Life*. Designed to be used with grades five to adult. Consists of nine reading measures of functional literacy (California Press).

14. *SRA Assessment Survey: Reading*. Contains levels that cover grades six through nine, yielding measures of vocabulary and comprehension (Science Research Associates).

15. *Stanford Diagnostic Reading Test*. Contains levels for use up to ninth grade; yields vocabulary and comprehension scores (Harcourt Brace Jovanovich).

16. *Stanford Reading Tests*. Contains levels for use up to tenth grade with measures of vocabulary and comprehension (Harcourt Brace Jovanovich).

17. *Traxler High School Reading Test*. Designed for grades ten through twelve; measures comprehension of easy ma-

       terial and finding main ideas of factual reading material
       (Bobbs-Merrill).
18. *Traxler Silent Reading Test*. Designed for use with grades
       seven to ten and measures word meaning and paragraph
       meaning (Bobbs-Merrill).

The tests listed above are not meant to be an exhaustive listing
of reading comprehension tests. There are many more reading
comprehension tests available. We have purposely not included
achievement tests that measure a variety of skills in different
areas, most of which contain measures of vocabulary and reading
comprehension.

It becomes clear that typical reading comprehension tests do
not measure all the comprehension skills we considered in chapter 6. To find published tests which contain items that measure
specific comprehension skills you must first identify the skill you
wish to measure and survey various tests until you find a corresponding section that measures the comprehension skill. In chapter 6 we described the skill or reasoning process that students
employ to answer particular questions. Understanding the relationship between a particular reasoning process and the kind of
questions that probe for the comprehension skill will enable you to
find appropriate test items in published tests that measure the
skill. It will be helpful to locate the comprehension skill you want
to teach in chapter 6 before searching for published test items to
measure it.

DIAGNOSING STUDY SKILLS

In our chapter on study skills, we discussed reading rate, reading flexibility, locating information, and organizing information
as aspects of the broad area of study skills. Additionally, the student's ability to read a variety of materials such as graphs, charts,
maps, and so on is considered an index of his or her study skills.
Many tests we have already mentioned contain subtests of study
skills. Below is a list of tests of study skills as well as study skill
checklists.

1. *EDL Reading Versatility Tests*. Contains several levels that
    range from fifth grade to college; yields measures of skim-
    ming, scanning, and reading fiction and nonfiction (Educa-
    tional Developmental Laboratories).
2. *Iowa Silent Reading Test*. Contains two levels with mea-

sures of directed reading and reading efficiency (Harcourt Brace Jovanovich).

3. *Iowa Test of Basic Skills.* Contains several levels that include subtests of map reading, reading graphs and tables, and knowledge and use of reference materials (Houghton Mifflin).

4. *McGraw-HIll Basic Skills System.* Includes measures of skimming and scanning, underlining techniques, and use of library (Science Research Associates).

5. *Study Habits Checklist.* Provides information about thirty-seven study skills and study habits (Science Research Associates).

6. *Study Habits Inventory.* A checklist of twenty-eight study skills and study habits (Stanford University Press).

7. *Spitzer Study Skills Test.* Provides measures of dictionary use, use of indexes, reading graphs and tables, map reading, use of information sources, and notetaking (World Book Company).

8. *Tyler-Kimberly Study Skills Inventory.* Designed for use in grades nine to college; yields measures of use of reference materials, card catalogues, the index, and interpreting maps and graphs (Consulting Psychologists Press).

DIAGNOSING READING POTENTIAL

We have, up to this point, discussed many tests of word identification abilities and reading comprehension that can be used to make diagnostic observations. The purpose of making these observations, we said, was to pinpoint specific reading skills students have mastered, need practice in, or have not mastered. In turn, this knowledge could be used to plan instruction in reading.

Many of the test instruments we have mentioned are used for additional purposes. One common use of test instruments in reading is to assign students to appropriate instructional programs. Based on his performance on a reading test, Johnny might subsequently be assigned to accelerated classes in one or more content areas, or content classes designed for the "average" or "slow" student. Depending upon the student's grade level and the availability of specialized reading programs, he might be assigned to "remedial" reading programs.

By definition, a remedial reader is a student who has a high potential for reading indicated by normal or above-average intelligence, but who is significantly retarded in reading ability. The degree of reading retardation the student must exhibit in order to be considered a remedial reader varies but is commonly considered to be two or more grade levels with students in the upper grades. The student in a remedial reading program receives instruction in the basic word identification and comprehension skills in a setting in which he or she can obtain more direct instruction from the teacher. The basic aim of the remedial reading program is to re-teach those basic skills the student either missed or failed to master, then to return the student to the regular classroom.

When we go about the task of identifying those students who are to go into a remedial reading program, our task is twofold: (1) to identify those students who are significantly retarded in reading but (2) who have a high potential for learning to read and growing in reading skill. In essence, we are predicting that these students will be the ones who will benefit most from remedial reading instruction.

Many of the tests we have already cited can be used in assessing the degree of reading retardation that a student has. Traditionally, intelligence tests have been used to assess reading potential. Harris and Sipay (1975), as well as many others, discuss a number of formuli that use reading and intelligence test scores in computing reading expectancy or reading potential.

In using intelligence test scores to estimate a student's reading expectancy or reading potential, we encounter several problems. First, many intelligence tests (especially group intelligence tests) require the student to read in order to perform well. Farr (1969) points out that these tests are little more than reading tests themselves. If we use intelligence tests like these to estimate a student's potential for reading, we are committing a logical error. On the other hand, if we use individualized intelligence tests to estimate a student's reading potential, we ultimately estimate reading potential based on the student's mastery of many intellectual skills that are only slightly related to reading ability. In either instance, we may not have a valid estimate of the student's reading potential.

Many specialists in the area of reading education recommend tests of listening comprehension as more valid estimates of a student's reading expectancy or potential. These tests are nothing more than silent reading tests administered orally; that is, the examiner reads passages to the student and assesses the student's listening comprehension of those passages. In this way, a student who is placed in the eighth grade, but who is reading on the sixth grade level, may be found to have a reading potential in excess of his or her reading level. Many times we find that reading-retarded students have a potential to read well above their grade placement. In the example of the eighth grader, he or she may well have a reading potential as measured by the listening comprehension test of tenth grade. By using a listening comprehension test to assess reading potential, we gain information about the student's level of comprehension of oral language which involves many of the same skills reading comprehension requires.

A number of oral reading tests that we have already cited are useful in assessing listening comprehension. Individualized reading diagnostic tests that contain passages of well-defined readability are also useful in assessing listening comprehension. Below are examples of several tests that can be used to measure the student's listening comprehension.

1. *Analytical Reading Inventory.* Contains three sets of graded passages across readability grade levels 1.5 to 8.5 (Charles Merrill).
2. *Classroom Reading Inventory.* Contains three sets of graded passages across eight grade levels (William C. Brown).
3. *Diagnostic Reading Tests.* Upper levels of this test include subtests of auditory comprehension (Committee on Diagnostic Reading Tests).
4. *Durrell Analysis of Reading Difficulty.* Contains reading passages for assessing listening comprehension across six grade levels (Harcourt Brace Jovanovich).
5. *Durrell Reading Listening Series.* Yields measures of listening vocabulary and listening comprehension of sentences (Harcourt Brace Jovanovich).
6. *Brown-Carlsen Listening Comprehension Test.* Designed for use in grades 9 to 13 to measure comprehension of spoken English (Harcourt Brace Jovanovich).
7. *Spache Diagnostic Reading Scales.* Contains sets of reading passages across eight grade levels, some of which are designed to assess listening comprehension (California Test Bureau).

DIAGNOSING PREDICTIVE ABILITY

We have emphasized the importance of predictive ability throughout the book. The Predictive Ability Test (Friedman, 1974) tests for this ability. A sample item followed by the answer is included in figure 11–2. The Predictive Ability Test is a nonverbal index of intelligence and learning potential. Because the respondent does not need to read to take the test, it can be used to estimate a person's reading comprehension potential. Although the *Predictive Ability Test* is objective and validity and reliability have been established for the test, the present form has been validated for persons seventeen years of age and older only.

DIAGNOSING READING IN THE CONTENT AREAS

We have in this chapter discussed a number of reading skill areas and described procedures for diagnosing student's abilities in these areas. Often, however, these procedures do not give a

PART III

DIRECTIONS:

On each of the pages in this section, you will see groups of pictures that can be arranged to show a correct order of events. On the top of each page you will see a picture of a beginning event on the far left and a picture of an outcome event on the far right. There are also a number of blank spaces in between. Some of the items have three blank spaces, and some have four blank spaces.

From the pictures shown on the lower portion of the page you are to fill in the blank spaces by selecting and ordering those pictures that lead from the beginning event to the outcome event. Each item has either two or three extra pictures that do not belong in the correct order.

SAMPLE ITEM:

Turn to page 8. At the top and far left of the page is Picture A which shows a boy about to make a high jump. Picture A represents the beginning event. On the far right is Picture F which shows the boy after he has made the jump. Picture F is the outcome event. Between the beginning and outcome events you see four spaces labeled B, C, D, and E.

Now examine the six numbered pictures on the lower portion of the page and select and order the four pictures that will show the way the boy could complete the high jump. In the spaces labeled B, C, D, and E, place the numbers of the four pictures in the correct order. The correct order would be Picture 1, then Picture 3, then Picture 6, and then Picture 2.

If all of your answers were correct for the sample item, it would be marked like the sample item on page 9. Turn to page 9 to see how the correct answers would appear.

Now turn to page 10.

FIGURE 11–2   Predictive Ability Test

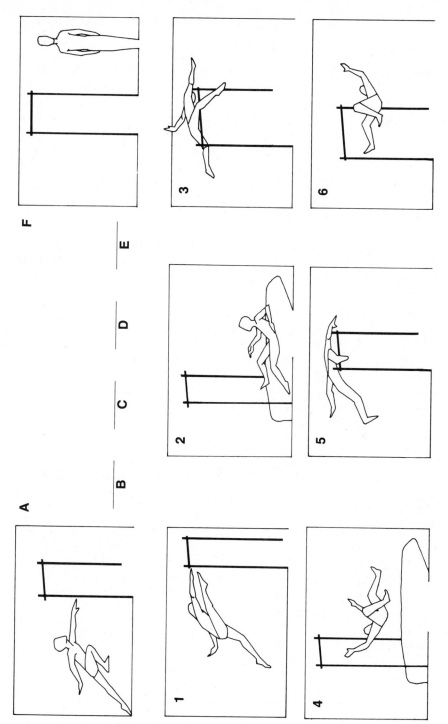

FIGURE 11–2 Predictive Ability Test (continued)

clear picture of how students function with the kinds of instructional materials they encounter in content areas. It is a difficult
task, for example, to find a published test that measures precisely
the map reading skills required in a particular social studies
course. If the teacher attempts to locate various published tests
that will be useful in diagnosing the range of reading skills necessary to effective reading and learning in the content areas, the list
could become quite lengthy and ultimately involve the teacher in
too much testing. For these reasons, we suggest informal content
reading inventories for diagnosing student progress in relevant
reading skill areas.

In constructing the informal content reading inventory, the
teacher should draw samples of reading materials and tasks from
the textbook and other materials being used in the content area.
By constructing the inventory around the actual instructional
materials being used and the tasks required of students, the inventory becomes a valid measure and predictor of student performance in the particular content area. The informal content
reading inventory, then, is an excellent device to use for determining quickly which students can be expected to have serious
difficulties with the textbook as well as determining what particular reading skills important in the content area individual students have or have not mastered.

Constructing the Informal Content Reading Inventory

Test Material

Choose a reading passage from the textbook being used in your
content area, and develop the test around it. A passage of about
three to four pages in length that is representative of the entire
textbook should be chosen. Other textbook materials such as
maps, graphs, index, and so on will also be utilized in the informal
content reading inventory.

Reading and Thinking Skills

The informal content reading inventory should be designed to
test for the student's ability to perform a variety of comprehension
and thinking skills. Obviously, the teacher cannot test for every
comprehension and thinking skill, so the teacher should select
those skills that are most important to successfully learning the

content he or she teaches. For example, a skill such as "identifying character traits and motives" is not a particularly important comprehension skill in math or science; it is a very important skill in English. The following list of specific skills should be included in the informal content reading inventory regardless of what content area it is used in:

- vocabulary and the ability to understand new vocabulary terms presented in content reading materials
- recalling specific facts, details, names, dates, and so forth
- following directions
- inferring details
- identifying supportive information and details
- getting the main idea
- predicting outcomes
- using parts of a book
- using reference and resource materials

Dependent on the content area, additional skills such as "reading maps, graphs, and charts," "identifying character traits and motives," or "identifying author's purpose and mood" may be included in the informal content reading inventory.

Guidelines in Constructing and Interpreting the Inventory

For each skill being tested, construct a minimum of five questions to assess the skill. In the above skill listing, skills one through seven can be tested using the reading selection chosen from the textbook. Skills eight and nine will necessarily involve parts of the textbook beyond the reading selection chosen for the test.

Inventory test questions can be written out and assembled in a short test booklet, written on the blackboard, or read orally to students after they have completed the reading selection in the text. If questions are read orally, they should be read at least twice and repeated if students request. Page references in the textbook should be included with those questions that require the student to read and interpret, for example, a map or graph contained in another part of the text.

An informal inventory is considered to be a formative diagnostic-progress test which is used to determine whether a student has mastered an instructional activity. As a rule of thumb, when the student gets 80 percent of the items correct on a diagnostic-progress test he is considered to have mastered the corresponding instructional activity and is ready to advance in his learning. When students get fewer than 80 percent of the test items correct it indicates that they need corrective instruction. After the corrective instruction they are tested again for mastery. In chapter 14 we describe further diagnostic-progress testing.

A record-keeping device that is often used in diagnostic testing is the skills chart that utilizes symbols indicating complete mastery ($\oplus$), partial mastery requiring review ($+$), and nonmastery ($-$). An example of such a skills chart is illustrated by figure 11–3.

DIAGNOSING SOCIAL RELATIONS, SELF-CONFIDENCE, AND INTERESTS

Classroom Social Relations

We know through research that the social climate of the classroom has a great effect on the learning that goes on in the classroom. Research has shown that students who have good friends among other students in the classroom tend to have better attitudes toward school and toward learning, tend to have better self-concepts, and tend to do better in school than students who have no friends or who are actively disliked. It appears, then, that the teacher should attempt to assess these patterns of social interaction so as to insure that students receive social and emotional support from other classrooom members.

Social interaction in the classroom is not an easy entity to measure and requires astute judgment on the part of the teacher. Few standardized instruments are available for the diagnosis of social relations in the classroom. Much of the diagnostic information available in this respect comes from the teacher's own interaction with and observation of students in the teaching-learning situation. Diagnosing social interactions in the classroom requires answering questions such as these:

- Which pupils have no friends in class? Which pupils have many friends in class? Which pupils are actively disliked by other class members?
- Why do some students have no friends? Why are some students actively disliked?
- Which students have the most influence over the group? What gives these students this influence?

SUBJECT	GRADE	SECTION	YEAR	SEMESTER	TEACHER

Name	General Reading Ability	Skills from Informal Content Reading Inventory											Comments
	Vocabulary Comprehension Study Skills	Vocabulary	Literal recall	Following directions	Inferring details	Supporting information	Main ideas	Conclusions	Predicting outcomes	Using book parts	Using references		

⊕ = Skill mastered   + = Need review in skill   − = Need to be taught skill

FIGURE 11–3 Class analysis chart

- What students are perceived by other class members as good students? As poor students? On what basis are these judgments made?

The teacher can construct a variety of informal diagnostic instruments that answer these questions. Listed below are ideas the teacher might use in constructing instruments to assess the classroom social environment.

1. Assessing the student's personal feelings about other class members.

   - Ask the student which three classmates he likes best; which three he likes the least.

   - Ask the student how many students in the class she knows well; how many she likes a great deal.

   - Ask the student who he likes best; who he would most like to work with given the opportunity.

2. Assessing the student's ideas about the perceptions of other class members.

   - Ask the student which three people are best able to get others to do things; which three people most often do things for other class members.

   - Ask the student which three people are most cooperative; least cooperative.

   - Ask the student which three people could improve their school work the most, if they wanted to.

   - Ask the student who she would most like to be if she couldn't be herself and had to be someone else in the class.

By analyzing the information that these questions yield, the teacher can begin to understand the social nature of the classroom. Close observation of students in group situations will also yield valuable information along these lines. Once the teacher has gained information regarding the social structure of the classroom, there are a number of ways he or she can use this information to adjust grouping and work patterns, as well as other factors, in order to restructure the social environment and change students' attitudes toward one another.

To begin with, the teacher can develop an inventory of students that shows specific skills and abilities that various students have. In this way, students learn more about one another and expand and broaden students' standards for acceptable and desirable assets. If, for example, Johnny is negatively perceived by other class members, this perception can be changed once the group learns that Johnny has a fishing trophy.

The teacher can also restructure in-class grouping patterns and work assignments to insure that pupils who have been neglected or rejected by the group have an opportunity to interact and participate in group activities. The assignment of rejected pupils to positions of leadership in the group or positions of responsibility in the group is another method of insuring that these pupils have the opportunity to interact and participate with other class members. The teacher can also select those students who are positively perceived by other class members and who are influential in the group to be peer tutors and helpers. This insures that low status class members have an opportunity to interact with pupils of higher social status. The teacher must, however, be cautious and not force interaction in this way. Furthermore, when the teacher establishes groups and subgroups of students, he or she should be cautious and insure that antagonism does not develop between groups; wholesome competition can be used to modify feelings of antagonism. Restructuring groups is another alternative open to the teacher in this respect.

Self-Confidence

We have discussed the importance of the students' sense of worth and their sense of their own ability to succeed as important factors in optimizing learning. Generally, these kinds of factors are measured with personality tests, self-concept inventories, and a multitude of other observation instruments that require clinical expertise on the part of the examiner.

There are a number of informal methods that the teacher can use in gaining information about students' self-confidence and self-concepts. One such method utilizes open-ended sentences that students complete themselves. For example, the teacher might present students with a number of open-ended sentences like the following and have the students complete them.

- What I like most of all is . . .
- My teacher thinks that I am . . .
- Other kids in class think that I . . .

- Sometimes I wish that . . .
- I am happy when . . .
- One of the things I dislike most is . . .
- One of the things I like most is . . .

The students' responses to open-ended questions such as these provide the teacher most useful information about how the students view themselves, how they think others see them, and particular things that might be troubling the students. Open-ended questions like these can also be used to assess reading interests and attitudes toward reading:

- Reading is . . .
- I have the most trouble reading . . .
- The thing I like to read about most is . . .
- Sometimes when I read I . . .
- My favorite school subject is . . .

Other informal methods of gaining information about students' self-confidence and self-concepts can be used. One such method utilizes descriptive adjectives; the students' task is to indicate which words describe them best. For example, students could be given a list of such descriptive adjectives and asked to tell which apply to them most of the time, part of the time, or practically none of the time. Descriptive adjectives the teacher might use in constructing such an instrument might include honest, friendly, good, bad, cheerful, warm, cold, smart, courteous, polite, lazy, helpful, popular, selfish, and so on.

Reading Interests

Diagnosing reading interests is an important aspect of diagnosis in general. Oftentimes, capitalizing on students' interests and providing related reading materials is the only reasonable course of action in promoting reading with retarded and reluctant readers. Many of the techniques we described for gaining information about the classroom social environment and self-concept can be used in determining students' reading interests. Below are examples of additional formats for reading interest inventories you may wish to use with your own students.

Checklists

Checklists are normally a listing of interest areas, specific themes and topics, book titles, and so on. Most often, the student responds to individual checklist items by checking blanks like "like," "indifferent," and "dislike." Some examples are presented below.

General Interest: 1. Mystery Stories ____ like ____ indifferent ____ dislike
Specific Topics: 2. Sports ____ like ____ indifferent ____ dislike
Specific Books: 3. Books like *The Outsiders* ____ like ____ indifferent ____ dislike

Annotated Fictitious Titles

This is a procedure for tapping students' reading interests in which the teacher makes up a number of fictitious book titles and provides a sentence or two explanation of what the book is about. An inventory using this procedure should use fairly mundane book titles and cover many, many interest areas. Each title is followed by a rating system like the one described above. Examples could include:

1. *The Forest Family* This is a book about how a family living in New York City decides to go to the country and live as people did 200 years ago.
2. *The Boy Who Never Said "Uncle"* This is a story of a fifteen-year-old boy who is faced with supporting his family after the death of his father.
3. *The Hobby Book* This is a collection of "how-to-do-it" articles about such hobbies as knitting, weaving, coin collecting, rock collecting, model building, and more than 100 more hobbies.

Open-Ended Questions

These inventories present the student with a number of incomplete sentences or open-ended questions that the student must complete or answer in writing (can be done orally in an interview format). Often, these inventories reveal many things about students the teacher might not learn otherwise. However, they require a good deal of interpretation on the part of the teacher.

Examples include:

1. School is . . .
2. I hate it when . . .
3. Most of all I want . . .
4. At home . . .
5. When I grow up I . . .
6. I usually read . . .
7. I'm different from other kids because . . .
8. I know I can . . .

Other Inventory Methods

There are many additional ways of assessing students' reading interests. The casual interview in which the teacher asks the students about books they like/dislike, as well as other interest areas, is probably the most effective since it communicates to the students that the teacher is interested in them. An excellent procedure is for the teacher to take a book from the library the students might be interested in and give it to the students, asking them to look it over and see what they think. Other techniques include book presentations by the teacher in class, having students complete book evaluation forms, having students list favorite and disliked books, asking students what they are reading now or what the last book was that they read voluntarily, and many more.

Quizzing students about favorite television shows, movies, and other activities also provides information useful in making inferences about students' interest areas. The teacher should also consult school and public librarians about which books are borrowed most often. Librarians are an excellent source of information regarding the reading interests of students.

SUMMARY

1. *Diagnosing sight word identification skills*. Few tests attempt to measure this skill, probably because informal tests are easily constructed by the teacher from basic sight word vocabulary lists. We advance a seven-step procedure for testing sight word identification and mention three published tests that include subtests of this skill.

2. *Diagnosing phonic identification skills*. Answers to the following questions assist us in diagnosing phonic identification skills: (a) Does the student possess the concept that letters represent sounds? (b) What is the extent and quality of the student's knowledge of sound-symbol correspondence? (c) Where in the word does the student fail to use phonic analysis skills—initial, medial, final? (d) Does the student exhibit a pattern of phonic identification errors? Ten tests are described that include measures of phonic identification skills.

3. *Diagnosing structural identification skills*. The diagnosis of structural identification skills ranges from diagnosing decoding skills to structural abstraction skills. In diagnosing structural identification skills we should attempt to answer the following questions: (a) What is the extent and quality of the student's knowledge of compound words? (b) What is the extent and quality of the student's knowledge of inflected and derived forms? (c) Is the student able to isolate discrete sound units (syllables) in words? (d) Is the student aware of familiar and frequent letter patterns that occur in words? (e) Is he or she able to see the "little words in the big words"? (f) Is the student able to utilize meaning clues contained in prefixes, suffixes, and roots? Eight tests are described that are useful in diagnosing structural identification skills.

4. *Diagnosing contextual identification skills.* Oral reading tests are most useful for diagnosing contextual identification skills. Answers to the following questions are helpful in diagnosing this skill: (a) When a student makes an oral reading error, to what extent is meaning preserved? (b) With what difficulty level (readability) of materials can the student effectively use context clues? (c) Does the student understand the concept of context but simply fail to use it during reading? Five tests are described that are useful in diagnosing contextual identification skills.

5. *Diagnosing vocabulary knowledge.* In diagnosing vocabulary knowledge the teacher determines the extent to which the student understands the meaning(s) of words. Diagnostic tests that require the student to deal with the relationship among words through categorization activities are of diagnostic utility. Two examples of such tests are presented.

6. *Diagnosing reading comprehension.* There are two purposes in diagnosing reading comprehension: (a) to determine the extent to which the student has mastered particular reading comprehension skills; and (b) to determine the reading comprehension level of the student in order to match the student with reading materials of appropriate difficulty. Choosing an appropriate diagnostic test depends upon the teacher's objectives in teaching new content. The comprehension skills measured by a test should correspond to those required to learn the new content. In addition to presenting guidelines for constructing informal content reading tests, we describe five individualized reading comprehension tests and eighteen group reading comprehension tests.

7. *Diagnosing study skills.* The diagnosis of study skills includes diagnosing reading rate and flexibility, the ability to locate and organize information, as well as the ability to read graphs, charts, and other nonverbal symbols. We describe eight tests that are useful in diagnosing various study skills.

8. *Diagnosing reading potential.* The purpose of diagnosing reading potential is to place students into reading instruction programs that will optimize their progress in learning to read. Quite often the diagnosis is to determine whether a student will benefit from a remedial reading program. Such a diagnosis attempts to identify (a) those students who are significantly retarded in reading but (b) who have a high potential for increasing their reading skill. We describe seven tests that are useful in estimating reading comprehension potential.

9. *Diagnosing social relations, self-confidence, and interests.* The purpose of diagnosing social relations, self-confidence, and interests is to determine the personal concerns of students which may enhance or impair learning. We describe ways of assessing social relations among students, their self-confidence, and their interests.

REVIEW QUESTIONS

1. What are the ways of diagnosing sight word identification? What is the purpose of diagnosing sight vocabulary?

2. How may phonic identification skills be diagnosed? What is the purpose of diagnosing phonic identification skills?

3. How can the teacher diagnose structural identification skills? For what purpose does the teacher diagnose structural identification skills?

4. What methods are there for diagnosing contextual abstraction skills? What is the purpose of diagnosing contextual abstraction skills?

5. What tests are used for diagnosing vocabulary knowledge? What is the purpose of diagnosing vocabulary knowledge?

6. How can reading comprehension be diagnosed? Why is it necessary to diagnose reading comprehension?

7. What are the various study skills? How may they be diagnosed? What is the purpose of diagnosing study skills?

8. How may reading potential be diagnosed? What is the purpose of diagnosing reading potential?

9. For what purpose do we diagnose social relations, self-confidence, and interests? How may they be diagnosed?

PART V
PREPARING TO TEACH READING

CHAPTER 12
Establishing Instructional Goals
PURPOSE

1. To show you how to derive desired learning outcomes and instructional goals as a basis for planning reading instruction and instruction in the various content areas.

BACKGROUND AND NEW INFORMATION

You already know what goals are from your everyday experiences and probably have some acquaintance with instructional goals as well. Instructional goals may have been given to you by the instructor of courses you have taken, you may have seen goals statements in course outlines, or you may have learned about instructional goals in the education courses you have taken. The desired learning outcomes listed at the beginning of each chapter in this book are an important element in deriving instructional goals.

The chapter opens with a definition of an instructional goal. The first major section of the chapter concerns deriving desired learning outcomes. In this section we discuss behavior references and content references as elements of desired learning outcome statements. Next, we discuss the types of behavior references included in desired learning outcome statements, preferences, motor skills, and reading and thinking skills. Next we deal with the analysis of behavior, the analysis of content, and the relationship between the two. We then show you how to construct a "table of specifications" for the purpose of deriving desired learning outcomes.

The second major section of the chapter involves deriving instructional goals. We begin this section by discussing the elements of an instructional goal statement and show the importance of each element. The elements of an instructional goal statement are references to (1) the person or manager responsible for achieving the desired learning outcome, (2) the instructional prescription to be selected or developed in order to achieve the desired learning outcome, (3) the student population who is to benefit from learning outcomes, and (4) the desired learning outcome to be achieved. Next we move to a discussion of readiness for learning. We consider readiness with respect to student interests and preferences, motor skills readiness, reading and thinking skills readiness, and content readiness.

KEY TERMS

table of specifications
component or task analysis

DESIRED LEARNING OUTCOMES

The student will be able to

1. Define an instructional goal and write desired learning outcome statements.
2. Enumerate the kinds of behaviors that may be included in a desired learning outcome statement.
3. Analyze content to form a content hierarchy.
4. Analyze behavior for the purpose of stipulating thinking procedures, motor skills, and preferences desired of the learner.
5. Relate behaviors and content to form a table of specifications and derive desired learning outcomes from a table of specifications.
6. Enumerate the elements of an instructional goal statement.
7. Describe the different kinds of learner readiness that must be taken into account as a basis for planning instruction.

If learning is to be purposeful, it must be goal directed. This means that the teacher must select goals to pursue as a basis for instructional planning. *An instructional goal is a commitment to move students with specific readiness characteristics to the achievement of a desired learning outcome.* When a goal is set the implication is that there is a commitment to pursue it and that resources have been appropriated to back up that commitment. A desire or a wish for something is not the same as a goal. A desire is not a goal if there is no intention or effort exerted to fulfill it. The establishment of an instructional goal carries with it a commitment to move students from their present state of readiness to a more advanced state of learning.

In this chapter we present a method for establishing instructional goals as a basis for planning instruction. Since setting goals is necessary in content area instruction as well as in reading instruction our presentation will be diverse. This will enable you to see how the method can be used to establish goals for better content area and reading instruction. In the next two chapters we will apply the method specifically to establishing goals for reading instruction.

DERIVING DESIRED LEARNING OUTCOMES

Before goal statements can be prepared, it is necessary to identify the desired learning outcomes to be achieved. We must now concern ourselves with the specification of learning outcomes as a basis for planning instructional strategies. Not all statements of desired learning outcomes are helpful in planning instruction. Meaningful statements should include (1) a behavior reference and (2) a content reference that together manifest the achievement of the desired learning outcome. The model for writing statements of desired learning outcomes looks like this:

The learner will (1) _____ (2) _____ .
                        (behavior reference)   (content reference)

All such statements may begin with "The learner . . .," or you may wish to refer to a particular kind of learner, for example, "The student in science . . .". In addition, a desired learning outcome statement should refer, if feasible, to an acceptable level of student performance. For instance: The learner will be able to spell correctly (behavior reference) 90 percent of the words on the seventh grade spelling list (content reference). From such a statement it would be possible to determine whether a desired learning outcome was or was not achieved; namely, learning to spell at least 90 percent of the words on the list. Moreover, it provides a reference for designing an instructional intervention to

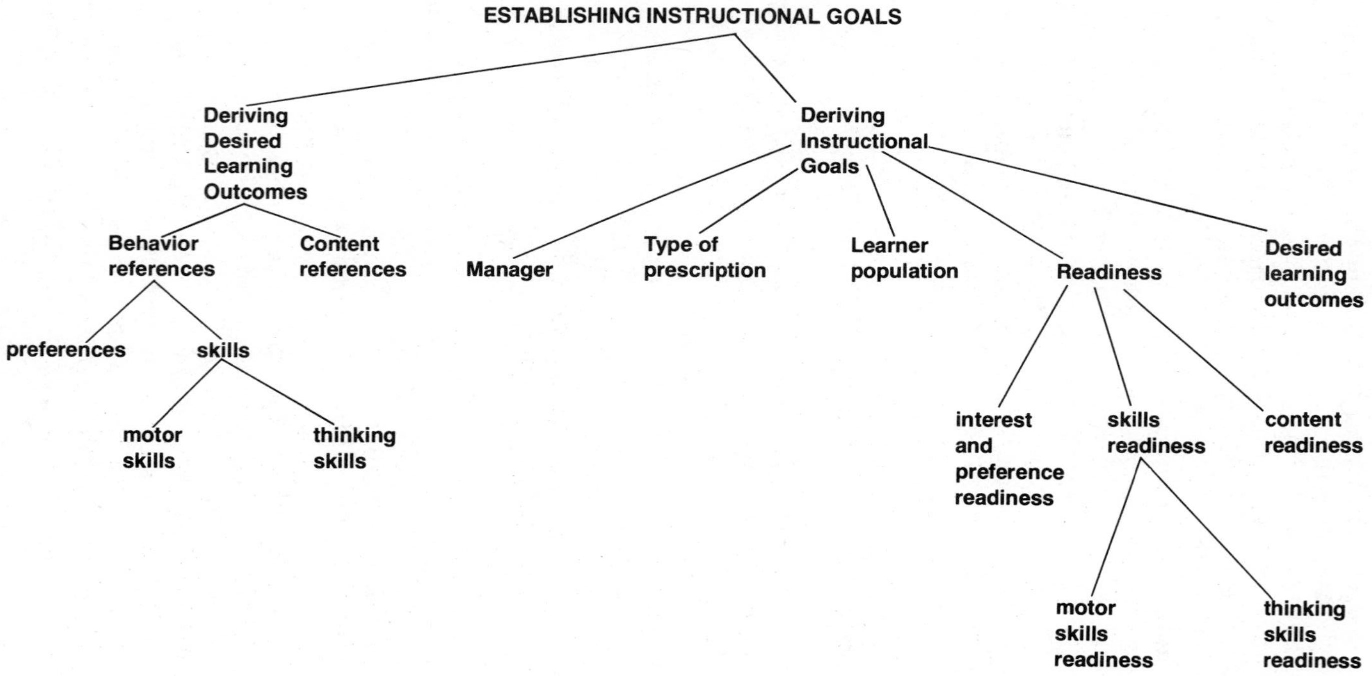

ESTABLISHING INSTRUCTIONAL GOALS

FIGURE 12–1   A hierarchy of topics in chapter 12

produce the desired learning outcome. Instructional planners should understand that they are to design an instructional plan to teach the words on the list.

Preference, Motor Skills, and Thinking Skills

Within this framework, we may specify statements that refer to different kinds of desired learning outcomes. These are changes in preferences and changes in skills. At least two skills can be distinguished: thinking skills and motor skills.

A desired learning outcome statement that pertains to a change in interest is written as follows: The learner will show an increased preference (behavior reference) for reading poetry (content reference). Such a statement implies that an instructional plan will be designed for students who are not interested in reading poetry to familiarize them with it. Afterward, when given a choice between reading poetry and other material, they will at least some of the time choose to read poetry. A change in preference implies a change in interest, thus a change in interest is inferred from a change in preference in a situation that offers a student alternative choices.

Moving to desired learning outcomes that pertain to skills, we may first consider motor skills. Desired learning outcomes that pertain to motor abilities concern the overt motor actions of the learner such as running and participating in sports. Examples of this desired learning outcome are: (1) The learner will be able to play (behavior reference) tennis (content reference). (2) The learner will be able to run a mile in five minutes or less. (3) The learner will be able to perform twenty push-ups. (4) The learner will be able to mold a statue out of clay. (5) The learner will be able to operate a tachistoscopic projector (or reading accelerator, or controlled reader). The content reference in the latter example is to teaching machines used in the teaching of reading.

Thinking skills as we have described them concern identification and prediction. Identification involves understanding similarities and differences. As a result, the individual is able to generalize about events that are similar and discriminate events that are different. An example of a desired learning outcome pertaining to identification is: The learner will be able to identify (behavior reference) examples of short stories (content reference).

Thinking skills pertaining to prediction involve programmatic thought. Knowing that events occur in a programmatic sequence allows the individual to predict that when an earlier event in a sequence occurs a later event will follow. Some desired learning outcome statements pertaining to prediction are: (1) The student will be able to predict what will happen (behavior reference) when an acid and a base are mixed (content reference). (2) The learner will be able to determine (behavior reference) the outcome when oil and water are placed in the same container (content reference). (3) The teacher trainee will be able to determine (behavior reference) the effect of prescribing reading material too difficult for the reader (content reference). (4) The teacher trainee will be able to foretell (behavior reference) the effect of reading material written in a dialect that is unfamiliar to the reader (content reference). Remember, a student may be able to describe a programmatic sequence without being able to use the program in making predictions. Desired learning outcomes that require students to describe sequences pertain to identification, not prediction.

As you can see, most, if not all, of the statements of desired learning outcomes that pertain to skill may begin: "The learner (or student) will be able to . . ." Statements of desired learning outcomes should not be complicated with extraneous additions. This unnecessarily adds to the work and may confuse the person who is attempting to design an instructional plan to achieve the outcome. It is advisable to follow the simple format offered above for composing a desired learning outcome statement.

In education we are concerned with the effectiveness of instruction in producing desired learning outcomes. It is pointless for us to study instruction and learning as separate entities. An instructional intervention is designed to produce a desired learning outcome. Therefore, the effectiveness of the intervention cannot be judged independently of the learning outcome it was designed to produce.

Because desired learning outcome statements include references to both content and behavior, it is necessary to determine the content and behavior you wish to teach in order to formulate desired learning outcomes. We suggest that you make content decisions first and then decide how you want your students to behave with respect to the content. Since content is what we think about, we are suggesting that you determine what you want your students to think about first. Then, determine how you want them to think about the content; that is, the thinking skills you want them to learn, use and apply to the content.

The Analysis of Content

As we said, content topics should not be taught in isolation from one another. Within any content area one topic is related to another. Although a topic may be learned in isolation, learning is enhanced when the student sees the relationship between one topic and another. In addition, if topics are related, the learning of one topic facilitates the learning of the other.

The appropriate way to analyze the relationships among topics in a content area is to derive a representational content hierarchy. We demonstrated how content hierarchies can be established working either inductively or deductively. We suggest now that for the purpose of planning instruction, it is more advantageous to work deductively.

The proper procedure is to first identify the most general reference to the course content you are teaching. In essence, you are identifying the content you intend to teach at the highest level of abstraction. The title of the course is often the most general reference to the content contained in it. Then, working deductively from the general to the specific, derive, level by level, a content hierarchy. You proceed until you reach the concrete level because it is at the concrete level that one can observe actual examples. This relates abstract ideas to tangible reality. Figure 12-2 shows how one proceeds to deduce a content hierarchy for literature. It displays that the most general content reference at the highest level of abstraction is literature. Working deductively, literature is subdivided on the next lower level into prose and poetry. On level 3 prose is subdivided into types of prose—short stories, novels, and so forth.

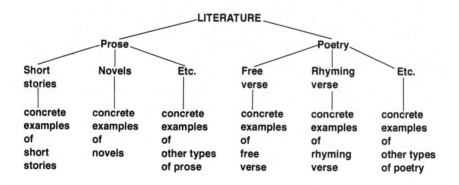

Poetry is subdivided into free verse, rhyming verse, and so on. On level 4 concrete examples of the categories on level 3 are provided. Figure 12–3 is the beginning of the derivation of a content hierarchy for zoology.

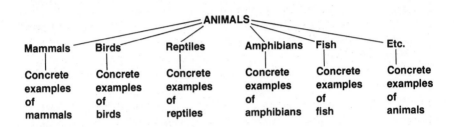

It is important that we again distinguish between an abstraction and an observable event. An abstraction is a label for a group of things that have similar characteristics. A name is given to the category of similar things to identify the abstraction. Abstractions cannot be observed directly. For instance, the term "mammal" denotes an abstraction. The term represents a category of living creatures that have in common such things as hair and mammary glands. However, one cannot observe "mammal" directly. You must observe examples of mammals such as dogs, apes, cats, and humans, and on the basis of their common characteristics identify them as mammals.

Much of what we teach in school is in the form of abstractions. No one has ever observed algebra, zoology, sociology, geography, and so on. In the construction of a learning outcome hierarchy we begin with higher level abstractions, subdivide them into lower level abstractions, and keep subdividing the lower level abstractions until we have reduced the learning outcomes to an observable form. The term animal represents a higher level abstraction, which in our previous example was subdivided into phyla, a lower level abstraction. Phyla were further subdivided into observable examples of the phyla. These examples are observable in that they can be seen to have the characteristics of the phyla. We can observe directly whether or not students know the characteristics of a phyla by asking them to name them. Because an abstraction cannot be observed directly, however, we must infer that a student understands the abstraction. For example, we infer that students know what the abstraction fish means by their ability to describe their common characteristics. Moreover, we infer that a higher level abstraction has been learned by inferring that lower level abstractions representing subdivisions of the higher level abstractions have been learned and the students know the relationship between the lower and higher level abstractions. Continuing with the example, we infer that students have learned what animal means when we establish that they know all about the phyla and their relationship to the higher level abstraction animal.

It is all right to believe that we understand what an abstraction such as patriotism means, but we must understand that patriotism, like other abstractions, cannot be observed directly. It must be inferred from observing such activities as standing and saluting when the flag goes by. Because much of education involves the teaching of abstractions, we need to define the criteria (common characteristics) that denote the learning of each abstraction. Moreover, we must reduce learning outcome hierarchies, which most often begin with higher learning abstractions, to observable forms of behavior.

One way to develop a content hierarchy is to use the textbook you have adopted for your course. The table of contents will reveal the content covered in the text. The more general topics (higher level abstractions) will be designated by the sections of the book. More specific topics will be indicated by the chapters within each section. Still more specific topics will be noted by the divisions and subdivisions of each chapter.

After forming the general content hierarchy from the table of contents, consult the index of the textbook; it will reveal the emphasis placed on each topic. The more listings there are under a heading in the index, the more emphasis the author is placing on the topic. From inspecting the index you will be able to determine when you need to supplement topics that you believe to be underemphasized in the text or when you need to delete a section that overemphasizes a subject. In using your textbook, determine whether the author gives sufficient concrete examples representing the abstraction categories being discussed. If not, you will need to provide additional concrete examples so that your students can better understand what the abstractions mean. Finally, if a teacher's manual accompanies the textbook, it may provide goal statements and/or a summary of the various topics covered in the textbook.

The Analysis of Behavior

The next step for the teacher is to determine the way he or she wants the students to deal with the content. This is a matter of determining the desired student behavior with respect to (1) thinking skills, (2) motor skills, and (3) the exercising of preferences. In this book we have done an elaborate analysis of thinking skills and have presented them in chapter 6. We dealt with preferences and motor skills to a much lesser degree. However, the major focus of the book is on thinking skills. For this reason, we will simply add preferences and motor skills to the thinking skills we discussed so that you will have a list of behaviors to consider. The list of behaviors is shown in the following outline. The skills in the outline will be elaborated and discussed in the next chapter. In this chapter we introduce them for the purpose of showing how behavior and content can be related for the purpose of deriving desired learning outcomes.

SUMMARY OUTLINE OF BEHAVIORS

I. Thinking Skills

    A. Identification skills

        1. Identifying similarities and differences
        2. Identifying concrete events
        3. Identifying through abstraction
            a. identifying through categorizing
            b. hierarchical identification
                (1) identifying through deductive reasoning
                (2) identifying through inductive reasoning
        4. Identifying to test predictions

    B. Prediction skills

        1. Predicting coming events
        2. Predicting the consequences of intervention

II. Motor Skills

III. Preferences

You can use this outline of behaviors when you wish to determine how you want your students to think about any content you are teaching them, the motor skills you want them to be able to perform, and the preferences you want them to develop toward the content. However, you may wish to develop subtypes of motor skills and preferences to specify in greater detail the motor skills and preferences you wish to teach.

Relating Behavior and Content

In the last twenty years, Leslie Briggs, Robert Gagné, Ivor Davies, Robert Glaser, Arthur Melton, and many others have advocated systematic "component analysis" as a means of deriving learning outcomes and tasks. In general, to perform a component analysis one first identifies the terminal learning outcome that is to be achieved. Then one proceeds deductively, level by level, until the most fundamental learning outcomes are derived. The result is a component hierarchy describing the learning outcomes that are to be achieved and their relationship to one another.

According to Davies (1973), component or task analysis is a process that utilizes both analysis and synthesis. That is, in analyzing a particular task, the teacher must first break the task down into its component parts or behaviors, then reassemble them in a logical and coherent manner. The ultimate aim of task analysis is to:

1. Describe the task which the student has to learn.
2. Isolate the required behaviors.
3. Identify the conditions under which the behaviors occur.
4. Determine a criterion of acceptable performance (Davies, 1973:36).

Davies (1973:38) goes on to describe the process of task analysis:

> A task analysis is really an audit and inventory. In it, knowledge, skill, and attitudes are identified and isolated, with the view to ultimately synthesizing them into a hierarchical organization relevant to the writing of a learning prescription. In carrying out such an analysis, the analyst or teacher must consider not only the physical components of the subject (i.e., materials), but also the mental components (procedures, decisions, abstractions).

We agree that component or task analysis is important as a reference for writing desired learning outcome statements and learning prescriptions to achieve these outcomes. However, we do not believe that the analysis of tasks alone is a sufficient basis. The analysis of tasks mainly yields the activities that are to be performed and the relationship between activities in a hierarchy. It is a little too much to expect a task analysis to reveal directly all the preferences, motor skills, and thinking skills to be learned. Nor does a task analysis reveal directly the content that is to be learned and the relationship between pieces of content. Further, we believe that focusing on content results in an overemphasis on teaching content and a neglect in teaching preferences, motor skills, and thinking skills. An overemphasis on the teaching of content may be responsible for the student's tendency to memorize content rather than to think about content in the variety of ways we have described.

We advocate analyzing content separately from analyzing behavior so that we can purposefully decide how we want students to behave and think about the content. By analyzing content and behavior separately at first, we can combine them for the purpose of specifying desired learning outcomes. In this way we can decide not only the content we want students to learn, but, equally important, the ways they are to deal with the content. This is especially important when you consider that the thinking skills we have described can be used to penetrate the content in any area and that most often the variety of thinking skills students may learn are more beneficial than the information they absorb about the content. For this reason we advocate construction of a two-dimensional (behavior by content) table of specifications from which desired learning outcomes can be derived.

The Table of Specifications

We will introduce the table of specifications in this chapter and show you how to use it with respect to reading in the next chapter. Assuming teachers have specified the content they want their students to learn and the behaviors they want their students to perform, they have the ingredients for constructing a two-dimensional table of specifications to integrate behavior and content. The list of topics to be learned would be taken from a content hierarchy after a content analysis had been performed. The list of behaviors might be taken from the list of behaviors on the summary outline of behaviors presented earlier in this chapter. A table of specifications serves as a basis for identifying (1) desired learning outcomes, (2) goals, and (3) test items for evaluating student progress. Table 12-1 is an example of a table of specifications for a course in zoology.

The content hierarchy you intend to teach is placed at the top of the table of specifications. This reminds you to teach the relationship between content and different levels of the content hierarchy. Furthermore, it reminds you that the thinking skills and other behaviors you wish to teach can be related to content at the various levels of the hierarchy. The Xs in the boxes represent the behaviors the teacher has chosen to teach with reference to the various content categories.

Beginning at the top of the content hierarchy, level 1, here are the desired learning outcome statements that would be written.

- The learner will be able to identify animals.
- The learner will be able to predict the behavior of animals.
- The learner will be able to handle and dissect animals.
- The learner will develop an increased preference for the preservation of endangered animals.

Seventeen desired learning outcomes can be written for level 2 of the content hierarchy. Under thinking skills, ten desired learning outcomes can be written, five for identification and five for prediction. The five under identification are:

The learner will be able to identify
1. fish
2. amphibians
3. reptiles
4. birds
5. mammals

The five under prediction are:

The learner will be able to predict the behavior of
1. fish
2. amphibians
3. reptiles
4. birds
5. mammals

TABLE 12–1
TABLE OF SPECIFICATIONS

	CONTENT ANIMALS				
BEHAVIOR SKILLS	FISH Concrete Examples of Fish	AMPHIBIANS Concrete Examples of Amphibians	REPTILES Concrete Examples of Reptiles	BIRDS Concrete Examples of Birds	MAMMALS Concrete Examples of Mammals
I. Thinking Skills The learner will be able to:					
A. Identify	X	X	X	X	X
B. Predict the behavior of	X	X	X	X	X
II. Motor Skills The learner will be able to:					
A. Handle					X
B. Dissect		X			
III. Preferences The learner will develop an increased preference for the preservation of endangered species	X	X	X	X	X

Two desired learning outcomes are noted under motor skills.

The learner will be able to handle mammals.
The learner will be able to dissect amphibians.

Five desired learning outcomes are indicated under preferences.

The learner will develop an increased preference for the preservation of endangered
1. fish
2. amphibians
3. reptiles
4. birds
5. mammals.

At level 3 the following desired learning outcome statements can be written:

IDENTIFICATION OUTCOMES

The learner will be able to identify examples of
1. fish, such as perch, bass, etc.
2. amphibians, such as frogs, newts, etc.
3. reptiles, such as snakes, alligators, etc.
4. birds, such as eagles, cardinals, etc.
5. mammals, such as apes, horses, etc.

PREDICTION OUTCOMES

The learner will be able to predict the behavior of specific examples of
1. fish
2. amphibians
3. reptiles
4. birds
5. mammals

MOTOR OUTCOMES

The learner will be able to handle examples of mammals such as hamsters.
The learner will be able to dissect examples of amphibians such as frogs.

PREFERENCES

The learner will develop an increased preference for the preservation of particular kinds of
1. fish
2. amphibians
3. reptiles
4. birds
5. mammals

Whenever content is taught within the framework of a content hierarchy, as it should be, there are always implicit additional desired learning outcomes pertaining to hierarchical thinking that should be taught.

IDENTIFICATION OUTCOMES

The learner will be able to identify similarities and differences among categories and events at the various levels of the content hierarchy. For example, the learner should identify the similarities and differences between fish and amphibians, and also the characteristics that fish share with animals in general.

PREDICTION OUTCOMES

The learner will be able to predict how all animals will behave alike. The learner will be able to predict the differences in behavior among various types of animals.

Although you may not need to actually write desired learning outcome statements, the importance of using a two-dimensional table of specifications cannot be overemphasized. It not only is a reference for identifying desired learning outcomes, it is a reference for planning instruction and constructing tests to evaluate the achievement of the desired learning outcomes. Once the teacher specifies a desired learning outcome in a cell of the grid, he or she knows that instruction must be planned so that students will achieve it. The grid informs the teacher of the content that must be covered in instruction and the behavioral performance that the student must learn, that is, what the student is expected to do with respect to the content. The teacher can plan instruction to cover every cell in the grid for which a desired learning outcome has been derived.

Teachers can also construct achievement tests referring to the boxes in the grid. The tests must cover the content they have decided to teach and must tap the behaviors they have decided to teach. The grid will indicate the content and the behaviors that must be probed by the tests, and can serve as a basis for writing goal statements.

Deriving Instructional Goals

Desired learning outcome statements alone are not a sufficient reference for planning instruction. Goal statements are. This is because goal statements include additional references that are needed to plan instruction. Desired learning outcome statements are included in goal statements. In addition, goal statements include references to the type of instructional prescription that is to be selected or developed, the learner population, and a learner readiness reference. All three of these additional references help in the planning of instruction. Although it is necessary to identify a desired learning outcome from a table of specifications in order to write a goal statement, it is not necessary to write the desired learning outcome statements on paper, since they will eventually be included in the written goal statement.

A model for writing a goal statement follows.

The educator will develop and implement (1) _____
$\overline{\text{type of prescription}}$

for the purpose of teaching (2) _____ (3)
$\overline{\text{population reference}}$

_____ (4) _____.
$\overline{\text{readiness reference}}$ $\overline{\text{desired learning outcome}}$

The statement of a desired learning outcome begins with: The learner . . . (or the specification of a type of learner, such as the math student . . .). A goal statement is a statement of a management objective. It begins with the name of the person or manager who is attempting to move the learner to the desired learning outcome. A goal statement can begin with: The educator . . . (or a type of educator such as a teacher, superintendent, or principal). Next, the goal statement should indicate the type of prescription to be developed, then the population who is to benefit from the prescription, then the readiness characteristics of the population, and finally the desired learning outcome to be achieved.

The following are examples of goal statements.

The (1) school district will develop and implement (2) a reading program for the purpose of teaching 40 percent of the (3) adult illiterates in the community (4) who read below the fifth grade level (5) to read above the fifth grade level in a six-year period.

The (1) instructional designer will develop and implement (2) an instructional plan to teach (3) first-grade students (4) who can count (5) how to add.

The (1) superintendent will develop and implement (2) a prescription to acquire the facilities necessary to teach (3) adult illiterates (4) who read below the fifth grade level (5) to read above the fifth grade level in accordance with the instructional plan.

The (1) teacher will develop and implement (2) a teaching strategy to teach (3) each sixth-grade student in the class (4) who is able to identify animals (5) how to classify them.

You will note that in the four goal statements given above, the first and third include a reference to an acceptable level of student performance with respect to the desired learning outcome. Although this is good practice, many times you actually determine the acceptable level of achievement after you select or prepare an achievement test to evaluate the achievement of a goal. The acceptable level of achievement is a high score on the test. Usually, the person who constructs the test determines the test score that indicates competency.

There are a number of reasons for adding the four extra references to the desired learning outcome in writing a goal statement. First, specifying the prescription is important because it is a reference to the specific program to be developed or selected. If the prescription has already been developed the name of the prescription can be included, such as the name of a commercial reading program. If the prescription needs to be developed, there must be some reference to the nature of the prescription.

Naming the person or type of person responsible for developing a prescription assigns management responsibility for completing the task. An administrator should be assigned to develop an administrative prescription. An instructional planner should be assigned to develop an instructional prescription, and a teacher or teaching specialist should be assigned to develop a teaching prescription. However, quite often the teacher develops the instruction plan and the teaching procedures for implementing it.

It is necessary to specify the learner population for whom the prescription is designed, because the characteristics of student groups vary and the prescription must take into account the characteristics of the learners. A learning prescription that is appropriate for teaching fourth graders to read probably is not appropriate for teaching adult illiterates to read. Taking the characteristics of the learner group into account allows the instructional planner to consider the learner's readiness in developing an instructional prescription.

READINESS

It is impossible to design an effective instructional plan to achieve a learning outcome without knowing the present readiness characteristics of the learner. The readiness characteristics define the starting point or point of entry. The instructional plan is designed to move students from this starting point to the desired outcome.

An instructional plan is appropriate for any student who has the readiness characteristics for which the plan is designed. However, it must be understood that certain learning outcomes cannot be achieved, given certain readiness conditions. To use an extreme example, it would be impossible to teach a two-year-old to do integral calculus no matter how desirable it might be.

Because there are so many personal traits that can contribute to learning, it is simplifying to regard them as readiness characteristics. After all, our main concern is with the learner's readiness to learn what we wish to teach. From this perspective we would assess a student's potential for learning by analyzing any personal characteristic only as it contributes to or limits the student's readiness to learn. Intelligence, maturation, prior learning, and other important factors are viewed as readiness factors which support or limit the individual's potential for learning. If we know individuals' readiness to learn, we should be able to decide what they can learn and how they can learn it.

In considering readiness for learning, let us first discuss the behavioral factors: preferences, motor skills, and thinking skills. Then, we can discuss content.

Interest and Preference Readiness

It may seem at first that interest is something different from readiness. However, from a teacher's point of view, if students are not interested in learning, they are not ready to learn, because they will not become involved in the instructional presentation. To insure student interest as a readiness condition, the teacher must, for example, provide students with material that is interesting to them, based upon such factors as age and sex, and allow them to select their preferences from among alternative reading materials.

Motor Skills Readiness

Motor skills must also be taken into account as a readiness factor. If we want students to use teaching machines and laboratory equipment, it is necessary that they have the manual dexterity to use the equipment. Otherwise, learning will be impaired. We are reminded of an experiment in which the teacher was compared to a teaching machine to see which was more effective in teaching spelling to second and third graders. The results showed that the second graders learned more from the teacher, while the third graders learned more from the teaching machine. It was found that second graders were not well enough coordinated to effectively use the machine, but the third graders were. Hence, the second graders could not benefit from using the machine. If a motor skill is a necessary readiness condition for learning, the best way to test and prepare for readiness is to monitor and correct the students while they are performing the motor task until they can execute it smoothly. Remember, a student may be able to describe a motor procedure accurately without being able to execute it.

Thinking Skills Readiness

We have discussed thinking skills comprehensively and suggested some possible readiness considerations. We suggested that identification is prerequisite to prediction. We also suggested that within the process of identification it is necessary to identify relationships, that is, similarities and differences, before any specific event can be identified. Furthermore, concrete events must be identified before they can be categorized. They must be identified categorically before the relative relationships of categories in a content hierarchy can be understood.

With respect to prediction, it seems necessary to be able to predict what is going to happen without intervention before one can predict the consequences of intervention. Also, one must make a prediction before formulating ways to test it. One must conceive of ways of testing predictions in order to be able to monitor feedback to determine whether events are turning out as predicted.

We said that skills were organized programmatically, both thinking and motor skills. A mastered skill is manifested by the successful execution of a program. Because programs contain subroutines, it may be necessary to be able to execute the subroutine of a program in order to be ready to implement the program. Or, to put it in terms of skills, if a skill contains subskills, then learning the subskills may be a readiness requirement for learning the skill. Because adding is a subroutine of the multiplication program, it is facilitating to learn how to add before learning how to multiply.

Content Readiness

As we suggested, we do not believe that it is necessary to learn content at a lower level of a content hierarchy before content at a higher level can be learned. Learning can proceed from the general to the specific or from the specific to the general, providing the various relationships within the hierarchy are taught.

A readiness condition for learning content in a hierarchy is to know what the word labels representing the content mean. Since most of the word labels in a content area represent abstractions, it is necessary for a student to learn the criteria for inclusion in a category represented by a word label and be able to distinguish examples that fit the category from nonexamples. To become ready to learn more about mammals, including their relationship to other animals, the student must first know the criteria for inclusion in the category mammals and be able to distinguish examples of mammals from nonexamples. We showed how categorical identification can be taught in chapter 4.

You may not need to actually write goal statements. However, you must always refer to the readiness characteristics of your students as a basis for programming instruction. All skills, including teaching skills, proceed programmatically. You will need to sequence the content you teach as well as the behaviors you teach based upon student readiness as we illustrate in chapter 13.

In this chapter we showed how a table of specifications is constructed and how desired learning outcomes and goals may be derived. We were purposefully diverse in our examples and applications so that the content area teacher might see how the method applies in the content areas. In the next chapter we show specifically how desired learning outcomes are derived to teach reading.

SUMMARY

1. An instructional goal is a commitment to move students with specific readiness characteristics to the achievement of a desired learning outcome.

2. Desired learning outcome statements should include a behavior reference and a content reference.

3. Behavior references in desired learning outcome statements may pertain to the expression of preferences, motor skills, or thinking skills.

4. To analyze the content you wish to teach, a content hierarchy should be constructed, indicating the hierarchical relationship of the various topics you intend to cover.

5. Once a content hierarchy is formed, the teacher needs to determine how he or she wants the student to deal with or behave with respect to the content. This is a matter of determining the thinking procedures and motor skills to be employed and the preferences to be expressed.

6. To relate behaviors and content for the purpose of deriving desired learning outcomes a table of specifications is constructed. One dimension of the two-dimensional table of specifications displays behavior, while the other dimension displays content. To derive desired learning outcomes the teacher reviews the cells in the table and decides which behavior and content relationships are to be taught.

7. Instructional goal statements include references to the educator or manager responsible for achieving a desired learning outcome, the kind of instructional prescription to be used to achieve the desired learning outcome, the population of students to benefit from the instructional prescription, the readiness

characteristics necessary to benefit from the instructional prescription, and the desired learning outcome to be achieved.

8. It is necessary to know the readiness characteristics of students in order to design an instructional prescription for them.
The readiness characteristics define the starting point or point of
entry. The instructional prescription is designed to move students
from this starting point to the selected desired learning outcome.

9. In order to design instruction, student readiness with respect to behavioral abilities and content knowledge must be
determined. Behavioral readiness pertains to interest and preference readiness, motor skills readiness, and thinking skills
readiness.

REVIEW QUESTIONS

1. What is the definition of an instructional goal?
2. What is the composition of a desired learning outcome statement?
3. What kinds of behavior references are included in desired learning outcome statements?
4. How should instructional content be analyzed?
5. How is a table of specifications constructed?
6. What is the composition of instructional goal statements? Why is each element included?
7. Why is it necessary to know the readiness characteristics of students in order to design an instructional prescription for them? What readiness characteristics must be taken into account?

CHAPTER 13
Desired Learning Outcomes in Reading Instruction

PURPOSE

1. To construct a table of specifications for reading instruction.
2. To derive desired learning outcomes for reading instruction from the table.
3. To show you how to accomplish these tasks.

BACKGROUND AND NEW INFORMATION

You are familiar with desired learning outcomes from our use of them in the advanced organizers at the beginning of each chapter. You learned more about desired learning outcomes and how to derive them from a table of specifications in the last chapter. The desired learning outcomes we will derive in this chapter pertain to the various word identification, vocabulary, and reading comprehension skills covered in earlier chapters. In chapter 3 we dealt with word identification skills, in chapter 4 with vocabulary skills, and in chapters 5, 6, and 7 with reading comprehension skills. In this chapter we will enumerate desired learning outcomes that manifest these skills.

The first section of this chapter involves the construction of a table of specifications for reading instruction. Content hierarchies for reading are discussed as well as behaviors that pertain to reading. Then behaviors are related to content to form a table of specifications. The remainder of the chapter concerns the derivation and statement of desired learning outcomes for reading instruction. First, desired learning outcomes pertaining to thinking procedures are discussed. These concern identification skills and prediction skills. Second, motor skills are considered; and finally, preferences.

KEY TERMS

hierarchical identification
making general and specific identifications
proving identifications

DESIRED LEARNING OUTCOMES

The student will be able to:

1. Construct a table of specifications for reading instruction.
2. Derive desired learning outcomes for reading instruction from a table of specifications.
3. Describe the various desired learning outcomes for reading instruction that pertain to thinking procedures, with respect to both identification and prediction skills.
4. Describe desired learning outcomes for reading instruction that pertain to motor skills.
5. Describe desired learning outcomes for reading instruction that pertain to preferences.

In this and the next chapter we will apply to reading instruction the general principles discussed in the previous chapter. In this chapter we will construct a table of specifications that covers desired outcomes pertaining to reading. You can refer to this table of specifications any time in the future when you want to select a desired learning outcome for your students to pursue. In the next chapter we will show you how to use the table of specifications to plan reading instruction.

In the previous chapter we showed you how to construct a table of specifications. We explained and illustrated how you identify the content for the table of specifications by deriving a content hierarchy covering the subject matter you wish to teach. We also explained how the summary outline of thinking skills can be used to identify the thinking skills for the table of specifications. In this chapter we derive a content hierarchy pertaining to reading and adapt the summary outline of behaviors presented in the previous chapter to reading. When these two dimensions for the table of specifications have been identified we will construct a table of specifications for reading instruction. Finally, we will describe the various desired learning outcomes that can be derived from the table.

We recommended that whenever feasible you use a course textbook as a reference for constructing a content hierarchy. Quite often the table of contents of the textbook defines a content hierarchy. The title of the textbook offers the most general reference to the content in the book; therefore, it can be used as a reference to identify the highest or most general level of the content hierarchy. The parts or sections of the textbook can be used to represent the next lower level of the hierarchy, and the chapters within the sections the next lower level. The headings within chapters can be used to define the next lower level of the content hierarchy.

Here is a diagram of such a content hierarchy:

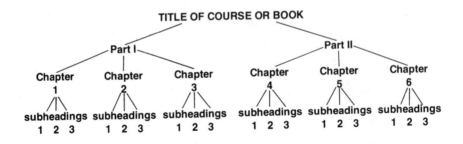

If you can use a textbook as a reference, you can modify it to suit your purpose and will not need to start from scratch. Your modifications will involve adding content that is not covered in the text and deleting content included in the text that does not serve your purposes. When you add content topics make sure you add them at the appropriate level of the hierarchy.

There are textbooks to guide instructional planning and teaching in most of the content areas. Unfortunately, there are few, if any, books that can reasonably be called textbooks in the area of reading. There are many readers and many publications that deal with various reading and thinking abilities but few comprehensively cover the reading and thinking that are taught by a reading teacher at particular grade levels. For this reason we need to con-

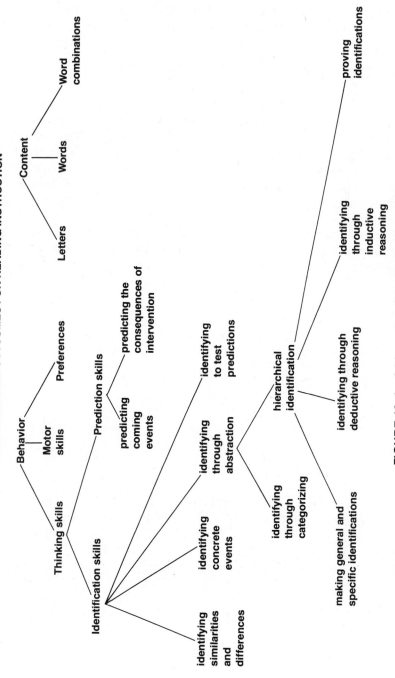

DESIRED LEARNING OUTCOMES FOR READING INSTRUCTION

FIGURE 13–1   A hierarchy of topics in chapter 13

struct a content hierarchy for reading so that we can use it to form a table of specifications for the teaching of reading.

CONTENT HIERARCHIES FOR READING

You will remember that reading is the extraction of meaning from word combinations which permits the reader to understand the author's message. The content of reading, then, involves printed letters, words, and word combinations. Students learn to identify letters so that they can recognize and extract meaning from words. They learn to extract meaning from words in order to understand the meaning of the word combinations presented by an author.

Letters, words, and word combinations are the ingredients for constructing a three-level representational content hierarchy for reading instruction.

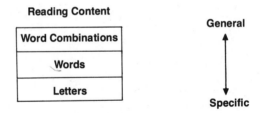

Letters are the most specific ingredient and form the lowest level of the content hierarchy. Letters are represented in words which form the next higher level of the hierarchy. Words are represented in word combinations which form the highest, most general level of the hierarchy. This three-level hierarchy is sufficient for our purpose, and we shall use it as the content dimension in constructing a table of specifications for reading instruction.

However, should you need a more extensive and elaborate content hierarchy for planning reading instruction, you might consider using the following hierarchy.

Reading Content

Subjects
Paragraphs
Sentences
Clauses
Phrases
Individual Words
Letter Combinations
Individual Letters

General

↑

↓

Specific

In the above representational hierarchy letters are represented in letter combinations, such as syllables. Letter combinations are represented in words, words in phrases, phrases in clauses, and clauses in sentences. Sentences are represented in paragraphs, and paragraphs are represented in the presentation of more general topics or subjects, such as chapters or subheadings within chapters.

BEHAVIORS THAT PERTAIN TO READING

We presented an outline of behaviors in chapter 12. It remains to apply these behaviors to the process of reading so that we may construct a table of specifications specifically adapted to reading. With respect to identification skills as they apply to reading, it is clear that readers must be able to identify the meaning of the word combinations on the printed page. To do this effectively they must be able to identify individual words and their meanings and to distinguish one letter of the alphabet from another. This requires good readers to use the many identification skills we have discussed throughout the book as they apply to reading.

In addition to making identifications students must learn to make predictions. They must be able to predict the coming message based on the words they are presently reading. Most of the thinking procedures presented in our outline may be applied to reading and used in relationship to letters, words, and word combinations to form a table of specifications for reading instruction.

A TABLE OF SPECIFICATIONS FOR READING INSTRUCTION

In the table of specifications, we present the most extensive list of behaviors in the book so that you may see most of the behaviors that are related to reading instruction. As we relate behavior to content in order to derive desired learning outcomes for reading instruction in the remainder of the chapter, we will make further elaborations of the various behaviors. When appropriate we will offer subdivisions of the major topics on the table of specifications. For purposes of review and synthesis we will present desired learning outcomes pertaining to reading comprehension skills where applicable.

TABLE 13-1
SPECIFICATIONS FOR
DERIVING DESIRED LEARNING OUTCOMES
FOR READING INSTRUCTION

BEHAVIORS	CONTENT		
	Letters	Words	Word Combinations
I. Thinking Procedures			
A. Identification Skills			
1. Identifying similarities and differences	X	X	X
2. Identifying concrete events: remembering			
a. sight identification	X	X	X
b. phonic identification	X	X	X
c. remembering programs for structural and contextual analysis	X	X	X
d. remembering programs for consulting authoritative sources	X	X	X

TABLE 13–1 (continued)

BEHAVIORS	CONTENT		
	Letters	Words	Word Combi-nations
e. remembering grammar programs	X	X	X
f. reading comprehension skills: remembering what the author said		X	X
3. Identifying through abstraction			
a. identifying through categorizing	X	X	X
b. hierarchical identification			
(1) making general and specific identification		X	X
(2) identifying through deductive reasoning		X	X
(3) identifying through inductive reasoning			
(a) producing concept categories from examples of the category		X	X
(b) producing concept categories from structural clues		X	X
(c) producing concept categories from contextual clues		X	X
(4) proving identifications		X	X
4. Identifying to test predictions			
a. formulating programs to test predictions			X
b. executing programs to test predictions			X
c. monitoring feedback to test predictions			X
d. making corrections based on feedback to confirm predictions			X
B. Prediction Skills			
1. Predicting coming events			X
2. Predicting the consequences of intervention			X
II. Motor Skills			
III. Preferences			

DESIRED LEARNING OUTCOMES FOR READING INSTRUCTION

The following desired learning outcomes are derived from the chart.

I. Thinking Procedures

    A. Identification Skills

In learning to read the student learns to identify letters, words, and word combinations.

       1. Identifying similarities and differences

In order to identify letters, words, and word combinations, the student learns to determine the similarities and differences among them.

Letters: Desired outcomes in the learning of letters

The student will be able to determine visually the similarities and differences among letters from their configurations.

The student will be able to determine the similarities and differences in the ways that letters are pronounced.

The student will be able to determine the similarities and differences in types of print such as cursive and manuscript print.

The student will be able to determine the similarities and differences among lower and upper case letters.

The student will be able to determine the similarities and differences among types of letter combinations such as prefixes, suffixes, blends, digraphs, and diphthongs.

Words: Desired outcomes in the learning of words

The student will be able to determine visually the similarities and differences in the configuration of words (from such aspects as their length and shape).

The student will be able to determine the similarities and differences in the pronunciation of words, for instance, words that rhyme and sound alike.

The student will be able to determine the similarities and differences in the meaning of words, for example, antonyms and synonyms.

The student will be able to determine the similarities and differences between a word and its abbreviation(s) and one abbreviation from another.

Word combinations: Desired outcomes in learning word combinations

The student will be able to determine the similarities and differences among phrases, clauses, sentences, topics, and titles.
    2. *Identifying concrete events: Remembering*
      a. Sight Identification: Desired outcomes in visual recognition

Letters: The student will be able to recognize by sight the letters of the alphabet.
Words: The student will be able to recognize words by sight.
Word combinations: The student will be able to recognize by sight word combinations such as at the door, in the house, the little puppy, and the red barn.

    b. Phonic Identification: Remembering pronunciation programs

Letters: Desired outcomes in the pronunciation of letters

The student will be able to remember programs for pronouncing letters and letter combinations. For instance, the student will be able to remember that, in general, the letters "c" and "g" have a soft sound when followed by "i," "e," or "y." Otherwise, they have a hard sound.

Words: Desired outcomes in the pronunciation of words

The student will be able to remember programs for pronouncing words. For example, the student will be able to remember vowel rules such as if there is only one vowel in a word and it is not at the end of the word, it usually has a short sound, unless it is followed by a controlling letter like r.

Word combinations: Desired outcomes in the pronunciation of word combinations

The student will be able to remember programs for pronunciation of word combinations. For instance, the student will be able to remember that in singing the word "the" is usually pronounced with a long "e" sound if it precedes a word beginning with a vowel.

c. Remembering programs for structural and contextual analysis

Letters: Desired outcomes in the structural and contextual analysis of letters

The student will be able to remember programs for analyzing the structure of letters in order to identify them. For instance, the student will be able to determine round, straight, tall, humped, curved, and tail letters.

The student will be able to remember programs for analyzing the context surrounding letters in order to make an accurate identification. For example, the student will be able to remember that a letter is capitalized when it is the first letter of a name.

Words: Desired outcomes in the structural and contextual analysis of words

The student will be able to remember programs for analyzing the structure of words in order to identify their meaning. For example, the student will remember to look for root words, prefixes, and suffixes in unfamiliar words in order to identify the meaning of the words.

The student will be able to remember programs for analyzing the context surrounding a word in order to identify the meaning of the word. For instance, if there are a number of definitions for a word the student will remember to identify the appropriate definition from the context surrounding the word.

Word combinations: Desired outcomes in the analysis of word combinations

The student will be able to remember programs for analyzing the structure of word combinations in order to extract meaning. For instance, the student will be able to remember that in English adjectives usually appear before the nouns they modify, and sentences usually are programmed in a subject-verb-object format.

The student will be able to remember programs for analyzing the context surrounding a combination of words in order to identify their meaning. For example, if a student does not gain meaning from a paragraph he may remember to look at preceding and succeeding titles and headings for clues.

d. Remembering programs for consulting authoritative sources

Letters: Desired outcomes in consulting authoritative sources to identify letters

The student will be able to remember programs to identify letters. For example, the student may remember to consult an alphabet chart, or if she is concerned with the pronunciation of a letter, she may consult a phonic record.

Words: Desired outcomes in consulting authoritative sources to identify words

The student will be able to remember programs to identify the meaning of words. For example, the student should know when and how to use the dictionary.

Word combinations: Desired outcomes in learning to consult authoritative sources to identify word combinations of interest.

The student will be able to remember programs to identify word combinations. For instance, the student should know when and how to use the resources of the library.

    e. Remembering grammar programs

Letters: Desired outcomes in applying the rules of grammar to letters

The student will be able to remember rules of grammar that apply to letters; for example, the rules for capitalizing letters.

Words: Desired outcomes in applying rules of grammar to words

The student will be able to remember rules of grammar that apply to words; for example, rules indicating when to pluralize words and when to use "a" or "an.".

Word combinations: Desired outcomes in applying rules of grammar to word combinations

The student will be able to remember rules of grammar that apply to word combinations; for instance, rules of punctuation and rules for using the correct tense.

    f. Reading comprehension skills: Remembering what the author said

In chapter 6 when we considered reading comprehension we

discussed reading comprehension skills that require literal comprehension or remembering what the author stated explicitly. To refresh your memory these comprehension skills are:

1. recalling a specific fact, detail, name, place, event, and so forth
2. following directions
3. recalling and retelling story events in order
4. paraphrasing what is read

> 3. *Identifying through abstraction*
>   a. *Identifying through categorizing*

Letters: Desired outcomes in categorizing letters

The student will be able to identify (1) letter categories such as vowels and consonants, (2) the defining criteria for inclusion in each category, and (3) examples and nonexamples of each category.

Words: Desired outcomes in categorizing words

The student will be able to identify (1) word categories such as nouns and verbs, (2) the defining criteria for inclusion in each category, and (3) examples and nonexamples of each category.

Word combinations: Desired outcomes in categorizing word combinations

The student will be able to identify (1) word combination categories such as sentences and paragraphs, (2) the defining criteria for inclusion in each category, and (3) examples and nonexamples of each category.

Reading comprehension skills: Desired outcomes in executing reading comprehension skills that require categorizing

The student will be able to identify (1) reading comprehension skills that require categorizing, (2) the defining criteria for the reading comprehension skills, and (3) examples and nonexamples of the skills.

In chapter 6 we described a number of reading comprehension skills that require categorizing. They are (1) classifying ideas, (2)

distinguishing fact and fantasy, (3) distinguishing real and unreal, (4) distinguishing fact and opinion, (5) distinguishing relevant and irrelevant information, (6) integrating new information with old, (7) evaluative reading, and (8) choosing correct and applicable meanings for multimeaning words.

In chapter 7 we advocated teaching all skills involved in reading comprehension as concepts. This requires the student to identify (1) the reading comprehension skill, (2) the defining criteria for the skills, and (3) examples and nonexamples of the skill.

b. Hierarchical identification

Hierarchical identification involves the understanding of the relationship among categories of a content hierarchy.

(1) Making general and specific identifications

Words: Desired outcomes in knowing that words denote more general and more specific categories of things

The student will be able to identify words that denote more general categories of things and words that denote more specific subcategories of the general categories. For example, the student may know that the word "animal" is a designation of a general category and that the word "fish" is a more specific reference to a subcategory of "animals."

Word combinations: Desired outcomes in learning that word combinations denote more general and more specific categories of things

The student will be able to identify word combinations that denote more general categories of things and word combinations that denote more specific subcategories of the general categories. For example, the student may know that the word combination "Things that fly in the air" is a reference to a more general category of objects than the word combination "Animals that fly in the air," which denotes a more specific subcategory.

(2) Identifying through deductive reasoning

Words: Desired outcomes in deducing words that exemplify a category

Given words that identify a category the student will be able to produce examples of the category and supply words that represent the examples. For example, given the word "animal," the student should be able to supply such words as fish, reptiles, and amphibians as denoting examples of the category animal.

Word combinations: Desired outcomes in deducing word combinations that exemplify a category

Given word combinations that identify a category, the student will be able to produce examples of the category and supply word combinations that represent the examples. For instance, given the word combination "things that live in the ocean," the student may deduce the subcategories "animals that live in the ocean" and "plants that live in the ocean." Or given the title of a book, the student may deduce topics that might be included in the book.

Reading comprehension skills: Desired outcomes in executing reading comprehension skills that require deductive reasoning

The student will be able to identify reading comprehension skills that require deductive reasoning and be able to execute the skills.

The reading comprehension skills mentioned in chapter 6 that require deductive reasoning are (1) identifying supportive information and details, (2) inferring details, (3) analyzing conclusions, (4) giving examples, (5) making applications, (6) applying information gained from reading to new situations, and (7) providing illustrations.

(3) *Identifying through inductive reasoning*

   (a) *producing concept categories from examples of the category*

Words: Desired outcomes in producing words that represent concept categories from words that represent examples of the category

Given words that identify examples of a category, the student will be able to induce the concept category. For example, given a list of words such as fish, birds, and reptiles, the student will be able to induce the category animals.

Word combinations: Desired outcomes in producing word combinations that represent concept categories from word combinations that represent examples of the category

Given word combinations that identify examples of a category, the student will be able to induce the concept category. For example, given the titles for chapters of a book, the student will be able to induce an appropriate title for the book.

(b) producing concept categories from structural clues

Words: Desired outcomes in producing concepts from structure clues in words

The student will be able to identify the meaning of an unfamiliar complex word from familiar structural components. For example, if the student had not seen the complex word "ultraconservative" before but knew the meaning of the root word "conserve," the prefix "ultra-," and the suffix "-ative," he could decipher the meaning of the word.

Word combinations: Desired outcomes in producing concepts from structural clues in word combinations

The student will be able to identify the meaning of an unfamiliar combination of words from familiar structural components. For instance, if the student did not know the meaning of the sentence, "He was higher than a kite," but the student knew the meaning of the individual words, and that the word "high" can mean elevated and elated she would have some idea of the meaning of the sentence. This amounts to producing a concept from the structural clues in a figurative and idiomatic language statement.

(c) producing concept categories from contextual clues

Words: Desired outcomes in producing words representing concepts from surrounding context

Meaning may be abstracted syntactically from the way words are grammatically programmed and/or semantically from knowing the meaning of surrounding words.

Syntactic abstraction

The student will be able to gain meaning of an unfamiliar word from syntactical clues. For instance, if the blank space in the following sentence represented an unfamiliar word, the student

might infer that the word is a noun from syntax: The _____
drives his car to the store.

Semantic abstraction

The student will be able to gain meaning of an unfamiliar word
from semantic clues. In the preceding example, the student
might infer that the unfamiliar word represented by the blank
space is a person rather than a place or thing because people drive
cars.

Word combinations: Desired outcomes in producing word combinations that represent concepts from surrounding context

Syntactic abstraction

The student will be able to gain meaning of an unfamiliar combination of words from syntactical clues. The term "for example"
following a statement cues the reader to look for a clarification of
the statement. If a student did not know the meaning of a statement but understood the example, he would learn something
about the meaning of the statement.

Semantic abstraction

The student will be able to gain meaning of an unfamiliar combination of words from semantic clues. For instance, if the student did not know the meaning of a sentence in a paragraph she
can infer meaning if she understands the surrounding sentences.

Although we gave examples of how syntactic and semantic
clues are used in contextual abstraction, it should be noted that
syntactic and semantic clues can be used to extract meaning
through structural abstraction as well. We demonstrated this in
chapter 3.

Reading comprehension skills: Desired outcomes in executing
reading comprehension skills that require inductive reasoning

The student will be able to identify reading comprehension
skills that require deductive reasoning and will be able to execute
the skills.

The reading comprehension skills mentioned in chapter 6 that
require inductive reasoning are (1) making generalizations, (2)

identifying character traits, (3) interpreting the author's style, bias, attitude, tone, or mood, (4) getting the main idea, (5) making summaries, (6) interpreting figurative and idiomatic language, (7) identifying the author's purpose, and (8) identifying character motives.

(4) Proving identifications

The student will be able to prove a conclusion arrived at inductively by reasoning deductively, and the student will be able to prove a conclusion arrived at deductively by reasoning inductively.

Words: For example, given the induced conclusion that the mood created by an author is "nostalgia," the student will be able to find specific statements made by the author that support this conclusion.

Given the deduced conclusion of the author that England, Israel, Canada, and the United States are "republics," the student will be able to find the general statement made by the author about republics which support this conclusion.

Word combinations: For instance, given the induced conclusion that the main idea the author is conveying is "overweight is harmful to your health," the student will be able to find specific statements made by the author that buttress this conclusion.

Given the deduced conclusion that *Playboy, Penthouse,* and *Hustler* magazines are "pornographic magazines," the student will be able to find the general statement made by the author that supports this conclusion.

4. Identifying to test predictions: Desired outcomes in testing predictions

a. Formulating programs to test predictions

To test predictions of the coming message while reading the student needs only to read the ensuing passages. In order to regain meaning, however, the student must learn to use word identification programs in combination.

The student will be able to combine phonic programs, structural and contextual abstraction programs, and programs for consulting authoritative sources in order to regain the meaning of the message.

b. Executing programs to test predictions

The student will be able to adjust his reading rate to the difficulty of the reading materials.

The student will be able to execute phonic programs, structural and contextual abstraction programs, and programs for consulting authoritative sources.

The student will be able to execute phonic programs, structural and contextual abstraction programs, and programs for consulting authoritative sources in combination.

c. Monitoring feedback to test predictions

The student will be able to determine whether her predictions of the coming message are turning out as expected.

The student will be able to determine whether the phonic programs, structural or contextual abstraction programs, programs for consulting authoritative sources, or a combination of these programs that he is using is helping him regain the meaning of the author's message.

d. Making corrections based on feedback to confirm predictions

The student will be able to understand why his predictions of the author's message did not turn out as he expected.

The student will be able to understand why the word identification program(s) he is using is (are) not helping him regain the meaning of the author's message and shift to a more promising program.

B. Prediction Skills

1. Predicting coming events: Desired outcomes in predicting the coming message

The student will be able to predict the coming message from preceding clues provided by the author. For instance, the student should be able to predict some of the content of a book from the title and table of contents.

2. Predicting the consequences of intervention: Desired outcomes in predicting cause-effect relationships

The student will be able to predict the effect of new information introduced by the author. For instance, the student should be able to predict the effect of the actions of characters in a story on future events in the story.

The student will be able to predict the word identification skills he can use to regain meaning when the meaning of the message is lost. These include phonic skills, structural and contextual abstraction skills, as well as skills for consulting authoritative sources.

II. Motor Skills

Desired Skills: Desired outcomes in performing motor programs that pertain to reading instruction.

Although reading is more closely associated with thinking skills than motor skills, some modes of reading instruction require students to perform motor programs. That is, some modes of reading instruction require students to operate teaching machines, tachistoscopes, reading accelerators, and the like. For this reason we will present one desired learning outcome to apply to motor skills as they might pertain to reading instruction.

The student will be able to execute efficiently motor programs she is to utilize in reading instruction.

III. Preferences

Desired learning outcomes pertaining to reading references

The student will develop an increased preference for reading as a means of acquiring information and enjoyment.

The student will develop an increased preference for mastering the skills that facilitate reading, such as the various identification and prediction skills described in this text.

The student will develop an increased preference for becoming actively involved in improving his ability to read (as opposed to being a passive recipient of reading instruction).

In enumerating desired learning outcomes we tried to be comprehensive in scope, but not exhaustive. Although we could generate many more desired learning outcomes pertaining to reading preferences, in the main they would be subdivisions and elaborations of the above desired learning outcomes.

The reading teacher must work to improve students' reading ability. This is the major desired learning outcome. To achieve this major objective, enabling objectives must be achieved, many of which we described. Within the constraints of his or her responsibility and sound "educational practice," the reading teacher selects and pursues the desired learning outcomes considered the most beneficial to students.

SUMMARY

1. The content dimension of a table of specifications for reading instruction should at least include, proceeding from the specific to the general, letters, words, and word combinations. A more elaborate content hierarchy for reading instruction might include proceeding from the specific to the general, individual letters, letter combinations, individual words, phrases, clauses, sentences, paragraphs, and subjects.

2. The behavior dimension of a table of specifications should include references to (a) thinking procedures, both identification and prediction skills, (b) motor skills, and (c) preferences.

3. The desired learning outcomes derived from a table of specifications should pertain to thinking procedures, motor skills, and preferences. Since reading primarily involves thought, most desired learning outcomes for reading instruction should pertain to thinking procedures.

4. Desired learning outcomes pertaining to thinking procedures relate to identification skills and prediction skills. The identification skills include (a) identifying similarities and differences, (b) identifying concrete events, and (c) identifying through abstraction which may involve making general and specific identifications, identifying through deductive reasoning, identifying through inductive reasoning, and proving identifications. The prediction skills include (a) predicting coming events and (b) predicting the consequences of intervention.

5. Desired learning outcomes for reading instruction also pertain to word identification skills, vocabulary skills, and reading comprehension skills. When students are identifying and predicting with respect to reading, they are employing word identification skills, vocabulary skills, or reading comprehension skills.

REVIEW QUESTIONS

1. What can a content hierarchy for reading instruction include?

2. What three major behavior divisions should be included in a table of specifications for reading instruction?

3. How does one construct a table of specifications for reading instruction?

4. How does one derive desired learning outcomes from a table of specifications for reading instruction?

5. What desired learning outcomes for reading instruction pertain to thinking procedures?

6. What desired learning outcomes for reading instruction pertain to motor skills?

7. What desired learning outcomes for reading instruction pertain to preferences?

8. What desired learning outcomes for reading instruction pertain to word identification skills?

9. What desired learning outcomes for reading instruction pertain to vocabulary building?

10. What desired learning outcomes for reading instruction pertain to reading comprehension skills?

CHAPTER 14
Planning Reading Instruction

PURPOSE

To show you how to plan and design reading instruction, including how to:

1. Establish student readiness for learning.
2. Select desired learning outcomes.
3. State instructional goals.
4. Prepare final exams.
5. Select instructional strategies.
6. Prepare instructional units.
7. Build instructional programs.

BACKGROUND AND NEW INFORMATION

In this chapter everything you learned previously in the book is applied to the planning of reading instruction. This chapter begins with a prescription for establishing student readiness for learning. Second, the selection of desired learning outcomes is discussed. Third, we deal with stating instructional goals. Fourth, we show you how to prepare a final examination (a summative exam). Fifth, we discuss the selection of an instructional strategy for teaching. Sixth, we show you how to prepare instructional units, which include instructional activities and diagnostic-progress tests. Finally, we discuss building an instructional program from instructional units.

KEY TERM

mastery learning

DESIRED LEARNING OUTCOMES

The student will be able to:

1. Establish readiness for learning.
2. Select desired learning outcomes for reading from a table of specifications.
3. State instructional goals as a basis for planning reading instruction.
4. Prepare formative and summative examinations for an instructional plan.
5. Select an instructional strategy for planning instruction.
6. Prepare instructional units to move students from a readiness state to a desired learning outcome.

We said that an instructional plan must be based on the readiness characteristics of the student. An instructional plan is designed to move students with common readiness characteristics to the achievement of more advanced desired learning outcomes. Therefore, the teacher must first determine the readiness characteristics of the students and then project desired learning outcomes the students are capable of attaining. Having established these two reference points, the teacher plans an instructional program to move students from their present readiness position, the entry level, to the attainment of the desired learning outcome, the exit level or terminal point for the program.

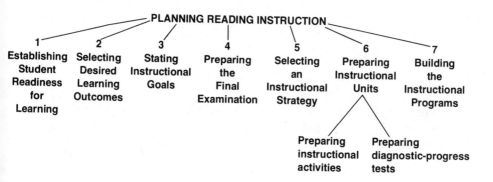

FIGURE 14–1 A hierarchy of topics in chapter 14

ESTABLISHING STUDENT READINESS FOR LEARNING

As soon as a teacher takes charge of a new group of students, he or she should become familiar with their readiness characteristics. This involves a thorough investigation of the students' present and past performance and other relevant factors.

Report Cards

The students' report cards provide a wealth of information. Students' grades in the content areas indicate how proficient they are in each content area. Grades in oral language, written language, spelling, and general language usage will inform the teacher of their competencies in language. Their grades in reading will indicate, in general, how well they are doing in reading and in executing the subskills used in reading. It also is wise to look at the students' grades for "effort" or "habits and attitudes." This will indicate whether a student's poor grades are attributable to lack of interest and effort. The comments of the students' previous teachers may also reveal subtle factors contributing to the students' grades.

Test Scores

Another index of student readiness is provided by the test scores that may be found in the students' files.

Standardized Survey Tests

Quite often the files contain scores from standardized survey tests of the student's achievement. These tests show how a student's performance compares to the performance of other students who have taken the test. Most often a percentile rank is given for each student indicating the percentage of students that scored above and below him on the test. Such tests often provide reading scores for the students in the form of a grade equivalent reading score.

The grade equivalent reading score can be used by the teacher to approximate a reading level. The teacher can select reading materials for the students based on their grade equivalent reading scores. If the reading material is to be in a particular content area, the teacher can check the students' grades in the content area on their report card or an achievement test and adjust readability level for the students based on these grades.

The reading scores on standardized achievement tests are of additional value to the teacher in assessing the relative reading abilities of the class. The teacher can compare the average reading achievement of the class to national norms, and sometimes data is provided on local norms. In addition, the teacher can identify the range of reading achievement in the class as well as identify the particular students who are performing above and below the grade level average. Although standardized achievement tests yield information pertaining to the relative abilities of students, it is difficult to determine from this type of test the particular skills a student has mastered. In general, the wider the range of achievement in a class, the less likely it is that one reading instruction program will serve for the entire class.

Criterion-referenced Diagnostic Tests

In reading, these tests measure the student's mastery of a number of specific reading-thinking skills. Typically, a student is said to have mastered a skill when she answers correctly 80 percent or more of the questions pertaining to a skill. A good many schools give these tests. The teacher can check the test files and learn the specific skills students have or have not mastered. The mastery of a specific skill indicates a student's readiness to master a more advanced skill. Thus, the teacher has a basis for selecting a desired learning outcome for the student to pursue.

Interest Inventories

Students must be interested in the reading material presented them in order to be ready to read. Otherwise, they may not become involved in the reading material. To approximate the reading interests of the students the teacher should take into account the ages of the students and determine the different interests of boys and girls at that age. To obtain the specific interests of students, the teacher must question them. Teachers can ask students what they have read in the past, the television shows they prefer to watch, and the activities they like to engage in. In short, the teacher finds the interests of students by determining their preferences.

SELECTING DESIRED LEARNING OUTCOMES

Once teachers are familiar with the readiness characteristics of their students, they are prepared to select desired learning outcomes for them to pursue. First, teachers examine the desired learning outcomes the school requires its students to pursue. Within these constraints the teacher makes selections.

After the parameters have been established, the teachers inspect the students' scores on the various portions of a diagnostic reading test. They note the skills the students have mastered. Then they look at the test items that comprise the sections of the test for which the students have shown mastery to familiarize themselves with the actual skills the students have mastered. The spaces not marked with an M represent possible desired learning outcomes the students may pursue.

Teachers study the possible desired learning outcomes and, within the constraints of their teaching assignments, they select one for the students to pursue. It is important to realize that the authors of diagnostic reading tests and instructional materials seldom presume to dictate the order in which various skills must be taught. Therefore, teachers must use their own judgment in sequencing the teaching of reading-thinking skills with the guidance we have provided.

Suppose you select "making predictions" as the skill you wish the students to master because they have not mastered this skill as yet. Further, you decide that you want to teach them specifically to predict coming events in a story. You now write the appropriate desired learning outcome for this skill as follows.

The student will be able to predict coming events in a story.

When the desired learning outcome has been selected we move to the statement of the instructional goal.

STATING INSTRUCTIONAL GOALS

You will remember that a statement of an instructional goal has two reference points for planning instruction: (1) the readiness characteristics of the student which represent skills required to enter the program; and (2) the desired learning outcome that is to be achieved at the end of the instructional program. Once the desired learning has been selected, it is necessary to be specific about the readiness or entry level skills required to achieve the desired learning outcome to be pursued in preparation for writing a goal statement.

In order to specify readiness characteristics a teacher inspects the table of specifications to identify the skills the students have mastered that are most logically prerequisite to and supportive of the desired learning outcome he has written. After inspection, he decides it is necessary to be able to identify programmatic sequences before one can use them to make predictions, so he notes that the ability to identify programmatic sequences is a most important readiness requirement.

The teacher then reviews diagnostic reading tests the students have taken for more information on their readiness. If relevant test scores are not available, he will need to administer diagnostic tests.

However, let us assume that he inspects the students' scores on a diagnostic reading test and finds that most of them have mastered a skill called "detecting sequences." He looks at the test items that comprise that section of the test and determines that the students can identify spatial and time sequences. They have demonstrated their knowledge of space sequence by ordering forms according to their size. They have shown their ability to identify time sequences by ordering events over time. This diagnostic information leads the teacher to believe that the students are ready to learn to predict what will happen next in a story. If he finds weaknesses in these skills, it indicates that he will need to prepare review material for the particular students who show weakness to bring them up to the required readiness level.

After reviewing the various capabilities of the students, the teacher decides that they are capable of identifying sequences in a story, which appears to be the most germane readiness skill for achieving the desired learning outcome. The teacher now is ready to write the instructional goal statement as follows.

> The teacher will develop and implement an instructional program to teach the eighth grade students in his English class who can identify story sequences to predict the coming events in the story.

PREPARING THE FINAL EXAMINATION: A SUMMATIVE TEST

After an instructional goal statement is written, the final exam is prepared to assess the achievement of the desired learning outcome in the goal statement. This serves two purposes. The selection of test items for the final exam clarifies in the teacher's mind the actual performances required of the students to exhibit achievement of the desired learning outcome. The test items are also suggestive of instructional activities that will lead to the attainment of the desired outcome. Therefore, they will assist the teacher in planning instructional activities.

If the teacher is familiar with sections of the various diagnostic reading tests and the test items in the sections, as she should be, she will be able to find many of the test items she needs to construct her final exams with little effort. The desired learning outcome statement we are using in our example suggests the kind of test items needed to assess the achievement of the outcome. The teacher would know that test items would require the students to read a passage and predict what may plausibly happen next. A teacher who is familiar with diagnostic reading tests would know where such test items could be found. Also, a teacher who is familiar with skill materials such as workbooks designed to teach reading-thinking skills might also remember books containing both instructional activities and companion test items that can be used to teach a desired learning outcome and test for achievement.

The importance of becoming familiar with available test items and instructional activities pertaining to the teaching and testing of the various reading-thinking skills cannot be overemphasized. The teacher should do more than read the headings; she should inspect the instructional activities and test items under each heading to see the actual learning and behavior that are being dealt with. As we said, titles in tests and instructional materials are often not sufficiently revealing of the content contained under them.

The final exam should enable the teacher to determine which students have and have not mastered the skill and to assign a grade to the students. Thus, it must be a criterion-referenced test rather than a norm-referenced test because we are concerned with how well a student has mastered the desired learning outcome. This is the criterion of achievement. We are not concerned directly with how well students have learned relative to their peers. Also, the final exam is a summative test in that it summarizes the students' competency in mastering a skill.

We offer the following procedure for constructing a criterion-referenced summative test. The procedure is derived from the work of Bloom, Hastings, and Madaus (1971). We include only a brief description of the procedures. We refer you to N. E. Gronlund, *Preparing Criterion-Referenced Tests for Classroom Instruction* (1973) and W. J. Popham, *Educational Evaluation* (1973) for more information on the construction of criterion-referenced tests.

1. Compile and construct test items. As we said, you can find many test items in existing diagnostic tests and instructional booklets. However, you may wish to revise them or construct your own test items. In either event, existing materials will be helpful.

Prepare twenty to forty test items for a desired learning outcome. You can file them under the heading of the desired learning outcome and combine them in different ways to vary your final exams on subsequent occasions. If time permits, the final exam for each desired learning outcome should contain at least twenty test items. Test items to measure the ability to "predict coming events from a story" can be found in many reading tests and instructional materials. The following is an example.

John's family was busy. They were happily looking forward to tomorrow. The guest had been invited. John's older sister had baked a cake and put twelve candles on it. John was visiting his uncle and was unaware of the plans for the next day.

1. We can guess that the next day John will be _____.
   a. upset
   b. twelve years old
   c. by himself
   d. away from home
2. Soon you would expect John to _____.
   a. go home
   b. leave town
   c. ride his bike
   d. recite a poem

As you can see, this kind of test item requires the student to read a story and determine what will happen next. The stories vary in length and usually more than one test item is written for each story. Another form of test item that is appropriate for this desired learning outcome is to present the student with statements that are arranged to depict a sequence of events. The student is asked to select from among alternatives what the next event will be.

2. Be certain that the test items correspond to your desired learning outcome. In selecting and constructing test items it is easy to drift from the desired learning outcomes. It is wise to check your test items to make sure they test for the behavior and the content specified in the desired learning outcome. For example, the desired learning outcome we are using requires the student to "predict coming events in a story." Thus, each test item must require the student to predict the future. Questions probing for other conclusions are inappropriate. The content is printed word combinations that tell a story. Thus, picture tests and oral tests are inappropriate. However, these additional skills may be tapped with respect to other desired learning outcomes and may be included in instructional activities for this desired learning outcome.

3. Develop a clear set of directions for responding to each type of test item. Students must be given directions they understand for a particular item type, and the teacher must make certain that the students understand the directions. Otherwise, the students' responses to the items will not be valid. R. L. Thorndike (ed.), *Educational Measurement,* 2nd edition (1971) provides excellent guidelines for writing test directions.

4. Establish a scoring procedure that will determine whether or not the student has or has not answered each item correctly. Scoring is greatly simplified and usually more accurate if "objective" test items are written. For objective test items, such as multiple choice, true-false, or matching, a simple right answer scoring key may be used. Thorndike (1971) explains test item types and provides guidelines for writing them. Remember, if you are not clear about the correct answer to a question, your students may be confused by the item. You can give your test to a colleague to check the accuracy of your scoring key.

5. Write general directions for the test. The student should be given instructions on such factors as (1) how to record answers, (2) the amount of time allowed to take the test, (3) the purpose of the test, and (4) how the test will be scored; for example, whether or not guessing at answers will be penalized. If possible, it is a good idea to give the test to a small group of students on a trial basis. Then, review the test with them for information on the clarity of the directions, as well as the clarity of the test items. Revise your test accordingly.

6. Establish a mastery performance standard. You now have completed your test items for the final exam. While the exam indicates what your students are to learn, it does not indicate how well your students are expected to learn it. To complete your final exam you must set a performance standard for the exam which you believe indicates mastery of the desired learning outcome. To insure competency we suggest that you set your performance standard at a high level. As a rule of thumb, students should answer correctly at least 90 percent of the test items to achieve mastery on a final exam of twenty items or more.

INSTRUCTIONAL STRATEGIES

Once the final exam is constructed, instructional activities can be planned to achieve mastery of the desired learning outcome. However, before becoming involved in the preparation of instructional activities, we need to consider instructional strategies that can influence instructional planning.

The Mastery Learning Strategy

In preparing instructional activities it is important to realize that most students can learn most of the material we teach in elementary, middle, and secondary school. The major difference between one student and another is rate of learning. Carroll (1963) suggested that the degree of school learning will depend on the time the student actually spends in learning relative to the amount of time the student needs to spend. Bloom (1968), elaborating on Carroll's position, argued that if students are given differential quality of instruction and differential opportunity to learn according to their needs, then the majority of students, perhaps as many as 95 percent, could be expected to attain mastery.

There has been sufficient research evidence supporting Carroll's and Bloom's positions for us to advocate the use of mastery learning strategies in the classroom. Block (1971) described the application of mastery learning strategy to classroom learning. Block and Anderson (1975) have published a booklet which summarizes the procedure.

To apply the mastery learning strategy the teacher defines instructional goals, prepares a final exam to test the achievement of the goals, and establishes a score on the final exam that indicates mastery of the goals much as we have described. In addition, the teacher prepares instructional activities to facilitate the achievement of the goals and a short diagnostic-process test to be administered at the end of each instructional activity to assess progress toward the goal and to diagnose impediments to student progress. The instructional activities are used initially to produce the desired learning and as corrective activities for students who do not show adequate progress on the diagnostic-progress tests.

The implications of the mastery learning strategy for instructional planning require the teacher to prepare a variety of instructional activities to facilitate the achievement of a desired learning outcome. Some activities are used in initial instruction, and some are used as correctives. The corrective activities are to be different from the initial activities so that a student who does not make acceptable progress as a result of the initial instruction may choose an alternative mode as a corrective. In addition, the teacher prepares short tests for administration at the end of each instructional activity. She uses the tests to provide feedback for herself and the student concerning student progress and reasons for lack of progress. She prescribes correctives for students who need to be directed back on the track that leads to the desired learning outcome. Students are given all the opportunities they need to achieve the desired outcome.

A Strategy for Teaching Reading-Thinking Skills

The mastery learning strategy pertains to instruction of any kind. The learning of reading-thinking skills can benefit from the use of the mastery learning strategy. However, there is an additional strategy that seems appropriate for the teaching of reading-thinking skills.

We suggest that in preparing instructional activity and diagnostic-progress test units you sequence these units as follows: (1) conversational units, (2) pictorial and graphic units, and (3) reading units. We recommend this sequence because a child first learns to think and express thoughts conversationally, then through pictorial modes, and finally by means of written words. If a student has a particular thinking skill, he may be able to demonstrate it conversationally without being able to demonstrate it through pictures or the written word. Further, diagnostic-progress tests are easily administered conversationally. A teacher may explain to the class how the understanding of a sequence permits predictions to be made, and immediately thereafter ask a student to predict what the class will do in school the next day. Instructional activity and diagnostic-progress test units are at the simplest and most fundamental level when they are in the conversational mode, and the teacher is able to keep an intimate running account of student progress.

Pictorial modes come next because we use pictures to bridge the gap between spoken words and written words. Reading primers are full of pictures that cue the message contained in the printed words. A student may well be able to sequence a group of pictures correctly without being able to sequence a set of statements describing the events in the pictures.

A thinking skill becomes a reading-thinking skill when the student is able to use it with respect to printed words. The student may have the thinking skill and be able to express it conversationally and pictorially, but the thinking skill does not become a reading-thinking skill until it can be applied through the media of printed words.

With these general instructional strategies behind us we can attend to the business of preparing instructional activites to achieve specific desired learning outcomes that pertain to reading.

PREPARING INSTRUCTIONAL UNITS

Establishing Readability Level

The first instructional decision the teacher needs to make concerns the readability level of the reading material he is going to present to the students. The grade equivalent reading scores of the students can be used as a general reference for establishing reading level.

Often, the desired learning outcome may not indicate that the reading level of the students is to be raised. Such is the case with the desired learning outcome we have been using as an illustration. The desired outcome is that students will be able to "predict coming events in a story." They may achieve this outcome without measurably increasing their reading level. Further, to be able to predict coming events in a story the students must at least have a literal comprehension of the reading material. This suggests that the readability level of the reading material should be low enough for all the students to literally comprehend. Otherwise, we cannot know whether a student's failure to predict the coming message is due to inability to predict or inability to literally comprehend the story.

We have made the point throughout the book that students seek optimum predictability. The learning situation should not be too predictable, lest the students become bored. The students should be presented with a challenge. They should reach to attain a learning outcome they have yet to attain. However, the learning situation should not be too unpredictable, or the students will become confused and unable to learn. The pursuit of one desired learning outcome at a time will tend to eliminate confusion, providing the students are ready to pursue the outcome and obstacles are not introduced into the learning environment.

Preparing Instructional Activities and Diagnostic-Progress Test Units to Achieve the Desired Learning Outcome

As we said, activities to achieve the desired learning outcome are suggested by the final exam questions. The teacher can review the questions and devise her own instructional activities and diagnostic-progress tests for these specific activities. Or she can find instructional activities and companion diagnostic-progress tests in many reading skills books, booklets, and program packages. Even if she finds all the instructional activities she needs to achieve the desired learning outcome in published materials, she will need to sequence them with respect to (1) conversational activities, (2) pictorial activities, and (3) reading activities. Also, she will need to insure that there is a variety of activities within each of the three areas so that students may choose among them according to their interests and so that she will have a sufficient number to use as correctives.

The Conversational Mode

To continue with our example the teacher first plans conversational instructional activity and diagnostic-progress test units to teach the students to predict coming events in a story. The teacher may read the beginning of a story to the students, make predictions about the coming events in the story and explain why his predictions are plausible based on what has gone before. Then the teacher may read the beginning of a story to the students and then pause and ask the students to state what they think will happen next and why they think as they do. The teacher can discuss with them the plausibility of their predictions based upon the sequence of events that was read to them.

Students should have it made clear to them that the author has the right to complete her story however she chooses, and that if they discover, when the story is finished, that their predictions were not entirely confirmed, it does not mean that they were "wrong." It is not their purpose to reword an author's story but to see how well they can predict what will happen next based on what they have already heard. There may be several appropriate possibilities at different points in the story, so the teacher should be careful to stop reading and allow discussion at a point where the coming event is fairly limited and obvious.

The Pictorial Mode

In preparing to instruct the students by means of the pictorial mode, the teacher can show them a sequence of pictures that tell a story and demonstrate that on the basis of viewing the beginning of the sequence they can predict the later events in the sequence. Diagnostic-progress tests can be prepared that require students to predict what will happen next in a story, based on a pictorial sequence of earlier events.

The Reading Mode

The reading mode involves students in reading passages that clearly cue coming events in a story and then answering questions that require them to predict the coming events. During instruction the students may make their predictions as part of class discussions. The companion diagnostic-progress test should require them to take a written exam.

Preparing Instructional Activities and Diagnostic-Progress Test Units to Insure Readiness

If all students mastered the readiness skills stated in your instructional goal, there would be little need to prepare instructional activities and companion diagnostic-progress tests to teach these characteristics. However, it is probable that some students in the class will not have mastered the readiness skills. Others who previously showed mastery may have forgotten the readiness skills and need a review. Further, a brief review of readiness skills is always a good way to introduce and show the connection with a more advanced skill, provided the review is not so extensive that it becomes boring. The format for preparing readiness instructional activity and diagnostic-progress test units, as well as all such units, is the same as we described earlier. In our example the readiness skill is "identifying sequences." The conversational, pictorial, and reading modes might be prepared as follows.

The Conversational Mode

The teacher might describe a sequence of events and explain to the class that because of our experience with events we learn to expect them to occur in a particular sequence. The sun rising and setting might be used as an example. The students can give examples from their experiences. Diagnostic-progress tests would require students to sequence events described by the teacher as a part of class discussion.

The Pictorial Mode

The pictorial mode involves students in looking at a number of events and indicating the sequence in which they would be expected to occur. The teacher can first demonstrate and explain sequences of pictorial events. Then students should have opportunities to arrange pictures that tell stories and give explanations about their sequential arrangements. This practice will help clarify their thinking about why pictures fit in certain orders and not in other orders. Then, in a diagnostic-progress test the students would be required to sequence pictures correctly.

The Reading Mode

Here the student would be involved in identifying sequences of written statements. The diagnostic-progress test may require students to sequence the activities described in a number of sentences.

Preparing Facilitating Instructional Activities and Diagnostic-Progress Test Units

The teacher may review the readiness skills and then move directly to the teaching of skills stated in the desired learning outcome, or he may attempt to identify intermediate skills that facilitate the learning of the desired learning outcome. It is the teacher's decision to make. However, if the gap between the readiness skill and the desired learning outcome is great and the teacher can think of intervening exercises that will facilitate the achievement of the desired learning outcome, he should prepare and use these facilitating exercises.

In our example, it is possible to review the readiness skill of identifying sequences and move directly to predicting coming events in a story, or the following facilitating activities might be considered for use. The teacher might think it a good idea to teach the students the relationship between sequences and predicting, and prepare conversational, pictorial, and reading modes to show the relationship.

The Conversational Mode

The teacher can show that knowing the counting sequence permits one to predict. The teacher might begin to count 1, 2, 3, and then pause and ask the students what they predict will come next if the counting continues. The same sort of illustration can be used with respect to the sequences of the notes of the scale and the sequencing of the words and notes of known songs such as the *Star Spangled Banner*.

The Pictorial Mode

In the pictorial mode the teacher might indicate that knowing growth sequences of living things allows predictions to be made about them. The teacher can demonstrate pictorially the life cycle of a butterfly and indicate that when one knows the stage of development the creature is in, one can predict what the next stage will be. A diagnostic-progress test can be constructed showing picture sequences. Students can be asked what they might predict, knowing each sequence.

The Reading Mode

In the reading mode the teacher can show that the events in a story often unfold in a sequence. The words one is reading will cue coming events in a story. Reading the sentence, "Sally's mother is taking her shopping," leads one to predict their future behavior. The statement, "Casey stepped up to bat, with runners on first and third," also leads one to predict certain coming events. For a diagnostic-progress test the class can be given written statements portraying common sequences and asked the kinds of activities a knowledge of these sequences permits one to predict. For instance, knowing the sequence of events that occur in a game permits one to predict how the players will behave.

Sequencing Instructional Activities and Diagnostic-Progress Test Units

By the time the teacher has planned the activities to insure readiness to achieve the desired learning outcome and facilitating activities, she should have a clear idea of the instructional sequence she intends to follow. In the example we have been developing the sequence can be displayed as follows.

	Readiness Units Identifying Sequences	Facilitating Units Relating Sequences to Prediction	Desired Learning Outcome Units Predicting Coming Events in Stories
The Conversational Mode	1	4	7
The Pictorial Mode	2	5	8
The Reading Mode	3	6	9

The instructional units are numbered in the order they would be taught. We have discussed instruction and diagnostic-progress testing with respect to all nine units shown above.

Establishing Points for the Formal Assessment of Student Progress

We have advocated diagnostic-progress testing after each instructional activity as a part of the instructional unit. Some of the diagnostic-progress testing will be done by the student. He will answer questions after viewing pictures or after reading a passage or two. The teacher may be aware of a student's problems only if the student solicits the teacher's help. This does not permit the teacher to carefully monitor student progress. Also, in the conversational mode the testing is quite informal. It requires the teacher in class discussions to question various students. Although some diagnostic and progress information can be obtained at these times, it is not sufficient for making sound judgments.

More formal appraisals must be made by the teacher to assess progress and to diagnose student problems for the purpose of prescribing corrective activities. Formal diagnostic-progress tests are formative tests. They need not be long. A five-to-ten item test is sufficient. They are administered at predetermined intervals as the students move toward the attainment of the desired learning outcomes. The results of the test allow the teacher to prescribe correctives for students who do not perform well on the test. If a student gets fewer than 80 percent of the test items correct, then corrective measures probably should be prescribed. The test results should be discussed with the students before the correctives are prescribed so that the students understand the purpose of the correctives. Feedback from diagnostic-progress tests serves another important purpose. It informs the teacher about the effectiveness of her instructional activities. If most of the students do not make acceptable progress, the teacher needs to review and probably improve the instructional activities.

Formal diagnostic-progress tests should be administered at least once every two weeks. If the teacher waits longer than two weeks to get students back on the track, it may become exceedingly difficult to help them. The teacher can inspect the prescribed sequence of units and determine logical milestones for assessing progress. For instance, in the example we are using a diagnostic-progress test might be administered after the reading mode units have been implemented. This would be after stage 3 when the unit on identifying sequences in written statements has been completed, after stage 6 when the unit on seeing the relationships between story sequences and prediction has been com-

pleted, and after stage 9 when the unit on predicting coming
events in a story is finished.

BUILDING THE INSTRUCTIONAL PROGRAM

The instructional unit the teacher plans first should be the unit
with which he chooses to begin his instructional program. Natu-
rally, the planning of an initial instructional unit will be suggestive of other units that may follow. The desired learning outcome
used in our example, "predicting coming events in a story," is
suggestive of desired learning outcomes that might be pursued
subsequently. Once the student learns how to predict coming
events in a story, she should learn how to test her predictions.
Therefore, a desired learning outcome that might be pursued next
is:

> The student will be able to test the predictions she makes of coming
> events in a story.

The related instructional goal might be expressed as follows:

> The teacher will develop and implement an instructional program
> to teach the eighth grade students in English to predict coming
> events in a story and to test their predictions.

With this instructional goal as a frame of reference the teacher
can plan instructional units to move students from the readiness
state to the desired learning outcome as we described previously
in this chapter.

The teacher can identify a tentative sequence of desired learning outcomes to be pursued in his instructional program during
his initial inspection of the table of specifications. Such sequencing implies that the achievement of a desired learning outcome
earlier in the sequence constitutes readiness to pursue the next
desired learning outcome in the sequence. This initial planning is
helpful to establish the scope of the instructional program and
sequential relationships among desired learning outcomes within
the program. However, the teacher must stand ready to revise the
sequencing upon a closer study of the readiness requirements for
pursuing each desired learning outcome.

PLANNING TO TEACH

Although it is not our purpose to discuss teaching in general, we will outline the mastery learning plan because we have described the planning of reading instruction within the mastery learning framework. We refer you to Block and Anderson (1975) for more information on the format.

Step 1: Orienting the Students To orient the student he is informed of *what* he is going to learn and *how* he is going to be taught.

To orient the student to the total instructional program the teacher can distribute to and discuss with the student the table of specifications. It shows what the student has mastered so far and what he is to learn. The teacher can discuss the mastery learning strategy to acquaint the student with how he will be taught.

As the teacher prepares to move students from a readiness state to a particular desired learning outcome, she can distribute and discuss the relevant goal statement. This acquaints the students with what they will learn next. To acquaint the students with how they will be taught, the teacher can describe the sequence of instructional activities she has planned as well as the diagnostic-progress tests she will use and when they will be administered.

Step 2: Administering Instructional Activities The instructional activities are administered according to plan.

Step 3: Administering Diagnostic-progress Tests The diagnostic-progress tests are administered on completion of each activity.

Step 4: Relating Feedback to Students The students are given feedback. The results of the test are discussed with the students privately and their strengths and weaknesses are described. They are also given encouragement.

Step 5: Moving to the Next Learning Activity Students who have made satisfactory progress move on to the next learning activity. Correctives are administered to students who do not make satisfactory progress. If the teacher desires to keep students moving at the same pace, he can have the students who made satisfactory progress tutor the others. Or he can involve students who make satisfactory progress in enrichment activities.

Step 6: Monitoring Corrective Activities The teacher monitors the corrective activities to make certain that the students who need correctives get as much guidance as they require in order to get back on the track.

Step 7: Administering the Final Examination The final exam is administered. The teacher certifies mastery for those who score above the mastery cut-off score on the test. If the feedback corrective procedures have been thoughtfully planned and carried out, most of the students will achieve mastery. The few who do not are recycled to an earlier stage of instruction and given more correctives so that they may achieve mastery.

SUMMARY

1. To establish student readiness for learning, the teacher should examine students' report cards, previous test scores, and interests.

2. Once the teacher is familiar with the readiness characteristics of his students, he is prepared to select desired learning outcomes for them to pursue. Within the constraints of school policy the teacher selects desired learning outcomes from a table of specifications for reading instruction.

3. Once a desired learning outcome is selected the teacher develops an instructional goal statement that incorporates the desired learning outcome.

4. After the instructional goal is stated, the teacher prepares a final exam to assess the achievement of the desired learning outcome in the goal statement. The final exam is a criterion-referenced summative test. The six steps involved in constructing a final exam are (a) compile and construct test items, (b) check to see that the test items correspond to the desired learning outcome, (c) develop a clear set of directions for responding to each type of test item, (d) establish a scoring procedure that will determine whether or not the student has or has not answered each item correctly, (e) write general directions for the test, and (f) establish a mastery performance standard for the test.

5. Next, the teacher selects or develops an instructional strategy to achieve mastery of the desired learning outcome. In general, we advocate the mastery learning strategy. For teaching reading-thinking skills we advocate, in addition, that three instructional modes be utilized—the conversational mode, the pictorial mode, and the reading mode.

6. After the instructional strategy is determined instructional

units are prepared. First, the teacher determines the readability level of the reading material she will present to the student. Then the teacher prepares instructional units (a) to achieve the desired learning outcomes, (b) to insure student readiness, and (c) to facilitate instructional units. Each instructional unit contains instructional activities and a corresponding diagnostic-progress test.

7. Next the teacher sequences instructional activities and diagnostic-progress test units.

8. To build an instructional program the teacher identifies a sequence of desired learning outcomes to be pursued while inspecting the table of specifications. Then the teacher plans instruction as we have prescribed to lead from one desired outcome to the next.

9. After the construction of the instructional plan the teacher executes the plan. We presented an outline of the mastery learning strategy for teaching or executing an instructional plan.

REVIEW QUESTIONS

1. How does the teacher establish student readiness for learning?

2. How does the teacher select desired learning outcomes for reading instruction?

3. How does the teacher develop an instructional goal statement for reading instruction?

4. How does the teacher prepare a final examination to assess the achievement of a desired learning outcome?

5. What is an instructional strategy? How may instructional strategies be applied to reading instruction?

6. How are instructional units prepared to achieve a desired learning outcome?

7. How are instructional activities and diagnostic-progress tests sequenced?

8. How does the teacher build an instructional program?

9. What is the mastery learning strategy for teaching or executing an instructional plan?

PART VI
TEACHING CONTENT READING

CHAPTER 15

Desired Learning Outcomes
in the Content Areas

PURPOSE

1. To review desired learning outcomes in the content areas, including desired behavioral outcomes and desired content outcomes.

BACKGROUND AND NEW INFORMATION

All the information you learned in the previous chapters concerning desired learning outcomes is applicable in this chapter. You have been familiarized with desired behavioral outcomes in chapters 12, 13, and 14, including motor skills, thinking skills, and preference outcomes. In addition, you were taught desired content outcomes for reading instruction in chapter 13, which acquaints you with content outcomes. In this chapter we consider desired behavioral and content outcomes in the various content areas.

The chapter begins with a discussion of desired behavioral outcomes in the content areas. First, interests and preferences are discussed, then motor skills, and then thinking procedures. The last section of the chapter is devoted to the consideration of desired content outcomes in the content areas. In this section, we consider content outcomes in English and language arts, social studies, science, and mathematics.

KEY TERMS

bibliotherapy
similies
metaphors
modularized scheduling

DESIRED LEARNING OUTCOMES

The student will be able to:

1. Describe how interests and preferences pertain to desired learning outcomes in the content areas.
2. Describe how thinking procedures pertain to desired learning outcomes in the content areas.
3. Describe desired learning outcomes in English and language arts.
4. Describe desired learning outcomes in social studies.
5. Describe desired learning outcomes in science.
6. Describe desired learning outcomes in mathematics.

In planning instruction we must take into account those skills and ideas that contribute optimally to effective living. Coleman (1972) catalogues the skills he believes students should learn in the educational system before the age of eighteen. These include:

1. intellectual skills
2. occupational skills
3. decision-making skills
4. general physical and mechanical skills
5. bureaucratic and organizational skills
6. skills in the care of dependent persons
7. emergency skills
8. verbal communication skills

According to Coleman, effective living is governed by the acquisition of these skills, and public schools generally only deal with a few of them. Those concerned with curricular reform in the content areas address themselves to many of the same considerations. Let us consider some of the desired learning outcomes in the content areas.

DESIRED BEHAVIORAL OUTCOMES

In Part III we described three major behaviors: (1) the expression of interests through the statement of preferences; (2) the use of motor skills; and (3) the use of thinking procedures. Let us examine desired learning outcomes that pertain to each behavior.

Interests and Preferences

As we said, interests are manifested by the preferences expressed by the individual. When he chooses a particular alternative from among a number of desirable options, he is showing an interest in that alternative. One way of capturing a student's interest in learning is to give him options in methods and materials and allow him to choose the one he prefers.

The teacher must be concerned with the student's interests. First of all, she must capture the student's interest in order to teach him. The teacher can lecture, write on the chalkboard, or conduct demonstrations, but if the student is not interested in what the teacher is doing, the student will not pay attention, and learning will not occur. Remember, the teacher controls teaching but not learning. The student decides whether or not he will learn what is being taught. Therefore, one of the teacher's goals must be to interest his students.

Second, a teacher in any content area must try to interest the student in the subject. Some students will have a desire to learn the content, while others may have an antipathy toward it. The

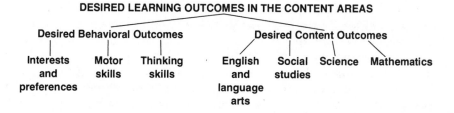

FIGURE 15-1   A hierarchy of topics in chapter 15

teacher can create an interest in a subject if she shows the student the relevance of the subject to his life. That is, she shows the student how learning the subject will improve his ability to predict what will happen in his world and to obtain his preferences.

Third, the teacher is usually concerned with interesting the students in particular aspects of a subject. An English teacher may not only wish to interest a student in English; he may also wish to interest the student in a particular author. A social studies teacher is not only concerned with interesting the student in that subject, she may want to interest the student in the democratic way of life. In all cases, the teacher's chances of interesting the student increase substantially if he shows the student how learning the subject will help the student predict in her life and achieve her preferences.

In order to interest your students in learning it is important for you to acquaint yourself with the problems and interests of the particular age group you are teaching. Each age group has particular problems and interests. Students in the age range of twelve to adulthood are involved in many mental, emotional, and physiological changes that greatly influence their behavior. Perhaps, as Erickson (1968) points out, the development of identity during this period of life is of overriding concern to students. Students are compelled to determine who they are as individuals, to develop a personal life style, to evolve a personal code of ethics—in short, to develop a self-identity. Students are also constantly involved in the process of recognizing how they relate to other people, integrating themselves into society, and learning how to become members of adult society.

These are difficult tasks for adolescents to deal with, and they are compounded by other factors. The development of a sexual identity, for example, is a significant part of developing both a self-identity and a group identity. The development of these various types of self-perspectives is made even more difficult by the fact that our society provides precious few markers along the way to indicate to students when they have achieved adulthood. In fact, the age of adulthood varies greatly depending upon whether one is going to the movies (age twelve), voting (age eighteen), or seeking lower auto insurance rates (age twenty-five). This is all very confusing and contradictory to adolescents.

Postman and Weingartner (1969), in their discussion of "What's Worth Knowing?" reproduce a set of questions that they have developed from conversations with children of many ages in an attempt to probe students for their interests and preferences insofar as what they learn in school. Generally, students are interested in answering questions about personal worries and concerns, coping with individual and societal change and causes of change, dealing with other people, understanding and communicating with other people, becoming members of adult society, deciding what kind of an adult to be, future aspirations, the quality and importance of ideas and knowledge, progress, the cycle of life, survival, threats to life, and the interrelatedness of different forms of life. A survey of studies dealing with the reading interests and preferences of students reveals that preferred reading materials deal with many of the same concerns.

Interests and Preferences in Reading

As Weintraub (1969) has pointed out, a number of problems exist in research that attempt to delineate the nature of students' reading interests. First, the studies of reading interests are limited by the categories examined in the studies and the way in which a researcher defines the categories. Second, we as adults may have different perceptions than children regarding what makes a story or book interesting. For example, a researcher might find intermediate grade students interested in reading materials about animals. Many of us might assume that students, then, like to read materials in which animals are the main characters and are endowed with human traits. On the other hand, closer examination may tell us that students are really more interested in reading about the care and feeding of animals. Thus, animal stories are of many varieties, and we are not always aware of the precise elements in stories about animals that students are interested in. These factors make the task of generalizing about what students prefer to read an arduous one indeed.

Shores (1964) found in studying the reading interests and preferences of students in grades four through twelve that interest in mystery and adventure literature remained high throughout these grades, while interest in animal stories declined. Both Shores and Wolfson (1960) found that boys and girls have a very strong interest in reading materials in the area of social studies. Ruth Smith (1962), analyzing library withdrawals, found the five general categories of humor-fantasy, real animals, nature-science, holidays-birthdays, and fairy tales to be of high interest. Nelson

(1966) examined the poems students in primary grades liked the most. He found that preferred poems had the following elements in common: they contained action but a minimum of description, had a discernible story line, many contained nonsense humor, and many were about the experiences of children. On the other hand, disliked poetry tended to be overly wordy.

Yarlott and Harpin (1971) found in studying 1000 high school students that they preferred reading fiction to nonfiction, novels and short stories over poetry and plays, historical novels to expository history, and science fiction to expository science material. They found that, generally speaking, both boys and girls preferred short stories, humor, and mystery. Desjardins (1972) administered an interest questionnaire to 196 ninth-through-twelfth graders. Results indicated that boys seemed to prefer car and sports stories, mysteries, and humorous stories. On the other hand, girls preferred stories of romance, but also liked mysteries, humorous stories, and adventure stories.

Johns (1973) analyzed the content of reading materials preferred by low socioeconomic level students. They preferred reading materials that depicted middle-class settings, characters with positive self-concepts, and characters in positive group interactions. Ojala and McNeill (1972) discovered that high school students were interested in reading about singers and singing groups, movie and television personalities, and sports figures. They also found that mysteries, science fiction, and biographies were among the most preferred types of books.

Pollan (1973) did an informal content analysis of books preferred by eleventh graders. Generally speaking, she found that preferred books had the following factors in common:

1. Most were first-person narratives.
2. Heroes were generally onlookers and/or outcasts from society.
3. Heroes were unique and portrayed as different from others.
4. Heroes often refused to join society and became "rebel-victims".
5. All preferred books dealt in some way with a quest for identity.

Carlsen (1975), in studying the reading interests of adolescents, attempted to group the kinds of reading matter preferred according to early, middle, and late adolescent periods:

EARLY ADOLESCENCE (AGES 11–14)

animal stories
adventure stories (preferred by boys)
mystery stories
tales of the supernatural
sports stories
growing up around the world (preferred by girls)
slapstick comedy

MIDDLE ADOLESCENCE (AGES 15–16)

nonfiction adventure stories and accounts
war stories (preferred by boys)
historical novels
mystical romance (preferred by girls)
contemporary stories of adolescent life

LATE ADOLESCENCE (AGES 16–18)

books dealing with a search for personal values and identity
books of social significance
books dealing with strange and unique human experience
books dealing with the transition into adulthood

In more recent studies, Carlsen (1975) has discovered a shift in the reading preferences of adolescents. Today's youth have moved from an interest in books about "doing your own thing" toward books about "getting it all together." They are looking for books that make a positive statement about people and the meaning of life and that communicate a hope for the future. In essence, according to Carlsen, today's teenagers prefer books that deal with "heroes worth modeling after, values worth upholding, and a sense of hope."

Preferred books often contain several levels of meaning within the context of a simple and easy-to-read style. Beyond these more superficial considerations, those books most often preferred by teenage readers:

1. contain a first-person narrative; a first-person account or "witnessing"
2. have heroes with a sense of uniqueness who are on the outside looking in and who have been unable to accept the human condition for what it is. Often, these kinds of characters are alienated "rebel-victims" who have rejected the in-

itiation rites of society and are portrayed as both saints and
madmen
3. demonstrate a strong antiintellectual bias, appealing more
to the reader's feelings, emotions, and intuitions
4. evidence a pervading theme of truth, gained only from personal experience
5. portray characters at a turning point in their lives and involved in a search for identity and self
6. treat childhood as a time of innocence and growing up with a
profound sense of loss due to a departure from childhood and
the innocence it entails.

Although this is a very brief review of what is known about students' reading interests and preferences, several guidelines can
be drawn in helping teachers to make appropriate reading materials available to students.

First, age and sex are the most potent factors influencing
students' choices of reading materials. Intelligence and
socioeconomic status have little influence in comparison. Students generally prefer characters in reading materials that are
roughly their own age and capable of what the students themselves are capable of. Seldom does a student tolerate a book about
a main character who is younger than he or she. Sex identification
is also relatively important in terms of character preferences.
Boys prefer action and adventure in reading materials to a greater
extent than girls. Both boys and girls prefer mysteries, realistic
and historical fiction, and biographic over many other types of
books.

Second, students prefer reading materials that have settings
different from those they encounter daily. While it is important for
students to be able to identify with story characters, it does not
necessarily follow that they need to identify with other elements
of the reading materials like setting. Third, students tend to prefer
reading materials that deal with the kinds of problems they themselves must deal with. The concept of bibliotherapy provides a
useful perspective in matching students to books. Essentially,
bibliotherapy is the prescription of certain books based on content
for certain students. For example, Haley (1974) provides a list of
books that deal with the "fractured family." The implication is
that students from broken homes can, by reading a prescribed
book, learn that other people have gone through the same experience and can see how at least one other person in the world dealt
with the very real problem of divorced parents. (See also: Fein and

Ginsberg, 1978; Pilgrim and McAllister, 1968; and D. G. Singer, 1977.)

Finally, as teachers, we must be aware that students are not necessarily interested in reading the things that interest us, or even the things we think they are interested in. Interests and preferences regarding the content of reading materials will vary so much from one individual to another that it is nearly impossible to generalize that all twelve-year-old boys, for example, are interested in reading about motorcycles. We must be aware also that students read on a variety of reading levels, just as we do, and we should not be overly concerned at what we might think of as poor choices of reading materials that our students might make. Reading interests and tastes constantly change and mature, and we must make a conscious effort not to discourage or stifle this process of maturation of reading tastes. There is evidence that a conscious effort to recommend books and other reading materials to students can greatly increase the amount of reading they do.

Motor Skills

Motor skills are important in many areas of learning. In physical education a student must learn to perform the physical feats that are involved in sports. In home economics the student must learn to cook, bake, and sew. In art he must learn to manipulate the art materials he uses to express himself. In music she may learn to play a musical instrument. To become accomplished she must learn to finger the instrument smoothly. In science a student must learn how to work with laboratory equipment. He learns to perform experiments in chemistry, to dissect frogs in zoology and to deal with physical matter in physics. Knowledge may be acquired in a short time, but a motor skill must be practiced for extended periods in order for smooth coordination to develop.

When motor skills are taught, the student is usually told the reasons for coordinating his movements in a particular way. This enables him to understand why he performs in a prescribed way. In addition, he is usually taught to conceptualize the correct performance. This allows him to think about what he is doing and to correct the mistakes he makes. It may be all right to train dogs and performing animals, but humans should be taught to conceptualize the correct coordination so that they may understand what they are doing and can correct their mistakes.

Although reading is more involved with thinking skills than motor skills, the introduction of teaching machines in the area of reading often requires the student to improve her reading by working with a machine. Otherwise, reading requires little more in the way of motor skills than finding a book in the library, eye scanning, and turning the pages.

Thinking Procedures

Most of what we teach in school requires the student to develop and apply certain thinking procedures, no matter what the content area may be and regardless of whether the student is learning from reading, lecture, or demonstration. To answer the questions on the teacher's tests, the student must be able to think. Consequently, one of our goals must be to teach the student how to think.

Researchers have devoted a great amount of effort to the discovery of developmental trends in these important abilities. Much of the work of Piaget, Gibson, Levin, and others has been directed toward these abilities. However, experimental stimuli, task variables, and so on differ from one experiment to another creating serious problems in our attempt to discover a developmental progression. The preponderance of these studies has been conducted with children in the age range of three to eight. Most of these researchers would agree that, developmentally speaking, nearly all of the abilities (or potential for learning these abilities) we associate with abstracting relationships, categorizing, and classifying have developed by the sixth or seventh grade. This does not imply that these abilities are systematically taught or even an important part of the middle and high school curriculum. However, the teaching of these abilities becomes increasingly important in the upper grade levels since the content to which students are exposed becomes increasingly more sophisticated. Similarly, students' life styles and the problems they encounter become increasingly more complex, making these abilities even more important from an instructional standpoint.

In almost everything we read we are required to identify similarities and differences and to think sequentially and in terms of cause and effect. In literature, we might read a poem. In the study of poetry, it is inevitable that we will be required to study literary devices such as metaphors and similies. These particular devices are used by poets to convey relationships of similarity. In history we are asked to study the events that led to the Civil War. More specifically, we study the events that caused the Civil War. We discover cause-effect relationships among events in history, how historical events are related. In science, we are asked to perform experiments step-by-step. We discover programmatic relationships in chemical reactions, in the evolutionary process, and in the life cycles of events as diverse as animals and stars. We discover the programmatic nature of the steps and strategies involved in problem solving. We discover how events are related, chronologically and hierarchically.

We make predictions about events, based on our discovery of the way in which events are sequentially related. Ultimately, the poem, the events leading to the Civil War, and the particular chemical process we studied are of less importance than the *thinking processes* we used in the study of these content areas. Ultimately, the similies and metaphors we studied will have a minimal effect on our lives. Similarly, knowing which events lead to the Civil War will provide us little help in understanding contemporary history. We will probably have little use for the information we gained from our study of the chemical reaction in our science class, that is to say, unless we specialize in a content area. However, the thinking processes we used in the study of these three subjects will transfer to other areas. We can see, for example, that the pollution problem in our community is similar to the problems in other communities. We can look at the sequence of events that led to the problem in another community and understand where our community is on that same continuum. We can predict what the outcome of the pollution problem will be if we do not deal with it. We can further predict the outcome of the problem if we take a particular course of action. In this instance, we have transferred the thinking procedures learned in three particular content areas to events outside the realm of school. We have transferred the thinking skills, not the content, to the problems that are confronting us in our daily lives. Certainly content can play an important role, but it is the thinking procedures that are of utmost value to effective living.

The written materials we use in instruction in content areas reflect these identification and prediction patterns. Many of the comprehension problems students have in content areas stem from their inability to follow the inherent structure of the written materials being used. That is, most students are not aware that paragraphs and larger units of prose are generally written in a format that promotes identification and prediction. When students discover and can use this inherent structure in written materials, they acquire a powerful tool to aid them in both comprehension and in their own writing.

This rationale supplies us with additional advantages, not the least of which is the enhancement of the relevance of learning and schooling. Specifically, if students and parents see a purpose and a use for what is taught in schools, then learning will be further facilitated. By teaching those skills that will help students identify and predict and gain their preferences from the environment, we help them to integrate themselves into society. Consequently, we will have made a great deal of progress toward enhancing students' self-confidence and toward actively involving students in the process of learning and living. In teaching reading-thinking skills in any content area our major concern should be to develop those procedures that will:

1. help students to better understand the environment and the society in which they live
2. provide students with a knowledge and understanding of societal and technological developments that have influenced their environment and the way in which they live
3. provide students with the opportunity to understand and critically evaluate factors that have a major influence on society
4. help students to better understand relationships among content areas, society, and people
5. help students acquire skills and competencies that will benefit them in their chosen vocation
6. develop in students an appreciation for change and the ability to cope with change in their society
7. help students refine all techniques of communication
8. improve students' abilities to identify and predict
9. help students to attain their preferences

DESIRED CONTENT OUTCOMES

At this point you know that the term "content" can be considered synonymous with "subject matter"; both terms refer to the information, ideas, concepts, and knowledge that comprise a given discipline. Content, then is *what* we think about. We have devoted a great deal of discussion to the thinking procedures that are necessary to mature reading. In essence, these skills comprise the processes we use in dealing with the information, ideas, and concepts that comprise a content area. The thinking procedures we teach affect what people *do* with the information they receive, not only from reading but from all aspects of life.

Curriculum experts, educators, and parents have debated for many years about what ought to be taught in the schools. This debate is reflected in the great amount of variation that exists among schools, school districts, and other educational agencies regarding what is taught. Recent trends in public schooling also reflect this change; many schools offer modularized scheduling of classes so that students are free to take a diversity of electives ranging from folklore to quantum chemistry. The debate is not over, nor will it ever be. The curriculum in any given school will continue to evolve and change to meet the needs of the students, as well as society. With the vast amount of information that is available today, the continued addition of information to our total knowledge base, and the ever-present fact that information is outdated almost by the time it reaches us, there is no reason to believe that curricular change is inappropriate or unnecessary.

Let us now inspect the content in various content areas so that you may be more familiar with instructional aims in these content areas.

English and Language Arts

Erickson (1965) points out five major aims of English and language arts instruction:

1. to think clearly and logically
2. to communicate clearly and correctly
3. to develop a sensitivity to beauty and the feelings of others
4. to develop the ability to find and use critically a variety of language materials
5. to become aware of the power and significance of language

Other writers in the area of English and language arts curriculum emphasize that the essential difference between English and other content areas is the emphasis in English on understanding an author's mood, tone, feeling, values, and so on. That is, in English and the study of literature, we deal primarily with the study of human beings through the medium of written language.

Odell (1973) emphasizes essentially the same point in describing the teaching of reading in the English classroom as a process of teaching students an awareness of different perspectives and viewpoints. Odell suggests that the English curriculum should be directed toward teaching students to:

1. get outside of their own frame of reference, to understand the thoughts, feelings, and values of other people
2. get outside of the immediate circumstances of the here and now, and project themselves into unfamiliar circumstances whether real or hypothetical
3. get outside of their immediate visceral reaction in order to understand why they react as they do to experiences

More specifically, Duke (1974) suggests that the teaching of literature should deal with seeing conflicts, understanding decisions and value judgments, sensing tone and mood, seeing and understanding character, and recognizing "stock" characters.

Another obvious consideration of the English and language arts curriculum is that of the teaching of grammar. The study of the language itself can be exciting and rewarding for students, but often is turned into drudgery. Current writers in the field of English curriculum see grammar and the study of language as a useful vehicle for understanding people of other cultures as well as our own cultural history. Additionally, the work of linguists such as Chomsky and Thomas has provided us an improved description of our language by emphasizing how changes in wording, syntax, and punctuation change meaning.

In short, the content of English and language arts instruction from the viewpoint of curriculum experts should be directed toward all processes of language and communication. The improvement of communication skills is seen as a vehicle for developing in students an understanding and appreciation of themselves and other peoples.

Social Studies

Bruner (1941) sees a number of areas that are of special importance in teaching social studies: (1) culture, (2) society, (3) role, (4) status, (5) social class, (6) socialization, (7) personality, (8) freedom, (9) justice, and (10) political behavior. Each of these subjects, according to Bruner, deserves attention in the social studies curriculum. Van Til (1976) describes a number of what he called "centers of experience" important in secondary education, many of which deal with social studies content. Among them are war, peace, international relations, overpopulation, pollution, energy problems, economic problems, government processes, consumer problems, intercultural relations, world views, and community living.

Other writers in the area of social studies curriculum emphasize the study of societies and social change as a major facet of the social studies curriculum. Other areas of emphasis include the environment, land-use, living patterns in cities, values, geographical and climatic influences on culture, social change, beliefs and attitudes of other social and ethnic groups, and so on. As Jarolimek (1974) points out, social studies curriculum development must address itself to many questions such as:

1. making social studies content more meaningful, in a personal sense, to students.
2. relating social studies to the out-of-school lives of students.
3. developing insights into the world in which we live through social studies.
4. depicting realistically the racial, ethnic, and national background of others.
5. using social studies to combat societal evils such as racism.
6. using social studies as a vehicle for teaching values.
7. building skills that will enable students to continue to learn about the world in which they live.
8. making the student a more effective decision maker.
9. helping students grasp the economic, military, and social reality of this country's international involvements

In essence, current thinking in social studies curriculum emphasizes the study of society and culture—that is, people. Change is an important consideration in the social studies curriculum. Understanding environmental and social change will enable students to live more effectively by successfully coping with change.

Science

Burkman (1972) reported the thinking of a large group of national leaders in science education attending a conference supported by the National Science Foundation. The following points regarding science teaching and the improvement of science teaching were made:

1. Group-centered and teacher-directed science instruction needs to be de-emphasized. More provisions should be made for individuals in terms of their learning rates, learning styles, and individual interests.
2. Applied science and technology should be dealt with as opposed to the current overemphasis on "pure" science.
3. The social implications, i.e., the cultural effects of science and technology should be dealt with as an important part of the science curriculum.
4. Science course offerings should go beyond the traditional biology-chemistry-physics sequence. Additionally, efforts should be made to integrate the life sciences and the physical sciences so as to demonstrate their relatedness.
5. Efforts should be made to individualize science instruction in terms of the materials available to teach science. Too many science instructional materials tend to be inflexible, requiring students and teachers to commit themselves to a sequence of topics for a full school year.
6. The goals and objectives of science instruction should be clearly specified in order that evaluation of the effectiveness of science education can be made.
7. Efforts should be made to insure that all high school graduates receive an adequate general education in science.

Yager (1976) elaborates on some of the content considerations in science that should concern us. He maintains that science instruction should be concerned with values. That is, students must be able to make judgments dealing with real problems. As implied above, these problems are primarily in the realm of science and society and the effects each has on the other. Secondly, science instruction should take on an interdisciplinary dimension that emphasizes a consideration of other areas such as politics, economics, sociology, communication, and change. Thirdly, Yager makes the point that science instruction should be "future oriented." In short, science teaching should be directed toward the "world we want" rather than a rehash of historic scientific discoveries. Finally, Yager indicates that science instruction should emphasize "inquiry skills that are oriented toward rational *decision making* rather than experimental skills." In addition, we need to make a stronger connection between inquiry skills—the *processes* of science—and similar skills required for effective living in a complex society.

Fundamentally, the science curriculum, from the perspective of current literature, should emphasize the relatedness of science to other areas of knowledge. In addition, the effect of science and technology on cultures and societies is an important facet of the total science curriculum. Finally, the usefulness of science content to effective living needs to be considered in determining the science curriculum.

Mathematics

Curricular concerns in the area of mathematics have, in the past several years, revolved around what is generally termed the "new math." Essentially, supporters of the new math have maintained that the introduction of topics in mathematics such as sets, field properties, symbolic logic, and so forth is needed as the mathematics curriculum continues to evolve. Opponents of new math are concerned that topics such as these are too abstract and are bringing about a decline in mathematics achievement.

Kline (1971), an opponent of the new math, maintains that whatever changes in the math curriculum of middle and secondary schools take place, they should embody efforts to:

1. Make mathematics more interesting and motivate students to achieve in mathematics.
2. Teach mathematics intuitively and as the deductive process it is.
3. Teach mathematics as a part of our total knowledge so that we emphasize its relatedness to other areas of knowledge, as well as the development of our civilization and culture.

Other writers in the field of mathematics curriculum have specified a number of topical areas that should be dealt with in the middle and high school mathematics program. Fehr (1971), for example, indicates that concepts and content hierarchies regarding the following topics should be taught at the high school level: number concepts, algebra, quantitative relations, concepts of measurement, and geometrical figures. Fehr also suggests that in preservice teacher education the following topics should be dealt with: relations, sets, laws of composition, structures, construction of numerical sets, logic, exploration of space, geometry through transformations, measures, and probability and statistics. Still others emphasize the teaching of general problem-solving abilities and the value of the structure of mathematics as a means for attaining understanding, application, and retention of mathematics content. A number of those writing in the area of mathematics education emphasize the teaching of deductive logic through geometry.

Still others concerned with curricular innovations and changes in mathematics place emphasis upon the application of knowledge of mathematics to problems encountered in daily living. Kline (1971) makes the point that too often mathematics becomes an abstraction for students when we make little or no attempt to communicate a purpose and usefulness of mathematics to our students.

Essentially, curricular concerns in mathematics currently revolve around a host of substantive issues. These issues will, in turn, influence both the teaching of mathematics and the content of the mathematics curriculum to be taught. In part, these issues might be summarized as follows:

1. Making the content of mathematics more purposeful and showing students how math content can be applied to other areas of knowledge as well as the practical problems students encounter daily.
2. Teaching mathematics in a topical sequence that will optimize students' mathematics achievement by emphasizing the structure of the content.
3. Emphasizing the relation of mathematics to other areas of interest, knowledge, and pursuit.
4. Showing how mathematics has influenced civilization and culture.
5. Teaching both deductive and inductive logic using mathematics as the vehicle.

Commonalities Among the Content Areas

Although it is our basic premise in content reading that reading and thinking skills required in particular content areas differ from one area to another, this should not imply that the goals and desired learning outcomes in different content areas are entirely dissimilar. In fact, from the foregoing discussion, there appears to be a certain unity regarding the goals and desired learning outcomes in different content areas.

Current thinking and trends in each of the content areas emphasize a number of common concerns. The curriculum in English (including literature and grammar), science, social studies, and mathematics has, according to current thinking, the following general factors in common:

1. That each content area is concerned with the language and thinking abilities required to understand the content, and that communication is of central concern.
2. That each content area should emphasize the relationship between the knowledge in that area and people, that is, how knowledge of the content helps one to understand individuals, societies, and whole cultures.
3. That each content area possesses structure and that this structure can be utilized in enhancing the learning that goes on in each content area.
4. That each content area is related to other disciplines and areas of knowledge and that the content should be presented, studied, and learned in the context of other disciplines.
5. That the knowledge in each content area has practical utility for improving students' abilities to live effectively in a complex society.

SUMMARY

1. Desired behavioral outcomes include desired motor skills, thinking procedures, and preference outcomes.

2. Teachers must be concerned with student interests because the teacher (a) must capture students' interest in order to teach them at all, (b) must try to interest the student in the content area, and (c) is usually concerned with interesting students in particular aspects of a content area.

3. Age and sex are the most important factors influencing student interests in reading materials. Student prefer reading materials that have settings different from those they encounter daily and reading materials that deal with problems they must deal with.

4. Teachers must be concerned with motor skills when instructional activities require the motor performance of students. Students should be taught to conceptualize correct motor performance so that they may understand what they are doing and can correct their mistakes.

5. Most of what we teach in school requires the student to develop and apply certain processes of thinking. In history students become involved in cause-effect thinking when they attempt to determine the cause of an historical event. In literature students are concerned with literary devices such as similies and metaphors which involve them in thinking in terms of similarities and differences. In science students think programmatically when they become involved in executing the steps of a laboratory experiment. In mathematics students become involved in categorical thinking when they deal with set theory. The essence of being able to think in a content area is the ability to identify and predict in the content area.

6. Desired learning outcomes in English and language arts include thinking and communicating clearly and correctly, developing a sensitivity for beauty, developing the ability to find and use language materials, and better understanding one's self and others.

7. Desired learning outcomes in social studies include understanding the concepts of culture, society, role, status, social class, socialization, personality, politics, values, social conflict, and economics.

8. Desired learning outcomes in science include an understanding of the relationship between life and physical science, applied as well as pure science, the social implications of science, the decision-making implications of science, and inquiry skills.

9. Desired learning outcomes in mathematics include an understanding of number concepts, algebra, quantitative relations, concepts of measurement, geometrical figures, sets, field properties, symbolic logic, and the application of math to problem solving.

10. The content areas share the following desired learning outcomes. Each content area should be concerned with thinking abilities, communications, the relationship between content knowledge and people, the relationship between one content area and another, and the relationship between a content area and effective living.

REVIEW QUESTIONS

1. Into what three areas can desired behavioral outcomes be subdivided?

2. Why must teachers be concerned with student interests?

3. What factors significantly influence student interests?

4. When must teachers be concerned with motor skills?

5. How do thinking procedures apply to teaching in the content areas?

6. What are some desired learning outcomes in English and language arts? In social studies? In science? In mathematics?

7. What are some desired learning outcomes that are common to the four content areas?

CHAPTER 16
Writing Patterns in the Content Areas
PURPOSE

To acquaint you with:
1. Premises underlying the teaching of reading in content areas
2. Reading and thinking in the content areas
3. The teaching of writing patterns in the content areas.

BACKGROUND AND NEW INFORMATION

The information you acquired from previous chapters provides a foundation for learning about writing patterns. In chapter 4 you were introduced to signal words. Signal words are discussed further in this chapter. The thinking procedures discussed since chapter 5 help you learn about writing patterns. The skill "detecting similarities and differences" is directly related to the "comparison/contrast writing pattern." The skills "identifying sequences" and "identifying cause/effect relationships" prepare you to understand the corresponding writing patterns that are discussed in this chapter.

The chapter begins with a discussion of basic premises underlying content area reading, including the direct skills approach and the content centered approach. Next we discuss similarities and differences in reading and thinking in content areas. The last section of the chapter is devoted to teaching writing patterns. In this section signal words are discussed, and then a number of writing patterns are described, including the listing, sequence, comparison/contrast, and cause/effect writing patterns.

KEY TERMS

rhythm
hyperbole
irony
concept load
deposition
typographical aids
diurnal

DESIRED LEARNING OUTCOMES

The student will be able to:

1. Describe basic premises underlying content area reading.
2. Describe similarities and differences in reading and thinking in the content areas.
3. Explain the importance of signal words in reading.
4. Describe the listing pattern, sequence pattern, comparison/contrast pattern, cause/effect pattern, purpose-setting pattern, and other stylistic patterns of writing and how to teach these patterns of writing to improve comprehension.

SOME BASIC PREMISES OF CONTENT AREA READING

Approaches to teaching reading skills in the content areas have received a certain amount of research attention and deserve increased attention in this respect. Basically, the methodology for teaching reading and thinking skills in the content areas is twofold. First, a *direct skills approach* has been advocated by many authorities in the field. The direct skills approach is carried out by the provision of direct instruction in skills associated with the particular content areas. For example, a social studies teacher might prepare a two-week unit for the purpose of teaching study skills including map reading, graph and chart reading, and reference skills. In this example, the study skills mentioned above would become the focus of instruction while the content or subject matter would be of little importance in comparison. Once students learn the particular reading and thinking skills being taught, they will transfer these skills and abilities to other content they study.

The direct skills approach has been criticized on the grounds that it assumes that the transfer of reading and thinking skills that

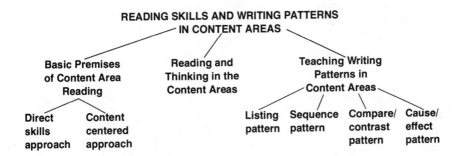

FIGURE 16–1   A hierarchy of topics in chapter 16

have been taught is automatic. Opponents of this method have shown that such transfer is not always automatic and cannot be assumed. These writers, in contrast, imply that the teaching of reading skills in content areas must take place in a way that requires the student to integrate the skills with the new content learned, letting the content learned determine the reading skills to be emphasized in content instruction.

Thus, the other major approach to teaching reading skills in the content areas is the *content-centered approach*. In other contexts, this approach has been referred to as the incidental approach in which reading and thinking skills are taught as the content material requires these skills of students. The advantages of the content centered approach include:

1. Reading skills are taught in a meaningful context; that is, they are taught when the material requires, giving students the opportunity to use and apply the skills in a meaningful situation.
2. The need for specialized reading classes (remedial, developmental, and so on) is lessened since content teachers assume the responsibility for teaching those reading skills necessary to understand and master the content they teach.

The content centered approach carries with it certain assumptions about the teaching that takes place in the various content areas. First, it assumes that the content area teacher possesses a basic understanding of the skills of reading. Second, it assumes a certain attitude on the part of the content area teacher such that the teacher sees a need for teaching reading skills and is willing to assume responsibility for teaching these skills. Third, the content centered approach requires the teacher to analyze the content in order to identify and clarify the nature of the skills that are necessary to understand and master the content being taught.

Another basic tenet of content area reading instruction becomes apparent here. That is, the instructional materials and tasks required of students differ among different content areas. Each content area requires a particular thinking style. Each content area emphasizes particular thinking skills. Each content area requires students to think in ways that are peculiar to that content area. There is an old adage that in order to effectively learn a foreign language, one must learn to think in that language. The analogy can be applied to reading and thinking in the content areas. In order to effectively learn in any content area, one must acquire the ability to think in that content area.

When students learn to think in the patterns that are peculiar to a given content area, they engage in the process of discovering the relationships that exist among events in the content area. When students learn to read in the various patterns that are peculiar to content areas, they likewise discover the relationships that exist among the events contained in the material they read. When students develop these abilities, they have, in essence, learned to identify and predict. Just as the fluent reader learns to use the inherent patterns in the printed language and to search for "fits" in terms of syntactic and semantic sense when reading, the fluent reader in the content area must also discover patterns of thinking and writing in content areas in order to make identifications and predictions about the content. This view of reading and thinking skills in the content areas is entirely congruent with views of reading offered by linguists and psycholinguists.

READING AND THINKING IN THE CONTENT AREAS

Smith (1963) investigated the idea that different writing patterns exist in content areas, analyzing 200 textbooks designed for use in grades 7 through 12. She found that there were "common" reading skills among all content areas of the type we have referred to in previous chapters. However, she did find that certain writing patterns were prevalent in particular content areas. In literature, she found that no single pattern or combination of patterns prevailed. Rather, literature contained a wide diversity of writing patterns. On the other hand, science, social studies, and mathematics textbooks exhibited less variation in the types of writing patterns used.

According to Smith, one of the most common patterns was what she referred to as the "classification" pattern. This pattern required students to engage in the process of categorizing information gained from reading. Within this pattern, the student must have a high degree of ability to understand relationships of similarity and contrast. The student must be able to group events based on their common elements. This, by necessity, also involves the ability to understand contrasts, differences, and discriminations. A second prominent writing pattern in science pervades Smith's "technical process" and "experiment" patterns. Both of these patterns require the student to deal with relationships of sequence. Following detailed instructions that ultimately lead to higher order skills is an important skill in the content area of science. Other patterns such as "statement of facts" and the "problem solving" patterns identified by Smith are prevalent in science. The "statement of facts" pattern involves the specific reading-thinking skills of determining the main idea and finding supportive details. The "problem solving" pattern places a premium on understanding relationships of programmatic sequence and relationships of cause and effect. The ability to read graphs, charts, diagrams, equations, abbreviations, and such is also important in the area of science.

In the content area of social studies, Smith indicates that the most prevalent writing pattern involves the use of cause-effect relationships. The ability to understand sequential relationships is also a frequent pattern in social studies, followed by relationships of similarity and contrast and by Smith's "statement of fact" pattern.

Reading in the area of mathematics presents some unique problems to students. Mathematics is replete with abstract symbols that stand for complex ideas. When students face the task of reading these symbols, they find that the reading material is a great deal less redundant and context aids are sparse. Smith's "problem solving" pattern is the most common in mathematics, again involving primarily relationships of sequence and cause and effect. Smith suggests a general strategy of close reading and concentration on what is being read in the content area of mathematics.

It becomes abundantly clear through an analysis of teaching

methods in the content areas, as well as an analysis of the content itself, that there are many "common" reading skills required in all content areas, that particular content areas require particular reading skills due largely to the nature of the content itself, and that in most instances a content centered approach is the more effective method for teaching these reading skills. Those skills considered "common" to all content areas would necessarily include the following:

1. Developing reading vocabulary.
2. Identifying and establishing purpose for reading.
3. Developing flexible reading strategies that suit the nature of the content being read and the purposes for reading.
4. Developing and refining specific reading skills including literal comprehension, understanding the main idea, predicting outcomes and events, deductive and inductive reading and thinking skills, and skills requiring classification and categorization.
5. Critical reading skills including the evaluation and application of the content that is read.

On the other hand, there are reading and thinking skills that are either peculiar to specific content areas or that are required to such a degree that their development and refinement can spell the difference between the student's success or failure in a content area. Reading in literature requires many reading and thinking skills dealt with in this and other chapters. Additionally, the following skills are fairly specific to reading in literature:

1. Dealing effectively with the many formats that are regularly used in literature, including short stories, novels, poems, essays, biographies and autobiographies, dramas, and so on.
2. Identifying and understanding literary devices such as personification, metaphor, rhythm, hyperbole, irony, and so forth.
3. Identifying and understanding stylistic devices peculiar to certain authors and the way in which an author develops tone, mood, characters, theme, and plot.

Reading in science, just as in social studies and mathematics, involves the mastery of reading expository materials. More specifically, the following reading and thinking skills are at a premium in dealing with science content:

1. Classifying and categorizing information gained from the content.
2. Following detailed instructions in a step-by-step manner.
3. Differentiating relevant from irrelevant information in solving problems.
4. Finding supportive information in determining main ideas and drawing conclusions based on content.

Length and volume of social studies materials, as well as vocabulary and concept load, create reading problems for students. Beyond these factors, social studies content consistently requires the student to have mastered the following skills:

1. Ability to use flexible reading strategies in order to effectively deal with lengthy reading assignments.
2. Identifying and understanding the way in which historical events are causally related.
3. Recognizing sequences and chronologies of events and understanding how they support the way in which events are causally related.

Finally, mathematics content requires students to develop facility in the following skills:

1. Mastering the many abstract and unfamiliar symbols used in math.
2. Developing the ability to read materials that contain a mixture of math symbols and language equivalents for math terms and symbols.
3. Developing strategies for solving mathematics problems including story problems.

While the skills previously mentioned are certainly not meant to be an exhaustive listing of those reading and thinking skills required in content areas, they do serve to point up the fact that different reading and thinking strategies are required in different content areas. This view of content area reading instruction implies two very important assumptions. First, the content that we teach and expect students to learn must be analyzed in order to determine what reading skills are required to master the content. Secondly, those reading skills we identify should be taught as an integral part of the content we expect students to learn.

We have attempted to show how the reading skills required in various content areas differ from one content area to another. We have also tried to differentiate these reading skills by content area. In the final analysis, however, we must closely examine the specific content we plan to teach in order to identify and provide instruction in these skills. Finally, we have indicated that the process of analyzing content for the reading skills it requires of students is the essence of the content centered approach to teaching reading, and we have emphasized that this approach, with few exceptions, tends to be an extremely effective approach to teaching reading skills and enhancing student achievement in content areas.

TEACHING WRITING PATTERNS IN CONTENT AREAS

The content reading materials we have students read reflect the relationships that exist among the ideas and concepts contained in the material. In addition, textbook authors utilize a variety of different writing styles and organizational formats to communicate the content. It becomes extremely important for students to be able to conceptualize the way in which content materials are organized and written if they are to comprehend the material they read. There are four major writing patterns that authors use in dealing with the content they write about: listing, comparison-contrast, sequence, and cause-effect. Our first task in teaching students how to deal with these writing patterns is to make them aware of those words that clue the reader in to the type of writing pattern the author uses.

Signal Words and Phrases

In reading, we have been conditioned to emphasize key words in new material that students are to read. The rationale behind this instructional method is simple. First, we identify and isolate those words that we predict might cause students problems. Then we preteach them in some fashion. This accomplishes two objectives: we lessen the student's anxiety about the new words by giving preexposure to them, and we immediately start to build a conceptual background for the new material since the concepts to be taught underlie the new vocabulary items. Finally, we can rationalize this procedure since it adds the dimension of repetition of the new vocabulary items; we do not learn a new word by one or two exposures to it but require repeated experience with the word in many contexts before we really know the word so that it becomes part of our vocabulary.

We regard many words in the English language as "function" words in that they carry little meaning and simply serve to string the more important content or key words together. However, many of these function words are extremely important because they tend to signal the relationships that exist between and among the more content-oriented words. We might regard words like *but* and *however* to be primarily function words. Yet they signal the relationship between ideas, events, people, and so forth. Consider the following example:

Ptolemy believed that. . . . However, Copernicus . . .

We know that the ideas of Ptolemy and Copernicus are opposed to one another. The relationship between their ideas is signalled to us by the word *however*. If the word *likewise* were substituted for *however*, this would signal that the ideas of Ptolemy and Copernicus were similar. By changing only one word, we completely reverse the relationship between the ideas of the two men from one of contrast to one of comparison. But the words *however* and *likewise* will not often be among those vocabulary items that the teacher extracts before the reading assignment and preteaches.

The preteaching of signal words is "hit and miss" at best. Few teachers consider the need for such instruction. It may not occur to many of us that instruction of this sort is even required. We, as teachers, probably learned on our own that certain words signal relationships. We look for these words and mentally note them in particular. The more able students often develop the ability to capitalize on signal words, largely on their own without instruction.

Below is a list of common signal words and phrases that denote particular writing patterns and, therefore, ways in which ideas and events are related. We will gain nothing, however, by teaching this list of words to our students. They already know these words and use them all the time. We can and should, on the other hand, help students to understand and sharpen their understanding of these kinds of words and what these words do in the context of reading material in subject matter areas.

Signal Words

Listing Pattern

the following	also		
then	in addition		
another	furthermore		
finally	likewise		
moreover	as well as		
besides	and		
next	many		
first	much		
second	some		
third	several		
	lastly		

Sequence Pattern

first	subsequent
second	until
third	while
last	meanwhile
soon	already
at last	next
then	after
now	during
immediately	in the meantime
ago	afterwards
at that time	before

Cause-Effect Pattern

for this reason	hence
in order to	thus
since	consequently
because	accordingly
so that	as a result
therefore	so

Comparison-Contrast

even though	on the contrary
but	nevertheless
however	notwithstanding
yet	rather
otherwise	not
although	in spite of
on the other hand	in comparison

We will now describe the four major content writing patterns, characteristics and examples of each, and strategies for teaching them. We refer to them as major patterns not because they are more important than other stylistic and organizational patterns of writing, but because they reflect the relationships that exist among the ideas and concepts contained in the content.

Simple Listing Pattern (Enumeration)

The listing pattern is often a collection of the most important information and main points presented in a chapter or section of a textbook. This pattern is frequently employed by the author at the end of a section or chapter as a summary statement of the main ideas of the section or chapter. Often an author uses the listing pattern to present a number of details. In either event, slow and detailed reading is often required. Example 1 is an illustration of a paragraph using the listing pattern.

EXAMPLE 1

In the mid-1800s the way in which scientists thought about the nature of man, as well as all animals, was forever changed. Charles Darwin, a young British scientist, undertook an extensive study of many species of animals throughout the world. After much study and observation, Darwin published his ideas which have come to be known as the "theory of the evolution of species." Darwin's theory of evolution was based on the following ideas and observations:

1. The fittest members of a species tend to survive, while less fit members do not.
2. Animal species adapt and change in a number of different ways over time such that all higher form animals evolve from lower forms.
3. The process of "natural selection" insures that those members of a species best adapted to survival will multiply, passing on the characteristics required for survival.

Strategies for Dealing with the Listing Pattern

1. Point out to students the signal words an author uses to key into the listing pattern.

2. Point out to students that the author can weave a listing of ideas or facts into a paragraph, or the author can stop in mid-paragraph and list the ideas or facts using indented arabic numerals. In the first example, attention to signal words will alert the student to a listing pattern, while in the second example differences in paragraph format will key the student into the listing pattern.

3. Help students to search the portion of the passage that immediately precedes the listing for a generalized statement of topic or main idea that might be supported by the information contained in the list.

4. Encourage students to establish the importance of the listed information to the overall reading assignment so that they will select an appropriate reading strategy (slow and intensive reading, skimming, and so on).

5. Since listing patterns are often a compilation of important points presented in a passage, encourage students to skim the

passage before they begin their reading in order to find listed information so that the listing can serve as an organizer and help to guide students in their reading.

Sequence Pattern

The sequence writing pattern is often confused with the listing pattern since the two are frequently similar in physical layout and in the signal words used to key into the patterns. If there is any significance attached to the ordering of information contained in the reading material, then the pattern is one of sequence. An author normally utilizes the sequence pattern for one or two purposes. First, an author may present a series of events that are ordered over time for the purposes of establishing a general chronological framework of events, and the ways in which chronologically related events can also be causally related. Second, an author may use the sequence pattern to present a series of steps in a process, usually requiring fairly close and detailed reading. Example 2 illustrates the use of the sequence pattern in presenting events in a chronological order, while example 3 illustrates how the sequence pattern is used to present steps in a process.

EXAMPLE 2

In the early 1800s, huge industries blossomed in the northeastern part of the United States. Workers in these factories faced many of the same problems English workers had experienced. As the industrial community grew and employed more and more people, workers became increasingly unhappy with poor working conditions, low pay, and the flood of immigrant workers. Laborers soon began to organize into unions to deal with these problems. Subsequent strikes and riots won for the labor unions a great deal of power. Finally, toward the end of the century the labor unions became so strong that they were able to force industries to provide better working conditions and wages and to exclude immigrant workers from their ranks.

EXAMPLE 3

The life cycle of a star is several billion years long and takes place in five stages. First, a dust cloud forms that is filled with particles of solids and gases. The particles in the cloud exert gravitational pull on each other, and soon the dust cloud begins to contract. A star enters the second stage when the star matter reaches a high enough temperature to cause a nuclear reaction. Stage three begins when so much hydrogen in the core has been converted to helium that the temperature of the star becomes too low for the nuclear reaction to take place. During stage three, the star expands and glows red and is sometimes called a red giant. A star enters stage four when the core of the star reaches temperatures of billions of degrees and the star becomes much bluer in color. Finally, in stage five the star goes through the nova stage and eventually becomes what scientists call a white dwarf.

Strategies for Dealing with the Sequence Pattern

1. Point out to students the signal words an author uses to key into the sequence pattern.

2. Help students to determine the nature of the sequential pattern the author uses. The author can use a variety of sequential patterns in content areas, the most frequent being "events in chronological order." Other sequential patterns that the author might use include "steps in a process" or listings of events from simple to complex, most important to least important, and other patterns where the author has attached some significance to the way in which events are ordered.

3. Once students understand the nature of the sequential pattern used, help them to understand the author's purpose in using the particular pattern. For example, in using the sequential pattern of "events in chronological order," as used in social studies content, the author's purpose may be to establish a time perspective for the events being discussed so that students will know when particular events occurred in relation to other events and establish in their own minds a broad chronological framework for the material being studied. The author might also use this pattern in order to clarify the cause-effect relationships that exist among the events being studied and to establish the importance of the chronology of events to the cause-effect relationships that exist among events. The sequential pattern in science, on the other hand, is often used to present a series of steps requiring very close and precise reading on the part of the student.

4. Encourage students to make use of sequential patterns in their own notetaking, using appropriate patterns dictated by the nature of the content. Encourage students to use the sequential pattern in their thinking in order to organize and make sense of the new content they study.

Comparison-Contrast Pattern

An author utilizes the comparison-contrast writing pattern most frequently to establish (1) the similarity between familiar or known content and unfamiliar or new content, (2) differences between highly confusable aspects of the content, and (3) an organizational structure that is inherent in the new content and helpful in learning the new content. In dealing with the comparison-contrast pattern, the reader should keep in mind the main point made by the author and the specific likenesses and/or differences used by the author in making the comparison or contrast. Below is an example of the comparison-contrast writing pattern.

EXAMPLE 4

There are four major kinds of tides which are primarily differentiated by astronomical relations of the earth, moon, and sun as well as ocean and coastal features. Diurnal and semidiurnal tides have tidal periods related to the lunar day. The diurnal tide has only one high and one low tide during each lunar day. The semidiurnal tide, on the other hand, has two high and two low tides in a lunar day, both of which are similar in nature. Mixed tides, like semidiurnal tides, have two high and two low tides during the lunar day; however, there are differences in the successive levels of the high and low tides. Solar tides are related to the length of the earth day. The high tide in a solar tide occurs at the same time each day, while the low tide occurs either six or twelve hours later.

Strategies for Dealing with the Comparison-Contrast Pattern

1. Point out to students the signal words an author uses to key into the comparison-contrast pattern.

2. Help students to determine whether the author is using primarily a comparison or primarily a contrast (or elements of both) in communicating the message.

3. Help students focus in on exactly what is being compared or contrasted so that they will have the most important ideas the author deals with clearly in mind.

4. When dealing with comparisons and contrasts of central importance to understanding the content, encourage students to list the resulting similarities and differences in their notes. The teacher is wise to demonstrate this technique with the group as an instructional strategy.

Cause-Effect Pattern

The cause-effect pattern in writing is similar to the sequential pattern in that cause-effect relationships are a special instance of sequential relationships. If two events are related causally, that is, one brings about (causes) the other (effect or result), then the relationship among the events is also sequential, since one event usually takes place before the other. However, the major focus is on the causal relationships since the sequential relationship that exists among the events is implicit. The cause-effect pattern is, perhaps, the most difficult to recognize by simply spotting the signal words to key into the pattern. Example 5 illustrates the cause-effect writing pattern.

EXAMPLE 5

Although the United States was still in its infancy during the late 1700s and early 1800s, its leaders were nonetheless intent on expanding its territorial boundaries. Spain claimed ownership of much of the territory along the Gulf of Mexico, from the present state of Florida to the port city of New Orleans. Eventually, the United States simply added this territory to its domain after it became evident that Spain was too weak to defend its claims. Soon after, Jefferson negotiated the Louisiana Purchase with the French leader Napoleon. While Napoleon had serious thoughts about a military invasion of the United States, things were going badly for him in Europe. In need of money to finance his army in Europe, Napoleon realized the necessity of selling the vast Louisiana territory rather than fighting for it. In a few short years, the physical size of the United States had doubled and redoubled.

Strategies for Dealing with the Cause-Effect Pattern

1. Point out to students the signal words an author uses to key into the cause-effect pattern.

2. Help students to determine if the author's purpose is to discuss causes of a particular event, effects of a particular event, or to show the nature of the causal relationship between two or more events.

3. Help students clarify in their own minds precisely which cause-effect relationships are of major importance to understanding the new content and which are of secondary importance.

4. Encourage students to question cause-effect relationships

stated or implied by the author. Help students to discriminate between direct and indirect causes and effects and to identify questionable cause-effect relationships stated or implied by the author.

5. Encourage students to list in their notes major events followed by their causes and/or effects that are important to understanding the content. The teacher can demonstrate this technique to the whole class while studying the new content.

ADDITIONAL PATTERNS OF WRITING

The major writing patterns we have discussed reflect the structure and organization of the concepts and ideas contained in the content. However, there are additional patterns of writing that pervade content reading materials which reflect specific functions that paragraphs serve as well as authors' writing styles. Just as with the major writing patterns, these additional writing patterns are often cued by the use of many of the signal words we have described. However, the various major writing patterns are often used within the context of more stylistic patterns of writing described below.

Purpose-Setting Patterns of Writing

There are particular patterns of writing that authors use in introducing new content. These patterns of writing tend to add structure and cohesiveness to the author's presentation of new content and emphasize less the actual presentation of new content. These additional patterns of writing are of particular importance since the proficient reader can key into these patterns and use these patterns in setting purposes for reading, in guiding reading, and in identifying innate structural units within the content itself.

Introduction Pattern

In presenting new content, an author often spends several paragraphs in introducing the new material. These introductory paragraphs serve several functions. First, they introduce the reader in a general way to the structure and scope of the material about to be read. Second, introductory paragraphs key the student into the author's purposes for writing, and therefore, the reader's purposes for reading. Below is an example of a paragraph of introduction.

EXAMPLE 6

A thorough understanding of the sedimentary processes that take place in our oceans is required to understand the history of the planet Earth. This involves studying the origin of the particles, how particles are moved from one place to another, the forces that change the characteristics of particles, the ways particles can be deposited, and how long it takes to deposit particles. Scientists have developed many techniques for analyzing and studying these things. In this chapter, we will examine a number of the techniques that are used in studying the history of our planet.

Strategies for Dealing with the Introduction Pattern

1. Point out to students the signal words and phrases often used in introductory patterns of writing that help the student key into the pattern. Some of these might include such words and phrases as "in this chapter," "in the pages to follow," "throughout," and so on.

2. Teach students how to recognize introductory paragraphs by their position in chapters and other reading selections and by the fact that they tend to be general in nature, containing very little specific information.

3. Teach students the functions and value of introductory paragraphs. Show students how introductory paragraphs set the stage for the remainder of a chapter or reading selection. Teach students how to use introductory paragraphs to help them set purposes for reading.

Transitional Pattern

Transitional paragraphs serve a number of functions. Simultaneously, they can summarize preceding information, introduce new information, and link together ideas and structural units contained in the content. Often, transitional paragraphs serve as stopping places for the reader and points where the reader can reconnoiter, allowing time to reflect on the information just read and to organize thinking about the new content covered in the reading. Finally, transitional paragraphs are also useful in helping the reader to set purposes for reading. An example of a transitional paragraph appears below.

EXAMPLE 7

We have studied several revolutions that have occurred in the history of countries like France and England. In the last unit, we read about the American Revolution, how it began, and the effects it had on the government and people of this country. In this unit, we will study another kind of revolution that took place more than 200 years ago—the Industrial Revolution. Like the revolutions we have already read about, the Industrial Revolution brought about many changes, but these changes were in many ways very different from the changes brought about by wars of revolution. In a sense, we are still in the midst of the Industrial Revolution even today.

Strategies for Dealing with the Transitional Pattern

1. Help students to note the transition pattern by noting changes of direction in the author's writing. Seldom is the transition pattern easily identifiable by spotting specific signal words. More often, several signal words and phrases are used in adjoining sentences to change the direction of the topic being dealt with, to present opposing viewpoints and arguments, or to extend the topic under study.

2. Teach students to use transitional paragraphs as places to reconnoiter and regain their bearings as they read new content.

3. Demonstrate to students the importance of transitional paragraphs in understanding how different topics the author deals with are related.

4. Help students to use transitional paragraphs to establish purposes for reading.

Summarizing Pattern

Paragraphs of summary, like introductory paragraphs, are general in nature and often provide a framework or structure for helping the student to organize the information read. Summary paragraphs also serve to remind the student of purposes for reading while the material is still fresh. An example of a summary paragraph is presented below.

EXAMPLE 8

To summarize, we have studied in this chapter how waves and currents make contact with land, as well as their depositional and erosional processes that constantly change the shoreline. Through the process of erosion, land is cut, sculptured, and leveled. Through the process of deposition, geographical formations such as beaches, bars, hooks, and islands are built. These constant changes in sea and land levels are evidence of submergence and emergence.

Strategies for Dealing with the Summarizing Pattern

1. Point out to students the signal words used to key into the summary pattern. Frequently, the author will label summary paragraphs in bold-faced type and utilize signal words within the summary paragraphs (for example, summary, review, in conclusion, and so on).

2. Encourage students to scan a reading selection or chapter for paragraphs of summary *before* they begin their reading. In this way, the summary paragraphs can be used by the student in setting purposes for reading and in establishing an overall framework or structure for learning new content.

3. Impress upon students the importance of summary paragraphs and encourage students to read and reread summaries. Help students to note internal summaries the author uses (summary sentences and paragraphs at the end of sections and subsections of a chapter.)

4. Teach students to paraphrase in their own words summary paragraphs.

Stylistic Patterns of Writing

There exist still other, more stylized patterns of writing with which students should become familiar. Within any given content area, an author is likely to use definitional, explanatory, narrative, and descriptive writing patterns in expressing and communicating new content.

Definitional paragraphs, as the term implies, define important words and concepts for the student. It is important for the student to determine *what* is being defined when he or she encounters paragraphs of definition. Explanatory paragraphs are similar to definitional paragraphs but tend to be more loosely structured and often explain terms and processes that are difficult to define in a precise manner. Descriptive paragraphs set out characteristics of whatever the author is describing and, in literature, tend to establish tone and mood. Narrative paragraphs can perform numerous functions but tend to present information in a personal or first-hand accounting. Regardless of the type of writing pattern the student encounters in reading, there are a number of general instructional strategies the teacher can use to guide students' reading of content materials.

General Strategies for Dealing with Various Writing Patterns

1. Encourage students not to skip unknown words. Help students search for definitions and explanations the author provides in text as well as to use the context to identify familiar voabulary words.

2. Encourage students not to skip graphic aids such as maps, graphs, charts, pictures, and so on. These aids are helpful in clarifying the terms and concepts the author uses to communicate new content. Provide specific instruction in helping students to read and understand graphic aids.

3. Teach students to search for typographical aids that an author uses to attach emphasis to particular words and concepts. Underlined words, italicized words, and words and phrases in bold-faced type point up important terms and concepts that require special attention and perhaps rereading by students.

4. Always encourage students to search for reading purposes by determining what the author's purpose is.

SUMMARY

1. There are two basic approaches to teaching reading and thinking skills in the content areas. The direct skills approach focuses on direct instruction of skills, subordinating the importance of the content being taught. The content centered approach focuses on the teaching of subject matter. Reading and thinking skills are taught as the content requires these skills of the students.

2. Reading and thinking skills common to all content areas include (a) developing reading vocabulary, (b) establishing purposes for reading, (c) developing flexible reading skills, and (d) developing reading comprehension skills.

3. Reading and thinking in literature involve (a) dealing with the many formats and types of literature, (b) understanding literary devices, and (c) understanding stylistic devices of authors.

4. Reading and thinking in science involve (a) classifying information, (b) following procedural instructions, (c) distinguishing relevant information in problem solving, and (d) finding supportive information in order to draw conclusions.

5. Reading and thinking in social studies involve (a) using flexible reading strategies, (b) identifying cause-effect relationships, and (c) detecting chronological sequences.

6. Reading and thinking in math require (a) mastering abstract symbols, (b) seeing the relationship between math symbols and language equivalents, and (c) solving various kinds of math problems including story problems.

7. Signal words are important because they signal the relationship between the author's ideas. In addition, signal words are used to denote particular writing patterns.

8. The listing pattern of writing is the presentation of a list of

the author's ideas. Sometimes the list presents a summary of important points, and sometimes a list of details is presented.

9. In the sequence pattern of writing the author presents a sequence of events. The sequence pattern is used to describe a chronological sequence of events and to describe a sequence of steps in a process.

10. The author uses the comparison-contrast writing pattern to point out similarities and differences in content and ideas, often to show the relationship between familiar and unfamiliar concepts or to clarify the meaning of complex concepts.

11. In the cause-effect pattern of writing the author attempts to show how a particular event produced a particular outcome. Authors use this pattern to show the consequences of particular actions.

12. Purpose-setting patterns are used to introduce new content, to make transitions from one subject to another, and to summarize new content.

13. Stylistic patterns of writing include definitional, explanatory, narrative, and descriptive writing patterns. Definition statements define new content. Explanatory statements clarify ideas that are not given to precise definition, with examples and illustrations. Descriptive statements provide the characteristics of the author's topic. Narrative statements provide a personal accounting of events.

REVIEW QUESTIONS

1. What are two basic approaches to teaching reading in the content areas?

2. What are the reading and thinking skills common to all content areas?

3. What are the reading and thinking skills typically required in literature? in science? in social studies? in mathematics?

4. Why are signal words important?

5. How and why does the author use the listing pattern in writing? the sequence pattern? the comparison-contrast pattern? the cause-effect pattern?

6. What purpose-setting patterns of writing are used by the author?

7. What stylistic patterns of writing are used by the author?

CHAPTER 17

Problems in Reading Content Materials

PURPOSE

1. To discuss reading problems in various content areas.
2. To prescribe strategies for dealing with these problems.

BACKGROUND AND NEW INFORMATION

Most of what you learned in earlier chapters about vocabulary building and the way the English language is programmed are applicable to this chapter. In this chapter you apply this knowledge to particular vocabulary problems in the content areas. In chapter 8 you learned about problems in teaching nonverbal symbols. This has particular applicability to teaching in social studies, science, and math. You learned earlier about syntax, that is, the way the language is programmed. In this chapter you will become acquainted with unusual syntactic organizations, especially in literature.

The chapter begins with a consideration of problems in reading English literature and strategies for dealing with these problems. Second, problems in reading social studies content and strategies for dealing with these problems are discussed. Third, problems in reading science content and strategies for dealing with these problems are discussed. Fourth, problems in reading math content, and strategies for handling these problems are discussed. Fifth, we deal briefly with reading problems in other content areas. Finally, we offer some general recommendations for making assignments to students and for promoting student reading.

etymology
affix

The student will be able to:

1. Describe problems in reading English literature, social studies content, science content, and math content and strategies for dealing with these problems.
2. Describe strategies for making student assignments.
3. Describe strategies for encouraging students to increase voluntary reading.

There exists a host of factors that makes content area reading materials difficult for students to read and comprehend. In other chapters we have discussed two important factors: readability of content materials and unique writing patterns used in content materials. In this chapter, we direct our attention to a discussion of additional trouble spots in reading content materials and strategies for effectively dealing with these trouble spots.

PROBLEMS IN READING ENGLISH LITERATURE

Just as in other content areas, reading materials in the English classroom present students with unique reading problems. Perhaps one of the major obstacles in reading literature is that of wide diversity in the materials to which students are exposed. This perspective is easily confirmed when one considers specific reading materials in literature according to writing style and format of presentation—reading in literature requires reading narratives, biographies, essays, articles, poetry, plays, short stories, and novels. Each style of writing requires the use of different strategies on the part of students.

Short Stories

Short stories are different from other forms of literature in that they contain only essential information required to advance the story. Much information is omitted, and therefore the student is

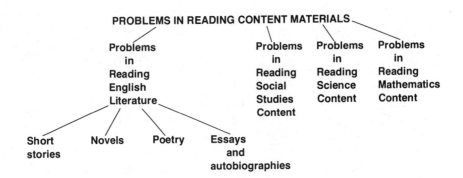

FIGURE 17–1   A hierarchy of topics in chapter 17

required to infer a great deal when reading a short story. Often, this concise presentation creates special problems when students begin reading. That is, they have a difficult time "getting started" because they are immediately immersed in the story without the help of a gradual buildup of background information. In short, students will lack structure for reading the short story. In this instance, preteaching and readiness activities are very important aids to insuring complete understanding. Students who constantly engage in predicting coming events in the story and filling in background information the author does not provide will have greater success in comprehending short stories. A slow, studious reading of the initial portion of a short story, followed by opportunities for discussion and prediction, is an excellent instructional approach to employ in reading short stories.

Novels

Novels, due to their length, present special reading problems for students. Often, we make the mistake of assuming that because students are reading on a particular grade level according to some standardized reading test, they can effectively read and comprehend an entire novel at the same level. This is not necessarily true. Such standardized tests require students to read relatively short passages (seldom more than 250 to 300 words in length) and answer related comprehension questions. This reading task is not representative of the task of reading a lengthy novel. Although we judge students to be on a reading level at which they can effectively read and comprehend a novel on a similar level, we often find that the task is a difficult one for them simply because of the amount of information the student must manipulate. It is advisable, therefore, to have students read novels that are somewhat below their effective reading levels if they have not had much experience in reading lengthy materials.

In reading a novel it is important for students to keep characters clearly in mind and to be aware of specific identifying traits of characters. It is also important to have a firm grasp of the plot or story line and to understand changes in plot that result from events in the story as well as subplots the author develops. In both respects, predicting coming events and outcomes relative to characters and plot is an excellent method of insuring understanding and enhancing the students' ability to keep characters and events from being confused. Recognizing conflicts and summarizing events are also important abilities in reading novels.

Poetry

Poetry is perhaps the most difficult form of literature for students to read and comprehend. This is true for a number of reasons. First, by its nature, a poem is a concise statement of an idea or mood the author wishes to express. That is, fewer words are used to express the author's meaning. This format requires the reader to possess many images and various meaning for words. Ideally, this is something that should be stressed in an instructional situation that utilizes poetry as the vehicle of instruction. Second, poetry regularly uses unfamiliar syntactical patterns that deviate from the more familiar subject-verb-object pattern of English. Mighty oaks do not grow from acorns . . ., mighty oaks from acorns grow. Syntactical patterns like this that are low in predictability influence the degree to which a reader extracts meaning from what is read. Third, poetry does not necessarily express the content of an idea. A poem can express a mood, a feeling, or an emotion. Students who are used to reading in order to acquire information or understand a story line are often confused by a poem that contains neither. For this reason, then, poetry requires an entirely different reading strategy than narrative and expository materials, largely dependent upon the author's purpose.

Drama

Reading plays also presents special problems for students. Plays are written to be performed, and without the benefit of the visual and auditory accompaniments of the dramatic performance, the student must infer a great deal from the dialogue alone. Plays generally contain information regarding the dramatic situation, proper staging, mood, and such in the form of italicized director's notes. Students often skim over these important reading aids too quickly in order to get to the heart of the play. As teaching aids, these notes are invaluable and deserve studious attention on the part of the student. Another aspect of plays that contributes to their difficulty level is that of the dialogue itself. Like poetry, dialogue is concise since much of the meaning a player communicates is carried on through intonation and gestures. A student reading the play simply does not have these aids available. The teacher is wise to select those portions of the play that reveal the most about the story line of the play and the characters in the play, then insure that these are fully understood by orally reading them or in some other way centering attention upon them. Like novels, plays are often rather long, and the teacher is again wise to have students recap and summarize various scenes and acts. Again, having students predict coming events, character traits, and so on, is an extremely useful instructional practice.

Essays and Autobiographies

Essays can take many forms, but perhaps the major factor in insuring that students understand an essay is their understanding of the purpose of the essay. Essays are meant to communicate an author's feelings, biases, attitudes, thoughts, and so on regarding a particular topic. Authors achieve this communication in many different ways, but paramount to comprehending the essay is the realization that it is not necessarily written to communicate a story line or a given body of information. Like the essay, the autobiography assumes no standard format. Like the essay, the autobiography does not necessarily advance a story line and should be read not with the purpose of understanding what the author did, but with the purpose of understanding the author him or herself.

STRATEGIES FOR TEACHING ENGLISH LITERATURE

Strategies for Teaching the Short Story

1. As readiness for reading a short story, introduce background information about the author, what prompted the author to write the short story, or any additional anecdotal information that might tend to build interest in reading the short story.

2. Explain to students the nature of the short story as a literary format. Explain that the author has intended for the reader to "fill in" much of the information about characters and other elements of the story.

3. Have students predict from minimal clues like the title and their knowledge of the author what the short story might be about before they begin their reading.

4. Have students skim the short story before they begin their reading in order to pick up specific pieces of information like character names, dates, locations, and so on. By learning ahead of time that a short story is set in the 1890s, for example, the students will be aware of this time frame throughout their reading, helping them to better understand the information contained in the short story.

5. If a short story is to be read as homework, have students do in-class reading of the initial portions of the short story. After they have completed the first portion of the short story, allow class time for discussing the information they have acquired and opportunities for predicting what is to come in the short story.

Strategies for Teaching the Novel

Many excellent books have been written regarding how to teach the novel as a literary form; the suggestions below should prove helpful in teaching the novel in the classroom.

1. With slower and less able readers, assign the novel chapter by chapter or in a fashion that breaks the novel up into more manageable pieces. In any case, do not assign several chapters to be read overnight with little or no explanation or establishment of purposes for reading. Take care to space the reading of the novel in such a way that no student is faced with an impossible reading task due to slow rate of reading.

2. Establish purposes for reading and help students to formulate their own purposes for reading the novel at regular intervals. If necessary, establish reading purposes for each separate reading assignment by indicating to students what you expect them to gain from their reading, special questions they should consider while reading particular sections, and what the students will be required to do after having completed their reading.

3. If you see fit, delete portions of the novel and summarize them for students. Oftentimes, whole chapters can be deleted from a reading assignment if they are not central to the understanding of the novel. You may want to do this only for the slower and less able readers in order to assure that the task of reading is not overwhelming to them. Individualize and tailor the reading assignment to the student.

4. Allow frequent in-class opportunities for oral reading of difficult passages from the novel. Read and do oral interpretations of more difficult portions as an instructional device to insure maximum understanding and comprehension.

5. As in the case of the short story and other literary pieces, allow frequent opportunities for students to predict coming events in the novel, giving them a chance to make and confirm hypotheses about action, characters, and so on. Present questions to students that are answered later in the novel; challenge students to predict the coming events in the novel.

6. As with any reading assignment, build a background of information about the novel itself, the author, public reaction to the novel, and additional anecdotal information that might pique the students' interests.

7. Recap and summarize the events of the novel at regular intervals through in-class discussion and questioning. Help students to keep the events in the novel as well as the characters clearly in mind.

Strategies for Teaching Poetry

1. Read poems to students in class and encourage students to read poems aloud when they are assigned. Fluent oral reading of poetry is a very helpful aid to understanding and comprehending poetry. Obtain, if possible, professional recordings of actors and poets themselves reading the poetry your students will study, and use these recordings as part of your instruction.

2. Help students understand the author's purpose, frame of mind, and intent in writing a particular poem, since understanding these kinds of things is crucial to understanding the poem. Encourage students to put themselves in the place of the poet.

3. Help students to assimilate new meanings for words they already know that are used by the poet; help them to gain new images for words and to search their own experiences for images they already possess for words. Help students to understand why a poet uses specific words in conveying a thought, a mood, or establishing a tone for a poem.

4. Teach students to recognize the author's use of literary devices and how these devices convey meaning, mood, and tone. Allow students an opportunity to construct their own literary devices. For example, in teaching the use of similes, give students several words or phrases they are familiar with and have them construct similes to show comparisons and convey meaning (new blue jeans are like . . ., a bubble bath is like . . ., waking up on a rainy Saturday is like . . .).

5. Establish readiness to read poetry by explaining to students the differences between poetry and more conventional styles of writing. For example, poems must be read slowly and thoughtfully and often reread, since they are very concise statements of the author's feelings, thoughts, and mood. Explain that the poet regularly uses unfamiliar word order to to achieve certain effects and that sometimes the only purpose a poet has is to create a mood in the reader. Establish readiness for reading poetry in other ways like providing background information on the poet, why the poem was written, and so on.

6. Take care in your selection of poetry for students to read. Often, students have had nothing but bad experiences with poetry, and one more will certainly not turn students into avid readers and lovers of poetry. Try to choose poetry that might have special meaning or a special message for your students and that possesses ideas and experiences familiar to the students. Try to avoid over-analyzing poetry from a strict literary perspective and requiring students to pick poems apart piece by piece.

7. Allow students an opportunity to write their own poems. Help them choose an incident or experience from their own lives that has special significance as the basis for a poem. Guide them in choosing words that best convey the meaning they intend and help them to use the literary devices they have studied in their own poetry. Encourage students to submit their poems to stu-

dent publications, the school newspaper, and other appropriate forums. The experience of having a poem published is like no other in generating interest in and appreciation of poetry.

Strategies for Teaching Plays

1. Emphasize the importance of the director's notes and other staging information to understanding the play. Encourage students to make suggestions about how a play might properly be staged, for example, lighting, props, or scenery that might be used, background sounds and background music, and so on.

2. Encourage understanding of characters by having students choose people from television, movies, books they have read, politics, and school to play the parts of the characters in the play. Have students support their choices.

3. Read orally in class portions of the play that are difficult or central to understanding the entire play. Have students perform portions of the play in class.

4. Try to select plays for classroom use that contain characters and themes familiar to students and within their frame of reference. Contemporary plays are useful in this respect since the language of modern drama is usually simpler, the characters easier to identify with, the action more familiar, and the plot often less complex.

5. Try to coordinate the reading of plays with school and community productions of the same or similar plays. Encourage students to attend dramatic performances.

6. Try to obtain professional recordings of plays and films of plays your students are reading. Use these aids as methods of building interest and readiness.

7. Through class discussion and questioning, recap and summarize the action of the play at regular intervals. Help students to keep the events and characters of the play clearly in their minds.

8. Invite amateur actors (there are probably a few among the teachers in your school) to come to the classroom and do dramatic readings in order to stimulate interest in reading plays.

Strategies for Teaching Essays and Autobiographies

1. Help students to understand that the essay is a forum for the author to express opinions, perspectives, biases, and feelings on a

variety of subjects. The quality of any essay is often judged by the extent to which the author influences the reader and causes the reader to adopt the ideas presented in the essay.

2. Encourage students to read essays critically and to examine the essay for use of supportive information and development of argument. Help students evaluate not only the individual ideas and thoughts presented in the essay but the total essay in light of the author's point of view.

3. Strive to help students evaluate and judge the ideas of the essayist in reference to their own opinions, experiences, feelings, and biases. Encourage students to consult additional resources for information on essay topics that are relatively unfamiliar.

4. For the less able readers and readers who have limited experience with essay reading, select essays that deal with contemporary concerns and problems like pollution, overpopulation, capital punishment, or mediocrity in television programming. Pursue these essay topics from the concrete to the abstract in an inductive manner. In pursuing a topic such as overpopulation, the concrete and specific aspects of the problem can be dealt with first. Gradually, guide students to the moral issues involved in the topic and relate the topic to additional and similar topics of concern.

5. Since biographies and autobiographies are often slanted and colored by the author, they too must be read with the intention of understanding the opinions, feelings, biases, and thoughts of the author and/or the subject of the narrative. Encourage students to read biographies and autobiographies with this purpose in mind.

6. On the basis of the author's feelings, biases, and opinions, encourage students to predict how the author might feel about other problems and concerns. Allow opportunities for the students to predict particular stands the author might take on related issues and problems.

PROBLEMS IN READING SOCIAL STUDIES CONTENT

As in other content areas, the reading materials that students deal with in social studies present problems for students. Since a great deal of the learning that goes on in any social studies class takes place via reading, it is important that social studies teachers be sensitive to the factors that serve to make social studies materials difficult to read. Many of the factors discussed here have been discussed in regard to other content reading materials, but there are aspects of reading social studies materials that are relatively unique to social studies.

Length and Volume

As we have pointed out in this and other chapters, the amount or length of reading material often has a direct bearing on the ease with which students comprehend the material. Students are often threatened and intimidated by books with many pages and small print. This, then, creates an emotional block to reading the textbook since the textbook becomes the symbol of an almost impossible task especially for the student who has reading problems. Since social studies textbooks tend to be lengthy, they represent for students a difficult and time-consuming task.

Vocabulary

As in other content areas, the introduction of new and unfamiliar social studies vocabulary words makes materials in this content area more difficult to read and lower in predictability. When the frequency of new vocabulary words becomes too great, comprehension is retarded. Additionally, students must gain very precise meanings for new social studies terms since these terms underlie the concepts and content hierarchies contained in the new material.

Relationships in and among Content Hierarchies

Social studies content is generally highly unfamiliar to students, and a great deal of new information is contained in social studies textbooks. Understanding social studies content places a premium on the students' ability to recognize and understand relationships among concepts. These relationships can be portrayed as elements of content hierarchies requiring students to engage in many higher-order reading and thinking skills.

Writing Style

Students are further faced with the task of developing reading, thinking, and study strategies for dealing with materials in social studies that are written in an expository format. Many of the reading materials, even those that are content oriented, that students deal with in the earlier grades are written in a narrative format that has been shown to be an easier format to deal with. Expository materials, like social studies textbooks, contain a great deal of information, in comparison to more narrative materials, and require close reading and different reading strategies.

Specialized Reading Skills

Finally, social studies materials regularly utilize a variety of pictorial aids that require special reading skills, and, therefore, special reading instruction. Social studies textbooks are replete with maps, graphs, and charts of many sizes and descriptions. Often, we neglect to teach the specialized reading skills that help students read and get information from these kinds of graphic aids.

STRATEGIES FOR DEALING WITH PROBLEMS IN READING SOCIAL STUDIES CONTENT

Length and Volume

1. Since social studies materials are often lengthy and represent a difficult task for many students, the teacher can differentiate reading assignments on this basis. For example, instead of having the slower and less able readers read an entire chapter, the teacher can assign specific sections to these readers. In this way, the teacher can insure that each reader is given a reading task that is "do-able."

2. If the teacher deletes less important sections from the reading assignment for the less able readers, the deleted sections might still contain a limited amount of information the teacher wishes for the students to obtain. In this instance, the teacher can specify exactly what information the student should get from the deleted sections and exactly where it is found in the material. Then, students can read perhaps two or three paragraphs from a deleted eight-page section and still not miss essential information.

3. Depending upon the way in which the teacher has organized the course, in-class time can be provided to less able readers for doing assigned reading.

Establishing Purposes for Reading

1. Preteach new vocabulary terms contained in the content as well as new meanings for known words by identifying those vocabulary items that might cause students reading problems and those terms that are central to understanding the new content. Follow the three-step strategy of placing the new terms on the board and pronouncing them, showing students where they appear in context and how the context can be useful in determining meaning and structurally analyzing the word for familiar affixes and roots.

2. Introduce the new content being studied with a general background of information, providing students with a framework for understanding the new content and relating the new content to what they have already studied and learned. This technique makes the new content more predictable and less threatening to students.

3. Stimulate students' interests in reading the new content with motivating anecdotal information related to the content. This can take the form of little-known facts about historical figures being studied, information about how some of the events being studied have affected contemporary history and our own lives, etomology of new vocabulary items that are introduced, and so forth.

4. Indicate to students what portions of the assigned reading are most important and which sections are of lesser importance. Encourage students to use study reading, skimming, scanning, and previewing strategies where appropriate.

5. Preteach the reading and interpretation of graphic aids such as charts, diagrams, and graphs that are contained in the material. Point them out to students and give them help in reading these aids so that they will be able to make full use of the information they contain.

6. Tell students before they begin their reading what you expect of them and what they are to do once they have completed the reading assignment. Communicate to the students the objectives you have set for reading the new content.

1. Augment important concepts and principles presented in the content with your own examples and descriptions to insure full comprehension. Often, textbook examples are not sufficient to adequately illustrate difficult concepts and principles.

2. Break up lengthy reading assignments, particularly for less

able readers, and allow opportunities for class discussion and questioning between segments of the reading assignment.

3. Before students begin their reading, after they have previewed the material they read, or after they have read initial portions of a reading assignment, engage them in predicting what they will encounter in subsequent reading.

PROBLEMS IN READING SCIENCE CONTENT

Vocabulary

Science materials introduce many new vocabulary words into students' reading. The high frequency of new vocabulary words and known words used in new contexts serves to lower predictability of science content and to make it more difficult to read. In addition, students are often required to gain a very precise meaning for new vocabulary words in science so that context aids are of less help than in many other reading materials.

Content and Content Hierarchies

Science materials frequently contain many more ideas and content hierarchies than other reading materials. Other authors have called science materials highly conceptually loaded. Also, the content and content hierarchies presented in science materials are usually more complex than those found in many other materials.

Relationships among Content Hierarchies

Another factor that serves to make science materials more difficult to read is the fact that students must recognize and understand the many relationships contained in the content hierarchies. That is, they must deal with the intrarelationships among the various components of content hierarchies, as well as the interrelationships among different content hierarchies.

Prerequisite Content Hierarchies

Since so many hierarchies are contained in science materials, often students must understand one content hierarchy in order to understand a related content hierarchy. Thus, prior experience is an important factor in reading and understanding science materials.

Writing Style

Many times, students have a difficult time making the transition from reading narrative materials to reading materials written in exposition style such as science content. More information and information of a more complex nature is presented in, for example, one page of science content than materials written in narrative format. Thus, a different reading strategy (study reading) is required for students.

Study Skills

Science content materials regularly require students to utilize various reading study skills. Skimming, scanning, reading graphs and charts, using book parts, using reference materials, and so on are often required in reading science content.

STRATEGIES FOR DEALING WITH PROBLEMS IN READING SCIENCE CONTENT

Since the problems in reading social studies content and science content are similar, the teaching strategies for dealing with the problems are similar.

Establishing Purposes for Reading

1. Expose students to new vocabulary terms contained in the content before they begin their reading of the new content. Preinstruction in science vocabulary in essence is preinstruction in the concepts and principles contained in new content. Therefore, the teacher is wise to include in vocabulary instruction examples that clearly describe the concepts underlying new vocabulary terms. Additionally, the teacher should place new terms on the chalkboard, having students pronounce them, find them in context of the reading assignment, and analyze them for familiar affixes and roots that help to unlock meaning.

2. In teaching new science content the teacher should decide what concepts and skills the students should already have mastered from previous content in order to effectively deal with new content. Reviewing related material that is central to understanding new content is an important aspect of teaching new content.

3. Stimulate interest in reading new content by relating in-

teresting anecdotal information to students about new content and establishing practical uses for new content that is to be studied. For example, in a geology unit that deals with the study of rocks and minerals, the teacher might relate the story of the Hope diamond, its history, and the mystery that surrounds it. Additionally, the teacher might explain some of the industrial uses of diamonds.

4. Inform students before they begin their reading which portions of the assigned reading are central to understanding the new content, as well as which portions are of lesser importance. Encourage students to use reading strategies like skimming, previewing, and study reading where they are most appropriate.

5. Communicate to students the objectives of reading new content material. Explain to students what they should gain from the new material, the concepts and skills they are expected to master, the nature of follow-up assignments and activities, and what they will be expected to do once they have completed their reading.

Clarifying the Content

1. Point out to students important graphic aids and materials contained in new content, the information they contain, and the importance of understanding the information to achievement of the unit objectives. Give students pointers on interpreting the graphic aids.

2. For less able readers, break up lengthy reading assignments and establish reading purposes for each portion of the total assignment. Allow in-class opportunities for discussion and questioning between reading assignments.

3. At intervals before, during, and after the reading assignment, have students predict what they will encounter in their reading in order to help them establish their own purposes for reading. Have students predict applications beyond those described in class and in the assigned reading for the information they gain from their reading.

PROBLEMS IN READING MATHEMATICS CONTENT

Reading in the mathematics content area presents some unique problems for students. Specifically, trouble spots in reading mathematics content include the following.

Vocabulary

Mathematics content materials introduce many new vocabulary terms, both new terms and words for which students must gain new meanings. Additionally, many of these vocabulary words signal operations that the student must learn, as well as concepts that are central to understanding new content. Therefore, students must gain very precise meanings for new vocabulary words in math since vocabulary deficiencies can also result in a lack of facility in math computation.

Symbols

Mathematics content requires students to master many new symbols—in essence, a new language. In addition, students must learn the language equivalents for new symbols and be able to use them interchangeably.

Story Problems

Perhaps the greatest problem to reading in the math content area is the reading and understanding of story problems in order to solve the problems. Vocabulary difficulty, mixtures of math symbols and their language equivalents, inclusion of too much irrelevant information, and so on make the reading and solving of math story problems a difficult task for students.

STRATEGIES FOR DEALING WITH PROBLEMS IN READING MATHEMATICS CONTENT

1. Verbal math problems (story problems) are often complicated by both difficult vocabulary and awkwardness due to difficult language structures that are used. The teacher should be constantly on the lookout for poorly worded and vaguely stated word problems. When such problems are found in content materials, the teacher is wise to point out the problems in wording and allow students an opportunity to reword or rewrite the problems themselves.

2. Since mathematics introduces many new symbols, the teacher should take care to insure that students possess a firm knowledge of the language equivalents for these symbols as well as a firm knowledge of the operations and relationships the symbols stand for.

3. Study reading and knowledge of special textbook features

(glossary, tables) are important ingredients to successful reading in mathematics. Instruction in math should deal often with these important abilities.

4. As in all content areas, vocabulary terms in mathematics can be a major cause of reading problems in mathematics. Besides new vocabulary terms that are introduced in the content, confusable vocabulary terms that are introduced in the content such as cardinal, foot, mean, radical, reduce, root, and so forth should be given special emphasis by the teacher. Vocabulary growth should also be included as part of the teacher's total evaluation of student achievement in mathematics.

5. The teacher should clarify the relationships and concepts in math by showing students language applications whenever possible. Three examples of concepts in mathematics, their mathematical application, and their language application are included below:

Concept	Mathematical Application	Language Application
Cumulative property	Addition: $4 + 7 = 7 + 4$	He ate ice cream and cake. He ate cake and ice cream.
Distributive property	$(8 + 4) \times 3$	The cows and horses were black.
Exponential notation	$10^6 = 1,000,000$	In language we abbreviate words: La. stands for Louisiana.

STRATEGIES FOR TEACHING THE MATH STORY PROBLEM

A common complaint of mathematics teachers is that their students have a great deal of difficulty in reading and working math story problems. Difficulty in this respect can be attributed to either specific reading and vocabulary problems or deficiencies in problem-solving ability. In the first instance, we have made numerous suggestions regarding the teaching of general reading and vocabulary skills. However, if the student's deficiency lies in the area of problem solving, the following instructional strategy should prove extremely helpful.

1. Read the problem through and identify what the problem is asking for. Is it the number of miles between two cities, or how

long it will take to get from one city to the other? Identify the units of measurement the problem deals with (miles, minutes, hours, feet, quarts, pounds, and so on).

2. Predict an approximate answer to the problem. Read the problem a second time and make a prediction based on a general consideration of the information contained in the problem. The prediction might take the form of a single approximated number or amount: around two hours, about forty feet, or in the neighborhood of ten tons. The prediction might take the form of a statement of approximate high and low values for the answer: between two and four hours, less than forty feet and more than twenty-five feet, or approximately ten to twelve tons. Making an initial prediction of an answer to the problem in this way will help the students to sort out relevant from irrelevant information in the problem and to identify when they are getting off the track in solving the problem.

3. Identify the facts given in the problem, then determine which facts are relevant to solving the problem and which facts are of no use in solving the problem. Convert different units of measurement so that all units are parallel.

4. Identify the mathematical operations required to solve the problem. Then, determine the sequence in which the mathematical operations should be carried out and proceed to solve the problem using the relevant facts previously determined.

5. Compare the final problem solution with the prediction made earlier. Determine whether or not the final problem solution is within the limits of the prediction, that is, the final solution is close enough to the approximate prediction to be accepted.

6. Finally, seek feedback regarding the correct and acceptable answer to the problem as soon as possible. Rework the problem if necessary.

The student who is deficient in problem solving skills will have the greatest difficulty with lengthy story problems, story problems that present a great deal of information, story problems that introduce a preponderance of irrelevant information, and story problems that require several mathematical operations and that require mathematical operations to be carried out in a precise sequence. It is advisable for the mathematics teacher to work through the steps stated above using simple examples, then progressing to more complex examples during in-class demonstrations. For the less able students, the teacher can provide varying numbers of additional "clues" that will help students to successfully solve the story problem.

READING PROBLEMS IN OTHER CONTENT AREAS

Reading is an important facet of learning in all content areas, including areas like auto mechanics, industrial arts, home economics, business education, music, and so on. The specific trouble spots in reading materials in these content areas largely overlap with those discussed in this chapter. For the most part, the specific reading problems students encounter in these other content areas center around the following:

1. Unfamiliarity with specialized and technical vocabularies used in a particular content area.
2. Inability to read and follow a set of steps or directions required to carry out a particular task in a given content area.
3. Unfamiliarity with the specialized reading materials used in a particular content area.
4. Lack of facility with all the skills associated with comprehension, locating information, organizing information, reading flexibly, and utilizing the information gained from reading.
5. Inadequate preparation for (establishing purposes for reading and readiness to read) and guidance in completing the reading task in the content area.

The strategies we have offered in this chapter regarding how to deal with specific trouble spots in reading content materials are applicable to other content areas and other instructional situations. They are also easily adapted to other areas and situations. The content area teacher in music, for example, should review the strategies offered in this chapter and employ those that are most appropriate for dealing with the reading problems of that content area.

GENERAL TEACHING STRATEGIES

Strategies for Making Student Assignments

As we have said, a great deal of difficulty develops when students are not clear about what they are required to do, what is expected of them, and the strategies for achieving the goals set by the teacher. When students are unclear about these factors, the teaching-learning situation becomes unpredictable for them and results in confusion and many student behaviors that are not conducive to learning. In other chapters, we have presented a highly structured format for giving a reading lesson that helps to ready students for reading new material and clarifies the nature of the goals and objectives they are to achieve.

The making of assignments is a key element in creating a predictable instructional situation for students in which they know what they are to do and how they are to go about the task set by the teacher. The assignment affords the teacher the greatest opportunity in providing pupil direction and promoting pupil growth and development in important skills. The classroom assignment, then, is one of the most important teaching devices available to the teacher. The teacher's skill in making classroom assignments can be greatly enhanced by following the strategies listed below.

1. Assignments should be made during the class period when they will best contribute to the overall objectives of the content being studied. Avoid making assignments when there is a lull in class or during the last few minutes of class.

2. Students should be informed as to the importance of an assignment, how it fits into the objectives of a given unit, the necessity of the assignment, what is to be accomplished in the assignment, and the skills and knowledges that students will gain as a result of completing the assignment. Assignments that are largely busy work will be difficult to explain to students in this way and should be avoided.

3. It should be made clear to students exactly what they are to accomplish in the assignment. A vague assignment is worse than no assignment at all. What is to be done, when is it to be completed, how should the task be approached? The teacher is wise to present students with several questions that will be answered by the completed assignment; in this way, students can refer to the questions while completing the assignment, and they will know when they are getting off the track and when their completed assignments have left out material that should have been included. The teacher is also wise to (a) have students copy the assignment in a notebook, (b) place the assignment in written form on the chalkboard, (c) allow ample time in class to make the assignment orally, (d) explain to students some of the pitfalls in doing the assignment that they should avoid, and (e) allow time in class for students to raise questions about the assignment.

4. Raise questions that will cause the student to become aware

of the reading and thinking skills required by the assignment. Emphasize those thought questions that are central to successful completion of the assignment and begin them with words like: why, what do you think, in what way might, and so on.

5. When required, be sure to tell pupils how to obtain the information they will need to complete the assignment, where it is located, and what they must do with the information once they have secured it.

6. If the assignment is complex, it is sometimes a good idea to give students a mimeographed explanation of the assignment that is clearly outlined step by step.

7. Review appropriate study and reading techniques (SQ4R, previewing, skimming, and so forth) and encourage students to utilize these techniques in completing the assignment.

STRATEGIES FOR PROMOTING WIDE READING

The Classroom Library

A teacher is wise to keep a classroom library of reference materials, paperbacks, magazines, and other high interest reading materials. The following suggestions will make the classroom library an effective addition:

1. Materials should exhibit much variety in terms of content and subject matter.
2. Materials should exhibit a wide range in terms of difficulty level, length, style, and format.
3. The teacher should control the contents of the classroom library to insure a diversity of materials are available.
4. The content of the classroom library should be changed periodically, with the addition of new materials and the deletion of materials that have not been used.
5. All students should have the opportunity to use the classroom library at regular intervals; it should not be reserved for those students who finish assignments early, nor should it be used as a reward for those students who do the best work or create no problems in the classroom.

Content teachers in highly specialized areas like auto mechanics, music, and other areas might wish to tailor the classroom libary to contain a wealth of reading materials that deal with that particular content area. Sources of reading materials for the classroom library are endless. The first sources the teacher might utilize are the school and local libaries. Local, state, and federal government publications are also an excellent source of reading materials for students. Whatever materials are chosen, the classroom library that makes available to students a wide diversity of reading matter has been shown to be an effective method for stimulating wide reading and developing the reading habit.

The Teacher as a Reading Model

If among our objectives in teaching reading is the objective of making our students lifetime readers and instilling in them the reading habit, then we as teachers must model the very behavior we wish to develop in our students. We must set aside time for our own reading and attach as much importance to reading as we would like our students to attach to reading. We must assume the role of an avid and voracious reader and daily demonstrate this attitude toward reading to our students.

The teacher who takes the task of being a model of reading seriously should carry the book being read for information and pleasure to and from school. In spare moments, the teacher should be seen by students reading. The teacher should also share with students the information and ideas gained from reading, whether or not the teacher's reading is directly related to the content dealt with in class. Above all, the teacher should be a visible model of a person who has the lifetime reading habit and for whom reading is an important source of entertainment and enjoyment.

Attractive classroom book displays, regular opportunities to utilize the resources of the school library, and in-class opportunities for students and teachers alike to share ideas gained from reading are all helpful ways of instilling interest in reading. Teachers should concern themselves with the reading needs of students and familiarize themselves with the wealth of adolescent literature that is available. Students also enjoy having their teacher read to them, and time should be set aside for such activities. Telling students that reading is enjoyable and that they should develop the reading habit is never enough; we, as teachers, must foster this attitude toward reading daily by being models of the very behavior we hope to develop in our students.

SUMMARY

1. Problems in reading English literature vary depending upon the type of literature in question.

2. Short stories are difficult to read because there is little background information or build-up and few elaborations and details.

3. Novels are difficult to read because they are long and intricate. The reader has problems assimilating the vast amount of information presented.

4. Poetry is difficult to read because it does not follow a logical format, and syntactical patterns vary from usual patterns.

5. Drama is difficult to read because the reader does not have the benefit of the visual and auditory accompaniments present in the dramatic performance. In addition, dialogue tends to be terse because much of the meaning is conveyed through intonation and gesture.

6. Essays and autobiographies are difficult to read because the reader must attempt to understand the author as well as the author's message.

7. To teach the short story the teacher should (a) introduce background information to build readiness and create interest, (b) explain the nature of the short story, (c) have students predict from the title what the story might be about, (d) have students skim the story before reading it intently, and (e) have the critical parts of the short story read in class.

8. To teach the novel the teacher should (a) have students read no more at one time than they can manage, (b) establish purposes for reading the novel, (c) allow oral reading in class, (d) allow frequent opportunities for students to predict coming events, and (e) supply background information and summarize events at regular intervals.

9. To teach poetry the teacher should (a) have poems read aloud in class, (b) establish the purpose of the author and purposes for reading the poem, (c) help students understand difficult words and the literary devices the poet uses, (d) explain the format and structure of poetry, (e) be careful in the selection of poems, and (f) have students write their own poems.

10. To teach plays the teacher should (a) emphasize the importance of staging information, (b) have students cast the play, (c) allow the play to be read and performed in class, (d) select plays that are interesting and relevant, (e) encourage students to attend plays, (f) summarize the play at regular intervals, and (g) present recordings and films of plays.

11. To teach essays and autobiographies the teacher should (a) help students understand that these are forums for authors to express themselves, (b) encourage students to decipher the author's viewpoint, biases, or mood, and (c) select interesting and relevant reading selections.

12. Social studies content is difficult to read because it usually is lengthy, vocabulary is specialized, hierarchical relationships among concepts must be learned, expository form is used, and it contains nonverbal symbols.

13. To teach social studies content reading the teacher should (a) assign reasonable amounts of reading at one time, (b) allow reading time in class, (c) establish purpose for reading, (d) provide background information, (e) stimulate student interest, (f) focus attention on major points, (g) preteach difficult vocabulary and nonverbal symbols, and (h) have students make predictions about the content of the reading selection.

14. Science content is difficult to read because of specialized vocabulary, the need to understand hierarchical relationships among science concepts, expository writing style, and the need to use reference materials often.

15. To teach science content reading the teacher should (a) preteach specialized vocabulary terms and graphic aids, (b) insure' readiness to understand new content, (c) stimulate student interest, (d) focus attention on important concepts, (e) establish purpose for reading, (f) break up lengthy reading assignments, and (g) have students make predictions about the content.

16. Math content is difficult to read because of specialized vocabulary terms, symbols, and graphs, and the difficulty of reading story problems.

17. To teach math content reading the teacher should (a)

clarify poorly worded statements, (b) insure that students learn math symbols and their language equivalents, (c) encourage study reading, (d) introduce special textbook features, and (e) show students language applications of specialized math concepts and symbols.

18. To teach the math story problems the teacher should help students (a) identify what the problem requires, (b) predict an approximate answer, (c) identify the facts given in the problem, (d) identify the mathematical operations to be employed, (e) compare the final solution with the predictions made earlier, and (f) obtain feedback on the correctness of students' work.

19. In making student assignments the teacher should (a) establish the purpose of an assignment, (b) provide clear instructions, (c) offer guidance for successfully completing the assignment, and (d) tell students how to obtain information used to complete the assignment and review appropriate study and reading techniques that will help in completing the assignment.

20. To promote wide reading the teachers should (a) build a classroom library, (b) present themselves as model readers, (c) provide classroom book displays, and (d) provide opportunities to utilize the school library and for in-class discussion of reading selections.

REVIEW QUESTIONS

1. What are the problems in reading short stories? How can the teacher deal with these problems?

2. What are the problems in reading novels? How can the teacher deal with these problems?

3. What are the problems in reading poetry? How can the teacher deal with these problems?

4. What are the problems in reading drama? How can the teacher deal with these problems?

5. What are the problems in reading essays and autobiographies? How can the teacher deal with these problems?

6. What are the problems in reading social studies content? How can the teacher deal with these problems?

7. What are the problems in reading science content? How can the teacher deal with these problems?

8. What are the problems in reading math content? How can the teacher deal with these problems?

9. What strategies can the teacher employ in making student assignments?

10. How can the teacher encourage students to become wide readers?

CHAPTER 18
The Organization of Content
in the Content Areas

PURPOSE

1. To analyze the organization of content in textbooks.
2. To show you how to organize content for instruction.
3. To show you how thinking procedures relate to content.
4. To analyze the thinking procedures probed in textbooks.

BACKGROUND AND NEW INFORMATION

This chapter applies what you have already learned to the organization of content in the content areas. Everything you learned previously about content hierarchies and concepts will be useful in this chapter as we show you how to organize content into content hierarchies in the various content areas. Everything you learned about thinking procedures provides a foundation for this chapter, because in this chapter we also relate thinking procedures to content in the different content areas.

The chapter begins with an analysis of English content. First, the organization of literature textbooks is considered. Second, we discuss organizing English content for instruction. Third, we relate thinking procedures to English content. Fourth, we analyze the thinking procedures probed in English textbooks. Next, we address the same four issues with respect to social studies content and then science content.

No new reading terms appear in this chapter.

The student will be able to:

1. Describe the organization of textbooks in English literature, social studies, and science.
2. Organize content for instruction, particularly in English literature, social studies, and science.
3. Describe how thinking procedures are taught with content, particularly in English literature, social studies, and science.
4. Describe the thinking procedures probed in English literature, social studies, and science textbooks.

THE ORGANIZATION OF ENGLISH CONTENT

The Organization of Literature Textbooks

Literature texts are most often anthologies or collections of writings by many authors. Thus, the English literature textbook varies tremendously in terms of authors' style, format (poetry, short stories, and so on), and in many other respects. Hence, the literature textbook can be lower in predictability for a host of reasons.

Organization by Literary Format

Often, literature textbooks are organized by placing similar forms of literature together. Poetry, short stories, essays, nonfiction, drama, and so on are each a separate and distinct category within the broad content hierarchy *literature*. This content hierarchy can be represented, then, as follows:

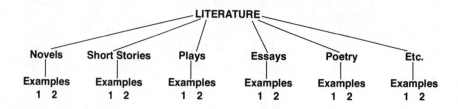

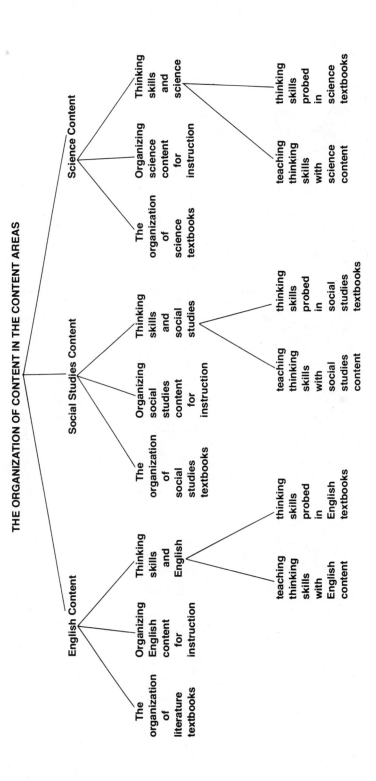

THE ORGANIZATION OF CONTENT IN THE CONTENT AREAS

English Content

- The organization of literature textbooks
- Organizing English content for instruction
- Thinking skills and English
  - teaching thinking skills with English content
  - thinking skills probed in English textbooks

Social Studies Content

- The organization of social studies textbooks
- Organizing social studies content for instruction
- Thinking skills and social studies
  - teaching thinking skills with social studies content
  - thinking skills probed in social studies textbooks

Science Content

- The organization of science textbooks
- Organizing science content for instruction
- Thinking skills and science
  - teaching thinking skills with science content
  - thinking skills probed in science textbooks

FIGURE 18–1   A hierarchy of topics in chapter 18

Organization by Literary Device

Within a particular category of the content hierarchy *literature*, textbook authors often group pieces of literature according to their emphasis of certain stylistic and literary devices such as plot, tone, setting, character, and so on. Each piece of literature under the category of tone, then, is considered a good example of the individual author's use of tone as a literary device. Again, using the broad content hierarchy of *literature*, we may represent this organizational arrangement in the following way:

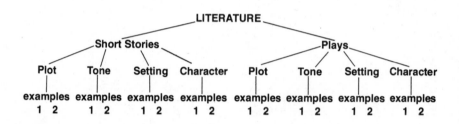

Common examples of such categories included in this type of textbook arrangement are understanding character, understanding sensory impressions, understanding author's purpose or viewpoint, understanding inferences and figurative language, getting the central idea, and so on. Within each of these categories, the textbook would include pieces of literature by individual authors that specifically require understanding these devices and that lend themselves to the teaching of these devices.

Organization by Theme

Another common way of organizing collected pieces of literature in a textbook anthology is according to the general theme with which the selections deal. Some examples of thematic categories used in this way are "people and problems," "courage," "search," "moments of decision," "the strange and eerie," and so on. All selections within the theme "moments of decision," then, are examples of literature in which the characters are confronted with circumstances requiring them to make a decision. Literary selections grouped in this fashion may also be similar in terms of literary devices used by individual authors. For example, the thematic category of "the strange and eerie" is probably more a category of selections similar in tone and mood than in topic and theme. In using this sort of organization, literary elements and devices such as plot, tone, character, and so on are relegated to a secondary role in terms of instructional emphasis. The emphasis is now placed upon the ideas being expressed by the individual authors so that different forms of literature (short stories, plays, poetry, and so on) will be used to study various topics and themes as opposed to placing instructional emphasis on the literary forms themselves. In terms of the broad content hierarchy *literature*, this textbook organization can be exemplified in the following manner:

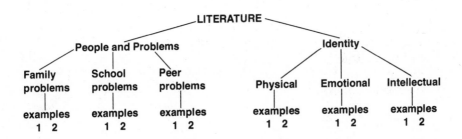

As you can see, the organizational arrangement of a literature textbook has a great deal to do with the instructional emphasis and content to be taught. A literature textbook organized by literary format emphasizes the study of literature according to form and style; poetry, for example, is studied as an art form first and for the ideas it might express second. Literature texts that utilize a thematic or topical organization first emphasize the ideas the individual authors express, and, second, the format the authors have chosen to express their ideas.

Organizing English Content for Instruction

As we have said, literature textbooks are loosely organized, and there is a great deal of variation from one textbook to another. As a result, the English teacher has an opportunity to manipulate and arrange the English content to facilitate learning in general and to pursue particular instructional objectives. Unless the English teacher imposes organization on the content taught, literature content will lack structure and predictability. Students, then, will have a more difficult time mastering new content, not because it is too difficult or too sophisticated, but because they perceive no organization to the content and they remain confused regarding what they are to do and what they are to learn.

Because English literature content is loosely structured, a content analysis of any given sample unit from a literature anthology can take many different directions. One of the topical themes mentioned previously was that of "people and problems." This theme unit is contained in a literature anthology designed for grade nine. A brief analysis of the selections in this unit reveals five short stories and two poems that deal with the following subtopics:

peer pressure
rationalization
discipline
peer relationships
parent-child relationships
growing up
peer love relationships
one's responsibility to others and to society
turning over a new leaf
making the break with the family

An extended analysis of the selections in this unit would, no doubt, reveal additional subtopics. However, for the purposes of structuring a unit of instruction based on a content analysis, these topics provide us enough information regarding the content of the unit in order to begin our analysis.

Each selection in the unit "people and problems" has as its main character(s) an adolescent(s). A quick examination of the previous list of subtopics indicates that many are among those areas of interest expressed by students and areas of concern expressed by curriculum experts which are discussed in chapter 13.

We know that among the chief concerns of adolescents is the transition to adulthood, as well as their own perceptions regarding the way they fit into their peer group and how their peers perceive them. Therefore, a workable content hierarchy might be represented as follows:

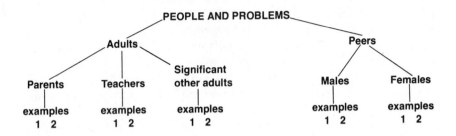

Since the content hierarchy "people and problems" implies two factors (people and problems), a second "subcategory" is provided in the hierarchy for kinds of problems adolescents might encounter with each of the groups of people listed.

Within the confines of the content hierarchy "people and problems," then, the major focus is correctly placed upon the interactions of the adolescent characters in the selections with significant other characters in the selections. The instructional thrust becomes the study of the ways in which adolescent characters deal with the problems that exist between themselves and the other characters in the selections.

Within the content idea hierarchy "people and problems," teachers might also wish to emphasize other characteristics of the selections contained in the unit. For example, they may wish to deal with literary devices such as plot, tone, mood, characterization, and so on. These elements might become an additional level in the content hierarchy or an additional content hierarchy may be constructed around them. In any event, structuring the content in English literature in this fashion serves to emphasizes the relationships in the content. If this structure is then communicated to students, their learning will be facilitated.

THINKING PROCEDURES AND ENGLISH

Teaching Thinking Skills with English Content

In discussing the thinking procedures required and those that can be taught with the content hierarchy "people and problems," we can begin with the first level of the hierarchy—adults and peers. In order to master the content hierarchy "people and problems," the students will necessarily have to be able to distinguish a host of factors that make some people adults and other people adolescents (as represented by the term "peers"). Obviously, students will be able to distinguish purely physical factors that separate these two groups. From this point, the teacher can guide instruction toward distinguishing more subtle factors that separate the two groups; for example, the responsibilities of adults and adolescents, things that interest and motivate adults and adolescents, behavior patterns of adults and adolescents, and many more. By including the next level of the content hierarchy, the teacher can begin to explore these distinguishing characteristics with regard to subcategories of adults (parents, teachers, significant other adults) and adolescents (males and females).

Up to this point, we have discussed relationships of similarity and differences regarding the levels and categories in the content hierarchy "people and problems." We can further emphasize relationships of sequence regarding this content hierarchy. For example, in distinguishing between adults and adolescents, the teacher can emphasize the sequence of steps, stages, behaviors, interests, motivations, and so on that a person goes through in becoming an adult. The interests, motivations, behaviors, and so forth that people exhibit become indicators of points in a general sequence we call "growing up." Therefore, the categories of "adults" and "peers" in the content hierarchy are related sequentially, and this relationship can be emphasized in instruction. Further, this particular content hierarchy can be justified for two very important reasons: 1) important reading-thinking skills can be taught by organizing instruction around this content hierarchy; and 2) the content itself is important to students and can be viewed as contributing to effective living (in fact, students themselves, as well as curriculum experts, have emphasized the importance of learning about the period between adolescence and adulthood).

We can further analyze the content hierarchy "people and problems" by emphasizing relationships of cause-effect among the categories of the hierarchy. That is, we can emphasize how a problem at school with those adults we call teachers can spill over into problems at home with those adults we call parents. Simply stated, the problems a character in a short story has are often caused or are the result of other problems and conflicts. By emphasizing these cause-effect relationships, we can teach students the general concept of how events cause other events and how events result from other events, and ultimately to apply this knowledge to the interactions students have with people in their environment.

There are many, many additional relationships contained in the hierarchy "people and problems" that teachers can emphasize in their instruction. The important point is, however, that by learning to recognize and understand these relationships, students can develop the ability to predict events. It is an important skill, for example, to be able to make accurate predictions about people and the behaviors they exhibit. It is an important skill to make accurate predictions regarding the effects of our own behavior. By organizing instruction around content hierarchies like "people and problems," we can teach the important reading-thinking skills required to master the content hierarchy as well as the reading-thinking skills required to deal with the people we encounter in our environment.

Thinking Skills Probed in English Textbooks

Most literature anthologies contain a variety of short stories, poems, plays, and so on. Short stories and other pieces of literature are usually followed by discussion questions that probe the students' understanding of the content. A survey of the content unit "people and problems" reveals that the discussion questions following related stories and poems deal with a number of comprehension areas. First, the general ability to understand the characters, their actions, and their motives is probed. This is most often accomplished by making a general statement about a character in the question and asking the student to find evidence and examples that support the general statement. Additionally, students are often asked to compare and contrast characters and to recognize character changes that may have taken place. In recognizing character changes, the student is often asked to tell when the change took place, what brought the change about, and what in the story clues the reader in to the fact that a character is undergoing change.

In reading poetry, discussion questions are generally designed to elicit from the student interpretations of specific words, phrases, images, and so on. With all types of literature, students are asked for qualitative judgments with questions like "in your

opinion . . .," "do you think . . .," "if you were the main character,
would you . . .". In asking for qualitative judgments from students, these questions most often require the students to furnish
proof or reasons for their responses.

A survey of the discussion questions contained in a literature
anthology also reveals that there are many thinking skills seldom
probed. While cause-effect questions are often included, seldom
do the questions probe for the student's understanding of cause-
effect relationships beyond a surface level. For example, a question that follows a short story may well ask the student to tell what
caused a particular conflict in the story or to tell what the result of
a particular character's actions were. In these instances, depending on the extent to which the author has explained these relationships, the student may only be required to repeat the words of
the author. In this example, the student certainly recognizes a
cause-effect relationship, but the relationship may have been very
explicit in the story, and the student, therefore, is required only to
recall information that was stated literally. To probe cause-effect
relationships at a higher level, questions can be constructed so
that they change the circumstances presented in the story and
require the student to explain further changes that may have
taken place. For example, consider the question "Suppose the
main character had *not* received the message; what do you think
he would have done and how might the story have turned out?" In
this instance, we have asked the student to make a whole new set
of contextual identifications based on new information. By changing the circumstances in the story somewhat, we have changed
the context. Now the student must make predictions about the
effects of these changes. The students must engage in probabilis-
tic thought and call upon information from past experience and
information about the specific characters gained from the story in
order to predict the effects of these new circumstances. The
quality of their responses will reflect the precision and validity of
the identifications they understand.

It can be seen even from a cursory analysis of textbook
questions that the major thinking skills being probed in literature
texts are skills that require the student to make identifications.
Many of the identifications required by these questions require
the identification of abstraction categories through structural and
contextual abstraction. Some questions require precise identification, for example, when the student must furnish supporting evidence for a general statement or must furnish an example of

something. These questions generally cause the student to engage in deductive thinking. Fewer questions require students to engage in inductive thinking in which they must generalize from specific instances. Judgmental questions often require inductive thinking, and the quality of the students' responses will be determined in large part by their ability to manipulate and organize a great deal of specific information in order to make generalizations. However, few questions require students to make predictions. This may be due to some extent to the format used by textbooks; normally, the student reads the required piece of literature, *then* attempts to answer questions. As Goodman points out, the better reader makes accurate predictions on the basis of less information. Perhaps a more useful instructional strategy is to ask students questions before and during their reading. In this way, we actively involve readers in making predictions and hypotheses about their reading, and they are more likely to seek to confirm their predictions.

THE ORGANIZATION OF SOCIAL STUDIES CONTENT

To discuss the organization of social studies content requires attention to the fact that the term "social studies" encompasses the study of literally hundreds of subtopics that comprise the discipline. Although in the elementary and middle schools students generally study "social studies," by the time students reach high school they are confronted with a multitude of course offerings such as geography, American history, world history, government, civics, economics, and so on. Recently, high school offerings in the area of social studies have been expanded to include the study of cultures, environmental issues, living patterns, and so on. The interrelationships between and among these subtopics are the essence of social studies.

Most of the subtopics of social studies can be grouped or categorized within five broad areas: history, government, geography, culture, and living patterns. These areas are not mutually exclusive; they overlap a great deal. To understand the relationship between one topic and another in social studies the student must employ reading and thinking skills.

Briefly, the study of history involves the study of the sequential and cause-effect nature of events that have shaped the world. To study government is to study the way in which men and women

have organized themselves to effect change and to achieve their
goals. The study of government and the processes of government
is, in actuality, the study of culture and civilization. Culture and
civilization are reflected in the forms of government human beings have invented. On the surface, geography is the study of a
collection of facts and names. However, an in-depth study of
geography cannot ignore the ways in which historical events, cultural patterns, and governmental processes have shaped and continue to shape the territorial boundaries that exist in the world.
Finally, the study of living patterns including environmental issues, land use, overpopulation, urbanism, and so on involves the
study of a new aspect of culture—technology. We might arbitrarily
conceive of the social studies content as a broad content hierarchy
that would look like this:

| History | Government | Culture and Civilization | Geography | Living Patterns |

In the final analysis, the content expert—the teacher—may well
perceive social studies content differently than it is organized
above. The important factor, however, is that the teacher analyzes
the content in such a fashion as to reveal the major ideas and
concepts (content hierarchies) contained in the the content, the
related but minor concepts (lower levels of the content hierarchies) contained in the content, and the relationships that exist
among the categories and levels of the content hierarchy.

This process of analyzing the content to be taught reaps many
benefits. First, it presents the content as an organized body of
knowledge. Second, it helps the teacher to make important decisions about what is relevant and what is irrelevant regarding the
content to be taught. Third, it helps to insure the teaching of
important reading and thinking skills. Fourth, it provides the student a structure and organization that ultimately facilitates learning the new content. Finally, it insures a strong match between
what is taught, what is learned, and what is finally tested; this
being the essence of evaluation of student achievement.

Let us now describe how social studies content is structured
and organized within the confines of textbooks and materials used

to teach social studies. This structure is reflected in the writing patterns used in social studies and the thinking patterns, therefore, required to understand social studies content. In the latter portions of this chapter we will present an extended example of a content hierarchy in social studies and an analysis of the reading and thinking required by the content hierarchy as well as the reading and thinking skills most often probed by social studies textbooks.

The Organization of Social Studies Textbooks

Unlike English textbooks, which vary a great deal in the way they are organized, social studies textbooks for the most part follow a regular and predictable pattern of organization. In most instances, the information contained in social studies textbooks is presented in a chronologically sequenced pattern. However, deviations from this pattern are frequent, and students must be able to cope with the writing and organizational patterns of social studies textbooks if they are to learn the content.

Sequence Pattern

Perhaps the most common pattern in which social studies textbooks and materials are written and organized is the sequence pattern. While the sequence pattern in science materials requires the student to follow a specific series of steps or directions, the sequence pattern in social studies is primarily one of chronology that pervades, for example, an entire textbook. The sequence pattern in social studies requires the student to follow a more general set of events in order to establish a time perspective and a general framework within which is set many specific events. In a traditional textbook, dealing for example with American history, the text begins with the exploration and colonization of America and follows with the American Revolution, westward expansion, industrial expansion, the Civil War, and so forth—all in a chronological sequence. Even more specialized textbooks like texts that deal with American government historically trace the development of government in a sequential pattern.

Cause-effect Patterns

Closely akin to the sequential pattern is the cause-effect pattern. We have, in other chapters, indicated that cause-effect relationships are a special kind or subset of sequential relationships. Part of the rationale for studying the events of history in a sequential fashion lies in the fact that the events of history also tend to be related causally. We might have students study, for example, the events prior to the American Revolution in the order in which they occurred. It is important for the student to understand that these events, to varying degrees, helped to cause the Revolutionary War. Events like the Stamp Act and the Boston Tea Party not only took place in a particular sequence before the Revolutionary War but in part can be studied as causes of the Revolutionary War. Since most social studies materials are written in a chronological and sequential pattern, the cause-effect pattern automatically becomes an aspect of reading and thinking about social studies content.

Deductive Pattern

Another common pattern that pervades social studies textbooks and materials is the deductive pattern. In this pattern, broad content hierarchies are introduced by the author followed by supportive information in the form of details, narratives, descriptions, and examples. This pattern is found within single chapters, units, and entire texts. A text unit written in the deductive pattern might begin with a broad content hierarchy like "culture," followed by additional units dealing with more specific cultural phenomena like "urbanism" and "industrialism." Each separate unit might also follow the deductive pattern. For example, the unit on "urbanism" would begin with the content hierarchy "urbanism," followed by specific examples and illustrations of the content hierarchy. The deductive pattern is similar to Robinson's (1975) generalization pattern. The task of the student in dealing with the deductive writing pattern in social studies is to recognize descriptions, examples, and illustrations in terms of the level of a content hierarchy they represent. When students fail to recognize relative levels in the content hierarchy, they are likely to attach much importance to relatively trivial information while underemphasizing or ignoring major points and ideas contained in the reading material.

Combinations of Patterns

Seldom do social studies textbooks and materials utilize the sequence pattern to the exclusion of the deductive pattern. These writing and organizational patterns are interwoven into the materials depending upon the nature of the specific content being dealt with. When the sequence pattern is followed in a text, content hierarchies are often introduced and further explored followed by a return to the sequence pattern. In this instance, the sequence and deductive patterns are being interwoven. Specifically, a social studies textbook in American history might begin with units about the exploration of the continent and the American Revolution. The text then might introduce the content hierarchy "The Birth of the American Government" within the deductive pattern, returning later to the sequence pattern with units about the settling of the West, the Civil War, and so on. Within the general sequence pattern, a text might also magnify the importance of the perception of cause-effect relationships in introducing a section entitled "The Years before the Civil War." This section will likely be laden with information regarding the causative factors leading to the Civil War. Although still within the general sequential pattern, a section following entitled "Reconstruction" will most probably be heavy with information about the effects of the Civil War. It is important for students to key into these various patterns and combinations of patterns if they are to perceive and understand the structure and organization of the content they are studying. In turn, the student's perception and organization of the content hierarchies will lead to increased and more in-depth understanding of the content.

Organizing Social Studies Content for Instruction

As we have said, social studies texts are fairly highly structured and exhibit a great deal of similarity in the way they are organized. However, the volume of information contained in a social studies textbook is often so great that it obscures the most relevant content hierarchies contained in the material. Students have particular difficulty in differentiating major and minor content hierarchies, relevant and irrelevant information regarding content hierarchies, and generally in perceiving the structure and organization of social studies content. For these reasons it is important that the teacher add structure and organization, and therefore predictability, to the content taught.

An analysis of social studies textbooks reveals that nearly all deal with the broad content hierarchy "government." While most

advanced texts treat the many concepts of government and the
various forms of government that exist in the world, textbooks in
American history deal specifically with the democratic and repub-
lican forms of government, since these are the forms of government under which we live. Central to the study of the government
of the United States (or any government, for that matter) is the
study of the ways in which governmental powers and authority
are divided. To begin with, governmental powers are divided
among the federal, state, and local governments. This division
can be represented as a broad content hierarchy in the following
way:

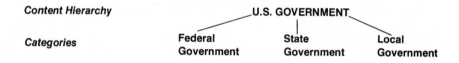

Content Hierarchy   U.S. GOVERNMENT

Categories   Federal   State   Local
                                Government   Government   Government

   Pursuing the analysis of the content hierarchy "U.S. Government" still further, we can show the divisions of the federal, state,
and local governments. Looking at only the further division of the
federal government, we can now deal with the more specific content hierarchy "federal government" and represent it in this way:

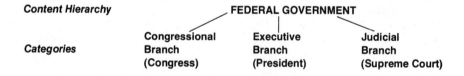

Content Hierarchy   FEDERAL GOVERNMENT

                                Congressional   Executive   Judicial
Categories   Branch   Branch   Branch
                                (Congress)   (President)   (Supreme Court)

While the state and local governments can be similarly portrayed,
we will deal with the development of the content hierarchy "federal government," since the inclusion of state and local governments will yield a rather unwieldy content hierarchy. Thus, by
adding an additional level to the content hierarchy "federal government," we have an extended hierarchy that can be portrayed
as follows.

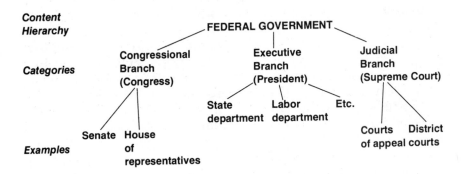

Within the content hierarchy "federal government," the major focus is correctly placed upon the three branches of government: congressional, executive, and judicial. Additionally, students are expected to learn about the specific governmental bodies associated with each of the three branches of government. This would include understanding who and what comprises each governmental body, how membership is determined within each governmental body, the duties and functions of each governmental body, the duties and functions of each member of each governmental body, the powers with which each governmental body is vested, and so on.

Teachers may wish to emphasize other characteristics of the elements in the content hierarchy "federal government" and make decisions regarding which of the above stated knowledges and understandings they want their students to master. Teachers may also wish to extend the content hierarchy; for example, they could include as an additional level under "Senate" and "House of Representatives" important committees within those governmental bodies. These added elements of the content hierarchy might also be used to construct an additional content hierarchy. In any event, structuring the content of social studies in this way helps to emphasize the relationships contained among the elements of the content hierarchy. If this structure is subsequently communicated to students, it can serve to facilitate and increase their learning of the new content.

THINKING PROCEDURES AND SOCIAL STUDIES

Teaching Thinking Skills with Social Studies Content

In discussing the thinking procedures required and those that can be taught with the content hierarchy "federal government," we can begin with the first level of the hierarchy—the congressional, executive, and judicial branches of government. In order to master the content hierarchy "federal government," students will be required to distinguish differences and note similarities among the three branches of government and the functions inherent in each. In terms of similarities, all are concerned to varying degrees with interpreting the Constitution of the United States and in carrying out the functions of government. Students must also understand the primary functions of each branch; that is, the primary function of Congress is to legislate or pass laws, while the main function of the executive branch is to execute or administer the laws. Finally, the judicial branch is responsible for interpreting the laws and judging them according to whether or not they violate the Constitution.

The recognition of similarities and differences in the content hierarchy "federal government" also includes lower levels in the hierarchy as well as the examples we utilize in teaching the content hierarchy. Students will be expected to identify similarities and differences between, for example, the Senate and the House of Representatives. As we have pointed out, these similarities and differences could involve such factors as the composition of these governmental bodies, their functions and duties, their powers, the way in which their members gain membership, and so on. These factors can then be compared to and contrasted with additional examples included in the content hierarchy like the various departments within the executive branch, the Supreme Court, and lower courts.

Up to this point, we have focused primarily on relationships of similarity and difference regarding the levels and categories of the content hierarchy "federal government." We can further determine, for instructional purposes, the relationships of sequence regarding this content hierarchy. For example, since the Senate and the House of Representatives are considered law-making bodies, we can emphasize the sequence involved in the proposal and passage of bills into law. The general sequence involves the introduction of a bill, committee discussion, discussion by all members of the governmental body, and voting. If the bill is then passed, it goes to the other congressional body for similar consideration. Finally, it is forwarded to the president. If the president vetoes the bill, another sequence is initiated in further consideration of the bill. Similar relationships of sequence exist among the departments of the executive branch and the courts of the judicial branch. Teachers must identify those relationships of sequence they consider important for students to understand so that they will ultimately master the content hierarchy "federal government."

In pursuing our analysis, we can identify and emphasize the relationships of cause and effect among the levels and categories in the content hierarchy "federal government." A consideration of the cause-effect relationship in this hierarchy leads us to another hierarchy—that of the system of checks and balances. At this point, the teacher may decide to introduce checks and balances as still another content hierarchy for instruction, or simply include instruction in this regard as part of the original content hierarchy. To exemplify the relationships of cause and effect in this content hierarchy, we might require the students to understand how one governmental body can intervene into the duties and functions of another. For example, the president has the authority to appoint justices to the Supreme Court, this being one of the knowledges within the content hierarchy already taught (similarities and differences in categories and levels of the hierarchy). However, the Congress can intervene by refusing to confirm the president's choice. Thus, the refusal of the Congress to confirm the appointment (cause) requires the president to make a new appointment (effect). This disagreement between the Congress and the president (cause) can lead to still further conflicts between the congressional and executive branches (effect). The content hierarchy "federal government" (or "system of checks and balances") is replete with cause-effect relationships that students must necessarily understand if they are to grasp the processes and procedures that define our system of government.

There are literally hundreds and thousands of additional relationships contained in the content hierarchy "federal government" that the teacher can emphasize during instruction. Some of these relationships may be too sophisticated, of low priority, or even irrelevant to the instruction the teacher provides. These are content decisions the teacher must make. The important point, however, is that by learning to recognize and understand these relationships, students can develop the ability to predict events. Studying the power structure of the federal government, for example, is important since all of us must live and function in a variety of power structures—in our home environment, in our jobs, in our communities, and so on. To understand how such structures are conceived and organized helps us to understand how to work effectively within them. We are in essence then able to predict our relationships, duties, authority, and roles within similar complex organizations—a skill that contributes to effective living. Further, in teaching the important reading and thinking skills required to master a content hierarchy, we teach skills that can be used in new contexts and situations. These skills are not specific, for example, to only learning social studies content. They are skills required for effective living and functioning in a complex society.

Thinking Skills Probed in Social Studies Textbooks

Most social studies textbooks follow the traditional chapter-by-chapter format, each chapter being followed by questions, activities, and projects. Questions contained in social studies textbooks and supplemental materials tend to take three forms: fact, main idea, and why questions.

Fact questions in social studies materials require the student to gain a literal understanding of the important points and information presented in the materials. Often, fact questions center on the student's literal understanding of new vocabulary terms, names, dates, and important events.

Questions probing the student's grasp of central points and main ideas are also contained in social studies textbooks and materials. Often, the student is called upon to identify the main idea of an entire chapter as well as main ideas of specific sections and topics within chapters. You will recall that perceiving the main idea involves inductive thinking on the part of the reader; the readers must integrate the knowledge of relevant and specific facts and points they have gained from their reading, then produce a generalized statement that encompasses all or nearly all of that relevant information. The wealth of information available in an average social studies text makes it imperative that the student reflect upon the main points and ideas the author presents.

Why questions occur frequently in social studies textbooks and materials and tend to deal primarily with the student's ability to recognize cause-effect relationships. These questions ask the student to tell "what caused" a particular event in history or to tell "what happened" or "what was the effect" of specific events discussed in the reading material. In many instances, however, these questions are answered directly in the text, requiring the student only to recall from the reading cause-effect relationships explicitly stated. Less often do cause-effect questions in social studies materials engage students in predicting causes and effects of events they have not directly learned about from their reading. Stated another way, few questions in social studies materials require the student to predict consequences of particular interventions. That is, few questions ask the student "what would happen if . . ." or "suppose _____ were true; how would this affect _____."

This brief analysis of the kinds of questions contained in social studies textbooks and reading materials is not meant to be exhaustive, nor is it meant to be generalized to all social studies materials. However, an examination of this sort does reveal that the preponderance of the questions contained in social studies materials tend to be identification level questions. In general, these identification level questions present the students with a question that requires them to understand a new vocabulary term from their reading; more specifically, these questions require descriptions, explanations, or the generation of an example or illustration. Again, most of these questions can be answered with descriptions, vocabulary terms, explanations, examples, or illustrations used explicitly in the text requiring little of the student above the literal level of reading comprehension.

In a similar manner, why questions often require little of the student above the literal level. In many instances, the student need only reproduce information presented in the text by keying in on signal words like "cause," "effect," "result," and so on. Few questions of this type really force the student to predict cause-effect relationships among events that were not specifically dealt with in the reading, or to link up the information in the reading with information from previous chapters, or to make predictions regarding what is contained in the remaining chapters. Seldom are students required to understand and think about the information they gain from their reading to the extent that they must make reasonable and accurate predictions about the content.

In conclusion, it should be noted that many fine social studies texts and supplemental materials are available. Although they do not always deal sufficiently with the higher level reading and thinking skills we have identified, they are easily adaptable to teaching these skills. If the questions we ask and the activities and projects we have students engage in require students to make predictions, test their predictions for confirmation or rejection, then we are actively involving students in important thought processes and teaching them how to master these important skills.

THE ORGANIZATION OF SCIENCE CONTENT

The Organization of Science Textbooks

Three basic earth science texts were chosen for analysis of content. Listed below are the major units in each. These three texts are designed for use in grades seven to nine, depending upon students' reading level.

Text 1

Unit 1 Our Planet Earth
Unit 2 Exploring Earth
Unit 3 Scientists Study Atmosphere and Weather
Unit 4 Space: Objects, Forces and Explorations
Unit 5 Preparations for Space Flight

Text 2

Unit 1 Physical Geology
Unit 2 Astronomy
Unit 3 Meterology
Unit 4 Oceanography
Unit 5 Historical Geology

Text 3

Unit 1 The Planet Earth
Unit 2 The Lithosphere
Unit 3 The Atmosphere and the Hydrosphere
Unit 4 The Earth's Crust Redesigned
Unit 5 Earth History
Unit 6 The Universe

An analysis of the units in three basic Earth science texts reveals a content hierarchy common to all three that can be represented as follows:

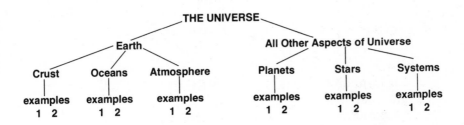

Further analysis of the content of the three texts reveals varying degrees of emphasis on the major categories in the content hierarchy "the universe." The table below portrays the approximate percentage of text devoted to the major categories in the content hierarchy.

THE UNIVERSE

	Earth	All Other Aspects of Universe
Text 1:	60%	40%
Text 2:	80	20
Text 3:	80	20

As you can see, Text 1 devotes a great deal more discussion to topics related to space, space exploration, other planets, stars, and so on. On the other hand, Texts 2 and 3 emphasize to a greater extent the study of our own planet. The point is that if a teacher has Text 1 available, he may feel that too little of the text deals with the study of the planet Earth and too much of the text deals with the study of the universe beyond the planet Earth. In this instance, the teacher may wish to augment the text with additional materials and supplemental readings that deal with Earth. The teacher may also wish to omit from study some of the material that deals with planets and stars. On the other hand, a teacher using Text 2 or 3 may feel that the study of the universe beyond the planet Earth is underemphasized. Under these circumstances the teacher may wish to supplement the study of other planets, stars, and solar systems. These are content decisions that teachers must make.

In Text 1, the first unit is entitled "Our Planet Earth." The outline below shows the topics covered in Unit One. Fully 25 to 30 percent of the entire textbook is devoted to coverage of the topics in Unit One.

Content Hierarchy of Unit One, Text 1

Chapter 1:
1. Lithosphere
   a. crust
   b. mantle
   c. core
2. Origin of Earth
3. Theories of Changes in Earth

Chapter 2:
1. Factors Affecting Earth Changes
   a. radiant energy
   b. weather and climate
2. Evidence of Changes
   a. volcanoes and earthquakes
   b. upheavals and erosion

Chapter 3:
1. Time Periods of Geologic History
   a. eons
   b. eras
   c. periods
2. Evidence of Time Periods
   a. fossils
   b. surface changes
3. Scientific Dating Methods
   a. radioactive carbon
   b. thermoluminescence

Chapter 4:
1. Climate Changes in Earth's History
2. Surface Features and Fossils Tell of Climate Changes

Chapter 5:
1. Earth Is Still Changing
2. Topographic Changes
3. Subsurface Changes

Organizing Science Content for Instruction

It is imperative that content teachers optimize the predictability of the content they teach. One method for accomplishing this task is to analyze new content for its inherent structure and organization. By analyzing content structure, communicating content structure to students, and following content structure in the teaching of new content, we can give students a powerful organizational tool to help them make sense out of the new information and content hierarchies we teach. Further, this procedure tends to clarify the goals and objectives students are to master in a content area, again optimizing the predictability of new content. Here are some examples of how to analyze new content in this fashion.

A teacher working with Unit One in the text would note that the outline emphasized *Changes in the Geologic History of Earth.* That is, the authors of this text emphasize that Earth has undergone many changes and is still changing today. To teach the content of *Earth Changes* to a class the teacher can construct a content hierarchy to facilitate the teaching of the content and the relationship between topics.

Using the content hierarchy of *Earth Changes* as the major thrust of Unit One, we can begin the process of content analysis in order to discover the structure of the content so that we might use that structure in presenting the new content to students. Further content analysis reveals that there are three varieties of changes that have affected Earth: subsurface, surface, and above-surface changes.

The content hierarchy can be represented as follows.

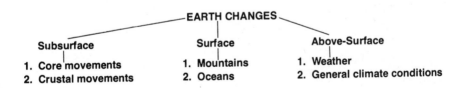

Additonal content analyses of Unit One in the first text can now be made based upon the content hierarchy *Earth Changes.* If the teacher wants to emphasize the factors or agents of change on earth to a greater extent, he or she may with to either extend the original content hierarchy to include several more levels, or use

the categories from the original content hierarchy to formulate
additional content hierarchies. The following example of an extended content hierarchy serves to outline perhaps six weeks of
instruction based on Unit One.

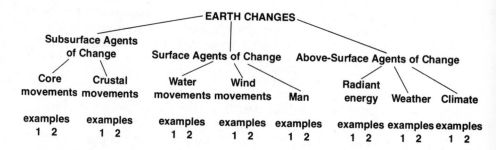

We might also take this extended content hierarchy and simply
break it down, and perhaps build two-week units of instruction
around the components. Using each major category from the original content hierarchy as a two-week unit heading, we might have
an outline of Unit One that would look like the example on p. 505.

Ultimately, the teacher must decide what aspects of the content
should be emphasized and what aspects should be deemphasized,
how much time to spend on each content hierarchy, the depth of
understanding students should reach on each content hierarchy,
whether or not supplemental materials are needed, and so on.
Using this method of constructing content hierarchies from the
content to be taught gives the teacher a way to organize his instruction based upon the structure of the content. By communicating this content structure to students, the teacher can
give students a way to organize the new content in order to optimize their mastery of the content.

THINKING PROCEDURES AND SCIENCE

Teaching Thinking Skills with Science Content

By identifying the content hierarchy *Earth Changes* and
categorizing these changes by type and location, we have
simplified for students the task of learning this new content. Now

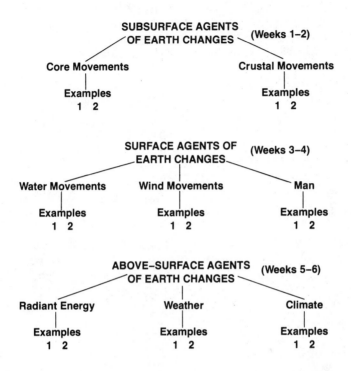

that we have established the content hierarchy (and there can be more than one) contained in Unit One, we need to perform further analyses to determine what kinds of reading-thinking procedures will be required in order to fully understand the content hierarchy *Earth Changes*.

To begin with, we will expect students to make identifications regarding the various categories and levels in the content hierarchy *Earth Changes*. We will expect them to understand that there are three general kinds or types of Earth changes and to identify the structural characteristics that make them different from one another. Further, we expect students to understand the relationships of similarity among the three categories of changes, identifying the fact that they are all examples of geologic changes and agents of change that affect Earth. We also expect students to understand the relationships of similarity and difference among the subcategories of subsurface, surface, and above-surface changes. Finally, we expect students to identify examples and nonexamples of the various categories and subcategories in the content hierarchy *Earth Changes*.

Further consideration of the content hierarchy *Earth Changes* and additional examination of the topics in the outline on page 504 suggest that programmatic or sequential thinking will be required of students in mastering the new content. The term "changes" itself suggests a sequence of events that attaches importance and significance to the order in which they occur. Unit One deals, in part, with the history of Earth; the term "history" also implies a sequence of events in which the ordering of those events is an important factor. Ultimately, it will be necessary for the student to understand the cycle of events from the origin of Earth to present Earth geologic history, keeping in mind the fact that these events can be categorized as subsurface, surface, and above-surface changes.

Programmatic thinking will also be required in understanding the cause-effect relationships among the categories and sub-categories in the content hierarchy *Earth Changes*. For example, core movements (causes) result in deposits of minerals (effects). In this particular example, the student must understand the relationships of cause and effect within one category (subsurface changes). Students must also understand the relationship among examples in different categories of the content hierarchy. They must understand, for instance, that crustal movements (causes) result in mountains (effects); stated another way, students are expected to understand that subsurface changes result in surface changes. The sequence and time ordering of these changes must be understood if students are to predict future events. Further, we might expect students to understand that certain agents of Earth changes like human beings interrupt these geologic sequences (causes) and that these interruptions result in additional changes or effects (For example changes in the ozone layer above the Earth—above-surface climatic changes).

It is evident, then, that the arrangement and structure of the content that we teach in the format of content hierarchies is a useful device for planning instruction. Content hierarchies tend to make the relationships that exist among the categories and levels in the hierarchy more apparent. Once we perceive and understand these relationships, we can then go about the task of teaching students the reading and thinking skills they will need in order to understand the new content.

Patterns of Writing in Science

The relationships that are portrayed through the construction of content hierarchies are also evident in the writing patterns authors use in writing about science content. That is, writing patterns and patterns of prose reflect the reading and thinking skills required to learn new content. Robinson (1975) cites six major writing patterns he has gleaned from analyses of contemporary science textbooks. Recognizing and understanding these patterns revolves, to a great degree, around students' knowledge of and ability to use "signal words" that cue the teacher regarding relationships among the ideas being presented in text (see chapter 4).

Robinson's *enumeration* pattern is what others have referred to as simple listing. An author may provide a separate list in text or weave a list into paragraphs using signal words like "first, second, then. . . ." The *comparison or contrast* pattern is also used frequently in science and is cued by signal words like "but, however, similarly, likewise," and so on. These patterns would seldom require reading-thinking skills beyond the identification level.

Robinson's *classification* and *generalization* patterns, again, are cued by many signal words. The *classification* pattern is essentially indicative of identification through categorization, and the *generalization* pattern is reflected in our discussion of inductive thinking in chapter 4 and chapter 6. Robinson's *problem solution* and *sequence* patterns both reflect the kind of thinking skills required in making predictions; that is, the following of a programmatic sequence of ideas.

Thinking Skills Probed in Science Textbooks

Most science content materials are presented in a chapter-by-chapter format, followed by questions for discussion, activities, and projects. A preponderance of the questions presented in science textbooks are devoted to making simple identifications, usually involving new science content vocabulary words.

Often, questions require students to structurally abstract when they ask the student to "list the properties" of something or "name three characteristics" of something. Questions frequently require the student to make deductive identifications when they ask for examples or illustrations. Questions less frequently present examples or illustrations, requiring students to inductively identify more general categories.

Many questions in science textbooks require the student to "discuss" or "describe" a multistep process. For example, describing how mountains are formed would involve describing various steps in the formation process in a sequential ordering and could involve the understanding of cause-effect relationships among the steps in the process. It should be noted, however, that questions like this can often be answered with only a literal understanding of the information presented in the textbook; questions may or may not require the thinking abilities described.

Other identifications are required by many questions in science textbooks that ask the student to "explain the difference" or "tell how _____ is different from _____." Instead of similarities among events that require those events to be grouped together under one or more categories, the student is asked to tell how events in categories or categories themselves are different from one another. This thinking ability is still an aspect of the identification of similarities and differences.

Cause-effect kinds of questions proliferate science textbooks. In these the student is asked to tell "what causes" a particular phenomenon or tell "what the effect is" of a particular phenomenon. In most instances, these questions are answered directly in text requiring the student only to recall from the reading cause-effect relationships explicitly stated. Seldom do cause-effect questions in science materials engage the student in predicting causes and effects of events not directly learned about from the reading. "Why" questions are used very often in science textbooks; they are usually loosely structured and are generally cause-effect type questions. Finally, few questions contained in science materials require the student to predict the consequences of a particular intervention. That is, few questions ask the student "what would happen if. . . ." or "suppose _____ were true; how would this affect _____."

Although this short analysis of textbook questions in science is certainly not meant to be generalized to all science textbooks, some trends in the kinds of questions we ask our students are descernible. First, most questions in science materials tend to be identification level questions. For the most part, identification level questions tend to be primarily questions that present students with a new vocabulary term from their reading and ask them to generate an example, description, or explanation of the new term. Generally, these questions ask the student to reproduce examples, descriptions, and explanations in such a way that they can be culled directly from the text—actually requiring little more than literal comprehension of what was read.

Another common question type has to do with the recognition of cause-effect relationships among the events treated in the textbook. In many instances, however, the student need only reproduce information presented in text by keying in on signal words like "cause," "effect," "result," and so on. Few questions of this variety actually require the student to predict cause-effect relationships among events that were not specifically dealt with in the reading. In too few instances are the students required to understand and think about the information they gain from their reading to the extent that they can make reasonable and accurate predictions about the content.

In conclusion, it should be noted that science textbooks and work books are often excellent materials to use in developing a number of predictive abilities. Many such materials require students to conduct experiments in which predictions and hypotheses must be made. If the experiments and projects required in science materials engage students in the process of making predictions, then testing them so they can be confirmed or rejected, then they deal with many of the predictive reading-thinking skills we have described in this and other chapters.

SUMMARY

English Content

1. Literature textbooks are organized by literary format, literary device, and by theme.

2. English textbooks are loosely organized. It is necessary for the English teacher to impose structure through the construction of content hierarchies to facilitate learning of English content.

3. To enhance the learning of English content, the teacher engages the student in applying thinking procedures to the content being taught. The full range of identification and prediction skills should be applied to the content.

4. The thinking skills probed in English textbooks are primarily identification skills that involve the student in a) remembering content that is literally stated, b) identifying similarities and differences in story characters, c) identifying character changes, d) evaluating story elements, and e) identifying cause-effect relationships. Prediction skills are seldom probed.

Social Studies Content

5. Social studies content usually covers history, government, geography, culture, and living patterns.

6. Unlike English textbooks, social studies texts are tightly organized in predictable patterns. Common patterns are the sequence pattern, the cause-effect pattern, the deductive pattern, or a combination of these.

7. In organizing social studies content for instruction the teacher can capitalize on and work within the framework of the textbook. The teacher needs to point out the hierarchical relationships among the content in the context.

8. To enhance the learning of social studies content the teacher should engage students in applying the full range of identification and prediction skills to the content. The more ways students are involved in thinking about the content, the more thoroughly they will understand the content and the relationship among topics.

9. Questions in social studies textbooks tend to be of three types: fact, main idea, and "why" questions. Fact questions require literal comprehension. Main idea questions require inductive reasoning. "Why" questions often require the identification of cause-effect relationships that are stated explicitly in the text. Seldom is the student required to exercise predictive abilities.

Science Content

10. Science textbooks are well organized and hierarchical relationships among science topics are evident in the organization. Nevertheless, there is considerable variation in the emphasis placed on science topics from one text to another.

11. Science textbooks are sufficiently well structured to provide a framework for organizing science content for instruction. However, teachers must construct content hierarchies to emphasize the content they wish to teach and to teach content not covered in the textbook. In addition, teachers should communicate to students the hierarchical relationships of science content to enhance learning.

12. Once content hierarchies are established, it is necessary to determine the thinking skills the student must apply to fully understand the content. First, students must apply identification skills in order to be able to identify science concepts and the relationship among the concepts. Then they should engage in applying prediction skills to the content.

13. Science textbooks tend to probe a wider range of thinking skills than textbooks in other content areas. Although science textbooks, as well as other textbooks, primarily probe identification skills, science texts include questions and instructions that engage students in employing prediction skills. Science texts involve students in projects and experiments which require them to test hypotheses.

REVIEW QUESTIONS

English Content

1. How are English literature textbooks organized?
2. How should English content be organized for instruction?
3. How should thinking procedures be applied in the teaching of English content?
4. What thinking skills are probed in English literature textbooks?

Social Studies

1. How are social studies textbooks organized?
2. How should social studies content be organized for instruction?
3. How should thinking procedures be applied in teaching of social studies content?
4. What thinking skills are probed in social studies textbooks?

Science

1. How are science textbooks organized?
2. How should science content be organized for instruction?
3. How should thinking procedures be applied in teaching science content?
4. What thinking skills are probed in science textbooks?

APPENDIX

INSTRUCTIONAL RESOURCES

Burmeister, Lou E. *Words: From Print to Meaning.* Reading, Massachusetts: Addison-Wesley, 1975. A collection of classroom activities for building sight vocabulary, using context clues, and acquiring knowledge of morphology and phonics.

Cheyney, Arnold B. *Teaching Reading Skills through the Newspaper.* Newark, Del.: International Reading Association, 1971. Provides concrete suggestions for developing vocabulary, critical reading, study skills, and attitudes through the creative use of the daily newspaper.

Ekwall, Eldon E. *Locating and Correcting Reading Difficulties* (2nd ed.) Columbus, Ohio: Charles Merrill, 1977. Presents hundreds of specific teaching suggestions in twenty-seven reading skill areas; also discusses the recognition of these skill deficiencies.

Engelmann, Siegfried. *Preventing Learning Failure in the Primary Grades.* Chicago: Science Research Associates, 1969. Contains many exercises and activities for developing language and concept skills and for sound-symbol drill.

Farguhar, Carolyn, Jennings, Bettye, and Weber, Elaine. *Personalized Approach to Reading.* Midland, Michigan: Pendell Publishing Co. Presents a wide variety of teaching activities and instructional strategies for dealing with a host of specific reading skills.

Forgan, Harry W. *The Reading Corner: Ideas, Games, and Activities for Individualizing Reading.* Santa Monica, Ca.: Goodyear Publishing Co., 1977. Presents a host of teaching suggestions for teaching word recognition, comprehension, and functional reading skills; also includes sample learning sheets for teaching these skills.

Forte, Imogene, Frank, Marjorie, and MacKanzie, Joy. *Kids' Stuff: Reading and Language Experiences.* Nashville, Tenn.: Incentive Publications, 1973. A collection of games, activities, and instructional approaches designed to improve a wide range of reading and language arts skills in intermediate and junior high school students.

Griese, Arnold A. *Do You Read Me? Practical Approaches to Teaching Reading Comprehension.* Santa Monica, Ca.: Goodyear Publishing Co., 1977. Provides hundreds of examples and activities for teaching concepts and comprehension skills in the areas of concept development, imagery, emotional reactions, character motives, perceiving relationships, making judgements and conclusions, and organizing ideas; also includes discussion of reading, listening, and thinking skills as well as demonstration lessons.

Hall, Nancy A. *Rescue: A Handbook of Remedial Reading Techniques for the Classroom Teacher.* Stevensville, Michigan: Educational Service, 1969. Presents hundreds of games and activities for use with the retarded reader in areas that include discrimination, phonics, language arts, directionality, and communications.

Herr, Selma. *Learning Activities for Reading* (2nd ed.) Dubuque, Iowa: William C. Brown, 1970. Offers a multitude of activities for teaching many specific reading and study skills.

Kaplan, S. N.; Kaplan, J. B.; Madsen, S. K.; and Taylor, B. K. *Change for Children: Ideas and Activities for Individualizing Learning.* Santa Monica, Ca.: Goodyear Publishing Co., 1973. Presents sample worksheets for a variety of skills including reading maps, graphing, and reading a variety of narrative materials; also includes descriptions of more than twenty specific learning centers, ideas on planning classroom time, and ideas for record keeping.

Keith, Joy L. *Comprehension Joy.* Naperville, Ill.: Reading Joy, 1974. Offers hundreds of games and activities for teaching comprehension and thinking skills.

Keith, Joy L. *Word Attack Joy.* Naperville, Ill.: Reading Joy, 1974. Presents hundreds of games and activities for teaching lower level word recognition and vocabulary skills.

Mallett, Jerry J. *Classroom Reading Games Activity Kit.* New York: The Center for Applied Research in Education, 1975.

Presents in kit form a wide variety of games and classroom activities for improving word recognition, comprehension, and study skills of young and disabled readers.

Mallett, Jerry J. *101 Make-and-Play Reading Games for Intermediate Grades.* West Nyack, New York: Center for Applied Research in Education, 1976. A collection of games and activities for teaching a host of reading skills at the intermediate grade levels.

Piercey, Dorothy. *Reading Activities in Content Areas: An Ideabook for Middle and Secondary Schools.* Boston: Allyn & Bacon, 1976. Presents hundreds of vocabulary, comprehension, and study skills activities for use in all content areas including business, English, speech, journalism, foreign languages, health, home economics, vocational arts, math, science, and social studies.

Platts, Mary E. *Anchor: A Handbook of Vocabulary Discovery Techniques for the Classroom Teacher.* Stevensville, Michigan: Educational Service, 1970. Offers a host of games and activities for teaching word recognition, vocabulary, and comprehension skills at the intermediate grade levels.

Platts, Mary E. *Spice: Suggested Activities to Motivate the Teaching of the Primary Language Arts.* Stevensville, Michigan: Educational Service, 1973. Presents a wide variety of games and activities for teaching of lower level word recognition, comprehension, and language art skills.

Reading Games. Greenwich, Conn.: Teachers Publishing Corporation. A reference and sourcebook of games and activities to be used in conjunction with reading instruction.

Resources in Teaching Reading. Gainsville, Fla.: University of Florida Reading Laboratory. Contains a wide variety of activities and specific suggestions for teaching a host of reading and reading-related skills.

Russell, David H., and Karp, Etta E. *Reading Aids through the Grades* (2nd ed.). New York: Teachers College Press, 1975. Compiles more than 440 activities for individualizing the teaching of word recognition, comprehension, and study skills; also includes a guide to materials for teaching reading.

Sanders, Norris M. *Classroom Questions.* New York: Harper & Row, 1966. Presents strategies for asking and constructing comprehension questions; includes many illustrations and examples.

Sargent, Eileeen E., Huus, Helen, and Andersen, Oliver. *How to Read a Book.* Newark, Del.: International Reading Association, 1970. Offers hundreds of practical suggestions for helping students learn to study textbook and narrative material effectively.

Source Materials for the Improvement of Reading (Research Bulletin No. 37). Brooklyn, New York: Board of Education, City of New York. Presents a reference list of sources of material for teaching reading skills.

Spache, Evelyn B. *Reading Activities for Child Involvement* (2nd ed.). Boston: Allyn & Bacon, 1976. Offers nearly 500 activities for improving the teaching of prereading, basic word recognition, comprehension, study, language development, vocabulary, and content reading skills; includes explanations of the skills, discussion of additional published materials for teaching reading, and a cross-referencing of skills and activities.

Spache, George D. *Sources of Good Books for Poor Readers.* Newark, Del.: International Reading Association, 1969. Lists hundreds of annotations and references for high interest-low vocabulary reading materials for the reluctant reader.

Thompson, Richard A. *Energizers for Reading Instruction.* West Nyack, New York.: Parker Publishing Co., 1973. Provides more than 250 practical teaching suggestions in the form of games and other activities for dealing with word recognition and comprehension skills.

Thompson, Richard A. *Treasury of Teaching Activities for Elementary Language Arts.* West Nyack, New York: Parker Publishing Co., 1975. Presents more than 300 games, puzzles, and specific learning activities for teaching language, reading, and communication skills.

Weber, Elaine, and Chappa, Jan. *Games that Teach within Your Reach.* East Lansing: Michigan State University, Mott Institute for Community Improvement. Keys a wide variety of exercises and activities to a range of specific reading skills.

West, Gail B. *Teaching Reading Skills in Content Areas: A Practical Guide to the Construction of Student Exercises.* Orlando, Fla.: Sandpiper Press, 1974. Describes hundreds of activities for testing, estimating readability, selecting textbooks, using book parts, interpreting graphics, extending vocabulary and comprehension, developing study skills, and making a variety of classroom materials for reading improvement.

NAMES AND ADDRESSES OF PUBLISHERS

Addison-Wesley Publishing Company
2725 Sand Hill Road
Menlo Park, California 94025

Allyn & Bacon, Inc.
Rockleigh Industrial Park
Rockleigh, New Jersey 07647

American Guidance Service, Inc.
Publishers Building
Circle Pine, Minnesota 55014

Bobbs-Merrill Company
4300 West 62 Street
Indianapolis, Indiana 46268

William C. Brown Company
2460 Kerper Boulevard
Dubuque, Iowa 52003

California Test Bureau/McGraw-Hill
Del Monte Research Park
Monterey, California 93940

Cal Press, Inc.
76 Madison Avenue
New York, New York 10016

Center for Applied Research
in Education, Inc.
521 Fifth Avenue
New York, New York 10017

Committee on Diagnostic
Reading Tests
Mountain Home, North Carolina 28758

Consulting Psychologists Press
577 College Avenue
Palo Alto, California 94306

Croft Educational Services
100 Garfield Avenue
New London, Connecticut 06320

Dreier Educational Systems, Inc.
320 Raritan Avenue
Highland Park, New Jersey 08904

Educational Development
Laboratories, Inc.
Division of McGraw-Hill
1121 Avenue of the Americas
New York, New York 10020

Educational Service, Inc.
Box 219
Stevensville, Michigan 49127

Educators Publishing Service
75 Moulton Street
Cambridge, Massachusetts 02138

Follett Educational Corporation
1010 West Washington Boulevard
Chicago, Illinois 60607

Goodyear Publishing Company
1640 Fifth Street
Santa Monica, California 90401

Harcourt Brace Jovanovich
757 Third Avenue
New York, New York 10017

Harper & Row, Inc.
10 East 53rd Street
New York, New York 10022

Houghton Mifflin Company
11000 South Lavergne Avenue
Oak Lawn, Illinois 60453

Incentive Publications, Inc.
2400 Crestmoor Drive
Nashville, Tennessee 37215

International Reading Association
800 Barksdale Road
Newark, Delaware 19711

Lyons and Carnahan, Inc.
407 East 25th Street
Chicago, Illinois 60616

Charles E. Merrill Publishing Company
1300 Alum Creek Drive
Columbus, Ohio 43216

Mott Institute for Community
Improvement
East Lansing, Michgan 48823

Mott Media
P. O. Box 236
Milford, Michigan 48042

New York City, Board of Education
 Bureau of Supplies
44-36 Vernon Boulevard
Long Island City, New York 11101

Parker Publishing Company
 Subsidiary of Prentice-Hall, Inc.
West Nyack, New York 10994

Pendell Publishing Company
1700 James Savage Road
P.O. Box 1666
Midland, Michigan 48640

Personnel Press
191 Spring Street
Lexington, Massachusetts 02173

The Psychological Corporation
757 Third Avenue
New York, New York 10017

Reading Joy
P. O. Box 404
Naperville, Illinois 60540

Reading Lab
University of Florida
15 N. W. 15th Street
Gainsville, Florida 32601

Sandpiper Press, Inc.
P. O. Box 1059
Oviedo, Florida 32765

Science Research Associates
259 E. Erie Street
Chicago, Illinois 60611

Stanford University Press
Stanford, California 94305

Teachers College Press
Columbia University
1234 Amsterdam Avenue
New York, New York 10027

Teachers Publishing
 Division of Macmillan
 Publishing Inc.
100 F. Brown Street
Riverside, New Jersey 08075

Richard L. Zweig Associates
20800 Beach Boulevard
Huntington Beach, California 92648

GLOSSARY

Abstraction the process of making an identification or prediction based on limited cues; for instance, identifying a friend from the sound of the voice only.

Affix a sound or sequence of sounds, or a letter or sequence of letters occurring as a bound form attached to the beginning or end of a word, base, or phrase, or inserted within a word or base and serving to produce a derivative word or an inflectional form.

Application Application as a comprehension skill may have one of two meanings: 1) application may refer to the correct utilization of information in different contexts or 2) application may refer to the demonstration by one's performance that he or she can correctly apply a learned skill.

Basal reader a series of reading textbooks that are eclectically designed and structured to teach reading skills.

Bibliotherapy the prescription of reading material related to readers' personal concerns and problems in order to interest them and help them solve their problems.

Blend consonant letters that blend together to make a distinct sound or a word (as brunch) produced by combining other words or parts of words.

Categorizing (as a thinking skill) distinguishing examples from nonexamples of a category. "Classifying ideas" and "evaluative reading" are examples of comprehension skills tht require categorizing.

Cloze procedure a procedure in which words in a reading passage are periodically deleted. Readers are tested to determine whether they can supply the missing words. One of its uses is to assess the compatability between students and reading material with respect to readability.

Concept a word label representing a category of items. The criteria for inclusion in the category are given indicating the attributes of items that belong in the category. Most words in the dictionary represent concepts. The definitions of the words enumerate the criteria for inclusion in the category.

Concept load   the number of concepts presented to the reader in a given number of words. Excessive concept load makes reading difficult.

Configuration analysis   the analysis of the shape or configuration of words to facilitate the recognition of the words.

Contextual abstraction   making an identification or prediction based on limited contextual cues; for instance, abstracting the meaning of an unfamiliar word by identifying the meaning of words that surround it.

Criterion-referenced tests   tests that measure the performance of individuals against a criterion to determine the extent to which an individual's performance meets the criterion.

Decoding   converting into intelligible language; for example; converting sight symbols into oral symbols as one does when pronouncing a written word. Decoding may or may not result in understanding.

Deductive reasoning   reasoning from a general principle to draw a specific conclusion. "Inferring details" and "making applications" are reading skills that require deductive reasoning. Deductive reasoning involves individuals in producing examples of a concept category they are given.

Defensiveness   the shutting out of traumatic events. When events are too unpredictable, defensiveness involves the shutting out of the confusing stimulation and the search for more manageable, familiar stimulation. When events are too predictable defensiveness involves the shutting out of the boring stimulation and the search for more novel, challenging stimulation.

Derived word forms   words constructed or derived from existing words by the addition of affixes; for example, "predetermined" is derived from the base word "term."

Digraph   a group of two successive letters whose phonetic value is a single sound (as "ea" in "bread" or "ng" in "sing") or whose value is not the sum of a value borne by each in other occurrences (as "ch" in "chin" where the value is "t" plus "sh").

Diphthong   a gliding monosyllabic speech sound (as the vowel combination that forms the last part of "toy") that starts at or near the articulatory position for one vowel and moves to or toward the position of another.

Direct observation   an observation made through the senses without the use of mediating devices such as paper and pencil tests.

Directed reading activity method   a method of structuring reading instruction to optimize learning. The method includes the following four steps performed in sequence: 1) establishing readiness to read, 2) guiding reading, 3) developing important concepts, and 4) providing follow-up activities.

Diurnal   recurring every day, having a daily cycle.

Errors of confabulation   errors made during reading that result in contextual/semantic violations; word substitutions that make no sense contextually.

Etymology   the study of the history of a linguistic form such as a word.

Evaluative comprehension   understanding which gives one the ability to judge the congruence between an existing state and a criterion state. The reader exhibits evaluative comprehension when he or she compares the author's position (the existing state) with a criterion. For example, a reader may be asked to evaluate whether an author's work meets the criteria for a good essay.

Flexible reading   the adjustment of reading rate to the purpose for reading and difficulty of reading materials. When reading materials are more difficult and a thorough understanding of the author's message is required one reads more slowly.

Formative tests   achievement tests that are designed to determine whether a particular portion of an instructional program is effective in moving a student toward an intended desired learning outcome.

Hierarchical identification   identifying the relationships among categories in a content hierarchy.

Hierarchy, representational   a hierarchy in which the lower levels are represented or included in the higher levels. Proceeding from the lower to the higher levels the references become less specific and more general. There are two kinds of representational hierarchies discussed in this text: 1) a *class inclusion hierarchy* in which the lower levels are subtypes or subclasses of the higher levels, for example, the lower level (dog) is a subtype of the higher level (mammal) and 2) an *activity or task hierarchy* in which the lower levels are activities represented in the higher levels, for example, pedaling is a lower level activity included in the higher level activity bicycle riding.

Hyperbole   extravagant exaggeration, for example, "mile-high ice-cream cones."

Indirect observations   observations made through mediating devices such as paper and pencil tests. Indirect observations are made to monitor traits such as learning and intelligence that cannot be directly observed as yet.

Inductive reasoning   reasoning from specifics to draw a general conclusion. Common elements are sought among specific events as a basis for generalizing about them. "Getting the main idea" from a reading passage is an example of inductive reasoning. Inductive reasoning involves the individual in producing a concept. given examples of the concept.

Inferential comprehension   the kind of understanding necessary to draw one's own conclusions about one's experiences. In reading, "interpreting the author's meaning" and "deriving meaning from figurative language" are examples of inferential comprehension.

Inflected word forms   word forms which have their function or usage altered by the addition of affixes; for example, "running" is the inflected form of "run."

Initiating events   events that attract our attention and stimulate our interest. We attempt to identify them in order to deal with them. Identifying initiating events is the first stage of the four-stage prediction program introduced in chapter 2 and applied throughout the book.

Intervention a change in an author's story line or some other alteration with respect to meaning that causes the reader to alter or refine the predictions he or she makes during reading.

Inverted sentence a sentence in which the predicate comes before the subject of the sentence. The use of inverted sentences increases the readability level of reading material.

Irony humorous or sardonic literary style that uses words to express something other than, and especially the opposite of, the literal meaning of the words.

Literal comprehension understanding and being able to recall directly stated facts from reading material. This is considered the most elementary and basic form of reading comprehension.

Literary definition provides the word label for a concept category and the defining criteria of the concept. A literary definition is the type of definition found in the dictionary.

Making general and specific identifications identifying words that denote more general categories and words that denote more specific subcategories of the general categories.

Mastery learning an approach to learning and instruction which provides students with all the practice, feedback, correctives, and time they need to achieve a desired learning outcome.

Metaphor a figure of speech in which a word or phrase literally denoting one kind of object or idea is used in place of another to suggest a likeness or analogy between them, such as "the ship plows the seas."

Modularized scheduling a flexible method of scheduling classes which enables students to diversify their learning and to choose a greater number of electives.

Norm-referenced tests tests that measure the individual's performance relative to others who have taken the same test.

Objectivity (of a test) a test is said to be objective when different scorers score the same subjects alike. Tests with scoring keys are objective tests because different scorers using the answer key will assign the same scores to test takers.

Operational definition specifies the operations or procedures one employs to produce a desired outcome. An operational definition specifies the steps one follows to produce an outcome such as in getting the main idea of a story.

Optimum predictability a situation in which individuals find events sufficiently familiar and understandable (not confusing) to enable them to make predictions and sufficiently novel (not boring) to challenge them to make predictions.

Paperback scanning technique a technique for teaching speed reading which utilizes reading material below the student's effective reading level and external pressure by covering the material at a rate the reader has no control over.

Passive voice   the use of a passive verb form. Passive voice increases the readability level of reading material.

Phonic generalization   rules of pronunciation. When rules of pronunciation are learned they usually generalize from one word to another of the same pattern.

Phonic identification   the association of written symbols with oral symbols for the purpose of identifying written words.

Power tests   tests that have no time limit or very lenient time limits. Such tests are designed to assess an individual's traits without the individual performing under restrictive time constraints.

Predicting   determining what will happen based upon an earlier trend of events.

Prepositional phrase   a group of words that begins with a preposition. An increased number of prepositional phrases increases the readability level of reading material.

Program   a sequence of activities that leads to specific outcomes. All procedures are programs including procedures for identifying the meaning of words and study procedures.

Proving identifications   the process of proving a conclusion arrived at inductively by reasoning deductively, or proving a conclusion arrived at deductively by reasoning inductively.

Psycholinguistics   the study of linguistic behavior as conditioning and being conditioned by psychological factors.

Readability   the level of difficulty of the reading material. Difficulty of reading material is commonly stated in terms of grade level; the higher the grade level the more complex the reading material.

Reading vocabulary   words the individual can read and understand.

Reality criterion   the ultimate aim of reading, which is extracting meaning from written words in order to get enjoyment and/or information.

Reliability coefficient   a correlation statistic that indicates the reliability of a test.

Reliability   (of a test) the internal consistency of a test. A test is said to be reliable when the items of the test measure the same characteristic.

Rhythm   the repetition in a literary work of phrase, incident, character type, or symbol.

Root word   a word that does not contain prefixes or suffixes, sometimes referred to as a base word.

Self-concept   one's ideas about himself or herself. Persons who have a positive or high self-concept think highly of themselves. Persons who have a negative or low self-concept think they are inadequate.

Semantics   the study of meaning in language. Reading is concerned primarily with extracting meaning from written words.

Sight vocabulary   those words the reader visually identifies instantly.

Signal words   words that indicate relationships among ideas in a reading passage. For instance, the signal word "next" indicates a sequential relationship, whereas the signal word "likewise" signals a similarity in a relationship.

Simile   a figure of speech comparing two unlike things that is often introduced by like or as, such as "cheeks like roses."

Skimming   scanning reading material in order to extract particular information.

Speeded tests   tests that measure characteristics of individuals while the individual is performing under time constraints.

Spontaneous reading   the continuous assimilation of the author's message as the reader perceives the words on the page. This is one of three stages in the reading program. In this stage reading proceeds without interruption because the reader is able to extract meaning from the written words and has little difficulty understanding what is being read.

SQ4R study method   a study method involving the following study steps performed in sequence: survey, question, read, recite, "rite" (write), and review.

Structural abstraction   making an identification or prediction based on limited structural cues; for example, abstracting the meaning of an unfamiliar word through identifying the meaning of familiar structural components of the word such as familiar prefixes, suffixes, or root words.

Study reading   careful and deliberate reading in order to understand and remember both details and major ideas presented in a text.

Summative tests   tests that summarize a student's achievement. A summative test is used to determine whether instruction has moved students to the achievement of a desired learning outcome for the purpose of certifying mastery of the desired learning outcome.

Syntactical density   a factor affecting the readability level of reading material. Sentence length and the complexity of sentence structure increase syntactical density and readability level.

Syntax   the systematic sequencing or programming of words; the way in which words are put together to form phrases, clauses, or sentences. The rules of grammar determine the way in which a language is programmed.

Table of specifications   a two-dimensional table that is used for the purpose of identifying desired learning outcomes, goals, and test items for evaluating student progress. One dimension of the table lists desired student behavior while the other dimension lists the content the student is to learn.

Task analysis   a method of breaking down a task into a hierarchy of component tasks. Task analysis is sometimes called component analysis.

Typographical aids   symbols that draw attention to ideas the author wishes to stress. Underlining, italicized words, and boldfaced type are examples of typographical aids.

Validity   (of a test) a test is valid when it measures what it is intended to measure. An IQ test is valid to the extent that it measures intelligence.

Vocabulary load   the quantity of words at a particular level of difficulty. The heavier the vocabulary load, the higher the readability level of the reading material.

Whole word method   the method of teaching students to recognize a word as a whole.

BIBLIOGRAPHY

Adams, J. A., and Xhigriesse; L. V. Some determinants of two-dimensional tracking behavior. *Journal of Experimental Psychology, 1960, 60,* pp. 391–403.

Aichelle, Douglas B., and Reys, Robert E. *Readings in secondary school mathematics.* Boston: Prindle, Weber & Schmidt, 1971.

Anderson, Lorin W. An empirical investigation of individual differences in time to learn. *Journal of Educational Psychology,* April 1976, *68,* pp. 226–233.

Asher, Steven R., and Markell, Richard A. Sex differences in comprehension of high- and low-interest reading material. *Journal of Educational Psychology,* 1974, *66,* pp. 680–687.

Athey, Irene J., and Holmes, J. A. Reading success and personality characteristics in junior high school students. *University of California Publications in Education,* 1969, *18,* pp. 22–51.

Ausubel, David P. Use of advance organizers in the learning and retention of meaningful verbal material. *Journal of Educational Psychology,* October 1960, *51,* pp. 267–272.

Barrett, Thomas C. (cited by Theordore Clymer) What is reading?: Some current concepts. In H. R. Robinson (ed.), *Innovation and Change in Reading Instruction: The Sixty-seventh Yearbook of the National Society for the Study of Education* (Part II), 1968, pp. 19–23.

Bazemore, Judith S., and Gwaltney, Wayne K. Personality and reading achievement: The use of certain personality factors as discriminatory. *California Journal of Educational Research,* May 1973, *24,* pp. 114–119.

Benz, D. A., and Rosemier, R. A. Word analysis and comprehension. *The Reading Teacher,* 1968, *21,* pp. 558–563.

Berg, Paul C. Flexibility in reading. In *Vistas in reading, proceedings of the International Reading Association.* vol. *11*, pp. 45–49, 1966.

Block, J. H., and Anderson, L. W. *Mastery learning in classroom instruction.* New York: Macmillan, 1975.

Block, J. H. Operating procedures for mastery learning. *Mastery Learning: Theory and Practice.* Edited by J. H. Block, pp. 64–76. New York: Holt, Rinehart and Winston, 1971.

Bloom, Benjamin et al. *Taxonomy of educational objectives: Cognitive domain.* New York: McKay, 1956.

Bloom, B. S. Learning for mastery. *Evaluation Comment,* 1968, *1*, pp. 1–11. Edited by J. H. Block.

Bloom, B. S., Hastings, J. T., and Madaus, G. F. *Handbook for formative and summative evaluation of student learning.* New York: McGraw-Hill, 1971.

Blount, H., and Johnson, R. E. Grammatical structure and the recall of sentences in prose. *American Educational Research Journal,* Spring 1973, *10*, pp. 163–168.

Bolles, C., Reinforcement, expectancy and learning. *Psychological Review,* 1972, *79*, pp. 394–409.

Bond, Guy L., and Dykstra, Robert. The cooperative research program in first grade reading. *Reading Research Quarterly,* 1967, *2*, pp. 5–142.

Bormuth, John. Cloze tests on reading comprehension. *Reading Research Quarterly,* Spring 1969, *3*, pp. 359–367.

Bormuth, John R. *Cloze tests as measures of readability and comprehension ability.* Bloomington: Indiana University, Ed.D. dissertation, 1962.

Bower, G. H., Clark, M. C., Winzenz, D., and Lesgold, A. Hierarchical retrieval schemes in recall of categorized word lists. *Journal of Verbal Learning and Verbal Behavior,* 1969, *8*, pp. 323–343.

Brown, A. S. Examination of hypothesis sampling theory. *Psychological Bulletin,* 1974, *81*, pp. 773–790.

Bruner, H. B., Evans, H. M., Hutchcraft, C. R., Wieting, C. M., and Wood, Hugh B. *What our schools are teaching: An analysis of the content of selected courses of study with special reference to science, social studies and industrial arts.* New York: Columbia University, 1941.

Burkman, Ernest. New directions for the high school science program. *The Science Teacher,* February 1972, *39*, pp. 42–44.

Buros, Oscar K. *The seventh mental measures yearbook.* Highland Park, N. J.: Gryphon Press, 1972.

Carlsen, G. R. Big change in adolescent reading. *Intellect*, 104, July/August, 1975, p. 8.

Carroll, J. B. A model of school learning. *Teachers College Record*, 1963, *64*, pp. 723–733.

Carter, R. P., Jr. The adult social adjustment of retarded and non-retarded readers, *Journal of Reading*, 1967, *11*, pp. 224–228.

Clymer, Theordore. Does 'can' mean 'should'? *The Reading Teacher*, January 1963, *16*, p. 217.

Clymer, Theordore. The utility of phonic generalizations in the primary grades. *The Reading Teacher*, January 1963, *16*, pp. 252–258.

Coleman, James S. How do the young become adults? *Review of Educational Research*, 42, Fall 1972, pp. 431–439.

Cramer, R. L., and Dorsey, Suzanne. Science textbooks—how readable are they? *Elementary School Journal*, 1969, 70, pp. 38–43.

Dale, Edgar. *Audio visual methods in teaching.* New York: Dryden Press, 1946.

Davies, Ivor K. *Competency based teaching.* New York: McGraw-Hill, 1973.

Davis, O. L., Jr., and Tinsley, Drew C. Cognitive objectives revealed by classroom questions asked by social studies student teachers. *Peabody Journal of Education*, 1967, 45, pp. 21–26.

Desjardins, Mary. Reading and viewing: A survey. *School Libraries*, Spring 1972, *21*, pp. 26–30.

Dolch, Edward A. *A Manual for Remedial Reading*, 2nd ed. Champaign, Ill.: The Garrard Press, 1945.

Duke, Charles R. Teaching the short story. *English Journal*, 1974, *63*, pp. 62–67.

Educational Measurement (2nd ed.). R. L. Thorndike (ed.), Washington, D. C.: American Council on Education, 1971.

Edwards, Peter. The effect of idioms on children's reading and understanding of prose. In Bonnie Smith Schulwitz (ed.), *Teachers, tangibles, techniques: Comprehension of context in reading.* Newark, Del.: International Reading Association, 1975, pp. 37–46.

Emans, Robert. The effect of verb simplification on the reading comprehension of culturally different high school students. *Reading World*, March 1973, *12*, pp. 162–168.

Emans, R. The usefulness of phonic generalizations above the primary grades. *The Reading Teacher*, 1967, 20, pp. 419–425.

Erickson, E. *Identity, youth and crisis.* New York: W.W. Norton, 1968.

Erickson, F. What are we trying to do in high school English? In Barton and Simmons (eds.), *Teaching English in today's high schools*, New York: Holt, Rinehart and Winston, 1965.

Estes, Thomas H., and Vaughan, Joseph L., Jr. Reading interest and comprehension: Implications. *The Reading Teacher*, November 1973, 27, pp. 149–153.

Estes, W. K. Reinforcement in human behavior. *American Scientist*, 1972, 60, pp. 723–729.

Farr, Roger, *Reading: What can be measured?* Newark, Del.: International Reading Association, 1969.

Fehr, Howard F. The mathematics program in Japanese secondary schools. In Douglas B. Aichelle and Robert F. Reys (eds.), *Readings in Secondary School Mathematics*. Boston: Prindle, Weber & Schmidt, 1971.

Fein, Ruth L., and Ginsberg, Adrienne H. Realistic Literature about the handicapped. *The Reading Teacher*, April 1978, 31, pp. 802–805.

Feldhusen, J. F., Thurston, J. R., and Benning, J. J. Classroom behavior, intelligence, and achievement. *Journal of Experimental Education*, 1967, 36, pp. 82–87.

Frase, L. T. Questions as aids to reading: Some research and theory. *American Educational Research Journal*, 1968, 5, pp. 319–332.

Frenzel, Norman J. Children need a multipronged attack in word recognition. *The Reading Teacher*, March 1978, 31, pp. 627–631.

Frerichs, Allen H. Relationship of self-esteem of the disadvantaged to school success. *Journal of Negro Education*, Spring 1971, 40, pp. 117–120.

Friedman, M. I. *Predictive abilities test*. Published by author. Columbia: University of South Carolina, 1974.

Friedman, M. I. *Rational behavior: An explanation of behavior that is especially human*. Columbia: University of South Carolina Press, 1975.

Friedman, M. I. *Word guessing test*. Published by author. Columbia: University of South Carolina, 1976.

Gagné, Robert T. *The conditions of learning*. New York: Holt, Rinehart and Winston, 1965.

Gallagher, James J. Expressive thought by gifted children in the classroom. *Elementary English*, May 1965, 42, pp. 559–568.

Gibson, Eleanor J., and Levin, Harry. *The psychology of reading*. Cambridge, Mass.: The MIT Press, 1975.

Glassman, W. E., and Levine, M. Unsolved and unsoluble problem behavior. *Journal of Experimental Psychology,* 1972, 92, pp. 146–148.

Goodman, Kenneth S. A linguistic study of cues and miscues in reading. *Elementary English,* 1965, 42, pp. 639–643.

Goodman, Kenneth S. Comprehension-centered reading. In E. E. Ekwall (ed.), *Psychological factors in the teaching of reading.* Columbus, Ohio: Charles Merrill, 1973.

Goodman, Kenneth S. Reading: A psycholinguistic guessing game. In H. S. Singer and R. B. Ruddell (eds.), *Theoretical models and processes of reading.* Newark, Del.: International Reading Association, 1970.

Goodman, Kenneth S., and Smith, Frank. On the psycholinguistic method of teaching reading. In E. E. Ekwall (ed.), *Psychological factors in the teaching of reading.* Columbus, Ohio: Charles Merrill, 1973.

Goodman, Yetta, and Burke, Carolyn. *Reading miscue inventory.* New York: Macmillan, 1972.

Greeno, James G., and Noreen, David L. Time to read semantically related sentences. *Memory and Cognition,* January 1974, 2, pp. 117–120.

Gronlund, N. E. *Preparing criterion referenced tests for classroom instruction.* New York: Macmillan, 1973.

Haley, Beverly A. The "fractured family" in adolescent literature. *English Journal,* 1974, 63, pp. 70–72.

Harris, Albert J. Reading and human development. In Nelson B. Henry (ed.), *Development in and through Reading: The Sixtieth Yearbook of the National Society for the Study of Education (Part I),* 1961, pp. 17–34.

Harris, Albert J., and Sipay, Edward R. *How to increase reading ability* (6th ed.). New York: McKay, 1975.

Helson, H. *Adaptation-level theory.* New York: Harper & Row, 1964.

Helson, H. Design of equipment and optimal human operation. *American Journal of Psychology,* 1949, 62, pp. 473–497.

Henderson, E. H., and Long, Barbara H. Decision processes of superior, average, and inferior readers. *Psychological Reports,* 1968, 23, pp. 703–706.

Henderson, E. H., and Long, Barbara H. Self social concepts in relation to reading and arithmetic. In J. A. Figurel (ed.), *Vistas in reading. Proceedings of the International Reading Association,* 1966, 11, pp. 576–581.

Hilgard, Ernest R. *Theories of learning*, (1st ed.). New York: Appleton-Century-Crofts, 1948.

Hilgard, Ernest R. *Theories of learning*, (2nd ed.). New York: Appleton-Century-Crofts, 1956.

Hilgard, E., and Bower, G. *Theories of learning*. Englewood Cliffs, N.J.: Prentice-Hall, 1975.

Hogg, James H. Development of verbal behavior through cognitive awareness training. *Journal of Educational Research*, 1973, 67, pp. 9–12.

Hunkins, F. P. What to ask and when. *Yearbook of the National Council on Social Studies*, 1974, 44, pp. 146–148.

Jarolimek, John. In pursuit of the elusive new social studies. In J. Jarolimek and H. M. Walsh (eds.), *Readings for Social Studies in Elementary Education* (3rd ed.). New York: Macmillan, 1974.

Jensen, Poul Erik. Theories of reading speed and comprehension. *Journal of Reading*. April 1978, 21, pp. 593–600.

Johns, Jerry. What do innercity children prefer to read? *The Reading Teacher*, February 1973, 26, pp. 462–467.

Johns, Jerry L. Reading preference of intermediate-grade students in urban settings. *Reading World*, October 1974, 14, pp. 51–63.

Johns, Jerry L. Reading preferences of urban students in grades four through six. *Journal of Educational Research*, April 1975, 68, pp. 306–309.

Johnson, Donald M., and Stratton, R. Paul. Evaluation of five methods of teaching concepts. *Journal of Educational Psychology*, 1966, 57, pp. 48–53.

Johnson, Donovan A. A pattern for research in the mathematics classroom. *The Mathematics Teacher*, May 1966, 59, pp. 418–425.

Johnson, M. S., and Kress, R. A. *Informal Reading Inventories*. Newark, Del.: International Reading Association, 1965.

Jongsma, Eugene. An analysis of the language patterns of standardized reading comprehension tests and their effect on student performance. *Journal of Reading Behavior*, December 1974, 6, pp. 353–366.

Kahn, P. Time organization and reading achievement. *Perceptual and Motor Skills*, 1965, 21, pp. 157–158.

Klare, George R. Assessing readability. *Reading Research Quarterly*, 1974–1975, 10, pp. 62–102.

Klausmeier, Herbert J., and Feldman, Katherine V. Effects of a definition and a varying number of examples and nonexamples on concept attainment. *Journal of Educational Psychology*, April 1975, 67, pp. 174–178.

Klein, Helen A., Klein, Gary A., and Bertino, Mary. Utilization of context for word identification decisions in children. *Journal of Experimental Child Psychology*, February 1974, 17, pp. 79–86.

Kline, Morris. The ancients versus the moderns; a new battle of the books. In Douglas B. Aichelle and Robert E. Reys (eds.), *Readings in Secondary School Mathematics*. Boston: Prindle, Weber & Schmidt, 1971.

Koenke, K., and Otto, Wayne. Contribution of pictures to children's comprehension of main idea in reading. *Psychology in the Schools*, 1969, 6, pp. 298–302.

Kucera, H., and Francis, W. N. *Computational analysis of present-day American English*. Providence, R. I.: Brown University Press, 1967.

Levine M. A transfer hypothesis whereby learning-to-learn, einstelling, the PREE, reversal/nonreversal shifts, and other curiosities are elucidated. In R. L. Lolo (ed.), *Theories in Cognitive Psychology* (The Loyola Symposium). Potomac, Md.: Laurence Erlbaun Associates, 1974.

Levine, M. Human discrimination learning: The subset sampling assumption. *Psychological Bulletin*, 1970 74, p. 398.

Lexier, Kenneth. Common oversimplifications of the reading process. *Journal of Reading*, April 1978, 21, pp. 601–605.

Lopez, Sarah H. Children's use of contextual clues in reading Spanish. *The Reading Teacher*, April 1977, 30, pp. 735–740.

McCann, Susan, and Barron, Richard F. The effect of student-conducted compenential analysis upon concept differentiation in a passage of social science content. In G. H. McNinch and W. D. Miller (eds.), *Reading: Convention and inquiry. Twenty-fourth Yearbook of the National Reading Conference*, 1975, pp. 274–278.

McCorquodale, K., Meehl, P., and Tolman, C. In W. K. Estes et al. (eds.), *Modern Learning Theory*. New York: Appleton-Century-Crofts, 1954.

Markle, S. M., and Tiemann, P. W. *Really understanding concepts: Or, in furious pursuit of the Jabberwocky*. Champaign, Ill.: Stipes, 1969.

Modern life is too much for 23 million Americans. *U.S. News and World Report,* November 10, 1975, *79,* p. 84.

Myers, Collin A. Reviewing the literature on Fernald's technique of remedial reading. *The Reading Teacher,* March 1978, *31,* pp. 614–623.

Nelson, R. C. Children's poetry preferences. *Elementary English,* 1966, *43,* pp. 247–251.

Odell, Lee. Teaching reading: An alternative approach. *English Journal,* March 1973, *62,* pp. 454–458.

Ojala, William T., and McNeill, Marda. A survey of adolescent interests in three schools. *Arizona English Bulletin,* April 1972, *14,* pp. 96–108.

Otto, W., and Koenke, K. Idiosyncratic word-association among adults at divergent levels of reading ability. In G. B. Schick and M. M. May (eds.) *Multidisciplinary aspects of college-adults reading, Yearbook of the National Reading Conference,* 1968, *17,* pp. 65–69.

Otto, Wayne, McMenemy, Richard A., and Smith, Richard J. *Corrective and remedial teaching.* Boston: Houghton Mifflin, 1973.

Palmer, William S. Research on grammer: A review of some pertinent investigations. *High School Journal,* March 1975, *58,* pp. 252–258.

Palmer, William S. The rip-off in reading. *English Journal,* November 1974, *63,* pp. 40–44.

Penty, Ruth C. *Reading ability and high school drop outs.* New York: Columbia University Press, 1956.

Pfeiffer, Isobel, and Davis, O. L., Jr. Teacher-made examinations: What kind of thinking do they demand? *NASSP Bulletin,* September 1965, *49,* pp. 1–10.

Pilgrim, Geneva H., and McAllister, Mariana K. *Young people and reading guidance.* New York: Harper & Row, 1968.

Pollan, Corrine. What high school students are really reading? *English Journal,* April 1973, *62,* pp. 573–576.

Popham, W. J. *Educational evaluation.* New York: Prentice-Hall, 1973.

Postman, Neil, and Weingartner, Charles. *Teaching as a subversive activity.* New York: Delacorte Press, 1969.

Preusser, D., and Handel, S. The free classifications of hierarchically and categorically related stimuli. *Journal of Verbal Learning and Verbal Behavior,* 1970, *9,* pp. 222–231.

Resnick, L. B., Wang, M. C., and Kaplan, J. Task analysis in curriculum design: A hierarchically sequenced introductory mathematics curriculum. *Journal of Applied Behavioral Analysis*, 1973, *6*, pp. 697–710.

Robinson, H. Alan. *Teaching reading and study strategies: The content areas*. Boston: Allyn & Bacon, 1975.

Rosenthal, Robert, and Jacobsen, Lenore. *Pygmalion in the classroom: Teacher expectation and pupils' intellectual development*. New York: Holt, Rinehart and Winston, 1968.

Rothkopf, E. Z. Some theoretical and experimental approaches to problems in written instruction. In J. D. Krumboltz (ed.), *Learning and the instruction process*. Chicago: Rand McNally, 1965.

Ruddell, R. B. Reading comprehension and structural redundancy in written material. In J. A. Figurel (ed.), Reading and inquiry. *Proceedings of the International Reading Association*, 1965, *10*, 308–311.

Ruddell, Robert B. The effect of oral and written patterns of language structure on reading comprehension. *The Reading Teacher*, January 1965, *18*, pp. 270–275.

Rupley, W. H. Relationship between behavioral problems and reading retardation. *Indiana Reading Quarterly*, 1971, *2*, pp. 4–7.

Samuels, S. J. Attentional process in reading: The effect of pictures on the acquisition of reading responses. *Journal of Educational Psychology*, 1967, *58*, pp. 337–342.

Shores, J. H. Reading interests and informational needs of high school students. *The Reading Teacher*, 1964, *17*, pp. 536–544.

Singer, Dorothy G. A look at some of the "New Wave" junior books. *Journal of Reading*, October 1977, *21*, pp. 9–14.

Singer, Harry. Active comprehension: From answering to asking questions. *The Reading Teacher*, May 1978, *31*, pp. 901–908.

Singer, Harry. The SEER technique: A non-computational procedure for quickly estimating readability level. *Journal of Reading Behavior*, Fall 1975, *7*, pp. 255–267.

Smith, Charlotte T. Evaluating answers to comprehension questions. *The Reading Teacher*, May 1978, *31*, pp. 896–900.

Smith, N. B. Textbook analysis grades 7–12. *Reading Teacher*, 1963, *17*, pp. 7–12.

Smith, Nila Banton. Some answers to criticisms of american reading instruction. *The Reading Teacher*, December 1962, *16*, pp. 146–150.

Smith, Nila Banton. The many faces of reading comprehension. *The Reading Teacher,* December 1969, *23,* pp. 249–259.

Smith, Ruth C. Children's reading choices and basic reader content. *Elementary English,* 1962, *39,* pp. 202–209.

Smith, William L. The controlled instrument procedure for studying the effect of syntactic sophistication on reading: A second study. *Journal of Reading Behavior,* Fall 1972/73, *5,* pp. 242–251.

Stauffer, R. A. A directed reading-thinking plan. *Education,* 1959, *79,* pp. 527–532.

Stoodt, Barbara D. The relationship between understanding grammatical conjunctions and reading comprehension. *Elementary English,* April 1972, *49,* pp. 502–504.

Tennyson, R. D., and Wooley, F. R. Conceptual model of classification behavior. *Educational Technology,* 1972, *12.*

Thomas, E. L., and Robinson, H. A. *Improving reading in every class: A sourcebook for teachers.* Boston: Allyn & Bacon, 1972.

Thorndike, R. L. *Educational Measurement,* 2nd ed. Washington, D.C.: American Council on Education, 1971.

Tolman, E. C. *Collected Papers in Psychology.* Berkeley: University of California Press, 1951.

Tolman, E. C. Principles of purpose behavior. In S. Koch (ed.), *Psychology: A Study of a Science,* vol. 2. New York: McGraw-Hill, 1959.

Tulving, Endel, and Gold, Cecille. Stimulus information and contextual information as determinants of tachistoscopic recognition of words. *Journal of Experimental Psychology,* October 1963, *66,* pp. 319–327.

Van Til, William. Crucial issues in secondary education today. *National society for the study of education yearbook* (Part 2), 1976, pp. 1–29.

Van Til, William. What should be taught and learned through secondary education? *National society for the study of education yearbook* (Part 2), 1976, pp. 178–213.

Velton, H. V. The growth of phonemic and lexical patterns in instant language. *Language,* 1943, *19,* pp. 281–292.

Weaver, W. W., And Bickley, A. C. Structural-lexical predictability of materials which predictor has previously produced or read. *Proceedings of the APA 75th annual convention,* 1967, *75,* pp. 289–290.

Weaver, W. W., Holmes, C. C., and Reynolds, R. J. The effect of reading variation and punctuation conditions upon reading comprehension. *Journal of Reading Behavior,* 1970, *2,* pp. 75–84.

Weintraub, Sam. What research says to the reading teacher: Reading graphs, charts, and diagrams. *The Reading Teacher,* 1967, *20,* pp. 345–349.

Weintraub, Sam. What research says to the reading teacher: Reading interests. *The Reading Teacher,* April 1969, *22,* pp. 655–659.

White, R. T. Research into learning hierarchies. *Review of Educational Research,* 1973, *43,* pp. 361–375.

Wisher, Robert A. The effects of syntactic expectations during reading. *Journal of Educational Psychology,* October 1976, *68,* pp. 597–602.

Wolfson, Bernice J. What do children say their reading interests are? *The Reading Teacher,* 1960, *14,* pp. 81–82.

Woolf, M. D. Ego strengths and reading disability. In E. L. Thurston and L. E. Hafner (eds.), *The philosophical and sociological bases of reading. Yearbook of the National Reading Conference,* 1965, *14,* pp. 73–80.

Yager, Robert E. Secondary science education: 1975 assessment. *High School Journal,* February 1976, *59,* pp. 198–207.

Yarlott, G., and Harpin, W. S. 1000 responses to English literature. *Educational Research,* 1971, *13,* pp. 87–971.

INDEX